CHILDREN'S SOURCE MONITORING

CHILDREN'S SOURCE MONITORING

Kim P. Roberts
*National Institute of Child Health
and Human Development*

Mark Blades
University of Sheffield, UK

LEA LAWRENCE ERLBAUM ASSOCIATES, PUBLISHERS
2000 Mahwah, New Jersey   London

Lawrence Erlbaum Associates, Inc., Publishers
10 Industrial Avenue
Mahwah, New Jersey 07430-2262

Cover design by Kathryn Houghtaling Lacey

Library of Congress Cataloging-in-Publication Data

Children's source monitoring / Kim P. Roberts and Mark Blades,
    (editors).
        p. cm.
    Includes bibliographical references and index.
    ISBN 0-8058-3326-9 (alk. paper)
    1. Memory in children. 2. Cognition in children. I. Roberts,
    Kim P. II. Blades, Mark.
    BF723.M4 C45 2000
    155.4'1312—dc21   99-056487
                                                           CIP

Books published by Lawrence Erlbaum Associates are printed
on acid-free paper, and their bindings are chosen for strength
and durability

Printed in the United States of America
10 9 8 7 6 5 4 3 2 1

Contents

Preface

Children need to be able to integrate information from different sources to build up a reliable knowledge base. In some situations, however, children need to be able to distinguish between different sources of information if they are to function competently in everyday life. They may need to know, for example, whether they have done their homework or just dreamed that they had, whether mom or dad spoke to them, or whether they learned information from a teacher or from a television show. Until now, the research on children's such source monitoring has been presented as scattered journal articles and as such, the picture of the development of source monitoring has been somewhat piecemeal. This has been the source of frustration for many scholars of children's source monitoring, and so the idea for this book was born from a need to provide a coherent account in this area, In this text, then, we sought to integrate current knowledge on children's source monitoring. We aimed for an easy-to-understand overview of source-monitoring theory complemented by critical discussions from an international set of leading investigators. Their research programs cut across different methodologies (e.g., nomothetic, individual differences, clinical) and are applied to a wide variety of areas of children's lives in which source monitoring is an important skill. Particular emphasis is placed on the effects of source monitoring on eyewitness memory and identification, learning and knowledge, and theory of mind development. This book was written at a level accessible to undergraduate and graduate students of psychology, researchers, and anyone interested in children's memory and applications of research in educational and forensic settings.

Acknowledgments

It has been a pleasure to work with so many talented individuals during the development of this book. First, we would like to thank the contributors for sharing the results of their research, and their persistent efforts during each stage of the writing. As with any active area of research, there are differences in interpretation across groups. These differences have been embraced by the contributors, however, who used them to think about their work in new and meaningful ways. It is to the contributors' credit that they spent time and effort rethinking their research conclusions and accounting for their findings in a way that has proved beneficial to the field in general. Through sharing their research in this volume, our understanding of the development and use of source-monitoring skills in children's lives has been greatly improved.

I would like to personally thank Michael Lamb for his support from conception to completion of this project. His advice and encouragement was gratefully received. I would like to thank Gabriela Marein-Efron, Cady Berkel, Nicole Sirrine, and especially Heather Lillemoe for getting up close and personal with the APA Publication Manual and editing the manuscripts so carefully. Mary Ann Foley has been a constant source of inspiration and support in the pursuit of understanding the development and the role of source monitoring in children's lives. Her insightful comments on drafts and research designs have made significant contributions to much of the work reported in this volume. Finally, I would like to thank Sashko Damjanovski for his patience, understanding, and encouragement over the past year.

—*Kim Roberts*

1

Introduction: Children's Source Monitoring

Kim P. Roberts
*National Institute of Child Health
and Human Development*

Fans of the television show *The Simpsons*, are familiar with the many mistakes of Homer, the main character. In one episode, Homer has a conversation with his wife in which he implies that he is going to work, but, after every work-related utterance, he thinks about how he intends to go to the local brewery instead. At one point, he gets confused between what he is saying and what he is thinking and mistakenly blurts out that he is going to the brewery. He thinks to himself "Uh, oh! Did I say that or just think it?" He finds the devastating answer to his question when his wife curiously asks him if he is going to the brewery (for further information, see Groening, 1997).

In this example, Homer engaged in an act of *source monitoring* (Johnson, Hashtroudi, & Lindsay, 1993; Johnson & Raye, 1981), a process needed to distinguish between memories from different sources of information. In Homer's case, he needed to decide whether he had said or thought about his brewery-trip idea. His future utterances would be highly dependent on the accuracy of his source-monitoring judgment.

Although Homer's example was trivial, humans need to make many kinds of source discriminations to function competently in everyday life. We need adequate levels of social and cognitive understanding to be able to protect ourselves from harm and interact with others. Occasionally, disruptions in regular functioning occur and the consequences may or may not be serious. Consider, for example, the

1

scenario in which Mrs. Fitzpatrick organized a surprise birthday party for her husband at their house. To make sure that he arrives home after the guests have arrived, Mrs. Fitzpatrick told her husband that she was having the carpets cleaned and that he should not return home until 7 p.m. As she is decorating for the party, she has an awful feeling that she may not have told him what time to return—she is not sure whether she *actually* told him to return after 7 p.m. or whether she just *intended* to tell him to return after 7 p.m. She eventually decides that she did tell him the time, and does not try to contact him again. It turns out that Mrs. Fitzpatrick did not tell her husband what time to return and he arrived home before the guests had arrived. In this hypothetical scenario, the consequences are unfortunate but not drastic.

Now consider the hypothetical scenario of Joe, who has suffered frontal-lobe damage because of an industrial accident. Since the accident, Joe can remember what people tell him, but not *who* disclosed the information to him. As a consequence, he often retells the same information (e.g., a joke) to the person who initially reported the information to him (i.e., the person who originally told him the joke). This habitual disruption of processes clearly lowers Joe's quality of life and can create frustration for those who regularly interact with him.

Both of the preceding examples detail a disruption of source monitoring because, in each instance, the content of the events was remembered (that the husband should not return before 7 p.m.; the information that Joe heard), but each person erred regarding the *source* of that content (said vs. thought about the time; Friend A vs. Friend B told the joke). Accurate source monitoring is also important in children's lives, and their "source errors" may also be disruptive. Recent developments in our understanding of source monitoring have also revealed that, in some circumstances, source errors may actually serve an adaptive function (see chap. 4, this volume).

Why is source monitoring an important skill for children? Source-monitoring skills mediate children's ability to carry out many functions, both cognitive and social. As a cognitive example, consider 4-year-old Diana, who is beginning to build up an autobiographical memory of events that she has personally experienced. Being a typical 4-year-old, however, Diana also has an active fantasy life. If Diana confuses memories of events that have actually happened to her and events that she has only imagined, the accuracy of her life history may be compromised. If the fantasies have negative aspects, her emotional well-being may also be harmed. As an example of a more social phenomenon, imagine that Karl tells his friend, William, a secret and asks him not to mention it to anyone else. William, however, is later confused about which of his friends asked him to keep the secret, and mistakenly talks to another friend, Alex, about the secret. The act of revealing this secret may harm the friendship between Karl and William. Throughout the rest of this book, the reader will see examples of how source-monitoring skills mediate the success of many different aspects of children's lives, such as their acquisition of knowledge (chap. 3, this volume), their event memory (chap. 6, this volume), and their suggestibility (chap. 8, this volume).

Pioneering work on the development of children's source monitoring began in the late 1970s and early 1980s (e.g., Foley & Johnson, 1985; Foley, Johnson, & Raye, 1983; Johnson, Raye, Wang, & Taylor, 1979). In these early studies, children's source monitoring for relatively simple stimuli, such as word lists, was examined. Contrary to the then-current conception of children as being hopelessly confused between memories of different events, these studies revealed that in some circumstances, children could actually be as accurate as adults (e.g., Foley & Johnson, 1985), or even show superior source monitoring compared with adults (e.g., Johnson et al., 1979). For example, Foley and Johnson (1985) found that 6-year-olds could distinguish which actions they had carried out (e.g., waving goodbye) and which a confederate carried out (further detail about these experiments is provided in chap. 2, this volume).

Although children showed some competence, they did have difficulty with some types of source monitoring. Specifically, Foley and her colleagues (e.g., Foley & Johnson, 1985; Foley et al., 1983) found that the 6-year-olds were confused between memories of overtly and covertly expressed items. For example, in Foley and Johnson's study on memory for actions, they found that the 6-year-olds confused memories of actions they had carried out with memories of actions that they had only imagined performing.

Two recent developments have marked a new wave of source-monitoring research. Studies of children's source monitoring of simple, unrelated stimuli (e.g., word lists) are helpful in specifying exact mechanisms because of the ease with which extraneous variables can be controlled. Recently, however, investigators have shifted their focus to children's source monitoring for information that is complex and related in meaningful ways. In addition, the relevance of studying source-monitoring processes carried out in the context of another task, such as recalling complex event memories, has also moved the field in new directions. Building on the early developmental studies, researchers have now documented a wealth of information about many kinds of source monitoring that children carry out in their everyday lives. This shift to studying source monitoring for complex events has been spurred by an acknowledgment of the role of source monitoring in many applied areas, such as educational and forensic settings.

Although research on children's source monitoring is now a common interest within the field of child psychology, until now, this work has only been published as scattered journal articles and chapters, and so a major aim for this book is to integrate divergent reports and be a starting point for students and researchers interested in children's source monitoring. It is helpful to synthesize what we know to provide an integrated account and to identify key areas for future research. To provide a representative account of current knowledge in the area, leading investigators of children's source monitoring were commissioned to discuss their programs of research. The authors have documented the different methodologies (e.g., nomothetic, individual differences, clinical) and applications of their research programs (e.g., eyewitness memory, "theory of mind," learning) to provide a rich analysis of children's source monitoring. Divergent programs of research are discussed that all tap into a different aspect or application of research on the development of source-monitoring skills. Although each program of research is unique, collectively, the chapters provide a much-needed integrated account of children's source monitoring.

There are several themes running through the chapters that contribute to the integrated flavor of the research findings. Some of the more prominent themes are the impact of source-monitoring processes on the information that is used by children as they learn about the world, the role of source monitoring in children's event memory, forensic and educational applications of source monitoring research, and comparisons with other theories of cognitive development (e.g., fuzzy-trace theory, Brainerd, Reyna, Howe, & Kingma, 1990). It was difficult, therefore, to meaningfully divide the chapters into strict subsections because each chapter straddles several different areas. The layout, therefore, should be viewed as indicative of general areas, rather than absolute, discrete categories of topics.

The book begins with an outline of source-monitoring theory and a historical review of the relevant developmental research (chap. 2, this volume). Rather than an exhaustive account of source-monitoring theory, which can be found in Johnson and colleagues' thorough *Psychological Bulletin* article (Johnson et al., 1993), a broad overview is presented with plentiful definitions and examples of the different types of source monitoring. This provides the reader with a theoretical grounding and a historical introduction to source-monitoring research to aid readers to synthesize the material contained in the following chapters. Much of the literature that forms the basis for the research programs described in the book is reviewed in detail in chapter 1, this volume, rather than duplicating background material in the empirical chapters. Current understanding about children's source monitoring discussed in chapter 1 is re-evaluated in chapter 12 by the same editor in light of the cutting-edge research reported between these two anchors.

The empirical chapters of the book are roughly split into three sections. The chapters in the first section (chaps. 3, 4, and 5), provide a review of the source-monitoring research that has clear implications for children's education. Although the importance of source monitoring to children's event memory has been discussed (e.g., Ceci, Huffman, Smith, & Loftus, 1994; Ceci, Loftus, Leichtman, & Bruck, 1994; Lindsay & Johnson, 1987), the role that source monitoring plays in the child's acquisition of declarative or procedural memory has not received much attention. Taylor, Esbensen, and Bennett (1994) showed that young children seem unaware of where they have learned information because they frequently report that they have always known what they have just been taught. If young children cannot identify where they learned information, this leaves open the (dangerous) possibility that they may absorb information regardless of the credibility of the different sources to which they are exposed. In chapter 3, this volume, Robinson presents a series of studies examining children's use of information from different sources. In particular, she discusses how young children (3- to 5-year-olds) assess a speaker's knowledge, and how children react when presented with contradictory or ambiguous information. Robinson finds a clear distinction in the behavior of 3-year-olds in their use of appropriate and inappropriate sources of information, and their ability to reflect and report on where they learned that information. Not only does this have implications for children's acquisition of knowledge, but it can also affect how they use information when describing memories of events that they have experienced.

Ratner, Foley, and Gimpert provide compelling findings in chapter 4 of this volume, illustrating that, in some circumstances, source confusions may underlie a mechanism that, rather than hindering learning, contributes to the acquisition of certain skills. An important aspect of their research is the emphasis of studying source monitoring in collaborative, goal-directed contexts. As demonstrated in recent research (e.g., Foley & Ratner, 1998), the kinds of processing that children engage in during different kinds of tasks leads to unique predictions about their source-monitoring behavior. Conceptualized this way, children's source errors are not regarded as negative indicators of their ability, but Ratner and colleagues' work signals a new perspective in which analyses of source misattributions reveal the kinds of processes that contribute to the rich schemas that children need to synthesize their knowledge.

In other circumstances, however, such as when source monitoring is the focus of a task, source-monitoring failures can be detrimental. Much of what we know about these source confusions and the development of accurate source-monitoring skills comes from studying the cognition of middle-class children with no known special educational needs. This narrow focus limits the confidence with which we can generalize our conclusions. Studying the patterns of source monitoring in other populations also serves theoretical purposes, because we can further explore the mechanisms underlying accurate source monitoring. In chapter 5, this volume, Lorsbach reviews the small number of studies that have been carried out with children who are not in educational mainstreams (e.g., children with autism or learning difficulties). By integrating the conclusions drawn about the memory and source-monitoring errors by children with learning difficulties, Lorsbach identifies the lack of effective reflective processing as being one of the mechanisms responsible for poor source monitoring, a conclusion echoed in other chapters. Lorsbach, therefore, outlines a cognitive profile that may prove useful in diagnoses as well as intervention efforts.

The contributors to the second section continue the theme of children's learning and focus on children's memories for one of the most pervasive forms of information in children's lives—television (see Gunter & McAleer, 1997; Jason & Hanaway, 1997; Van Evra, 1998). The research reported by Roberts and Blades (chap. 6, this volume) and Thierry, Spence, and Memon (chap. 7, this volume) also reflects the new wave of research in which investigators focus on children's source monitoring for complex material in the context of event memory. Both groups of researchers specifically focus on children's discrimination for information they learned in engaging, real-life events from that gleaned through watching television programs, and find that, in some situations, children inaccurately report that information seen on television actually occurred in real life.

As outlined in chapter 12 and elsewhere (see Johnson et al., 1993, for a full account), one way that people distinguish memories of different events is by an examination of the qualitative characteristics of those memories. Memories that contain distinctive characteristics are easier to distinguish than memories containing the same information. Roberts and Blades (chap. 6, this volume) describe how memories of television may be particularly likely to be confused with memories of real-life events because television can evoke the same kinds of perceptual, sensory, and affective processing typically evoked when children are involved in real-life events, thus leading to confusion. Events that are similar are more likely to be confused than events that are unique (e.g., Lindsay, Johnson, & Kwon, 1991), and Roberts and Blades extend our understanding by showing that it is not only similarity in the content of real-life events and television that cause confusion, but they discuss numerous other ways in which the representations of both types of events take on similar characteristics. In chapter 7 of this volume, Thierry and her colleagues compare the usefulness of source-monitoring and fuzzy-trace theories to explain children's confusion between televised and real-life events. Like other contributors, Thierry et al. investigated the source-monitoring skills of young children (3 to 5 years). Both groups of researchers cautiously note that their results may have implications for children's *eyewitness memory* (chap. 6, this volume) and *suggestibility* (Thierry, Spence, & Memon, this volume), topics that are addressed more explicitly in the third section of the book.

Understanding the role of source monitoring in children's memories of complex events was partly motivated by the desire to investigate the accuracy of children's eyewitness testimony in light of the well-publicized daycare sexual abuse cases in the 1980s (see Ceci & Bruck, 1995). Since then, research has implicated source-monitoring failures as contributing to children's reports of events that have not happened (e.g., Ceci, Huffman, et al., 1994; Ceci, Loftus, et al., 1994) or confusions between different sources of information to which children have been exposed (Ackil & Zaragoza, 1995). The exact mechanisms through which source errors contribute to inaccurate eyewitness reports, however, have not been specified. In the third section (chaps. 8, 9, 10, and 11), several groups of researchers discuss their investigations of various aspects of children's eyewitness memory.

Beginning the third section, Quas, Schaaf, Alexander, and Goodman (chap. 8, this volume) outline why source monitoring may be particularly important in a forensic context. Quas et al. present a theoretically driven examination of the potential impact of several characteristics of child abuse investigations on children's source monitoring. Many investigations of source monitoring have not assessed children's memory of forensically relevant events, thus limiting the generalizability of the conclusions. Children's memory of touching and being touched is clearly relevant to our understanding of eyewitness memory, as many of the incidents that police question children about involve bodily touch (e.g., during an investigation of sexual abuse; Goodman, Quas, Bulkley, & Shapiro, in press). Not only is the actual touch itself important, but the child's interpretation of the touching may also affect the accuracy of children's memory and source monitoring (Foley, 1997). Quas et al. discuss some of their research in which they investigated children's reports of an actual or fictitious touching experience over a series of repeated interviews. Quas et al. specifically assess whether young children can identify a suggestive interviewer as the source of information when they are asked to describe their experiences.

In the next two chapters, the importance of source monitoring in children's suggestibility is tracked, although both groups of researchers investigated a different aspect of the source monitoring—suggestibility relationship. Welch-Ross (chap. 9, this volume) returns to some of the links made earlier by Robinson (chap. 3, this volume) between source monitoring and theory of mind development. Welch-Ross considers the impact of memory, source monitoring, and various forms of representational understanding on children's suggestibility. A *mental-state reasoning model of suggestibility* is outlined and a series of experiments that test the claims of the model are presented. As discussed in chapter 2, this volume, now that many of the factors affecting the development and accuracy of children's source monitoring have been identified, one of the challenges for researchers is to understand the complex interactions of individual and situational variables. A similar shift in perspective has been recommended in the eyewitness literature (e.g., Poole & Lindsay, 1999). Welch-Ross' approach is symptomatic of this challenge.

Accounting for the individual variation in the accuracy of children's eyewitness reports is a question that is receiving much attention of late (e.g., Eisen, Goodman, Davis, & Qin, 1998). In chapter 10 of this volume, Leichtman, Morse, Dixon, and Spiegel specifically address the role that individual differences in source monitoring plays in young children's false reports of complete events that never happened.

Some researchers have presented direct evidence showing that some people accept misleading information because they genuinely believe that the misleading detail was present in the target event (i.e., a source confusion). Lindsay and Johnson (1989) and Zaragoza and Koshmider (1989) found that asking adults to choose from which source they learned certain information reduced their suggestibility relative to a control group who were merely asked to say whether the details were in the original event (see chap. 2, this volume, for further detail). In independent investigations, Thierry et al. (chap. 7, this volume) and Leichtman et al. (chap. 10, this volume) present procedures that they designed to "inoculate" children against such source errors. The results were modest, but encouraging, and the effects of these training techniques further inform us on the mechanisms of source monitoring in event memory.

As previously described, Quas et al. (chap. 8, this volume) review the importance of source monitoring in eyewitness testimonies; that is, verbal reports of events. The research program discussed by Foley, Foley, and Cormier (chap. 11, this volume) illustrates the usefulness of using the source-monitoring framework to investigate a nonverbal aspect of eyewitness memory—face identification. Their research indicates that using a source-monitoring perspective to investigate identification processes reveals important aspects of the kinds of perceptual mechanisms that occur when encoding and identifying faces.

In summary, the research programs discussed in this book highlight current issues in the study of children's source monitoring. The chapters provide an overview of the diversity of situations in which source monitoring is important, as well as the variety of techniques available to investigate these skills. The conclusions drawn from the different research endeavors are integrated in chapter 12, this volume, and discussed in relation to our current knowledge of children's source monitoring.

REFERENCES

Ackil, J. K., & Zaragoza, M. S. (1995). Developmental differences in eyewitness suggestibility and memory for source. *Journal of Experimental Child Psychology, 60,* 57-83.

Brainerd, C. J., Reyna, V. F., Howe, M. L., & Kingma, J. (1990). The development of forgetting and reminiscence. *Monographs of the Society for Research in Child Development, 55,* 1–111.

Ceci, S. J., & Bruck, M. (1995). *Jeopardy in the courtroom.* Washington, DC: American Psychological Association.

Ceci, S. J., Huffman, M. L. C., Smith, E., & Loftus, E. F. (1994). Repeatedly thinking about a non-event: Source misattributions among preschoolers. *Consciousness and Cognition, 3,* 388–407.

Ceci, S. J., Loftus, E. F., Leichtman, M. D., & Bruck, M. (1994). The possible role of source misattributions in the creation of false beliefs among preschoolers. *International Journal of Clinical and Experimental Hypnosis, 42,* 304–320.

Eisen, M. L., Goodman, G. S., Davis, S. L., & Qin, J. (1998). Individual differences in maltreated children's memory and suggestibility. In L. M. Williams & V. Banyard (Eds.), *Trauma and memory* (pp. 31–46). Thousand Oaks, CA: Sage.

Foley, M. A. (1997, April). Where to go next? Discussion presented in Roberts, K. P. (Chair), *Children's source monitoring and eyewitness testimony.* Symposium presented at the biennial meeting of the Society for Research in Child Development, Washington, DC.

Foley, M. A., & Johnson, M. K. (1985). Confusions between memories for performed and imagined actions: A developmental comparison. *Child Development, 56,* 1145–1155.

Foley, M. A., Johnson, M. K., & Raye, C. L. (1983). Age-related changes in confusion between memories for thoughts and memories for speech. *Child Development, 54,* 51–60.

Foley, M. A., & Ratner, H. H. (1998). Distinguishing between memories for thoughts and deeds: The role of prospective processing in children's source monitoring. *British Journal of Developmental Psychology, 16,* 465–484.

Goodman, G. S., Quas, J. A., Bulkley, J., & Shapiro, C. (in press). Innovations for child witnesses: A national survey. *Psychology, Public Policy, and Law.*

Groening, M. (1997). *The Simpsons: A complete guide to our favorite family.* Edited by R. Richmond, & A. Coffman. New York: Harper Collins Publishers, Inc.

Gunter, B., & McAleer, J. L. (1997). *Children and television.* London: Routledge & Kegan Paul.

Jason, L. A., & Hanaway, L. K. (1997). *Remote control: A sensible approach to kids, TV, and the new electronic media.* Sarasota, FL: Professional Resource Press.

Johnson, M. K., Hashtroudi, S., & Lindsay, D. S. (1993). Source monitoring. *Psychological Bulletin, 114,* 3–28.

Johnson, M. K., & Raye, C. L. (1981). Reality monitoring. *Psychological Review, 88,* 67–85.

Johnson, M. K., Raye, C. L., Wang, A. W., & Taylor, T. H. (1979). Fact and fantasy: The roles of accuracy and variability in confusing imaginations with perceptual experiences. *Journal of Experimental Psychology: Human Learning and Memory, 5,* 229–240.

Lindsay, D. S., & Johnson, M. K. (1987). Reality monitoring and suggestibility: Children's ability to discriminate among memories from different sources. In S. J. Ceci, M. P. Toglia, & D. F. Ross (Eds.), *Children's eyewitness memory* (pp 92–121). New York: Springer-Verlag.

Lindsay, D. S., & Johnson, M. K. (1989). The eyewitness suggestibility effect and memory for source. *Memory and Cognition, 17,* 349–358.

Lindsay, D. S., Johnson, M. K., & Kwon, P. (1991). Developmental changes in memory source monitoring. *Journal of Experimental Child Psychology, 52,* 297–318.

Poole, D. A., & Lindsay, D. S. (1999). *Children's eyewitness reports after exposure to misinformation from parents.* Manuscript under review.

Taylor, M., Esbensen, B. M., & Bennett, R. T. (1994). Children's understanding of knowledge acquisition: The tendency for children to report that they have always known what they have just learned. *Child Development, 65,* 1581–1604.

Van Evra, J. P. (1998). *Television and child development* (2nd ed.). Mahwah, NJ: Lawrence Erlbaum Associates.

Welch-Ross, M. (this volume). A mental-state reasoning model of suggestibility and memory source monitoring. In K. P. Roberts & M. Blades (Eds.), *Children's source monitoring.* Mahwah, NJ: Lawrence Erlbaum Associates.

Zaragoza, M. S., & Koshmider, J. W., III. (1989). Misled subjects may know more than their performance implies. *Journal of Experimental Psychology: Learning, Memory, and Cognition, 15,* 246–255.

2

An Overview of Theory and Research on Children's Source Monitoring

Kim P. Roberts
*National Institute of Child Health
and Human Development*

In chapter 1, this volume, several examples are given of how source monitoring can disrupt everyday functioning in both cognitive and social domains. As described, the reader will see examples throughout the book of the importance of source monitoring in children's acquisition of knowledge, organizational skills, reasoning, and event memory. Before examining these topics in detail, however, a theoretical overview of source monitoring is necessary. This chapter is intended to put the research discussed in the following chapters in perspective and to allow the reader to review the work with a critical and informed eye.

This chapter is not intended to be an exhaustive review of source-monitoring theory; rather, this chapter teases out the main ideas in the source-monitoring framework, with a discussion of factors known to have significant effects on the accuracy of children's source monitoring. All readers are strongly urged to carefully read Johnson and colleagues' (Johnson, Hashtroudi, & Lindsay, 1993) excellent overview of the source-monitoring framework. This chapter is split into four parts. In the first section, I clarify the nature of source monitoring and present examples of some of the types of source discriminations that children and adults make in their everyday lives. The theoretical underpinnings of this framework are discussed in the second section as I describe how we actually carry out these source discriminations. In the third section, presented is an overview of developmental differences in source monitoring and draw on the early, pioneering studies in this area. Finally, in the final section, significant factors are discussed that impact children's source monitoring. These factors are grouped into five main areas: characteristics of the sources to be discriminated (similarity, complexity of the sources), characteristics of the person (imagery ability, representational understanding, other individual differences), the role of the agent who is carrying out the source distinction (self-generation effect, elaborative processing, the importance of the perspective adopted), interaction with the sources (feedback, employment of cognitive operations, and the goal-related nature of the task), and, finally, the impact of processes carried out at the time of remembering (gist interference, orientation to source). The historical overview summarizes the current state of our knowledge on the development of children's source monitoring and takes us to the current wave of research reviewed in the following chapters.

WHAT IS SOURCE MONITORING?

Source monitoring describes "the set of processes involved in making attributions about the origins of memories, knowledge, and beliefs" (Johnson et al., 1993, p. 3)[1] and the theoretical framework developed out of reality-monitoring theory (Johnson & Raye, 1981). *Reality monitoring* refers to source decisions regarding internally derived and externally derived events. For example, one may try and distinguish whether you actually watched the Orioles baseball team beat the Yankees (an event that originated external to the individual carrying out the source monitoring) or whether you just had a daydream that the Orioles won the World Series (an event derived from within the individual).[2] This example requires reality monitoring for the status of the remembered events (i.e., public vs. private). In this case, external events are defined as publicly perceived events (e.g., a television show, words spoken by a friend on the telephone, dentist filling a cavity), whereas internal events originate in the individual and, in the case of status-reality monitoring, are not public (e.g., thinking through a solution to a problem, dreaming).

---

[1]A point on grammatical notation: When referring to the *process* of source monitoring, common procedure is to write it as two separate words (e.g., "children's source monitoring can be accurate"). When 'source monitoring' is used as a description, a hyphen is used (e.g., "in a study on factors affecting source-monitoring accuracy"; "Source-monitoring theory can guide the research in this area").

[2]*Event* refers to any instance in the past—not necessarily a memory of a complex event like a birthday party, but *event could also refer to hearing a word, learning the day of the week, and so on.*

Another kind of reality monitoring refers to distinguishing the origin of internal and external events. For example, you may want to decide whether you booked the family vacation or whether your husband did that. This example requires a decision about the self—other nature of events (i.e., Did I or my husband carry out this action?). Just as with status reality monitoring, external events refer to those that originated outside the individual (i.e., something your husband did) and internal events refer to those that were generated by the individual carrying out the source monitoring (i.e., what you did). In contrast to status-reality monitoring, however, in the case of origin reality monitoring, both internal and external events were publicly perceived. The distinction of interest here is between the self versus other nature of events.

As well as distinguishing between memories of internally and externally derived events, there are other kinds of source comparisons that children need to learn, and these are summarized in Table 2.1, although this list is not exhaustive (Johnson et al., 1993). One distinction is known as *external source monitoring* and refers to the process of distinguishing between memories of different external events (i.e., events that originate outside the individual and are publicly perceived). For example, a young boy may need to remember whether Anne or Jessie asked him to a birthday party, or a girl may want to remember whether she learned that there is life on Mars from watching a reputable television news show or from a children's science fiction program.

A final kind of source distinction is known as *internal source monitoring*. An example of internal source monitoring (distinguishing between memories of events generated by the individual carrying out the source monitoring), is the case of a teenager deciding whether she told her mom that she had been given detention in school before she told her dad. This requires a decision between two self-generated, publicly perceived events. Internal source monitoring also refers to those occasions when a distinction between memories of self-generated, private events is necessary, such as a child deciding whether he imagined the ending to Lewis Carroll's *Alice in Wonderland* or whether he dreamed about it. Similarly, one may need to distinguish between two self-generated events, one of which was public and the other private, such as a child deciding whether he had actually tidied his room or just pretended to tidy it. This latter kind of internal source monitoring is also known as *realization judgments* (Foley, Johnson, & Raye, 1983). Just as with reality monitoring, then, the definition of what is an *internal event* can refer to the status (public vs. private) or the origin (self vs. other) of the information. As discussed by Johnson et al. (1993),

TABLE 2.1
Classification of Source-Monitoring Discriminations

Label	Sources	Example
Reality Monitoring		
a. Status (public vs. private discrimination)	External (other-generated and publicly perceived) vs. Internal (self-generated and private)	Did John Glenn really land on the moon or did I just dream he did?
b. Origin (self vs. other discrimination)	External (other-generated and publicly perceived) vs. Internal (self-generated and publicly perceived)	Did he switch the channel on the TV or did I?
	External (other-generated and publicly perceived) vs. Internal (self-generated and private	Did he switch the channel on the TV or did I just imagine he did?
Internal Source Monitoring	Internal (self-generated and public) vs. Internal (self-generated and public)	Did I tell Mom or Dad that I would call?
	Internal (self-generated and public) vs. Internal (self-generated and private)	Did I actually turn the oven off or did I just intend to turn it off?
	Internal (self-generated and private) vs. Internal (self-generated and private)	Did I dream about winning the Lottery or winning the Nobel Prize?
External Source Monitoring	External (other-generated and publicly perceived) vs. External (other-generated and publicly perceived)	Did Sonny or Cher sing the song?

neither categorization scheme is more correct than the other, but the definitions provide an indication of the many different kinds of source distinctions. In addition, the definitions outlined here provide a conceptual foundation for reasoning about source monitoring, especially for newer scholars of source-monitoring theory.

Source monitoring for the public—private dimension of events does not refer to reality testing, or the process of distinguishing between the real and fictional status of entities, although developmentally, this may precede the formation of some source-monitoring skills. Rather, source monitoring refers to the processes involved in distinguishing the sources of *memories* of events.[3] Suppose that little Christopher visits his friend, Jonathan, on Monday and plays with Jonathan's toy car. On Tuesday, Jonathan goes on vacation so Christopher cannot visit, but Christopher imagines what games he would play if he had the toy car. Christopher knows that he isn't really playing with the toy car, but is just imagining so. When Jonathan returns from vacation two weeks later, he asks Christopher what he did while he was on vacation. Christopher says that he played with the toy car and Jonathan replies that Christopher could not have played with the car because Jonathan took the toy car with him on vacation. In other words, Christopher knew the reality status of his actions at the time in question (that he didn't really play with the car), but was later confused when trying to *remember* what he did and what he imagined; that is, he made an internal source-monitoring error for the public—private dimension of the events.

It is important, at this point, to draw attention to the conceptual underpinnings of source-monitoring theory. Within the source-monitoring framework, source is not conceptualized as a label or a tag in a memory representation containing source information that can be directly retrieved. (Note that this is in contrast to some other frameworks such as fuzzy-trace theory, Brainerd et al., [1990], in which source is considered to be a verbatim representation; see Thierry, Spence, & Memon, this volume, for a comparison between source-monitoring and fuzzy-trace theories.) Rather, controlled or automatic decision processes that take place at the time of remembering result in an *attribution* of source. The decision processes may use information that was encoded in memory, but source is attributed rather than recalled. Take the preceding example of Christopher needing to distinguish between a memory of imagining playing with a

---

[3]I use *memory* in the broadest sense of the word and include, for example, episodic, autobiographical, declarative, and procedural memory to show that we need to distinguish the origin of knowledge and beliefs as well as more explicit memories of events.

toy car versus a memory of actually playing with a real toy car. He may remember both events, but because he remembers so well what he did when he was actually playing, he may reason that he must have been playing with the car because he would not have remembered the incident so well if it did not actually happen. In other words, Christopher has attributed the source of his memory (derived from his imagination) to the time when he was actually playing with the toy car.

There are several reasons why source information is unlikely to be encoded as a tag in memory, and, again, readers are referred to Johnson et al.'s (1993) review for more detailed arguments. First, many researchers have found accurate old/new recognition for items, but poor identification of the items' source, and this occurs for all age groups (e.g., Ackil & Zaragoza, 1998; Ferguson, Hashtroudi, & Johnson, 1992; Foley & Johnson, 1985; Powell & Thomson, 1997; Roberts & Blades, 1995; Schachter, Harbluk, & McLachlan, 1984). Indeed, several contributors to this volume have found that children can use or remember factual content without remembering its source, or inaccurately attributing its source (e.g., chap. 3, this volume). Second, manipulations that alter source-monitoring accuracy may not affect old/new recognition, and vice versa (e.g., Lindsay & Johnson, 1991; Rybash, Rubenstein, & DeLuca, 1997). Third, conceptualizing source as a tag does not explain the specific asymmetries in misattribution errors (e.g., Anderson, 1984; Foley et al., 1983). Fourth, more recently, studies on the time course of reality-monitoring judgments demonstrate that recognition processes use different information than that required for source judgments, or at least a less differentiated form of the information (e.g., Johnson, Kounios, & Reeder, 1994). This is not to say that recognition memory and source monitoring are unconnected. Rather, Johnson et al. argue that the association between the different processes depends on the extent to which the same information is used for each skill. Finally, as discussed more fully in the sections entitled "How Do We Source Monitor?" and "Factors Affecting Source Monitoring," what information is encoded at the time of the event has direct implications for the accuracy of the source attribution.

One of the appealing features of this framework is that source-monitoring theory offers an explanation of the times when people make memory errors that are not based on inaccurate memory for content. Rather, source memory is conceptualized as a set of processes carried out at the time of remembering, which affects accuracy in varying degrees. For example, an eyewitness may see a youth in a blue sweater steal candy from a convenience store. While the witness is waiting for the police to take his statement, he talks to another witness who mentions that the suspect was wearing a red sweater. When the original eyewitness gives his statement to the police, he recalls that the account of the other witness was inconsistent with his account, but mistakenly recalls that he saw the suspect in a red sweater and the other witness described the suspect as dressed in a blue sweater. In other words, our witness remembers both his own and the other witness' account of the suspect's attire, but is thoroughly confused regarding the sources of the information—he genuinely believes that he saw the suspect wearing a red sweater (when, in fact, this description was merely suggested to him).

An astute reader may be thinking: "But, are all source-monitoring judgments this straightforward?" Clearly, they are not. Consider, for example, the situation when a mother and daughter are reminiscing about the child's birthday party the previous year. The mother (inaccurately) suggests that the daughter wore a Jack-in-the-Box costume, when the child actually wore a rabbit costume and her brother was the Jack-in-the-Box. The daughter's teacher asks the daughter what costume she wore last year. There are several different source distinctions that the daughter may consider to give an accurate answer:

1. The daughter needs to engage in reality monitoring for the status of the event (perceived vs. nonperceived event) and decide whether she actually wore the Jack-in-the-Box costume (perceived) or whether it was only a suggestion that she wore it (nonperceived).

2. She may engage in reality monitoring for the origin (self-generated or other-generated event) and decide whether she put the Jack-in-the-Box costume on or whether her brother wore the costume.

3. She may engage in a combination of status and origin reality monitoring (self-generated, private event vs. other-generated, public event) and decide whether she imagined she put the Jack-in-the-Box costume on, or her mom told her that she wore the costume.

These are examples of the variety and levels of source decisions. Different source discriminations may take precedence depending on the specifics of the decision required. For example, if the teacher asked the child "Who wore the Jack-in-the-Box costume?" the child may focus most of her source attributional reasoning on origin reality monitoring (did she or her brother wear the costume) because the important source distinction is the person who wore the costume (although the other source discriminations may also affect the accuracy of her answer). If her teacher asked her "Did you really wear the

Jack-in-the-Box costume?", the daughter's answer may be more influenced by reality-monitoring judgments for the status of the event (actually wore costume or suggestion that she wore costume) because the public–private (actual–fictitious) dimension is the most important distinction in this case.

We can see from this example that it is likely that, depending on which source distinctions are of interest, children's source monitoring may show different patterns. A recent investigation with adults supports the suggestion that source-monitoring decisions are likely to be related to the characteristics of the source query. Marsh and Hicks (1998) asked college students to read a word (seen items), or to swap two letters in an anagram to produce the word (generated items). After a delay, the participants in one condition were given a test containing the words plus distracters not presented before, and they were required to choose whether the word was previously presented in the experiment and, if so, whether they saw or generated the word. The source question varied, however, to focus attention on different qualitative characteristics. Marsh and Hicks found that accuracy for generated items was better than for seen items when participants were asked "Did you generate the word?", and accuracy for seen items was better than for generated items when asked "Did you see the word?" In other words, how the participants were probed affected the accuracy for their source judgments because they used the cues in the question as a basis for their source attributions. When the cue in the question was a useful distinction for a particular item, source attribution was enhanced; when it was a less useful cue, source attribution deteriorated.

In summary, we have covered a variety of source distinctions: those according to a reality dimension (e.g., Was it real or a dream?), a person dimension (e.g., Did Jack or Jill say it?), an action dimension (e.g., Did I jump or skip to the store?), and a temporal dimension (e.g., Did it happen yesterday or the day before?). There are also other dimensions on which we may want to discriminate memories and knowledge, such as deciding whether a complete, complex event happened or not (e.g., Did I go to Hawaii or not?). In the next section, I present a concise version of the different ways in which we monitor the sources of our memories. Readers who are interested in a more detailed account of source monitoring are referred to Johnson et al.'s (1993) *Psychological Bulletin* article.

HOW DO WE SOURCE MONITOR?

The accuracy of source monitoring is determined both by the quality of the encoding at the time of the event and the quality of the decision processes performed at the time of remembering. There are basically two ways in which we monitor the sources of our memories: The most common way is relatively automatic and involves examining the characteristics of memories; the second way is more deliberate and effortful and comprises systematic judgments. Many tests of source-monitoring theory have been carried out with adults, although there are similarities in the processes involved in children's and adults' source monitoring (Foley, Durso, Wilder, & Friedman, 1991). However, source-monitoring skills may not be as well developed or stable in children (e.g., Roberts & Blades, 1995) and some issues are especially pertinent with respect to children's cognitive development. In this section, research with children and adults is discussed.

Examining the Characteristics of Memories

Examining the characteristics of our memories may be carried out automatically as we recall past experiences (Johnson et al., 1993). Memories derived from external and internal sources are qualitatively different and these differences are used in source-monitoring judgments. Specifically, memories derived from externally generated events contain, on average and in comparison with memories derived from internally generated events, more information that is perceptual (e.g., colors, sounds), contextual (spatial: e.g., location of event; temporal: e.g., the time of day the event occurred), semantic (what the event was about), and affective (e.g., feeling scared), and less information about cognitive operations. *Cognitive operations* refer to thoughts and cognitive processes that took place at the time of the event and could include reasoning, remembering, generating, inferencing, imagery, and so on. In contrast, memories derived from internally generated sources contain less perceptual, contextual, semantic, and affective information (because the event was not, in fact, perceived), but more cognitive-operations information than do events derived from externally generated sources.

An examination of the characteristics of memories can induce a conclusion that the event was internally or externally generated. For example, suppose you need to remember whether you have entered some data or just intended to enter the data—you engage in internal source monitoring for the status of the events: "Did I enter the data (actual, public event) or just imagine entering the data (private event)?" As you are trying to remember, you recall that your finger joints hurt from typing, that your eyes hurt from the glare of the computer screen, and that you had to rush to finish before the meeting with your supervisor. As your memory contains sensory, perceptual, and temporal information, you may attribute the memory to an event

that actually occurred. If, on the other hand, as you are trying to remember, you think about how you made a mental note to yourself to
buy the latest spreadsheet software so that data entry would be easier
and you do not remember any perceptual and contextual details associated with entering data. In this case, you may attribute your memory
to a nonperceived, imagined event. In the first scenario, the memory
contained characteristics that were typical of memories derived from
actual, perceived experiences, leading you to conclude that you had
actually entered the data; in the second scenario, your memory was
more typical of that of an imagined event, and so you conclude that
you merely intended to enter the data.

Memories of different events, then, contain different qualitative
profiles. For example, a memory of daydreaming that the Orioles won
the baseball championship (private, internally generated event) is
likely to contain fewer perceptual and contextual details and more information about the imagery and generation processes that gave rise
to the daydream than would a memory of actually being at Yankee sta-
dium and seeing the team win (public, externally derived event). Memories of tidying a bedroom (public, internally generated event) and
carrying out the actions in pretense (private, internally generated
event) may also contain perceptual information associated with the
actual or mimed actions of tidying, but these memories also contain
cognitive-operations information because both events were derived
from within the individual who is carrying out the source monitoring.
Hence, the useful differences in qualitative characteristics are relative
and not absolute.

This source-monitoring process may be disrupted either at the
time of encoding or during the decision-making processes at the time
of remembering. Let us return to the data example previously described to see how encoding processes can disrupt later source monitoring. Imagine that, as you entered the data, you were highly
cognitively engaged because you were noting the number of outliers in
your sample. Your memory may contain a large amount of cognitive-operations information relative to the amount of perceptual and
sensory characteristics. Your memory is now more typical of a memory derived from an internally generated, private event, so source
monitoring based on the retrieved characteristics of your memory
may lead to a decision that you did not actually enter the data. Even if
your memory was rich in characteristics typical of an action that you
have actually carried out, source errors may occur during the source
decision-making processes carried out at the time of remembering.
This could happen if the person was engaged in a demanding task
while they were source monitoring, for example, as in the case of di-

vided attention (e.g., Jacoby, Woloshyn, & Kelley, 1989). In addition, intervening events between the time of encoding and the time of remembering could alter the accuracy of the information reported. For example, if a second person was entering the data and told you about some variables that you had not created, then your memory may be contaminated by this misleading information. Source attributions based on this hybrid memory will therefore be affected.

That internal and external memories contain these characteristics was demonstrated in a study by Johnson, Foley, Suengas, and Raye (1988). Johnson et al. asked adults to rate their memories of actual and imagined events for the presence of a wide range of criteria. They found that memories of events that had actually happened contained more visual detail, more details of sounds, smells, tastes, the setting, location, spatial arrangements of objects and people, time references, and descriptions of memories from before and after the target event. This evidence supports the unique characteristics of memories of externally and internally derived events that are outlined in the source-monitoring framework. Similar profiles have also been documented in children's reports (e.g., Alonso-Quecuty, 1996; Roberts, Lamb, Zale, & Randall, 1998).

What evidence is there that people actually do use the unique characteristics of memories from externally and internally derived events to judge their source? Some direct demonstrations for the use of these criteria have come from experimental manipulations of the characteristics of different sources (e.g., Johnson & Suengas, 1989; Suengas & Johnson, 1988). If memories differ according to the characteristics previously outlined, and participants use these average differences to attribute source, then it should be possible to manipulate the accuracy of source-monitoring decisions by manipulating the qualitative characteristics of those memories. Johnson and Suengas (1989) asked adult participants to actually carry out six short events (e.g., wrapping a parcel) and to imagine carrying out six events. Before giving descriptions of their memories to judges for them to rate as perceived or imagined events, half of the participants rehearsed perceptual aspects of the events and half rehearsed apperceptive aspects. Rehearsing perceptual details should lead to memories that contain more perceptual information than if the apperceptive details had been rehearsed, and rehearsing apperceptive details should lead to memories containing less perceptual details. Johnson and Suengas found that the descriptions of imagined events given by participants who rehearsed perceptual aspects contained as much perceptual detail as descriptions of the events that were actually carried out. If judges use the presence of perceptual information as indicative of a memory of a publicly perceived event, then both the descriptions of perceived and imagined events should be rated as perceived if they were given by participants who rehearsed perceptual details. The judges did, in fact, rate descriptions containing the greatest perceptual detail as memories of a perceived event regardless of the actual source of the memory (perceived or imagined), demonstrating that the qualitative differences in memories are used as cues to the source of a person's memories.

Support for the examination of the qualitative characteristics of memories in source discriminations also comes from studies showing that when the memories to be distinguished are from the same class, source discrimination is difficult, even when those memories contain the prototypical characteristics of that class of memories (Foley et al., 1983; Foley & Johnson, 1985; Lindsay, Johnson, & Kwon, 1991). For example, Foley et al. found that children had more difficulty distinguishing between memories of what they had said and what they imagined they said (both internal events) than they did distinguishing between what they had said and what another person had said (internal and external events, respectively). Interestingly, this did not explain all of their difficulty because Foley et al. also found that children were as good as adults at distinguishing between what two different people said (i.e., two externally derived events). Lindsay et al. argued that the within-class difficulty reflects a more general difficulty with discriminating between memories that share similar characteristics, and this is discussed later in the "Factors Affecting Source Monitoring" section.

The presence of cognitive-operations characteristics can be a particularly useful cue in status-source monitoring (distinguishing between the public and private nature of events), as demonstrated in experiments in which an increased amount of encoded cognitive operations resulted in more accurate source discriminations (Foley et al., 1991; Finke, Johnson, & Shyi, 1988). Foley et al. (1991) showed 6-year-olds, 9-year-olds, and adults a set of words and pictures and asked the participants to either state the function of the item, or to generate an image of the item and rate the vividness of their image. When later asked to distinguish whether they had seen the item presented as a word or a picture, the participants in the function condition made more external source-monitoring errors than children in the imagery condition because they were more likely to say that they saw a picture of an item, when the item was actually presented as a word. Foley et al. reasoned that the children and adults in the imagery condition used more deliberate and extensive cognitive processing than did those participants who were asked to perform a more automatic rating of function. The extensive cognitive processing led to memories that contained more cognitive operations than did the memories of the participants in the function condition, and this information was used in the source judgments. Furthermore, half of the items were previously categorized by Snodgrass and Vanderwort (1980) as simple or complex. Foley et al. found that participants in both conditions were more accurate at identifying the source of complex items (which would require more cognitive processing) than simple items. This study demonstrates that differences in the characteristics of memories can be used to successfully identify the source, and that children can use the same criteria as adults to judge the source of their memories.

In summary, one way that we can accurately monitor our memories is through an examination of the characteristics of those memories. Memories of events that were externally generated and have public status contain more information about perceptual, contextual, semantic, and affective information than memories that are internally generated and private. External memories also contain few details of the cognitive operations carried out at the time of the event. Relative to memories of externally generated events, memories of internally generated events contain a lack of perceptual, contextual, semantic, and affective information; but will contain more cognitive-operations information. These profiles can be used to attribute the source of memories, and this method will be most effective when memory characteristics are distinctive. When there is a disruption in the encoding of details that give rise to these characteristics, source-monitoring accuracy may suffer. Similarly, anything that affects the quality of the characteristics in the time between experiencing the events and making the source judgment will affect the accuracy of the discrimination (e.g., a loss of perceptual information will make it more difficult to distinguish between a memory of performing an action and a memory of imagining an action). This process of source monitoring can be carried out automatically during the course of remembering the event.

Deliberate Judgment Processes

Source distinctions can sometimes be strategically invoked and involve reasoning, retrieving other memories, and noting relations (Johnson et al., 1993). For example, suppose that you are at a conference and a participant who is staying in the same hotel as you offers to give you a ride back to the hotel in her car. She suggests that you meet her in the parking lot. As you are walking to the parking lot, you think about what her car looks like and you imagine a red car. You are not sure, however, whether you have actually seen her car before, and so you must engage in reality monitoring for the origin of the memory (memory of a car vs. memory of an imagination). You can picture the shape, color, and noise of the car—it is a small, red, convertible car, with an exhaust that rattles. An examination of the characteristics of your memory may lead you to conclude that you have actually seen her car because your memory contains perceptual details that are typical of memories of actually perceived events. You want to be absolutely sure, however, and so you also engage in more strategic decision making and accurately conclude that you cannot have a memory of a perceived event, because you only met the participant for the first time earlier that morning and, hence, could not have seen her car before. Later that evening you realize that the conference participant reminded you of a friend, and it was actually your friend's car that you imagined.

Evidence for the role of strategic source monitoring comes from experimental demonstrations of systematic biases in source attribution. If people do not engage in deliberate decision making, then there will be a random distribution of different kinds of errors; if people do make strategic source decisions, however, then there will be systematic misattribution biases shown in the pattern of errors. Consider another example: Suppose Mike told Margaret a joke that she had not heard before. Margaret (inaccurately) thinks that she and Mike had discussed the joke before. She tried to decide whether she had told Mike the joke, or whether he had told her the joke. She concludes that Mike must have told it to her because she reasons that she would have had a better memory for the joke if she had told it to Mike. This is known as the "it-had-to-be-you" effect, which has been empirically demonstrated in several investigations (Anderson, 1984; Johnson & Raye, 1981) and this bias has been observed in both adults' and children's source monitoring. For example, some of the children in Foley et al.'s (1983) study were asked to distinguish between words that they had said and words spoken by a confederate. Some of the children (and adults) inaccurately claimed that distracter words presented at the test were present when the words were spoken, and there was a distinct pattern to these false positive errors. Specifically, participants were more likely to claim that the confederate had said the word than to claim that they had said the word. This is an example of a strategic source decision process that goes something like this: A (new) item seems vaguely familiar, and source attribution is attempted; people reason that if they had said, done, or thought the item, they would have remembered it more clearly; they do not remember the item clearly; therefore, they must not have generated the item.

As strategic source-monitoring processes are deliberate and effortful, they are also subject to disruption. For example, Dywan, Segalowitz, and Webster (1998) show that younger adults (mean age 24 years) show better source discrimination for words previously presented on a study list and new words that were repeatedly presented on a test than did older adults (mean age 70 years). In a second experiment, they found that when the attention of the younger adults was disrupted during the study trial (by asking them to listen to a string of numbers and identify when three identical numbers occurred together), their subsequent source monitoring was at a similar level to the older participants. This led Dywan et al. to conclude that a lack of attentional control explains why older adults show source-monitoring deficits compared with younger individuals.

In summary, people can engage in systematic judgment processes when monitoring the source of their memories. Evidence for these processes is seen in systematic biases, such as the "it-had-to-be-you" effect. At times, these strategic processes can be disrupted, leading to inaccuracies in source attributions. If, for example, a person is distracted when making the source judgment, or if the person uses an heuristic that is in error, failures to accurately identify source can occur. In the next section, I discuss the relationship between automatic and strategic decision processes.

Stringency of Decision Processes

Automatic and strategic processes may work together or alone to result in a source decision. The accuracy and deployment of these processes may depend on the criteria that is used as a comparison for the information that has been activated. Stringent source monitoring usually entails using both heuristic and strategic judgments and setting strict criteria (Johnson et al., 1993). It may be helpful to conceptualize the use of criteria as "if X, then Y" judgments. Consider the example of the conference participant attempting to distinguish between a memory of a red car and an imagination of the car. If the criteria was set at "if there is vivid information in my memory, then it must be a memory of an actually perceived event," the source attribution may have been made on the basis of the automatic examination of the characteristics of the activated information (small, red, noisy car) without continuing with any strategic processes. In this example, however, strategic source monitoring (reasoning that you could not have seen her car, therefore, your memory was not one of an actual event) prevented an error that would likely have been made if source attribution had been based solely on automatic appraisals. Of course, sometimes strategic processes can result in inaccurate source monitoring. If, for example, you knew that the participant's favorite color was red, you may have (inaccurately) concluded that you had actually seen her car because it fits with your knowledge about the participant. The "it-had-to-be-you" effect can also be explained by an interaction between automatic and strategic processes. When items are falsely recognized, any automatic source-monitoring process that is carried out must fail because no encoded characteristics of the item should be available to examine because they were not, in fact, perceived. The judgment of source (i.e., that the other person must have said it) was made through strategic judgments about likely sources.

These if–then judgments are not set in stone. Rather, they can change with the demands of the task, can be influenced by metamemory biases, and can be affected by assumptions and beliefs about memory (Johnson et al., 1993). In some situations, a strict criterion may be set; in other situations, this same criterion may be more lax. Imagine that you have come across the information that males are more aggressive than females, but you are unsure where you learned that information—you may have read about it in a scientifically controlled study in a psychology textbook, you may have seen it expressed as an opinion on a personal web page, or it may have come from a number of other sources. If you were participating in a friendly discussion in a bar, you may set a fairly lax criterion and decide to bring up this information because you know you "read it somewhere." If you were taking a psychology test, however, you may expend more effort in accurately determining the source of the information and, hence, set more stringent criterion levels. Rather than using a, "if I read it, then it must have come from a credible source," heuristic you now use, "if I read it *in a psychology textbook*, it must have come from a credible source" heuristic.

Evidence from the changes in criteria levels comes from experimental studies showing that increasing the importance of source decisions (e.g., by orienting participants to source, or varying the task demands) leads to more accurate source monitoring. Lindsay and Johnson (1989) showed college students a slide of an office scene and later asked them to read a narrative about the slide. Some participants read a narrative that contained inaccurate information. Participants were then tested for their memory of the slide in one of two ways: (a) a yes/no recognition test and asked to indicate if the item was in the picture, or (b) a source-monitoring test and asked to indicate if the item was in the picture, text, picture and text, or neither picture nor text. Lindsay and Johnson found that participants given the source-monitoring test less often claimed that a misleading item from the narrative was in the slide than the participants who answered a yes/no recognition test. In other words, orienting the participants' attention to source decreased (but did not eliminate) the number of confusions between the narrative and the slide. Lindsay et al. argued that participants given the yes/no test may have responded on the basis of a familiarity judgment ("if I recognize it, I must have seen it") without an appraisal of where the information was presented; other participants who were oriented to source, however, set stricter decision levels because the source-monitoring test required them to recognize and identify the source of the presented information. Similar results were also found by Zaragoza and Koshmider (1989). More extended discussions of the relation between source monitoring and misinformation effects in children can be found in Ceci, Huffman, Smith, and Loftus (1994), Lindsay and Johnson (1987), Powell, Roberts, Ceci, and Hembrooke (in press), and several chapters in this volume (Leichtman, Morse, Dixon, & Spiegel, chap. 10; Quas, Schaaf, Alexander, & Goodman, chap. 8; Thierry, Spence, & Memon, chap. 7; Welch-Ross, chap. 9).

As well as the stringency of the source-decision criteria, different weights may be assigned to different factors used in the source judgment (Johnson et al., 1993). For example, when distinguishing between a memory of an action that you have carried out and an intention to carry out that action, you may assign significant weight to the presence of cognitive-operations information in your memories. This is because the presence of cognitive-operations information is a useful cue to use in this situation: The memory of the intention is likely to include cognitive operations information (e.g., imagery about what the action would feel like, planning the steps to carry out the action, thinking about intended consequences, etc.), whereas a memory of an action that has actually been carried out is unlikely to contain such a large proportion of cognitive-operations information relative to other kinds of information, such as sensory details. If, however, you had an external source-monitoring judgment to make between which one of two coworkers told you a joke, then the presence of cognitive-operations information is likely to be of limited use in this situation, as both events were generated by sources external to you. In this situation, a more useful cue to use would be perceptual information that is distinctive to each person (e.g., one person has a deep voice, the other person waves their hands emphatically when telling a joke). In this case, then, you might assign more weight to the perceptual information in your memories when you make your judgment than you would to cognitive-operations information. This simplifies the matter, of course, because source judgments are most effective when multiple cues to source are used (Ferguson et al., 1992; Johnson et al., 1993).

In summary, automatic and strategic decision processes can be used alone or together when making source attributions. Each type of process can provide a check on the other, although errors can occur. When automatic and systematic processes are used together, more stringent source monitoring will occur. The weight assigned to each kind of process varies depending on the nature of the source distinction and the demands of the current task.

THE DEVELOPMENT OF SOURCE MONITORING

Important developments in source monitoring take place in childhood. It is believed that source monitoring is fairly stable through most of adulthood, with some decline in abilities in elder years. Several researchers have encouraged research, particularly with children aged 3 to 8 because important changes in source monitoring are evident in this age range (Roberts & Blades, 1995; Welch-Ross, 1995), and this conclusion is borne out by many of the contributors to this volume (e.g., Robinson, chap. 3; Thierry et al., chap. 7; Welch-Ross, chap. 9).

There are several issues that are particularly important to bear in mind when thinking about children's source monitoring and its development. First, children's development is typically not evidenced as a series of Piagetian-like jumps. Rather, the development of children's source monitoring, like many other childhood developments, is shown in gradual steps, rather than sudden flashes of understanding (Johnson et al., 1993; Lindsay et al., 1991). Dissociation between different types of source monitoring has been found in developmental investigations (e.g., Foley et al., 1983, 1985; Hashtroudi, Johnson, & Chrosniak, 1989; Welch-Ross, 1995) and in people who have suffered brain damage (e.g., Harvey, 1985). Children may appear competent at source monitoring using one measure, but using another measure in the same experimental context, they may make source misattributions (see chap. 6, this volume). Children's source-monitoring skills may also be unstable over delays (e.g., Roberts & Blades, 1995; chap. 7, this volume). The second, related issue refers to children's development and to the characterization of source in general. I described earlier that there are many different kinds of source comparisons that we may need to make in our everyday lives. I also presented some examples showing that even when it appears to be a relatively straightforward source judgment ("Did I play with the real toy or the block?"), there are often several different levels at which source must be determined. According to source-monitoring theory, source is not considered an all-or-none concept (Johnson et al., 1993) and recent experimental evidence has shown that adults can make partial source judgments, even when they cannot make 'full source judgments' (Dodson, Holland, & Shimamura, 1998). With these issues in mind, the reader should regard age as an indicator of children's source monitoring, rather than a guaranteed predictor of children's competence. We now turn to experimental investigations of source-monitoring development and an analysis of the factors that influence children's competence.

Early Investigations of Children s Source Monitoring

To see whether children's source monitoring differed from that of adults, Johnson, Raye, Hasher, & Chromiak (1979) showed 8-, 10-, 12-, and 17-year-olds pictures of familiar objects one, two, or three times. The participants were also asked to imagine each of the items one or three times, or they did not imagine the item at all. When the participants were asked to estimate the frequency with which each item was presented, Johnson et al. found that the more an item was imagined, the more often it was judged to have been presented. Although the magnitude of this effect varied for the 17-year-olds and the younger children, the same pattern was observed for all age groups.

Systematic studies of children's source monitoring were published by Foley and her colleagues in the early 1980s (Foley et al., 1983; Foley & Johnson, 1985). Some time will be spent explaining the 1985 study as the techniques employed have been used in many subsequent investigations of source monitoring and are still used today. Foley and Johnson (1985) compared 6- and 9-year-old children's source monitoring to that of college students. Three types of source monitoring for simple actions were assessed. To investigate reality monitoring for the origin of the actions, some participants performed some actions (e.g., wave goodbye) and watched someone else perform other actions (Do–Watch condition). External source monitoring was investigated by asking other participants to watch two different people perform actions alternately (Watch–Watch condition). Finally, to investigate internal source monitoring, the remaining participants performed some actions and imagined performing other actions (Do–Pretend condition).

Several minutes later, participants were presented with the items from the experiment as well as distracter items that were not part of the session and tested to see whether they could remember the source of the actions. They were asked to make a choice between the two sources (e.g., said vs. heard) or to say that it was a new item that they had not come across during the activity phase. For example, in Foley et al.'s (1985) study, the children in the Do–Watch condition could be asked to decide whether they touched their knee, whether someone else touched their knee, or whether no one touched their knee. The source questions were modified for children in the other conditions so that those in the Watch–Watch condition could be asked to decide whether Person A touched their (Person A's) knee, Person B touched their (Person B's) knee, or whether noone touched their knee, and those in the internal source-monitoring condition could be asked to decide whether they really touched their knee, pretended to touch their knee, or no one touched their knee. Questions of this nature—that provide a forced choice between the different sources required in the source discrimination—are referred to throughout the book as "traditional source-monitoring questions."

Using this testing procedure, it was possible to obtain an index of source monitoring by dividing the number of correct source attributions by the total number of items that were recognized as being part of the activity phase. This gives a measure of source identification that is independent of recognition memory. Recently, some researchers (e.g., chap. 11, this volume) have split assessments of source identification into two parts such that a recognition question is asked first (e.g., "Did someone touch their knee?"), and if the participant asserts that they recognize the item from the first phase, a source–discrimination question is then administered (e.g., "Did you really touch it, or did you pretend to touch it?"). Of course, it is important to counterbalance the order of the alternatives to prevent response biases from skewing the results.

Returning to Foley and Johnson's (1985) study, the authors found that all of the children and adults were quite accurate in the Do–Watch and Watch–Watch conditions. The 6- and 9-year-olds, however, made more errors than the adults in the Do–Pretend condition. In other words, internal source monitoring and external source monitoring, as indexed by the action tasks in this study, appears to be developed by age 6, and both of these aspects of source monitoring develop before internal source monitoring for performed and pretended actions. Foley and her colleagues had also found the same pattern of results using words instead of actions as stimuli (Foley et al., 1983).

Research building on these pioneering studies has provided information that gives us a fuller picture of the complexity of children's source monitoring. For example, in the Do–Pretend condition of Foley and Johnson's (1985) study, the experimenter asked the children to "be careful not to give me any clues or hints about what you are pretending to do" (p. 1148). Further research (Roberts & Blades, 1995) has shown that children younger than 6 years can distinguish between performed and pretended actions when they are allowed to physically act out the actions (i.e., a developmentally appropriate form of pretense). Similarly, using Foley et al.'s methodology, Welch-Ross (1995) found that most improvements in Do–Pretend (i.e., physically acting out the pretense) and Do–Imagine (i.e., imagery with no corresponding actions) discriminations occur between ages 3 and 4. Discriminating between memories of pretended and imagined actions, however, does not develop until after age 5.

FACTORS KNOWN TO AFFECT CHILDREN S SOURCE MONITORING

Source monitoring is a complex skill and, as documented by others (e.g., Johnson & Raye, 1981; Johnson et al., 1993), many factors from the time of encoding (e.g., quality of encoding, qualitative aspects of the sources) to the time of remembering (e.g., attention, stringency of criteria, demands of source query) can influence the accuracy of the source attribution. The following section should not be taken as an exhaustive account of factors affecting the accuracy and quality of children's source judgments. Rather, I have pulled together those factors that have consistently been shown to have reliable effects on children's source monitoring. I focus particularly on the characteristics of the sources, the characteristics of the person, the role of the agent, interaction with the sources, and the processes carried out at the time of remembering. The research and conclusions reviewed in this section provide a foundation and a context for the innovative research programs discussed in the following empirical chapters. Each factor discussed does not exist in isolation but researchers are currently documenting the interactions between different variables (e.g., similarity of sources and the role of the agent, Day, Howie, & Markham, 1998; Foley & Ratner, 1998).

Characteristics of the Sources

In this section, I discuss how the similarity and the complexity of the sources to be distinguished affect source monitoring.

Similarity. In Foley et al.'s (1983) study, children and adults were asked to carry out different kinds of source monitoring. Foley et al. found that the 6- and 9-year-olds were as accurate as the adults when required to distinguish between words said by two different speakers, or when distinguishing between words they had spoken themselves and words spoken by another person. The 6-year-olds, however, had difficulty distinguishing between words that they had said and words they had imagined saying. Foley and colleagues concluded that the conceptual distinction of self–other is well developed in children of this age, although they do not use the same metamemory rules as adults to distinguish between overt and covert verbalizations.

Markham (1991) designed a study to determine what caused the difficulty expressed by the children in Foley et al.'s (1983) study when distinguishing between words said and imagined. Markham argued that the difficulty may be a result of (a) the problems associated with distinguishing memories when the *same actor* was involved, as was found with adults' source monitoring (Johnson, Foley, & Leach, 1988), or (b) the involvement of the self in both the overt and covert acts (Foley et al., 1983). In Markham's study, 6- and 9-year-olds and adults performed some actions and imagined performing actions (Do condition), or they watched someone perform actions and imagined that person performing other actions (Watch condition). Because there were no differences in source discrimination by the participants in either condition, Markham reasoned that source monitoring is more difficult whenever a discrimination is required and the same actor is involved (either self or another person).

Taking this explanation further, Lindsay et al. (1991) presented a series of experiments to show that source monitoring is more difficult whenever the sources to be discriminated are similar (c.f. the "discriminability principle," see Reyna & Lloyd, 1997). For example, children had more difficulty distinguishing between words spoken by two speakers of the same gender than those spoken by a male and a female (Lindsay et al., 1991, Experiment 1). In another experiment, children had difficulty deciding from which of two television screens they had heard items that were similar in content than when the content was unique to each story (Lindsay et al., 1991, Experiment 2). Finally, in a modification of Foley and colleagues' (Foley et al., 1983; Foley & Johnson, 1985) studies on overt and covert expression of words and actions, Lindsay et al. (Lindsay et al., 1991, Experiment 3) found that children (aged 7 to 10 years) and adults were more confused when the same actor was the subject of the actual and imagined actions.

Researchers have found that the effects of similarity extend beyond perceptual and semantic similarity because functional similarity of sources also affects source monitoring. In a series of studies, children between the ages of 3 and 8 years enacted everyday actions (e.g., talking on the telephone) using a toy or using a substitute (e.g., a wooden block; Foley, Harris, & Hermann, 1994). When they were asked to say how they had carried out each action (i.e., with toy or substitute), the children could accurately identify the actions they had performed with actual toys, but the younger children were more likely than the older children to inaccurately claim that they had used a toy when they had only used a substitute. Because the number of source misattributions was equal for object or gestural substitutes, Foley et al. concluded that the 3-year-olds were confused because of the *functional* similarity of the actions rather than any perceptual similarity between the toys and the substitutes. These results reveal that the basis for similarity effects in source monitoring for actions may lie in the activation of motoric representations (Day et al., 1998). As shown later in the section on prospective processing and in chapter 4, this volume, the kinds of cognitive operations engaged in during the activity has striking effects on source monitoring and learning.

In summary, any sources that are perceptually or functionally similar are more difficult to discriminate than those that differ. Similarity, therefore, appears to have an effect in at least two ways at encoding: First, similar properties of the items may be laid down in memory representations; second, the items may elicit similar motor or cognitive operations that are also represented in memory. Discriminating between memory representations that are similar is clearly more difficult. The similarity effect is further explored with complex real-life and televised events later in the book (chap. 6, this volume) and several authors apply this principle to their research (e.g., chap. 6 & 7, this volume). Although similarity clearly makes source monitoring more difficult, it is unclear whether this explains developmental differences in source monitoring for thoughts and actions or verbalizations carried out by the self. As shown in the following section, "The Role of the Agent," and discussions by Day et al. (1998) and Foley and Ratner (1998), the agent also matters.

Complexity. Arguing that the complexity of the stimuli to be discriminated affects source monitoring is misleading. Rather, it is the processing of those stimuli at encoding that has effects on source-monitoring accuracy. In particular, any stimuli that evoke cognitive operations that are subsequently encoded and later used in source decision processes are more likely to be accurately attributed to source than are stimuli that do not evoke distinctive cognitive operations information. For example, Finke et al. (1988) found that half-shapes split along the vertical axis were easier to imagine whole than half-shapes split along the horizontal axis. Other adults were then shown these half-shapes and asked to imaginally complete them, as well as whole shapes. They were later given a source-monitoring test to see whether they confused the whole and half-shapes. Finke et al. found that participants were more likely to (inaccurately) claim that a vertical half-shape was presented whole than making the same error for a horizontal half-shape. They argued that it was easier to distinguish between whole and horizontal half-shapes because participants encoded the cognitive operations that were carried out to imaginally complete the figure; in contrast, the whole shapes were automatically perceived. Memories of horizontal half-shapes and whole shapes, then, contained distinctive characteristics that could be used in the source judgment. As the vertical half-shapes were easy to imaginally complete, however, the memory representations of the half-shapes contained less cognitive operations information, making their representations more like those of the whole shapes.

A simple prediction follows with respect to the complexity of stimuli: Memories of stimuli that require effortful processing will be easily distinguished from automatically encoded stimuli. Because complex stimuli inevitably require more processing than simple stimuli, complex stimuli will be misattributed to other sources less than simple stimuli. This is exactly what Foley et al. (1991) found in their study with 6-year-olds, to 9-year-olds, and adults. They presented a set of words and pictures. Half of the words and half of the pictures were of simple items, and half were of complex items as standardized by Snodgrass and Vanderwort (1980). All participants were later more confused about the origin (word or picture) of simple rather than complex items. Because the simple items required little cognitive effort to process, Foley and colleagues argued that this automatic process resembled perceptual processing, thus making source discrimination difficult.

In summary, the properties of the events or items to be distinguished affect the accuracy of the source-monitoring judgment. In particular, sources that are similar in content or function are more difficult to distinguish than those that contain unique properties because these latter items are more likely to give rise to memories that contain characteristics distinctive enough to enable successful discrimination. The kinds of processing carried out during the time of encoding also affects source monitoring because the effortful processing evoked by complex sources provides useful source-specifying information.

Characteristics of the Person

As with most other types of cognition, there is variability between the source-monitoring skills of different people in the same situation. There is an increasing amount of research aimed toward identifying predictors of this variation and, in this section, I review work on imagery, representational understanding, and other individual differences. Although there is little conclusive data, several of the chapters in this volume document how researchers have used an individual-differences approach to better understand children's behavior, and readers are urged to consult chapters 4, 9, and 10, this volume, in particular, for state-of-the-art research in this area.

Imagery.   One factor that has received fairly consistent attention is *imagery* ability. Several studies have shown that when imagery is automatic and effortless, source confusions between actually perceived and imagined stimuli are increased (Dobson & Markham, 1993; Foley et al., 1991; Markham & Hynes, 1993). For example, recall that Foley and colleagues showed children and adults a set of words and pictures (Foley et al., 1991). Half of the participants were asked to image the item, and the remaining participants were asked to state the function of each item. On a later source-monitoring test, those who had rated the function of the item were more confused between which items were presented as words and which were pictures than were those who had been explicitly instructed to image. Foley and colleagues argued that, when asked to state the function, participants spontaneously imaged the item. Spontaneous imagery is an automatic process and is likely to require few effortful cognitive operations. This means that reality monitoring was more difficult because memories of the words took on the characteristics of memories of perceiving a picture (i.e., containing visual information) making source discrimination more difficult.

Foley et al. (1991) found that both the children and the adults in the study showed a similar propensity to spontaneously image in the Function condition, and further research has shown that age-invariant individual differences in vividness of imagery can have significant effects on source-monitoring accuracy. Specifically, forming vivid images appears to have a detrimental effect on a variety of different types of source monitoring. Given that there are individual differences in the ease with which images are formed, there is variation in the degree of confusion evidenced by people. For example, Markham and Hynes (1993) categorized adults as high or low imagers, depending on their scores on the Vividness of Imagery Questionnaire (Marks, 1973), which measures the ease and vividness with which people form images. All participants were then shown whole and half shapes and asked to rate the picture for complexity. One half of the participants in the high-imagery and low-imagery groups were also asked to image the half shapes as whole before the complexity rating. On a later source-monitoring test, the high imagers who were instructed to form images were more confused than those who were not told to image, although their scores were still good. Markham and Hynes argued that the images created of the half shapes by the high imagers in the imagery-instructions group were as perceptually detailed as the whole shapes, thus making source discrimination difficult. Consistent with Foley et al.'s (1991) results, low-imagery participants who were instructed to image were less confused than those who were not told to image, and presumably created images spontaneously, thus leading to memories containing few cognitive operations cues that could be used to distinguish between memories of the whole and half shapes.

In summary, source confusions between perceived and not-perceived stimuli are difficult when the memory characteristics are similar. In particular, the lack of cognitive operations information hinders source accuracy. There may be little distinguishing information because of the task demands (e.g., evoking spontaneous imagery) or because of individual differences in the ease and richness of images formed. Finally, the propensity to engage in imagery on multiple occasions may also predict the degree of source confusion between perceived and nonperceived events because repeatedly imaging a fictitious item or event can lead to a memory that is as rich and perceptually detailed as a memory of an actual event (Ceci et al., 1994; Johnson, Raye, Wang, & Taylor, 1979; see Roberts, 1996, for a review).

Representational Understanding. Very young children may not make accurate source decisions because they do not see the need to distinguish memories of different sources of information. For example, in a series of experiments, Taylor, Esbensen, and Bennett (1994) taught preschoolers facts that they did not know prior to the study (e.g., cats chase mice, bears are brown). When they subsequently asked the preschoolers to state where they had learned the information, children under 5 years and some 5-year-olds reported that they had always known the information. It was only when the learning 'event' was made salient (by explicitly telling the children that they were going to be taught something new) that they could identify the time at which they learned the facts. Taylor and colleagues argued that the children did not understand that access to a source of knowledge is a necessary condition of knowing. This does not mean that children younger than 5 years cannot source monitor at all—young children can accurately distinguish some types of action memories as well as older children (e.g., Foley, Ratner, & Passalacqua, 1993; Roberts & Blades, 1995). Rather, it seems that attributions for knowledge may be impaired because these young children have not yet realized that the connection between knowledge and its source is important.

Not only must young children appreciate knowledge-source connections, but they must also learn to make assessments about the reliability of the sources of information to which they are exposed. Some researchers have argued that young children treat information that they have gained through direct experience as more reliable than information that an adult tells them (e.g., Perner, 1991). Others, however, have presented evidence to show that, in some circumstances, children do make appropriate distinctions between information gained through direct experience and presented by an adult who has no direct experience (Robinson, 1994). A more complete review of research in this area is presented by Robinson (this volume), who shows that being able to use knowledge sources appropriately is particularly important when those sources contradict each other.

On an applied level, this research has been implicated in the case of children's eyewitness reports because sometimes interviewers can present information to children that conflicts with what the child remembers about the event (Quas et al., this volume). The way that children handle conflicting representations and the consequences for source monitoring can have a significant impact on the accuracy of their event reports (Welch-Ross, Diecidue, & Miller, 1997). A model relating children's understanding of mind and source monitoring, and its effects on children's suggestibility, is presented in a later chapter (Welch-Ross, this volume).

Other Individual Differences. Once again, it is important to bear in mind that source discrimination accuracy and relationships with individual differences may depend on the discrimination of interest. Durso, Reardon, and Jolly (1985) found that there was no difference in the internal or external source monitoring of 'field-dependent' individuals (who are thought to consider self and nonself information separately and to rely on internally generated information) and 'field-independent' people (who do not differentiate self and nonself information as clearly and rely more on externally generated information (Witkin, Goodenough, & Oltman, 1979). The authors did find, though, that field-dependent individuals were more accurate than field-independent individuals when asked to distinguish between memories of self- and other-generated information. Durso et al. argued that the reality-monitoring advantage of field-independent individuals occurred because they could appropriately weigh the cognitive operations information produced by self-generated acts, whereas the field-dependent individuals made little use of this information.

The field-independence personality variable has not been investigated with relation to source-monitoring accuracy in children. However, a related concept, that of dissociation, has been receiving much attention in the empirical literature recently, largely because of proposed relationships between dissociation, trauma, and suggestibility in eyewitnesses (e.g., Eisen & Goodman, 1998). The connection between dissociation and source monitoring is unclear. Several of the items on the Dissociative Experiences Scale (DES; Bernstein & Putnam, 1986) seem straightforward source-monitoring situations (e.g., Item 15: "Some people have the experience of not being sure whether things that they remember happening really did happen or whether they just dreamed them"; Item 24: "Some people sometimes find that they cannot remember whether they have done something or have just thought about doing that thing"). However, in a recent investigation with adults, Koppenhaver, Kumar, and Pekala (1997) found no relationship between scores on the DES and a reality-monitoring measure. Other researchers have found correlations between DES scores and suggestibility (Hyman, Husband, & Billings, 1995), but the extent to which source monitoring mediates this relationship is not clear. A productive goal of future research would be to create interesting and testable models to predict how these factors explain the variability in children's and adults' memory reports.

In summary, individual differences may affect source monitoring and functions involving source monitoring (e.g., event memory) because of differences in the kinds of processing evoked. For example, memories of high imagers may be more perceptually detailed than those of low imagers if they visualize information; if, however, visual images are created spontaneously with little effort, their memories will contain less cognitive operations cues that could be used in the judgment of the origin of the memory. If young children do not understand the representational nature of memories and the connection between knowledge and source, then they may not even attend to potential source cues. Individual differences will need to be considered in future research to further our understanding of children's source monitoring.

The Role of the Agent

In this section, I focus on the salience of self-generated items and its effects on later source distinctions, and how this is affected by differences in elaborative processing and the perspective adopted at the time of the event.

The Generation Effect.   Not only may personal characteristics affect source monitoring, but some researchers have noticed that source-monitoring decisions regarding the self may be unique compared with other kinds of source monitoring. In many studies, source attributions regarding activities carried out by the self were more accurate than source attributions regarding activities carried out by other people (e.g., Anderson, 1984; Baker-Ward, Hess, & Flannagan, 1990; Foley et al., 1983; Foley & Johnson, 1985; Roberts & Blades, 1998). This preference for discrimination of self-related items has been considered an extension of the "generation effect" (Slamecka & Graf, 1978), which describes the phenomenon of improved recall and recognition of items generated by oneself compared with memory for items generated by another person. Applied to source monitoring, the advantage of self-related items is not restricted to those times when an item is overtly expressed; the same result occurs for self-generated, covert thoughts (Johnson, Raye, Foley, & Foley, 1981).

In Foley et al.'s (1983) and Foley and Johnson's (1985) studies, children aged 6 and 9 years demonstrated preferential recall for self-generated items. Foley and her colleagues argued that the self–other distinction is well developed in school-age children and provided evidence to show that they use this conceptualization to cluster their recall. Preferential discrimination of self-generated items appears to develop gradually in the preschool years. Roberts and Blades (1998) found that 6- and 9-year-olds made less source misattributions when they answered details related to actions they had performed compared with attributions related to actions they had watched a confederate carry out. In contrast, the 4-year-olds in their study made more source confusions in response to questions about the confederate's actions than they did about their own. The 4-year-olds did, however, report more intrusions (details that never occurred) in response to the other-performed questions than the self-performed questions showing that the self-related advantage seems to be somewhat developed. It is during the preschool years that children develop a sense of self, leading some researchers to argue that this is one of the main reasons for the development of autobiographical memory and the offset of childhood amnesia (Howe, 1998; Howe, Courage, & Peterson, 1994). Children's understanding of other people's minds is also developing during this time (see Frye & Moore, 1991; Olson, Astington, & Harris, 1988; Wellman, 1990), and further research based on the self-related source-monitoring preference described here and these other aspects of children's development is likely to prove fruitful (e.g., Welch-Ross, 1995).

That even young children show some advantages for source attribution of self-generated items does not guarantee that children will always make accurate source attributions for these items. As described earlier, although the children in Foley et al.'s (1983) study could carry out some kinds of source attributions (i.e., they could distinguish memories of what they had said from what another had said), the 6-year-olds were less accurate than the adults when required to distinguish what they had said from what they imagined. An analysis of the false positives (claiming that a new distracter item was in the list of say or think words) revealed that the 17-year-olds showed a tendency to claim that they had imagined saying the item, but the children did not show this tendency. Hence, similar to the "it-had-to-be-you" generation effect (see the section "Deliberate Processes"), strategic processes are revealed through this misattribution bias. Foley and colleagues explained the bias in terms of metamemory assumptions: As people are aware that memories vary in strength, they will attribute a vague 'memory' of an item (they could not have a memory of the distracter from the trial because it was not presented) to something that they thought in a say or think task because they know that memories of deeds are stronger than memories of thoughts. According to Foley et al., the children who did not exhibit this bias do not yet use the same metamemory rules. Furthermore, children are more likely to say that an imagined action was performed than claim a performed action was imagined (Foley & Ratner, 1998). It appears that children do show a self-preference, but this is not always manifested until later school age.

Elaborative Processes. To explain the development of the self-preference effect, Baker-Ward et al. (1990) presented an "elaboration hypothesis." Specifically, they argued that it is not the involvement of the self, per se, that aids memory and source monitoring, but rather the advantage is dependent on "the extent to which preexisting knowledge is utilized to provide a meaningful mnemonic representation" (p. 67). Support for the hypothesis came from a study in which children performed some actions and watched either a familiar or a less familiar peer carry out other actions (Baker-Ward et al., 1990, Experiment 2). On a later source discrimination test, children who had watched a less familiar peer carry out actions remembered the actions they themselves had performed better than those of their partner. Children who had watched a familiar peer perform actions, however, remembered those actions as well as their own. Baker-Ward et al. argued that the improvement in memory of the peer's actions occurred because children could relate the peer's actions to a rich self-schema, which increased the availability and accessibility of the items. Hence, the self-generated advantage occurs because the self is a rich construct of supporting knowledge that promotes elaboration of encoded information (see Symons & Johnson, 1997, for a recent review).

The results of other research shows that the kinds of processing carried out by children at the time of encoding and at the time of source monitoring determines the accuracy of the source judgment, and items related to the self appear to promote certain kinds of processing. In another study, Foley, Santini, & Sopasakis (1989) asked 7-year-olds, 10-year-olds, and adults to say words and imagine another person saying other words. The person that participants imagined varied depending on condition. Participants imagined either a friend, a parent, or themselves, and it was found that they were most confused when they imagined themselves saying the words. Although the confusion may have come about because the same person was the actor in the say and the think trials, Foley et al. argued that a more likely explanation is that the elaborations that were activated when people imagined a familiar person aided later source discrimination, and metamemory responses collected in this study were consistent with this view. In a second study, elaborations were constrained by asking people to imagine a word from a sentence-completion task that elicited almost automatic responses. Discrimination in this experiment was poor. Further experiments showed that discrimination was enhanced for items associated with personalized rather than generic encodings.

It seems, then, that it is not the personalized content of the elaborations per se, but the kinds of processing evoked that aids source discrimination. In a study with 6-year-olds, 9-year-olds, and adults, participants were given a cued-recall task with various instructions to help remember the words (Foley, Wilder, McCall, & Van Vorst, 1993). Memory was most accurate when participants generated personalized referents during the exercise. To see whether the content or the cognitive operations performed to generate the imagery was responsible for the effects, the children were yoked so that each child who generated the imagery was matched with another child who was instructed to image the exact content of the imagery generated by the first child. The children who generated the imagery were more accurate at recalling the words than those who imaged the same content, but did not generate the imagery. These results are consistent with a source-monitoring account that proposes the unique value of cognitive operations cues. Hence, the source-monitoring framework can be used to guide research in various areas of cognition, and several later chapters document the application of source-monitoring theory in diverse areas (e.g., chaps. 4, 5, and 11, this volume).

Differences in Perspective.   Another mediating factor for effects regarding the self concerns the perspective that children adopt during tasks. As noted in the section on the Similarity of Sources, children are more confused when the same actor is involved (e.g., when distinguishing between what you said and what you thought) than when discriminating between two different actors (e.g., distinguishing between what you said and what another person said). The degree of this confusion is mediated by the perspective adopted, and, hence, discriminating between similar actors may be explained by similarities in the perspective adopted and the consequent processing induced. Foley and Ratner (1998, Experiment 2) asked 6-year-olds to participate in a typical say–imagine actions task. For the imagine items, half of the children were told to imagine what it would *feel* like to perform the actions (kinesthetic condition) and the other children were told to imagine what they would *look* like if they performed the actions (visual condition). The children in the kinesthetic condition made a significant amount of source errors for the imagined actions, showing that the perspective children adopt during imagination has consequences for source monitoring. These results are also consistent with the finding that kinesthetic feedback is a cue that is used in some source-monitoring decisions (see the following section, "Visual and Kinesthetic Feedback").

Foley and her colleagues (see Ratner & Foley, 1996) have proposed that the pattern of source attributions made by children reveal the prospective processing that entails before actions are performed and imagined. Cognitive operations such as planning and anticipating the actions may be retrieved at the time of source monitoring and cause confusion because this kind of processing would occur for both the prospect of performing or imagining performing the actions (Foley & Ratner, 1998). In other studies, Foley et al. (1993) showed that children recode actions performed by someone else as their own, suggesting that the kinds of prospective processing previously described should also occur when children are watching and imagining other people perform. The bias to call imagined actions performed should occur, therefore, even when actors other than the self are involved, and this was demonstrated (Foley & Ratner, 1998, Experiment 1). Further work by Foley and Ratner examine this issue in more depth and highlight the role and value of such processing (see chap. 4, this volume).

Hence, the self plays a complex role in source judgments: older children may show an advantage for source monitoring related to the self, whereas younger children may not; sometimes there is an advantage for self-involvement, but at other times the involvement of the self hinders source-monitoring accuracy. Much depends on the nature of the source distinction (distinguishing between thoughts and deeds that are self-generated, distinguishing between self- and other-generated deeds), and the elaborative and prospective processing carried out.

Interaction With the Sources

In this section, I discuss how the child's involvement in the event and the way in which they act upon the sources to be distinguished affects the quality and accuracy of source judgments. First, I discuss the use of feedback cues established through active participation, and then discuss more recent research that investigates the role of cognitive operations and prospective processing.

Visual and Kinesthetic Feedback. It was described in the section "Characteristics of the Sources" that the similarity and complexity of the sources to be discriminated can partially determine the accuracy of source discrimination. A person's interaction with those sources also affects the encoding and cognitive processing involved in the source decision, as shown in the preceding section, "The Role of the Agent." In addition, the special kinds of perceptual processing evoked by involvement in the events affects source monitoring. Anderson (1984) showed that adults were more confused when they tried to decide whether they had traced an item or imagined tracing an item than they were when deciding whether they traced the item or just looked at the item. She argued that the greater imagine–perform trace confusion occurred because these activities led to the coding of similar information in memory, thus making it difficult to identify the source from the memories.

Foley, Aman, and Gutch (1987) went on to specify the kinds of information in memory that may be similar when children engage in tracing activities. In this study, 7- and 10-year-olds traced pictures using a pencil and a finger, a pencil and a stylus (pencil without lead), or a stylus and a finger. When later asked to identify how they had traced the pictures (e.g., with a pencil or a finger), there was less confusion between items traced with a pencil and those traced with a finger than for the two other comparisons. In a second experiment in which children traced and imagined tracing with a pencil, a stylus, or a finger, the most imagine–perform trace confusions were made by children in the finger condition, and the least by those in the pencil condition. Foley et al. argued that the visual consequences of using a pencil and the kinesthetic feedback when using a writing utensil (pencil or stylus) provided distinctive memorial cues that were used in source attributions. When children traced pictures using their fingers, however, there were no visible consequences and the actions were similar. Hence, the sources were likely to be confused. The mere presence of feedback cues, however, is not sufficient to guarantee accurate source monitoring if those cues are not distinctive. This is discussed more fully later in the book (see chap. 6, this volume).

Cognitive Operations. As mentioned earlier, in early investigations of the development of children's source monitoring, tasks were designed that used relatively simple stimuli (e.g., word lists), although interesting cover stories were employed so that the tasks 'made sense' to the children (e.g., Foley & Johnson, 1985). More recently, and partly motivated by the realization of the importance of source monitoring in children's eyewitness memory (e.g., Johnson & Foley, 1984; Kail, 1990; Lindsay & Johnson, 1987; see chap. 8, this volume), researchers have begun to investigate source monitoring after children have actually *interacted* with someone else. To investigate children's memory for interactive actions, as may be required when a child is questioned after making an allegation of sexual abuse, for example, Gordon, Jens, Shaddock, and Watson (1991) asked 5- to 7-year-olds to perform and imagine performing some actions. One half of the imagined and performed actions were carried out alone (e.g., "stand up and sit down") and the other half were carried out with a confederate (e.g., "let's stack blocks together"). Although the interaction had no effects on source discrimination immediately after the task, when questioned 8 weeks later the children identified the source more accurately when probed about the interactive activities than activities they had performed alone.

Generalizing from the results of laboratory studies of children's source monitoring carries many cautions. To increase the applicability of research to real-world concerns, such as the accuracy of children's testimony, source-monitoring skills have been investigated using complex and involving events (e.g., Ackil & Zaragoza, 1995; Ceci, Huffman, Smith, & Loftus, 1994; Ceci, Loftus, Leichtman, & Bruck, 1994; Parker, 1995; Poole & Lindsay, 1995, 1999; Roberts & Blades, 1998; Roberts, Lamb, & Sternberg, 1999). As well as concerns about the validity of research, this is an important development because children's source monitoring for sequential and nonsequential items differs (Markham, 1991). As noted by Goodman, Quas, Bulklay, & Shapiro, (in press), one of the major reasons that children become involved in the legal system is because they have made allegations of physical or sexual abuse. In many incidents of sexual abuse, the child is actively involved, he or she is likely to be the only witness, there may be many instances of touching, and there are complex interactions between the child and perpetrator. Researchers have, therefore, carried out studies to improve our understanding of how interacting in complex events affects children's source monitoring.

For example, in a study by Parker (1995), 6- and 9-year-olds performed and imagined performing actions in short vignettes, such as dressing-up activities. The activities were carried out either alone or with a confederate. To increase the forensic generalizability of the results of the study, the interactive vignettes were based on those used by Goodman, Rudy, Bottoms, and Aman (1990), who designed the events to parallel the kinds of actions that take place in incidents of sexual abuse. Parker found that interacting in the events had different effects on children's discrimination of performed and imagined actions and this varied with age. Specifically, the 6-year-olds could identify the source (perform or imagine) of imagined actions from the interactive vignettes more accurately than they did the source of imagined items in the noninteractive vignettes. There was also a developmental difference in the source discrimination of imagined actions from the interactive vignettes, such that the 9-year-olds were more accurate than the 6-year-olds. In contrast, discrimination for the origin of performed actions did not vary with the extent of the interaction. Parker argued that more cognitive operations were executed when imagining actions in the interactive than noninteractive vignettes, and this information could be used as cues to source attribution. The 6-year-olds, however, either did not encode the cognitive operations (although other research shows that cognitive operations information has clear effects on preschoolers' source monitoring, see Ratner et al., this volume) or they could not use these cues effectively. The latter explanation is consistent with Foley and Ratner's (1998) observation that children have difficulty 'looking inward.'

In summary, physical interaction in events may affect children's source monitoring not only because of the visual and kinesthetic feedback produced, but through the engagement of various cognitive operations involved in carrying out those actions or interacting with another person.

Goals. The nature of the interaction studied naturally affects the conclusions drawn about children's source monitoring in complex, interactive events. Researchers have differed in their operational definitions of *interaction*. In one sense, "interaction" is defined as any activity carried out by children in an event, as in the bystander–participant distinction in the eyewitness field (e.g., Roberts & Blades, 1998; Rudy & Goodman, 1991). According to this operationalization, children who are physically involved in an event are interacting and those who do not carry out any actions but merely watch the event do not interact. Much research on children's source monitoring for self-generated versus other-generated actions and words, therefore, has relevance here.

Another definition of the concept of interaction focuses more on the *collaborative* nature of interaction as studied by Gordon et al. (1991) and Parker (1995). According to this definition, the child is interacting whenever the event revolves around a shared exchange with another person. Collaboration affects source monitoring in important ways. In collaborative activities, there is a shared end goal and the resulting cognitive processing related to the goals affects source monitoring. Although researchers have started to examine children's source monitoring after engaging in complex, sequentially related events with end goals (e.g., the puppet-making activity in Roberts and Blades' [1998] study), the children's actions do not actually affect the end goal (e.g., the puppet was made regardless of the children's actions). In contrast, Foley et al. (1993) examined 4-, 6-, and 8-year-old children's source monitoring after they had taken turns with an adult to place pieces on a collage. The child and the experimenter alternately placed pieces on the collage in the presence of an Identifiable or an Abstract model of the collage. They found that the children were more confused between who placed which pieces when in the presence of the Abstract model than when using the Identifiable model. Foley and her colleagues argued that this was because the model detracted attention from source and hence reduced the information available for source monitoring at the later test.

When the children's role as decision maker was reduced by the experimenter instructing the child about which pieces to place on the collage, the children made more source-monitoring errors than if they were allowed to choose their own pieces (Foley et al., 1993). This suggests that the cognitive operations necessary to choose the pieces and coordinate actions with the experimenter were represented in the memory of making the collage. Cues from these cognitive operations could be used in source attribution (Foley et al., 1993). The nature of the interaction and the shared goals, therefore, have specific effects on children's source monitoring and Ratner and Foley have developed these findings into a person-based model of activity memory (see Ratner & Foley, 1996; Ratner et al., this volume).

In summary, a child's interaction with an event elicits complex modes of functioning. In contrast to being passive recipients of instructions, when children are encouraged to participate in goal-related tasks they plan and predict actions before they carry them out. This may be particularly important when children have been subjected to repeated events, such as multiple incidents of sexual abuse, because the child is likely to be able to predict aspects of each scenario. In addition, the meaning of the actions (e.g., touching) may affect the kinds of processing carried out at the time of the event (Foley, 1997).

Processes When Making the Source Judgment

In this final section, I briefly review two factors that are receiving much attention in research on children's source monitoring: the effects of interference from gist, and directing children's attention to source. Each of these areas of research is promoting fruitful hypotheses about the mechanisms involved in source monitoring.

Gist Interference. As discussed earlier, source monitoring can be carried out automatically or with deliberate effort, and both processes may be used together (Johnson et al., 1993). Distracting attention away from deliberate source monitoring, therefore, should increase errors in source discrimination. This was demonstrated by Ackerman in a series of studies linking source errors, inferential reasoning, and story recall (e.g., Ackerman, 1992, 1994). Ackerman found that when conditions promoted gist abstraction, the incidence of source errors increased. Children heard stories in which they were required to make an inference to resolve inconsistencies in the story. Under these conditions, they made more source errors by attributing information about an object in the story to the story itself, even though the child had actually inferred the information. The number of source errors was decreased when children were directed to the inconsistencies, and increased after a delay.

Ackerman's explanation was grounded in fuzzy-trace theory (e.g., Brainerd, Reyna, Howe, & Kingma, 1990), in which 'source' is characterized as a verbatim detail and is represented in memory separately to representations of gist. According to Ackerman's representation hypothesis, the gist reasoning performed to resolve the inconsistencies in the story interfered with the processing of the verbatim (source) details. As source is conceptualized as verbatim information, a failure to retrieve this information results in a source error. This effect increases when children have to resolve ambiguous utterances by integrating information from different sources (Ackerman, 1994). Memory-reasoning dissociations such as this have been amply demonstrated (e.g, Brainerd & Reyna, 1990) and can explain source errors if source is conceptualized as a tag in memory. A full comparison between fuzzy-trace theory and source-monitoring theory is not possible here, but readers are referred to the articles by Johnson et al. (1993) and Reyna and Lloyd (1997). In addition, the value of both theories to understanding source monitoring within the context of suggestibility research with children is discussed in Thierry et al. (this volume) and Powell et al. (in press).

Orienting to Source.   As found by Ackerman, children's source monitoring is sensitive to instructions directing attention to or from source information. Several investigators have demonstrated improvements in source attribution accuracy by encouraging adults to focus on the source of memories. Lindsay and Johnson (1989) and Zaragoza and Lane (1994, Experiment 3) carried out experiments using the standard misinformation paradigm. In both experiments, participants view a slide or slides and read a narrative about the slide(s) that contains misleading details. The memory test comprised either a yes/no recognition (e.g., "Was there a X?") or a source-monitoring test (e.g., "was there a X in the video, the narrative, both, or not at all?"). Consistently, participants who answered the source-monitoring questions less often claimed that they saw a misleading detail in the video than did participants given the yes or no test. The misinformation effect was not completely eliminated, however, with the source-monitoring test.

It is possible, of course, that the suggestibility evidenced by participants in Lindsay and Johnson's (1989) and Zaragoza and Lane's (1994) studies was the result of "aware uses of memory" (Lindsay, Gonzales, & Eso, 1995), such as demand characteristics (e.g., believing that the experimenter desires the postevent detail to be reported, or knowing that the misled detail was in the postevent information, but not realizing that it was different to the target event) rather than genuine source confusions. Aware uses of memory are unlikely to explain all of the misinformation effect, however, for several reasons. First, Zaragoza and Lane (1994, Experiment 5) collected confidence ratings and showed that some people *genuinely* believed that they had seen the misleading detail in the video (as opposed to response bias or demand characteristics). Second, even when participants are informed that everything in the narrative is inaccurate and that they should not report any items from the narrative (i.e., Jacoby's opposition procedure; see Jacoby, 1991), source confusions can still occur (e.g., Lindsay, 1990).

Developmentally, the presence of the misinformation effect varies. Preschoolers appear to be the most susceptible and children grow more resistant to suggestions with age (see Ceci & Bruck, 1993, 1995, 1998). Lindsay et al. (1995) estimated how much of children's suggestibility is the result of genuine source confusions. Lindsay et al. used Jacoby's (1991) formula to reveal the separate contributions of aware and unaware uses of memory (calculated by comparing the number of errors made in response to a standard yes/no recognition test and the number of errors made after receiving opposition instructions) and found that preschoolers make more unaware than aware errors after a delay (21% aware, 14% unaware), whereas older children showed the reverse pattern (11% aware, 20% unaware). This shows that younger children are clearly susceptible to social pressures during misinformation experiments, but genuine source errors are still possible even when opposition instructions are given.

In another experiment using the misinformation paradigm, Newcombe and Siegal (1996) found that when the source of the target event was made explicit, children's reports were more accurate. Children aged 3 to 5 years were told a story about Loren eating her breakfast and then heard a narrative containing misleading details about what Loren ate and why she was sick (taken from Ceci, Ross, & Toglia, 1987). They compared children's responses with the question "Do you remember how Loren was sick when you heard the story?" with a question that made the source explicit: "Do you remember how Loren was sick when you heard the story *the first time*?" They found that the children who had been asked the latter, source-explicit question gave the accurate answer (i.e., the detail from the story and not the postevent narrative) more than those in the control group. It is not clear from this study whether it was the specific reference to time or a more general effect from making the source explicit that aided the children's reports, but it is clear that children have an ability to monitor their sources that may not be revealed with all kinds of memory questions.

In Parker's (1995) study on discriminating between performed and imagined actions (see the section, "Interaction With the Sources"), she found that children who were interviewed immediately and after two weeks accurately identified the origin of more actions than did children who were interviewed about the event only at the 2-week delay. On the basis of these results, Parker suggested that children can be inoculated against losses in source-monitoring capabilities. Poole and Lindsay (1995) tried to improve children's source monitoring by highlighting the different sources to children, but found that preschoolers still appeared confused. Children interacted with "Mr. Science" and carried out some simple science experiments. Three months later, the children's parents read them a story three times about the science experiments and included experiments that the children had never actually carried out with Mr. Science. When later interviewed, the two different sources (event and story) were highlighted to the children, and they were given practice in discriminating which detail came from which event. The preschoolers, however, were still inaccurate when asked about the source of information they had only encountered once (event or story). Hence, one of the current challenges in this area is successful training of online monitoring skills, and chapters 7 and 10, this volume, discuss how they have addressed this issue.

CONCLUSIONS

Source monitoring is a skill that plays an integral part in many aspects of children's and adults' lives. Without the ability to monitor sources of information, we would be confused between which of our friends spoke to us, whether we have carried out actions or not, or whether we acquired information from reputable or noncredible sources, to name just a few common scenarios. Source distinctions take many forms (e.g., distinguishing between internal events, distinguishing between external events, and distinguishing between internal and external events), and can be made regarding the status (public vs. private) or the origin (self vs. other) of the events. The nature of the source judgment can depend on the current task demands.

According to source-monitoring theory (Johnson & Raye, 1981; Johnson et al., 1993), source is attributed to a memory based on decision-making processes carried out at the time of remembering. We can distinguish between different sources of information (e.g., memories, knowledge, beliefs) automatically and without awareness or through more effortful and deliberate processing, and these processes can be used together for the most accurate source judgments. The qualitative profiles of information determines the accuracy of some source judgments. If memories, for example, contain distinctive characteristics, then the sources of these memories are likely to be accurately discriminated. Typically, memories derived from publicly perceived sources contain more perceptual, sensory, semantic, and affective information than do memories of internally-derived events, which contain more cognitive operations information. Knowledge of these characteristics is used to make source-monitoring judgments for one's own as well as other peoples' memories. More strategic source discriminations may be made using commonsense assumptions or by using knowledge of the sources themselves.

The emergence of source-monitoring skills in children does not have an all-or-none factor. Rather, children can be competent at some source-monitoring judgments (e.g., reality monitoring regarding who performed certain actions), but be confused with other judgments (e.g., whether they performed or imagined performing action; Foley & Johnson, 1985). Furthermore, children can have difficulty in one situation but be competent in another (e.g., Roberts & Blades, 1995; Welch-Ross, 1995). I reviewed several of the main factors known to affect children's source monitoring. As well as the characteristics of the sources to be distinguished, the child's relationship to those sources affects their later source monitoring. The kinds of cognitive operations (e.g., elaboration, prospective processing) that the child engages in when exposed to the sources affect later source judgments. In some circumstances, these cognitive operations can be used as cues to source (e.g., Foley et al., 1991). In addition, individual differences (e.g., imagery ability) affect the kinds of processing carried out at encoding and during remembering, which in turn impacts source monitoring. Finally, the nature of the task at the time of remembering will affect the source judgment.

The research reviewed in this chapter provided an account of our understanding of the mechanisms contributing to source monitoring and the development of this skill. In the remainder of the book, the authors present state-of-the-art research building on this knowledge base that, collectively, reflects the current state of source-monitoring research. In contrast to the earlier studies of source monitoring, some of the researchers have investigated children's source monitoring for complex and meaningful stimuli (e.g., chaps. 6, 7, and 8, this volume), and others have focused on investigating source monitoring in areas not addressed before (e.g., representational understanding, chap. 3, this volume, and chap. 9, this volume; face identification, chap. 11, this volume; clinical populations, chap. 5, this volume). Finally, some researchers have addressed complex interactions between individual differences in source monitoring and other skills (e.g., chaps. 4, 9, and 10, this volume). In the final chapter (chap. 12, this volume), the conclusions discussed by the contributors are integrated and assessed with respect to the research reviewed in this chapter.

REFERENCES

Ackerman, B. P. (1992). The sources of children's source errors in judging causal inferences. *Journal of Experimental Child Psychology, 54*, 90–119.

Ackerman, B. P. (1994). Children's source errors in referential communication. *Journal of Experimental Child Psychology, 58*, 432–464.

Ackil, J. K., & Zaragoza, M. S. (1995). Developmental differences in eyewitness suggestibility and memory for source. *Journal of Experimental Child Psychology, 60*, 57–83.

Ackil, J., & Zaragoza, M. S. (1998). Memorial consequences of forced confabulation: Age differences in susceptibility to false memories. *Developmental Psychology, 34,* 1358–1372.

Alonso-Quecuty, M. L. (1996). Detecting fact from fallacy in child and adult witness accounts. In G. Davies, S. Lloyd-Bostock, M. McMurran, & C. Wilson (Eds.), *Psychology, law, and criminal justice: International developments in research and practice* (pp.74–80). Berlin, Germany: Walter de Gruyter.

Anderson, R. E. (1984). Did I do it or did I only imagine doing it? *Journal of Experimental Psychology: General, 113,* 594–613.

Baker-Ward, L., Hess, T. M., & Flannagan, D. A. (1990). The effects of involvement on children's memory for events. *Cognitive Development, 5,* 55–69.

Bernstein, E. M., & Putnam F. W. (1986). Development, reliability, and validity of a dissociation scale. *The Journal of Nervous and Mental Disease, 174,* 727–735.

Brainerd, C. J., & Reyna, V. F. (1990). Gist is the grist: Fuzzy-trace theory and the new intuitionism. *Developmental Review, 10,* 3–47.

Brainerd, C. J., Reyna, V. F., Howe, M. L., & Kingma, J. (1990). The development of forgetting and reminiscence. *Monographs of the Society for Research in Child Development 55,* 1–111.

Ceci, S. J., & Bruck, M. (1993). The suggestibility of the child witness: A historical review and synthesis. *Psychological Bulletin, 113,* 403–439.

Ceci, S. J., & Bruck, M. (1995). *Jeopardy in the courtroom.* Washington, DC, American Psychological Association.

Ceci, S. J., & Bruck, M. (1998). Children's testimony: Applied and basic issues. In W. Damon, I. E. Sigel, & K. A. Renninger (Eds.), *Handbook of child psychology: Vol. 4* (5th ed., pp. 713–773). New York: John Wiley & Sons.

Ceci, S. J., Huffman, M. L. C., Smith, E., & Loftus, E. F. (1994). Repeatedly thinking about a non-event: Source misattributions among preschoolers. *Consciousness and Cognition, 3,* 388–407.

Ceci, S. J., Loftus, E. F., Leichtman, M. D., & Bruck, M. (1994). The possible role of source misattributions in the creation of false beliefs among preschoolers. *International Journal of Clinical and Experimental Hypnosis, 42,* 304–320.

Ceci, S. J., Ross, D. P., & Toglia, M. P. (1987). Suggestibility of children's memory: Psycholegal implications. *Journal of Experimental Psychology: General, 116,* 38–49.

Day, K., Howie, P., & Markham, R. (1998). The role of similarity in developmental differences in source monitoring. *British Journal of Developmental Psychology, 16,* 219–232.

Dobson, M., & Markham, R. (1993). Imagery ability and source monitoring: Implications for eyewitness memory. *British Journal of Psychology, 32,* 111–118.

Dodson, C. S., Holland, P. W., & Shimamura, A. P. (1998). On the recollection of specific- and partial-source information. *Journal of Experimental Psychology: Learning Memory and Cognition, 24,* 1121–1136.

Durso, F. T., Reardon, R., & Jolly, E. J. (1985). Self-nonself-segregation and reality monitoring. *Journal of Personality and Social Psychology, 48,* 447–455.

Dywan, J., Segalowitz, S. J, & Webster, L. (1998). Source monitoring: ERP evidence for greater reactivity to nontarget information in older adults. *Brain & Cognition, 36*, 390–430.

Eisen, M., & Goodman G. (1998). Trauma, memory, and suggestibility in children. *Development and Psychopathology, 10*, 717–738.

Ferguson, S. A., Hashtroudi, S., & Johnson, M. K. (1992). Age differences in using source-relevant cues. *Psychology and Aging, 7*, 443–452.

Finke, R. A., Johnson, M. K., & Shyi, G. C. W. (1988). Memory confusions for real and imagined completions of symmetrical visual patterns. *Memory and Cognition, 16*, 133–137.

Foley, M. A. (1997, April). Where to go next? Discussion presented in Roberts, K. P. (Chair), *Children's source monitoring and eyewitness testimony.* Symposium presented at the biennial meeting of the Society for Research in Child Development, Washington, DC.

Foley, M. A., Aman, C., & Gutch, D. (1987). Discriminating between action memories: Children's use of kinesthetic cues and visible consequences. *Journal of Experimental Child Psychology, 44*, 335–347.

Foley, M. A., Durso, F. T., Wilder, A., & Friedman, R. (1991). Developmental comparisons of explicit versus implicit imagery and reality monitoring. *Journal of Experimental Child Psychology, 51*, 1–13.

Foley, M. A., Harris, J. F., & Hermann, S. (1994). Developmental comparisons of the ability to discriminate between memories of symbolic play enactments. *Developmental Psychology, 30*, 206–217.

Foley, M. A., & Johnson, M. K. (1985). Confusions between memories for performed and imagined actions: A developmental comparison. *Child Development, 56*, 1145–1155.

Foley, M. A., Johnson, M. K., & Raye, C. L. (1983). Age-related changes in confusion between memories for thoughts and memories for speech. *Child Development, 54*, 51–60.

Foley, M. A., & Ratner, H. H. (1998). Distinguishing between memories for thoughts and deeds: The role of prospective processing in children's source monitoring. *British Journal of Developmental Psychology, 16*, 465–484.

Foley, M. A., Ratner, H. H., & Passalacqua, C. (1993). Appropriating the actions of another: Implications for children's memory and learning. *Cognitive Development, 8*, 373–401.

Foley, M. A., Santini, C., & Sopasakis, M. (1989). Discriminating between memories: Evidence for children's spontaneous elaborations. *Journal of Experimental Child Psychology, 48*, 146–169.

Foley, M. A., Wilder, A., McCall, R., & Van Vorst, R. (1993). The consequences for recall of children's ability to generate interactive imagery in the absence of external supports. *Journal of Experimental Child Psychology, 56*, 173–200.

Frye, D., & Moore, C. (1991). *Children's theories of mind.* Hillsdale, NJ: Lawrence Erlbaum Associates.

Goodman, G. S., Quas, J. A., Bulkley, J., & Shapiro, C. (in press). Innovations for child witnesses: A national survey. *Psychology, Public Policy, and Law.*

Goodman, G. S., Rudy, L., Bottoms, B. L., & Amans, C. (1990). Children's concerns and memory: Issues of ecological validity in the study of children's eyewitness testimony. In R. Fivush & J. A. Hudson (Eds.), *Knowing and remembering in young children* (pp. 249–284). Cambridge, MA: Cambridge University Press.

Gordon, B. N., Jens, K. G., Shaddock, A. J., & Watson, T. E. (1991). Children's ability to remember activities performed and imagined: Implications for testimony. *Child Psychiatry and Human Development, 21,* 301–314.

Harvey, P. D. (1985). Reality monitoring in mania and schizophrenia: The association of thought disorder and performance. *Journal of Nervous and Mental Disease, 173,* 67–73.

Hashtroudi, S., Johnson, M. K., & Chrosniak, L. D. (1989). Aging and source monitoring. *Psychology and Aging, 4,* 106–112.

Howe, M. (1998). Language is never enough: Memories are more than words reveal. *Applied Cognitive Psychology, 12,* 475–481.

Howe, M. L., Courage, M. L., & Peterson, C. (1994). How can I remember when "I" wasn't there: Long-term retention of traumatic experiences and emergence of the cognitive self. *Consciousness and Cognition, 3,* 327–355.

Hyman, I. E., Jr., Husband, T. H., & Billings, F. J. (1995). False memories of childhood experiences. *Applied Cognitive Psychology, 9,* 181–197.

Jacoby, L. L. (1991). A process-dissociation framework: Separating automatic from intentional uses of memory. *Journal of Memory and Language, 30,* 513–541.

Jacoby, L. L., Woloshyn V., & Kelley, C. (1989). Becoming famous without being recognized. *Journal of Experimental Psychology: General, 118,* 115–125.

Johnson, M. K., & Foley, M. A. (1984). Differentiating fact from fantasy: The reliability of children's memory. *Journal of Social Issues, 40,* 33–50.

Johnson, M. K., Foley, M. A., & Leach, K. The consequences for memory of imagining in another person's voice. *Memory and Cognition, 16,* 337–342.

Johnson, M. K., Foley, M. A., Suengas, A. G., & Raye, C. L. (1988). Phenomenal characteristics of memories for perceived and imagined autobiographical events. *Journal of Experimental Psychology: General, 117,* 371–376.

Johnson, M. K., Hashtroudi, S., & Lindsay, D. S. (1993). Source monitoring. *Psychological Bulletin, 114,* 3–28.

Johnson, M. K., Kounios, J., & Reeder, J. A. (1994). Time-course studies of reality monitoring and recognition. *Journal of Experimental Psychology: Learning, Memory, & Cognition, 20,* 1409–1419.

Johnson, M. K., & Raye, C. L. (1981). Reality monitoring. *Psychological Review, 88,* 67–85.

Johnson, M. K., Raye, C. L., Foley, H. J., & Foley, M. A. (1981). Cognitive operations and decision bias in reality monitoring. *American Journal of Psychology, 94,* 37–64.

Johnson, M. K., Raye, C. L., Hasher, L., & Chromiak, W. (1979). Are there developmental differences in reality-monitoring? *Journal of Experimental Child Psychology, 27,* 120–128.

Johnson, M. K., Raye, C. L., Wang, A. W., & Taylor, T. H. (1979). Fact and fantasy: The roles of accuracy and variability in confusing imaginations with perceptual experiences. *Journal of Experimental Psychology: Human Learning and Memory, 5,* 229–240.

Johnson, M. K., & Suengas, A. G. (1989). Reality monitoring judgments of other people's memories. *Bulletin of the Psychonomic Society, 27,* 107–110.

Kail, R. (1990). *The development of memory in children.* New York: W. H. Freeman & Co.

Koppenhaver, J. M., Kumar, V. K., & Pekala, R. J. (1997). Dissociativity, imagery vividness and reality monitoring. *Dissociation: Progress in the Dissociative Disorders, 10,* 21–28.

Lindsay, D. S. (1990). Misleading suggestions can impair eyewitnesses' ability to remember event details. *Journal of Experimental Psychology: Learning, Memory, and Cognition, 16,* 1077–1083.

Lindsay, D. S., Gonzales, V., & Eso, K. (1995). Aware and unaware of memories of postevent suggestions. In M. S. Zaragoza, J. R. Graham, G. C. N. Hall, R. Hirschman, & Y. N. Ben-Porath (Eds.), *Memory and testimony in the child witness* (pp. 86–108). California: Sage.

Lindsay, D. S., & Johnson, M. K. (1987). Reality monitoring and suggestibility: Children's ability to discriminate among memories from different sources. In S. J. Ceci, M. P. Toglia, & D. F. Ross (Eds.), *Children's eyewitness memory.* New York: Springer-Verlag.

Lindsay, D. S., & Johnson, M. K. (1989). The eyewitness suggestibility effect and memory for source. *Memory and Cognition, 17,* 349–358.

Lindsay, D. S., & Johnson, M. K. (1991). Recognition memory and source monitoring. *Bulletin of the Psychonomic Society, 29,* 203–205.

Lindsay, D. S., Johnson, M. K., & Kwon, P. (1991). Developmental changes in memory source monitoring. *Journal of Experimental Child Psychology, 52,* 297–318.

Markham, R. (1991). Development of reality monitoring for performed and imagined actions. *Perceptual and Motor Skills, 72,* 1347–1354.

Markham, R., & Hynes, L. (1993). The effect of vividness of imagery on reality monitoring. *Journal of Mental Imagery, 17,* 159–170.

Marks, D. F. (1973). Visual imagery differences in the recall of pictures. *British Journal of Psychology, 64,* 17–24.

Marsh, R. L., & Hicks, J. L. (1998). Test formats change source-monitoring decision processes. *Journal of Experimental Psychology, Learning, Memory and Cognition, 24,* 1137–1151.

Newcombe, P. A., & Siegal, M. (1996). Where to look first for suggestibility in young children. *Cognition, 59,* 337–356.

Olson, D. R., Astington, J. W., & Harris, P. L. (1988). Introduction. In J. W. Astington, P. L. Harris, & D. R. Olson (Eds.), *Developing theories of mind* (pp. 1–15). Cambridge, MA: Cambridge University.

Parker, J. F. (1995). Age differences in source monitoring of performed and imagined actions on immediate and delayed tests. *Journal of Experimental Child Psychology, 60,* 84–101.

Perner, J. (1991). *Understanding the representational mind.* Cambridge, MA: MIT Press.

Poole, D. A., & Lindsay, D. S. (1995). Interviewing preschoolers: Effects of nonsuggestive techniques, parental coaching, and leading questions on reports of nonexperienced events. *Journal of Experimental Child Psychology, 60,* 129–154.

Powell, M. B., Roberts, K. P., Ceci, S. J., & Hembrooke, H. H. (in press). The effects of repeated experience on children's suggestibility. *Developmental Psychology.*

Powell, M. B., & Thomson, D. M. (1997). Contrasting memory for temporal-source and memory for content in children's discrimination of repeated events. *Applied Cognitive Psychology, 11*, 339–360.

Ratner, H. H., & Foley, M. A. (1996). A unifying framework for the development of children's activity memory. *Advances in Child Development and Behavior, 25*, 33–105.

Reyna, V. F., & Lloyd, F. (1997). Theories of false memory in children and adults. *Learning and Individual Differences, 9*, 95–124.

Roberts, K. P. (1996). How research on source monitoring can inform cognitive interview techniques: Commentary on Memon and Stevenage (1996). *Psycoloquy, 7(44).*

Roberts, K. P., & Blades, M. (1995). Children's discrimination of memories for actual and pretend actions in a hiding task. *British Journal of Developmental Psychology, 13*, 321–333.

Roberts, K. P., & Blades, M. (1998). The effects of interacting with events on children's eyewitness memory and source monitoring. *Applied Cognitive Psychology, 12*, 489–503.

Roberts, K. P., Lamb, M. E., & Sternberg, K. J. (1999). Effects of the timing of postevent information on preschoolers' memories of an event. *Applied Cognitive Psychology, 13*, 541–559.

Roberts, K. P., Lamb, M. E., Zale, J. L., & Randall, D. W. (1998, March). Qualitative differences in children's accounts of confirmed and unconfirmed incidents of sexual abuse. In A. Crossman & M. Scullin (Chairs), *Avenues for assessing the reliability of children's statements: A panoply of approaches.* Symposium presented at the biennial meeting of the American Psychology-Law Society, Redondo Beach, CA.

Robinson, E. J. (1994). What people say, what they think, and what is really the case: Children's understanding of utterances as sources of knowledge. In C. Lewis & P. Mitchell (Eds.), *Children's early understanding of mind: Origins and development* (pp. 355–381). Hillsdale, NJ: Lawrence Erlbaum Associates.

Rudy, L., & Goodman, G. S. (1991). Effects of participation on children's reports: Implications for children's testimony. *Developmental Psychology, 27*, 527–538.

Rybash, J. M., Rubenstein, L., & DeLuca, K. L. (1997). How to become famous but not necessarily recognizable: Encoding process and study-test delays dissociate source monitoring from recognition. *American Journal of Psychology, 110*, 93–114.

Schachter, D. L., Harbluk, J. L., & McLachlan, D. R. (1984). Retrieval without recollection: An experimental analysis of source amnesia. *Journal of Verbal Learning and Verbal Behavior, 23*, 593–611.

Slamecka, N. J., & Graf, P. (1978). The generation effect: Delineation of a phenomenon. *Journal of Experimental Psychology: Human Learning and Memory, 4*, 592–604.

Snodgrass, J. G., & Vanderwort, M. (1980). A standardized set of 260 pictures: Norms for name agreement, image agreement, familiarity, and visual complexity. *Journal of Experimental Psychology: Human Learning & Memory, 6*, 174–215.

Suengas, A. G., & Johnson, M. K. (1988). Qualitative effects of rehearsal on memories for perceived and imagined complex events. *Journal of Experimental Psychology: General, 117*, 377–389.

Symons, C. S., & Johnson, B. T. (1997). The self-reference effect in memory: Meta-analysis. *Psychological Bulletin, 121*, 371–394.

Taylor, M., Esbensen, B. M., & Bennett, R. T. (1994). Children's understanding of knowledge acquisition: The tendency for children to report that they have always known what they have just learned. *Child Development, 65*, 1581–1604.

Welch-Ross, M. K. (1995). Developmental changes in preschoolers' ability to distinguish between memories of performed, pretended, and imagined actions. *Cognitive Development, 10*, 421–441.

Welch-Ross, M. K., Diecidue, K., & Miller, S. A. (1997). Young children's understanding of conflicting mental representation predicts suggestibility. *Developmental Psychology, 33*, 43–53.

Wellman, H. M. (1990). *The child's theory of mind.* Cambridge, MA: MIT Press.

Witkin, H. A., Goodenough, D. R., & Oltman, P. K. (1979). Psychological differentiation: Current status. *Journal of Personality and Social Psychology, 37*, 1127–1145.

Zaragoza, M. S., & Koshmider, J. W., III. (1989). Misled subjects may know more than their performance implies. *Journal of Experimental Psychology: Learning, Memory, and Cognition, 15*, 246–255.

Zaragoza, M. S., & Lane, S. M. (1994). Source misattributions and the suggestibility of eyewitness memory. *Journal of Experimental Psychology: Learning, Memory, and Cognition, 20*, 1–12.

3

Belief and Disbelief: Children's Assessments of the Reliability of Sources of Knowledge About the World

Elizabeth J. Robinson
University of Birmingham, UK

What do we do when new information contradicts an existing belief we have about the world? For example, I hold the view that the coffee jar contains coffee. I see you look inside, and you announce that it contains tea bags. I am likely to believe you without checking the jar myself, because I assume that you are better informed about it than I am. I assume that you are right and I was wrong, and I can explain that by assuming that someone added tea bags to an empty coffee jar in my absence. To take a more complex example, suppose you are a 14-year-old who makes the reasonable assumption that physical objects such as tables are as solid as they appear to be. Her teacher gives a lesson on particle theory. Does the student believe what she is told? It may be difficult: "Well you can't see any particles or owt, so it's just—just can't believe it. You know, that this table's made out of particles—hundreds of millions ... " (Driver, 1989, p. 103). A similar problem arises for younger children who are told that the earth is round, when their own experience tells them it is flat (Vosniadou & Brewer, 1992). Our naïve theories about physics or biology are often contradicted by scientifically accepted theories (e.g., Atran, 1996; DiSessa, 1996). Similarly, a young child with a misconception about the conditions under which quantity can change (a nonconserver) may be contradicted by another nonconserver who is judging from a different perspective, or by a conserver (Doise, 1988; Roazzi & Bryant, 1998; Russell, 1981, 1982). The young child has the choice of rejecting the contradicting view or of trying to integrate it into his or her own interpretation. A final example is a child or adult who has experienced an event and is subsequently given a misleading suggestion about what occurred, as happens in research on suggestibility (as reviewed by Ceci & Bruck, 1993) or as may happen to a witness in court (Qin, Quas, Redlich, & Goodman, 1997), and this is discussed thoroughly in chapter 8, this volume. In each of these examples, the new input comes via an utterance (although this may be accompanied by a visual illustration or a practical demonstration) and it contradicts a belief based on one's own direct experience—of coffee jars, tables, relative quantity, or the world in general. In some cases, as with the coffee jar example, the contradiction can be explained easily. In the case of "scientific knowledge," which apparently contradicts our own experiences or naïve theories, the contradictions may take more effort to resolve—it is not easy to simply discount one's own direct experience of how things are, or one's naïve theory about how an aspect of the world works, but on the other hand it would be unreasonable to assume that the teacher is lying or grossly mistaken. If we are to maintain both beliefs, one solution might be to hold them in separate mental compartments, one for real life and the other for school science. Another solution might be to try to understand how a table can appear to be solid despite being made up of hundreds of millions of particles, or how the earth can appear to be flat despite really being round, or how quantity can remain unchanged despite a change in appearance. Of course these ways of resolving the apparent contradiction may be offered by a speaker who is aware that what he or she is saying contradicts the listener's prior belief, but often listeners will be left to solve the problem themselves.

However we decide to deal with contradictions like these, we are likely at some point in the process to assess the relative reliability of the sources of the contradicting inputs. There may or may not be source-specifying information attached to our existing belief, and if such information is attached, it may be more or less accurate. That we recall some things as conscious experiences but others just as "knowledge," and the memory systems that could be responsible for these different types of memories are of interest to researchers of adults' remembering. Tulving (1972) gave the label *semantic memories* to things we "just know" and which are not recalled as particular experiences, such as a belief about the solidity of physical objects like tables. He distinguished these from memories that are recalled as experiences, "episodic memories," which tend to have more or less source-specify- ing information attached. Within memory for events (as opposed to facts), a further distinction has been made between "remembering" as a conscious experience that an item was recently presented, and "knowing" or recognizing that the item was presented, but without any conscious recollection of its presentation (Gardiner & Java, 1993; Tulving, 1985). Research on adults' ability to make attributions about the origins of memories, knowledge, and beliefs has focused on the circumstances in which accurate or inaccurate attributions tend to be made (see Johnson, Hashtroudi, & Lindsay, 1993; Roediger, McDermott, & Robinson, 1998 for reviews), and on the variables that influence the incidence of remembering as an experience as opposed to knowing (e.g., Jacoby & Hay, 1998). Understanding the mechanisms involved in attributing a source to a belief is clearly relevant to understanding how we resolve a contradiction between that belief and new input. But even if the circumstances surrounding the acquisition of the initial belief are recalled accurately and completely, there still has to be an evaluation of the reliability of the source. Which sources do we consider to be reliable and which unreliable?

When making evaluations of reliability, adults presumably draw on their assumptions about the various ways in which the things people say or think can be in error. We know that people can lie or make slips of the tongue, but adults also assume that well-intentioned speakers can make false statements that are based on a misunderstanding of the matter in question, on out of date knowledge, or on forgetting something relevant. I might have suggested that you make yourself a cup of coffee while I was ignorant of the fact that the coffee jar now contains tea bags. Adults also accept that their own interpretation of events directly perceived can be in error: The dead animal I see on the road ahead can turn out to be a paper bag. More broadly, adults assume that minds interpret incoming information, and that errors of interpretation can occur for a whole variety of reasons. Some errors are more likely to occur than others and it is our (often implicit) assessments of these likelihoods that help us decide how to resolve contradictions between inputs. I am ready to accept your statement that the coffee jar contains tea bags because I find it plausible that the tea bags could have been added in my absence: I think that my belief could easily be wrong. If the coffee jar in question was a new one straight from the supermarket shelf, then I would be much less likely to believe your statement that it has unexpected contents, and would probably want to check for myself.

I hope this introduction makes the case that deciding how to handle contradicting inputs is no straightforward matter, and that the decisions we make are influenced by our assumptions about how peoples' minds work. This immediately leads us to wonder how young children, whom many researchers believe to have an immature conception of the mind, will handle conflicting inputs. Later in this chapter I draw on the literature about children's theory of mind to make specific predictions, but first of all let us see how young children behave in a situation similar to the one just described, in which you tell me that a newly purchased jar of coffee contains tea bags. In my thought experiment, I had doubts about the reliability of your utterance and wanted to see for myself. On this occasion I place less trust in what you tell me than in what I see for myself. Do young children discriminate between seeing and being told in the same way that an adult might?

Making an adultlike judgment in this situation may *not* require an adultlike understanding of the mind. Both Perner (1991) and Zaitchik (1991) make the assumption that very young children, despite their immature conception of the mind, treat information gained via an utterance as less reliable than information gained directly. Perner (1991) argued that this must be the case, because information gained via utterances is so unreliable that the child's knowledge base would be unstable if such information were given the same weight as information gained directly. In Zaitchik's (1991)[1] paper the assumption remains implicit. On the other hand, Robinson (1994) pointed out that children in the early stages of mastery over language would find it particularly difficult to become an active member of a communicating network if they constantly doubted the truth of what people said to them.

In this first investigation, as in the subsequent ones, I focus on circumstances under which a speaker contradicts the child's belief derived from direct experience (such as seeing), and the speaker apparently intends to be informative and cooperative.

DO PRESCHOOL CHILDREN DISCRIMINATE KNOWLEDGE GAINED BY SEEING FROM KNOWLEDGE GAINED BY BEING TOLD?

Further details of this work appear in Robinson, Mitchell, and Nye (1995) and in Robinson (1994). The question of interest was: When preschool children receive new information that contradicts a prior belief, is that new information treated as less trustworthy when it is obtained via an utterance rather than by seeing directly?

---

[1]For a discussion of Zaitchik's view and an alternative interpretation of her evidence, see Robinson, Mitchell, and Nye (1995).

Children aged 3 to 4 years were taken individually into the headmistress's (principal's) office in their nursery, and saw a set of new boxes containing toys, which had supposedly just arrived. On each box was a clear picture depicting the toy inside. The child was asked about one of the boxes, "What do you think is in this box?" and inferred the content, for example, a car. The experimenter then had a look inside, and told the child, "There's only one thing in the box, and it's a teddy bear!" Shortly after, a second adult who had been quietly reading in a corner of the room came over and asked the child what was in the box. We were interested in whether the child maintained her or his initial belief based on the picture on the outside of the box, or whether he or she believed what the experimenter had said. About 42% of the children maintained their initial belief, but if we exclude those who could not recall what the experimenter had said, this dropped to 24%.[2] In a comparison trial, children saw for themselves the unexpected content of the box, and as we would expect, hardly anybody maintained their initial belief that had been based on the picture on the outside. Therefore, in this investigation, and in several replications, children aged 3 to 4 years clearly discriminated between seeing for themselves and being told, treating the latter as less reliable. Although they often did revise their initial belief on the basis of what they were told, they were significantly less likely to do so than when they saw for themselves what was in the box, in line with Perner's (1991) argument.

Also consistent with Perner's view that this differential weighting occurs despite an immature understanding of the mind, children were no *less* likely to believe what they were told when the experimenter announced the surprising content of the box without having looked inside. In this condition in our study, the experimenter said, "I'm not going to have a look inside" before saying what the box contained. Children apparently could treat the information contained in an utterance as unreliable without yet understanding why it is unreliable—because it comes via another's mind, which is subject to error. If this explanation is correct, then we would expect to find that as children's understanding about the mind improves between the ages of around 3 to 5 years, so would their sensitivity to how well informed the speaker is (Robinson, 1994; Robinson, Mitchell, & Nye, 1995).

This suggestion links with the argument made by Welch-Ross, Diecidue and Miller (1997), who demonstrate a relationship between

---

[2]The failures to recall the utterance are interesting. They could arise just through failure to pay attention, but they could also arise if children cannot handle false utterances, as described by Riggs and Robinson (1995).

children's understanding of the mind as representational, and their willingness to resist a false suggestion. In their research, children aged between 3 and 5 years were told a story illustrated with pictures (and so they both saw and were told about the true state of affairs), and shortly after were asked either straightforward questions about what happened such as, "Did Sally play basketball?", or misleading questions such as, "Sally played dress up, didn't she?" when Sally did not play that game. Several days later, children were asked to recall the events of story. Children were more likely to be (wrongly) influenced by the misleading questions if they performed less well on tasks that assessed their understanding of the mind as representational. Welch-Ross et al. (1997), concluded that children who fail to understand that the mind can misrepresent are inclined to "overwrite their event representation with the most recent or salient informative experience" (1997, p. 48). Astington and Gopnik (1988) put forward a similar view. Yet our evidence shows that young children do not simply believe the most recent input about the content of a box, but are sensitive to the source of that input. To that extent, they were not simply overwriting their prior event representations.

There are, however, important differences between our procedure and that of Welch-Ross et al., apart from the obvious one of the difference in delay before recall. The children in Welch-Ross et al.'s (1997) study had no information about the knowledge of the experimenter who asked the misleading questions and so had no obvious way of deciding whether their own belief was likely to be more or less reliable than the experimenter's. Our children, in contrast, knew that the experimenter had or had not seen inside the box and so had a basis for deciding whether or not to believe what she said (but see the information that follows). We would expect that children with a more advanced understanding of the representational mind are more likely to be influenced by a suggestion from an experimenter who is apparently better informed than they are, than by one from a less well-informed experimenter. Recent work by Welch-Ross suggests that this is indeed the case (Welch-Ross, 1999, chap. 9, this volume), although in her study the "knowledgeable" experimenter was as well informed as, rather than better informed than, the child. Children were read a story by an experimenter and were subsequently interviewed either by that same adult or by an adult who professed ignorance of the story. Children's scores on a battery of false belief tests predicted the tendency to be misled by the leading questions of the knowledgeable interviewer more than by those of the naïve interviewer. Children who gained low scores on the false belief tests were equally misled by the naïve and by the knowledgeable interviewer.

A second difference between our procedure and that of Welch-Ross et al. (1997) is that, in their study, the interest was on the effect of giving children a misleading suggestion rather than no further input, whereas our interest was in the relative effects of further inputs of different kinds—being told by a well- or ill-informed adult, or seeing inside the box for oneself. Our children's willingness to revise their initial belief about the content of the box on the basis of the suggestion from an experimenter who announces she has not seen inside seems similar to the effects of suggestibility found by Welch-Ross, although our children's initial beliefs were based on much more flimsy evidence than those of the children in the Welch-Ross study.

To return to our results: Children gave less weight to what they were told than to what they saw for themselves, but failed to take into account the level of informedness of the speaker. Children could be predisposed to behave in the former way, but the latter, finer discrimination does seem to require understanding the link between information access and knowledge state. There is, though, another possible reason why the children in our study failed to give more weight to a well-informed than to an ill-informed speaker, which does not deny them understanding about the link between information access and belief formation. The children could have been misled by the confident manner in which the experimenter announced the surprising content of the box and just assumed that she knew, even though she had not seen. The same might be said for the experimenter who offered the misleading suggestion in Welch-Ross et al.'s (1997) study without giving the children any indication of how well informed or ill informed she was. Children's trust in the information given by an adult interviewer has also been used to explain children's suggestibility. Usually an ignorant speaker would qualify her comment with something like, "Maybe it's a teddy bear," or "It could be a teddy bear." But we could not include such qualifications in our procedure because then the content of the utterance would have conveyed unreliability, rather than just the fact that it was an utterance. To get over this problem, and to probe more deeply into children's sensitivity to the level of informedness of the speaker, we developed a new procedure in which we avoided the social peculiarity of an ignorant speaker announcing the content of a box.

DO CHILDREN BELIEVE A WELL-INFORMED SPEAKER MORE THAN AN IGNORANT ONE?

Further details of this series of experiments appear in Robinson, Champion, and Mitchell (1999). In our new procedure, the child and the experimenter opened two identical containers (e.g., two blue plastic trash cans) and found that one contained a teddy bear and the other a snowman. The teddy bear and the snowman were returned to their trash cans, the lids put on, and the trash cans were put away in a bag. Shortly after, one was taken out at random, nobody knew whether it was the one with the teddy bear or the one with the snowman. A monkey puppet, operated by the experimenter, invited the child and the experimenter in turn to guess which they thought it was, asking, "Which one do you think it is, the one with the teddy bear or the one with the snowman?" The child guessed (e.g., "Teddy bear"), and whatever the child said, the experimenter contradicted her or him ("Snowman"). With this procedure, it was perfectly acceptable to announce the content, whether or not one really knew what it was and without qualifying a guess with "I think." The monkey then asked the child in a puzzled voice "So which one is it?" Now the child had the opportunity to repeat what he or she had said originally, or to switch to agree with the experimenter. When both players were guessing, it was equally appropriate for the child to repeat what he or she had originally said or to switch and be consistent with the experimenter. But on half the trials, the monkey puppet had allowed the experimenter to look inside the trash can before she answered the question "Which one do you think it is?" Now, the child should switch to agree with the better-informed experimenter. If children more frequently switched to agree with the experimenter when the experimenter had seen inside than when she was just guessing, we could conclude that children were sensitive to the level of informedness of the speaker. We included two filler trials on which the experimenter agreed with the child, just so children were not constantly being contradicted.

We tested children aged 3 to 4 years, 4 to 5 years, and 5 to 6 years in nursery (preschool), reception (kindergarten), and first year (first grade) classes, respectively. Children in each of the three age groups discriminated between the two types of experimental trial, switching to the experimenter's view more frequently when the experimenter had seen inside than when she had not. There was no age-related improvement: Our 3- to 4-year-olds performed just as well as the 5- to 6-year-olds. Note that the children were not willing to agree with the experimenter just because of their own feeling of uncertainty about the contents of the trash can; if they had been, they would have switched to agree with the experimenter even when she was no better informed than they were.

This result suggests that our failure to find sensitivity to speaker informedness in Robinson, Mitchell, and Nye's (1995) experiment was due to children assuming the speaker was well informed because of the confident manner in which she announced the content of the box. We cannot tell whether this led some children to believe the utterance without reflecting at all on the experimenter's source of knowledge ("she said what's inside so it must be true"), or whether they inferred that she must have some prior knowledge, even though she had not looked in the box ("she said what's inside so she must have had some kind of information access"). The latter seems quite justifiable, and adults might interpret the situation in this way. The former, in contrast, seems less justifiable and could imply that children may treat the giving of an utterance as a sign of knowing rather than as a means of conveying knowledge.

Whatever the reason for the discrepancy between our two experiments in the way children treat an utterance from an ignorant speaker, it is clear that under some conditions at least, 3- to 4-year-olds can discriminate appropriately between well- and ill-informed speakers. They were behaving as if they understood that the person who had seen inside the container knew what the content was, and the person who had not seen inside did not know. In our next two experiments, we compared children's behavior under this procedure with their explicit judgments of the knowledge of the two players. If, as suggested previously, the mere giving of an utterance tends to mislead the child into thinking that the speaker is knowledgeable, then we would expect that children would be better at judging knowledge when no utterances are given, than in the procedure just described in which players announce what they think is in the trash can.

In these experiments, children played a modified version of the game previously described (hereafter described as "utterance" trials) and, on other trials ("knowledge" trials), they judged the knowledge of a player who had or had not looked inside the trash can but did not announce what she or he thought was inside. We were interested in the possibility that children tend to treat the giving of an utterance as a sign of knowing. If they do, they are at risk of giving too much weight to what they are told compared with what they have seen directly. This could be particularly important with respect to eyewitnesses who may be coached by other people to change their testimony, or be exposed to interviewers who ask leading questions (see chap. 8, this volume). Although we have shown that the children in our studies are sensitive to the unreliability of what they are told, there remains the possibility that they are overweighting information gained via utterances.

Let us consider first the children's behavior on the utterance trials. These were somewhat different from those we used in the previous experiment: Then, the child always guessed what was in the container, and the experimenter either guessed or was knowledgeable. This time, we omitted trials on which both players guessed, and replaced them with trials on which the child saw inside the trash can and the experimenter guessed.[3] On each trial, either the child or the experimenter knew and the other was guessing. The appropriate pattern of responding to the monkey's final puzzled question, "So which one is it?" was for the child to repeat her or his initial belief when he or she had seen inside, but to update to agree with the experimenter when it was the experimenter who had seen inside. In our first experiment using this procedure, 28 out of 64 (44%) of the 3- to 4-year-olds showed this correct pattern, and in a second experiment with exactly the same procedure and the same experimenter, the success rate rose to 30 out of 40 (75%). Presumably, differences in our samples account for this difference: The intake of the school used in the second experiment was of a higher socioeconomic group than that of the school used in the first experiment. In any case, it is clear that in line with our previous experiment, a substantial proportion of young children discriminate between informed and ignorant speakers.

Now we consider children's behavior on the knowledge trials. On these, the procedure was the same in that either the child or the experimenter saw inside the container, but this time neither person announced what they thought was inside. Instead, the child was asked either, "Who knows best which one it is, Helen (experimenter) or you?" or "Does Helen know which one it is, yes or no? Do you know which one it is, yes or no?" Contrary to our expectation, children made significantly more errors on knowledge trials than on utterance trials. Of the sample that showed 44% success on utterance trials, 25% gave correct judgments of "Who knows best?" Of the sample who showed 75% correct responding on utterance trials, only 28% made correct knowledge judgments on behalf of both child and experimenter. Children behaved as if they knew which player was the better informed when they decided whether or not to believe what the experimenter said, but they failed to judge correctly who knew best when no utterances were given.

These results are relevant to the discussion of children's implicit and explicit knowledge about the mind (Chandler, Fritz, & Hala, 1989; Clements & Perner, 1994; Freeman, Lewis & Doherty, 1991; Robinson et al., 1999), and to developmental work on procedural and declarative knowledge more generally (e.g. Parkin, 1997), but that will not be

---

[3]We made this change so that we could classify an individual child as showing the correct or incorrect pattern of responding and so make within-child comparisons between utterance and knowledge trials. When both players are guessing we cannot do this because it is equally correct for the child to repeat or switch her or his judgment; we can only show more switching on a group basis on trials when the experimenter has seen than on trials when she is guessing.

elaborated here. The possibility that the contradicting utterance served as a signal to the child to attend to the speaker's information access is also interesting, but not relevant here (see Robinson et al., 1999). Rather, we are concerned with the implications for children's evaluations of the reliability of sources of knowledge. So far we have no evidence that children are at risk of giving too much weight to information conveyed in an utterance simply because they treat the giving of an utterance as a sign of knowledge. The evidence so far suggests that many children aged 3 to 4 years treat information contained in utterances with appropriate caution, at least under the kind of conditions we have used here.

REPORTING THE SOURCE OF KNOWLEDGE GAINED BY SEEING

Now we make closer links with the published literature in which children are asked to report the source of a belief recently formed (Gopnik & Graf, 1988; O'Neill & Gopnik, 1991; Wimmer, Hogrefe, & Perner, 1988). Results of these studies suggest that many 3-year-olds are poor at reporting how they know what is in a drawer, for example, when they have just been shown or told the content by the experimenter. The explanation offered by the authors listed previously is that children who do not yet conceive of the mind as representational fail to understand the connection between information access and consequent knowledge or belief state, and so simply do not know how they know. O'Neill and Gopnik (1991) discussed the implications of this account for children's memory, suggesting that children who fail to understand the causal relationship between information access and belief state may not retain any information about the origin of their belief. This may also be important for future source monitoring because children may not encode useful source-specifying information that they can use later to make source attributions. Perner and Ruffman (1995) elaborated on the suggested link between understanding about belief formation and memory. They demonstrate an association between children's ability to remember events as having been experienced (assessed by free recall) and their understanding about the relationship between information access and consequent knowledge state. Applied to our research, we would expect that a child who does not know how he or she knows something would be poor at evaluating the relative reliability of conflicting beliefs; he or she should make errors in our task. In the study described next, we examined the relationship between children's decisions about what to believe, and their ability to report the source of their final belief.

This time children not only decided which of two conflicting inputs to believe, as in the previous studies, but they also reported the source of their final belief. Would the children who made correct judgments about what to believe also be able to correctly report the source of their belief? Our procedure was a modification of the one used in the second series of studies: On each trial, one person was informed about the chosen object and the other person was guessing, their views were contradictory, and the child had to make a final decision about what to believe. The experimenter was Emma Whitcombe (see Whitcombe & Robinson, 1999, for more details). The children were aged between 3 and 5 years. On each trial, the task was to identify which of a pair of pictures had been chosen to go in a frame. The child knew that the chosen picture was of either, say, a banana or some cheese (both yellow). The chosen picture could be viewed directly in its frame, in which case the viewer had complete information about what was depicted, or it could be viewed through a window, in which case the viewer saw a patch of color that was not sufficient to identify with confidence what was depicted. For example, on one type of trial, the experimenter might look at a patch of yellow through the window, suggest that it showed cheese, and then the child saw the entire picture of a banana. The child was the victim of contradicting views and the experimenter was less well informed than the child. On another type of trial, the roles would be reversed. On each trial the child was asked an identity question (what the picture depicted) and a source question (how she or he knew). The source question was asked first in open form: "How did you know it was an X?", and if the child did not answer, options were offered, "How did you know it was an X, was it because you saw it or because I told you?" (order of options counterbalanced between children). To give children the best chance of understanding the source question on the experimental trials, they were given two initial single-source warm-up trials in which the experimenter gave them feedback on their answers to the source question, such as, "That's right, you saw the X" or "No, I told you about the X, you didn't see it."

To enable us to make a straightforward comparison with the literature on children's source-monitoring skills (e.g., Gopnik & Graf, 1988; Wimmer, Hogrefe & Perner, 1988), each child also had single-source trials in which he or she either saw the complete picture in its frame, or was told what the picture depicted by the experimenter who had seen the complete picture. Again, the child was asked an identity question and a source question. The results for these single-source trials were in line with the published literature (Gopnik & Graf, 1988; O'Neill & Gopnik, 1991). As expected, children nearly always answered the identity questions correctly: They simply had to report back what they had seen or what they were told, and they had no reason to doubt the accuracy of either input. For reporting sources, as in the previous research, the 4- to 5-year-olds performed near ceiling, but the 3- to 4-year-olds made more errors. Their mean scores were 1.67 when seeing the source and 1.43 when told the source, out of a maximum of 2. Consistent with Wimmer, Hogrefe, and Perner (1988), who used an open question to assess children's understanding of sources, none of the 3- to 4-year-olds could consistently answer the open question, and all had to be offered the forced choice options on one or more trials. The 4- to 5-year-olds, in contrast, nearly always answered the open question and usually did so correctly. This pattern was also found in the dual-source (experimental) trials, and suggests that the younger children were less aware of sources than the older ones.

On dual-source trials, when children were the victims of contradicting input, they had to make a choice about which source to believe. In answer to the identity questions, the 4- to 5-year-olds virtually always made the correct choice, and the performance of the 3- to 4-year-olds was also near ceiling: They gained mean scores of 1.83 when seeing was the informative source, and 1.66 when being told was informative, out of a maximum of 2. To the extent that children made correct decisions about what to believe both on seeing and being told trials, they were monitoring their sources accurately. They generally believed the interpretation based on seeing only when they were better informed than the experimenter, and they generally believed what they were told only when the experimenter was the better informed. The good performance of the 3- to 4-year-olds in this study goes beyond that in the second series: Then, the child just had to compare the knowledge of someone who had seen inside the trash can with that of someone who had not seen, whereas in this study the comparison was between somebody who had seen the whole picture, and somebody who had seen a part through the window. Our children who were successful demonstrated a working understanding of the relative reliability of utterances from well-informed and partially-informed speakers.

In marked contrast to the good performance on the identity question, the source question on dual-source trials proved to be quite difficult for the 3- to 4-year-olds. Their mean score was 1.14 when the informative source was being told and 1.35 when seeing was informative (out of 2). Overall, children were inclined to report that they knew because they had seen, even when, in fact, they had had to be told what the picture depicted. Children were much more likely to perform completely correctly on identity questions than on source questions—20 children out of the sample of 47 consistently accepted information only from the well-informed speaker, yet failed to report explicitly the source of their belief, whereas none performed perfectly on source questions but made errors on identity questions.

A further result of interest is that children were more accurate at answering the source question on single source than on dual-source trials. One possible explanation for this is that when forced-choice options are given, the child can choose the correct option in a single-source trial just by recalling what happened—that they saw or were told something—without understanding that that is how they know the identity of the item. On dual-source trials, because children both saw and were told something, their performance using that strategy would be at chance if the two sources were equally salient. If this is correct, there is a risk of false positives in the previous single-source studies (e.g., Gopnik & Graf, 1988), and children may actually be poorer at reporting how they know than we previously assumed. It could be, though, that children performed more poorly in dual-source conditions because of the increased information-processing load of the dual source task[4]. Whichever is the case, we can be confident that children who responded correctly in dual-source conditions, reporting seeing or being told as their informative source as appropriate, did have access to their modality of input. Only 21% of our 3- to 4-year-olds gained the maximum score in response to the source question, compared with 69% of the 4- to 5-year-olds. This, along with the finding that, unlike the older children, the younger ones nearly always needed to be prompted with "was it because you saw it or because I told you?" suggests that there are substantial improvements in children's ability to reflect on their sources of their beliefs between the ages of about 3 to 5 years.

The relatively good performance of our young children at deciding what to believe perhaps offers reassurance that in their everyday lives they are not seriously at risk of disbelieving what is true and believing what is false, even if they would be unable to justify their decisions to an observing psychologist. The results reported here suggest that children may be able to monitor sources when the decision processes are automatic and require no effortful reflection, but may nevertheless

---

[4]The results of a further experiment by Emma Whitcombe suggest information overload was unlikely. Children watched a video in which one person looked inside a box and another felt, and they gave conflicting views about the box's content. As in the preceding experiment, there were two contradictory sources so the information processing load was similar, yet children were very rarely confused in reporting which person had which form of access.

have difficulty when they are required to engage in more deliberate and strategic decision making (see the introduction by Roberts, this volume, for a fuller account of different source decision processes). As suggested by Lorsbach (chap. 5, this volume), children with learning difficulties who are delayed in many cognitive tasks also exhibit a difficulty with reflective processing.

WHY DO CHILDREN MISREPORT THEIR SOURCES OF KNOWLEDGE?

Why did children in the previous experiment misreport their sources of knowledge? I suggest four possibilities, all of which could occur: First, children might have no conscious experience of the circumstances under which their final belief was acquired, like adults who make a "know" rather than a "remember" judgment in a word-recognition task (Gardiner & Java, 1993). When asked the open-source question "How do you know it's a … ?" they would have no idea what to say, like most of our 3- to 4-year-olds. When offered prompts, "Did you see it or did Emma tell you?" they would simply guess, with a 50% chance of being correct if the two response options were equally available to them. The adult literature on recognition memory suggests that this kind of error can occur in people who certainly do understand the link between information access and consequent belief state, but on the basis of Perner and Ruffman's (1995) research we might expect errors of this kind to be common among 3- to 4-year-olds who do not yet have that understanding: As mentioned previously, these authors argue for a developmental link between ability to remember events as having been experienced, and understanding about the relationship between information access and consequent knowledge state.

The second possible type of error is that children may be making reality-monitoring errors by reporting having seen events that were only suggested to them (e.g., Ackil & Zaragoza, 1995; Lindsay & Johnson, 1987; Quas et al., chap. 8, this volume; Roberts & Blades, 1996). Specifically, children may mistakenly attribute the experimenter's experience to themselves, so they imagine that it was they who saw the whole picture, whereas actually it was the experimenter. Alternatively, when the experimenter announces what she sees (e.g., a banana), the child might imagine a banana and later mistake the imagined banana for a banana really seen in the picture (Foley & Johnson, 1985; Roberts & Blades, 1995; Welch-Ross, 1995). In our experiment, children making either of these source-monitoring errors would say, "I know it's a banana because I saw it" because they wrongly believe they did see the whole banana.

As with the first type of error, this could occur among people who understand the link between information access and belief state. Indeed, it might be more prevalent among such people, because what could be happening is that having decided correctly to believe what the experimenter says, the child then wrongly attaches that belief to the original informative source. The child might infer from "I know what the object is" to "So I must have seen it." Indeed, some types of internalizing source errors are used in collaborative learning as shown later (chap. 4, this volume).

The third and fourth possible types of error would only occur if there was a failure to understand the link between information access and belief formation. The third is the one mentioned earlier, which could account for successful answering of a source question in a single-source trial: The child can recall accurately what happened (that he or she saw, or felt, or was told something) but does not realize that that is how she or he knows what the object is. The child makes no link between knowing something and having had access to relevant input. When asked an open-source question, "How do you know it's a ... ?" he or she cannot answer, but when offered prompts, "Did you see it or did Emma tell you?" the child answers correctly simply on the basis of her or his recollection of what happened. He or she is not reporting how he or she knows, but responding to the prompts in a superficial way. When there are two sources the child has no basis for choosing between them and answers at chance if the two are equally salient. As I argued previously, this can account for the greater difficulty of reporting sources in the dual-source task compared with the single-source task.

The final type of error is perhaps the most interesting. Again, the child recollects the circumstances surrounding the belief, he or she recalls accurately that he or she only saw part of the picture through the window, but wrongly assumes this is how he or she knows that the picture depicts a banana. The child says, "I know it's a banana because I saw it," but means something different from the child who makes the second type of error (i.e., who wrongly remembers having seen the whole banana). Unlike the child who makes the third kind of error (i.e., recalls object but does not realize that is how they have knowledge of the object), this child knows that information access leads to belief formation, but fails to understand what beliefs arise from a particular kind of access. She or he wrongly assumes that seeing an uninformative part of a picture enabled her or him to know what it depicts. In our next experiment we examined the source reporting errors in more detail.

SEEING AND FEELING

In the next experiment, conducted by Katherine Antcliff, we again made comparisons between 3- to 5-year-olds' (3 years, 3 months to 5 years, 4 months) ability to make the correct decision about which of two conflicting inputs to believe, and their ability to report the source of their belief. Each trial began with the child seeing and examining a pair of objects, which either looked the same and felt different (e.g., identical cereal packets, one empty and one full), or felt the same and looked different (e.g., identical balls, one red and one blue). A puppet chose one of the objects from the pair in secret and placed it in a tunnel that had a window in one side. The tunnel was placed so that one person (either the child or the experimenter) could see through the window, and the other person was allowed to feel inside the tunnel. Each child had two trials under one of four conditions—either the child saw and the experimenter felt, or the experimenter saw and the child felt, and either the object was chosen from a pair that looked the same and felt different, or from a pair that felt the same and looked different. Therefore, the child was better informed when he or she felt an object chosen from a pair that felt different, or when he or she saw an object chosen from a pair that looked different. The experimenter was better informed when the child felt an object chosen from a pair that felt the same, or when he or she saw an object chosen from a pair that looked the same. As usual, on each trial the child expressed her or his view about which object had been chosen, was contradicted by the experimenter who was either more or less well informed than the child, and the child was asked a final identity question "So which one is it?" Then the child was asked a source question, for example, "How do you know it's the red one … (if necessary) because you felt/saw it or because Kate told you?"

As in all the previous studies, in their identity judgments, children discriminated correctly between the trials on which they were knowledgeable and trials on which the experimenter was knowledgeable: They were more likely to believe what they were told when the experimenter was better informed than they themselves. There was no age-related improvement in this measure. Children generally made the correct decision about what to believe, and this was equally true, whether seeing or feeling was the informative source. When color was the differentiating feature, no child (out of 20) who had seen the chosen object through the window agreed with the experimenter's guess, and when weight was the differentiating feature, no child (out of 18) who had felt the chosen object agreed with the experimenter's guess. When the experimenter was the better informed, the great majority of children agreed with her, although 4 out of 19 consistently (i.e., on both trials) maintained their guess about weight (compared with 10 who consistently agreed with the experimenter), and 3 out of 18 consistently maintained their guess about color (compared with 11 who consistently agreed with the experimenter).

As in the previous study, children were much worse at reporting their sources than at deciding which source to believe. For source judgments, the younger children were significantly worse than the older ones. As in Whitcombe's experiment, the older children were much more likely than the younger ones to be able to answer the open-format source question, and answers to the open question were nearly always correct: 32 children consistently answered the open-source question correctly (having also believed the informed source on both trials), and only one child consistently offered the wrong source in answer to the open question. Therefore, nearly all the source errors followed prompts, " ... because you felt or saw it, or because Kate told you?" The majority of these errors consisted of children reporting their own source (seeing or feeling), when in fact they had believed what they had been told.

What can the results tell us about the incidence of the four kinds of possible errors just described? No child consistently said he or she knew because he or she had been told when in fact he or she believed his or her own direct source (seeing or feeling), although one child responded in this way on one of her two trials, and seven reported both sources, although their final belief was necessarily based on only one. These data do not suggest that the first type of error was occurring with any frequency: Children with no conscious experience of the event who simply guessed when offered the prompts should have been equally likely to choose "told" as "saw or felt." With a longer delay between experience and recall, this type of error could appear.

No child suggested that he or she had seen or felt when in fact that was the experimenter's informative source, so we have no evidence that the second kind of error (i.e., internalizing experimenter's experience) was occurring either. That error could only have occurred in response to the open question, because the experimenter's source was not offered as a prompt. Again, with longer delays before recall of the source, such errors might occur. We have, then, no strong evidence of this kind of error with this immediate recall procedure.

We are left with errors that could be based on a failure to understand the link between information access and knowledge or belief state. I suggested previously that these could arise either from gross ignorance of the link (the child simply recalls what happened in response to prompts) or from partial understanding (the child might link the wrong input with her or his belief). Children who made source errors nearly always reported that they knew because they had seen or felt the chosen object, when in fact they had correctly believed what they were told. How can we tell whether these children were just reporting that they had seen or felt something, which was perhaps more salient than having been told something, or whether they were genuinely linking their experience with their knowledge of the chosen object's identity? The procedure does not permit us to be sure, but listening to the tape recordings of the testing gives me the impression that some children were doing the latter. Although no child consistently answered the open source question inaccurately, several children did so on one of their trials, for example, by answering enthusiastically to "How do you know it's the red one?" with "Cos I felt it!" This response could indicate accurate recall of the child's own experience of feeling or seeing, but wrong identification of this as the source of knowledge. If so, these are the interesting children whom I suggested realize that knowledge arises from information access, and so understand to some extent the question, "How do you know?" but as yet do not realize what kinds of knowledge are acquired by particular kinds of access.

Other researchers have also identified children who fail to understand what knowledge can be gained by a particular kind of access, and I discuss their work in the next section. Note that for the moment the focus is on children's reflective understanding about the knowledge to be gained from a particular source rather than on their decisions about which of two conflicting sources to believe.

JUDGMENTS ABOUT THE KNOWLEDGE GAINED FROM FEELING OR SEEING

O'Neill, Astington, and Flavell (1992) reported a series of studies involving children aged 3 to 6 years. As in Antcliff's experiment just described, children experienced pairs of objects that either looked the same but felt different, or felt the same but looked different. One object from the pair was chosen, and children had to indicate in a variety of ways whether the chosen object could be identified just by seeing it, or just by feeling it. That is, in O'Neill et al.'s procedures, children had to predict what knowledge would be gained by seeing or feeling, rather than report the source of knowledge already gained, as in the experiment described in the section on Seeing and Feeling. Young children found these tasks quite difficult, and O'Neill et al. conclude that it is not until the age of around 5 or 6 years that children begin to understand the modality-specific aspects of knowledge in the same way as adults. Pillow (1993) reached a similar conclusion on the basis of similar evidence. These authors conceive of the 4- to 5-year-old child as learning something about the links between input via a particular modality, and the consequent knowledge state. Although they do not draw inferences for the child's source-monitoring skills, the implication would seem to be that children who fail to understand these links would make source-monitoring errors of the kind I identified previously. For example, they would not be able to report that the reason they know a money box is empty is because they felt it, rather than because they saw it.

If this is right, can we account in a similar way for the errors children made in Whitcombe's experiment reported in the section "Reporting the Source of Knowledge Gained by Seeing?" Recall that, in her procedure, one person saw an entire picture and the other person saw an uninformative part of it. Children correctly believed the experimenter when the experimenter had seen the entire picture, but misreported how they knew: They said, "I know because I saw it." Generalizing from Antcliff's results, it seems reasonable to assume that some children in Whitcombe's study correctly remembered that they had seen only a part of the picture, but wrongly believed that is how they knew what was depicted in the picture. Yet these children did not have access via an inappropriate modality, like the children in Antcliff's experiment who felt one of a pair of objects that differed only in color. The children in Whitcombe's experiment saw something, but just did not see enough to identify what was in the picture. We can not argue that they misunderstood the link between access via a particular modality and consequent knowledge state. In both cases children had information access that was inadequate to allow the chosen object to be identified: Feeling is inadequate if you need to identify color, and seeing a patch of color is inadequate if you need to identify shape. Children may not have had limited understanding about modality of access in particular, but rather about inadequacy of access more broadly.

Robinson, Thomas, Parton, and Nye (1997) considered this issue. We argued that children's overestimation of the knowledge to be gained via a particular modality can be construed as part of a broader problem children have with identifying an input as ambiguous, that is, as permitting more than one possible interpretation. We examined children's attributions of knowledge to an observer who had to decide which one of a pair of objects he was looking at through a window in a box. The objects might be bars of chocolate, one red and one blue, so that seeing the color of the chosen bar through the window allowed the observer to identify it. Alternatively, the objects might be dishwashing liquid bottles of the same color, one full and one empty. This time, seeing the color through the window did not allow the observer to know which one had been chosen. Finally, the objects might be cans of baked beans, one large and one small, but identical in color. Again, seeing the color through the window was insufficient to identify, which can had been placed in the box. We found that children aged 4 to 6 years were just as likely to overattribute knowledge to the observer in the case of the large and small cans, as in the case of the empty and full bottles. In the latter case, one might argue that children failed to understand the information to be gained from seeing rather than feeling (in line with O'Neill et al., 1992, and Pillow, 1993), but with the large and small cans the problem cannot be failure to understand about modality-specific knowledge. Rather, the problem is failure to understand the knowledge to be gained from seeing a small part rather than the whole can.

We concluded that the children's tendency to judge that an object's nonvisual properties can be identified on seeing the object can be subsumed as part of a more general difficulty evaluating ambiguous input. If this is right, children in Antcliff's experiment who reported "I know it's the red one cos I felt it" should, under Whitcombe's procedure, judge "I know it's a banana cos I saw a small patch of yellow." We do not know whether this is the case, because, like other researchers into children's source-monitoring skills, we only asked our participants to report the modality of their input. Yet in the adult literature on source monitoring, the "source" of a memory can be defined much more broadly as the conditions under which it was acquired (e.g., Johnson et al., 1993). At the moment we simply do not know how much the children in our tasks would be able to tell us about the conditions under which their final belief was acquired.

SUMMARY AND CONCLUSIONS

The results so far strongly suggest that young children can make the correct decisions about which of two conflicting sources to believe without being able to report explicitly which of the two players knows best (see earlier section, "Do Preschool Children Discriminate Knowledge"), and without being able to report which source they judged to be the more reliable (see the section, "Do Children Believe a Well-Informed Speaker," and the section, "Why Do Children Misreport?"). Children seem to have a working understanding of the link between information access and knowledge state, sufficient to allow them to make correct evaluations of the reliability of sources, but without necessarily being able to reflect on how they acquired their belief. It would not be accurate to describe children's correct source reporting as explicit knowledge about the source of their belief, because even when our children reported accurately which source they believed (that they saw, felt, or were told), they did not reveal explicit understanding of why they treated one source as more reliable than the other. Our children were not expected to say, "I know it's the red one because you told me and you saw it," or "I know it's a banana because you told me and you saw the whole picture." As mentioned previously, we do not know whether our children had conscious experience of the circumstances surrounding the acquisition of their belief, but neither do we know whether they could reflect on why they made the decisions they did. These are two separate questions; as I discussed in the section "Reporting the Source of Knowledge" and the section "Who Do Children Misreport?" some children may remember correctly what happened, but make the wrong inference about the basis for their belief because they only have a general idea that information access leads to knowledge without yet recognizing the more precise mapping between modality of input and knowledge gained.

I do not argue that children who make correct decisions about what to believe "really" understand about sources of knowledge and that their understanding is underestimated or masked when they are asked to report their sources. There are obvious benefits in being able to reflect on how one knows something in the way that adults can, although of course adults' reflections can be inaccurate, as in the case of false memories (e.g., Conway, Gathercole, Collins, & Anderson, 1996; Loftus, 1998). However, developmental research on source monitoring and theory of mind has tended to focus exclusively on children's ability to verbally make explicit their views, and has neglected to examine children's working assumptions about knowledge and the mind as revealed in their ongoing interactions in the social and physical world. The accuracy of children's judgments about what to believe clearly impacts on their learning. The research presented here suggests that, in some circumstances at least, young children seem not to be at risk of making wrong decisions.

REFERENCES

Ackil, J. K., & Zaragoza, M. S. (1995). Developmental differences in eyewitness suggestibility and memory for source. *Journal of Experimental Child Psychology, 60*, 57–83.

Astington, J. W., & Gopnik, A. (1988). Knowing you've changed your mind: Children's understanding of representational change. In J. W. Astington, P. L. Harris, & D. R. Olson (Eds.). *Developing theories of mind* (pp. 193–206). Cambridge, MA: Cambridge University Press.

Atran, S. (1996). From folk biology to scientific biology. In D. R. Olson & N. Torrance (Eds.), *Handbook of education and human development* (pp. 646–682). Cambridge, MA: Blackwell.

Ceci, S. J., & Bruck, M. (1993). Suggestibility of the child witness: A historical review and synthesis. *Psychological Bulletin, 113*, 403–439.

Chandler, M., Fritz, A. S., & Hala, S. (1989). Small-scale deceit: Deception as a marker of two-, three-, and four-year-olds' early theories of mind. *Child Development, 60*, 1263–1277.

Clements, W. A., & Perner, J. (1994). Implicit understanding of belief. *Cognitive Development, 9*, 377–396.

Conway, M. A., Gathercole, S. E., Collins, A. F., & Anderson, S. J. (1996). Recollections of true and false autobiographical memories. *Journal of Experimental Psychology: General, 125*, 69–95.

DiSessa, A. A. (1996). What do "just plain folk" know about physics? In D. R. Olson & N. Torrance (Eds.), *Handbook of education and human development* (pp. 709–730). Cambridge, MA: Blackwell.

Doise, W. (1988). On the social development of the intellect. In K. Richardson & S. Sheldon (Eds.), *Cognitive development to adolescence* (pp. 199–218). Hillsdale, NJ: Lawrence Erlbaum Associates.

Driver, R. (1989). The construction of scientific knowledge in school classrooms. In Millar, R. (Ed.), *Doing science: images of science in science education* (pp. 83–106). London: Falmer Press.

Foley, M. A., & Johnson, M. K. (1985). Confusion between memories for performed and imagined actions. *Child Development, 56*, 1145–1155.

Freeman, N. H., Lewis, C. & Doherty, M. J. (1991). Preschoolers' grasp of desire for knowledge in false-belief prediction: Practical intelligence and verbal report. *British Journal of Developmental Psychology, 9*, 139–157.

Gardiner, J. M., & Java, R. I. (1993). Recognizing and remembering. In A. F. Collins, S. E. Gathercole, M. A. Conway, & P. E. Morris (Eds.). *Theories of memory* (pp. 163–188). Hillsdale, NJ: Lawrence Erlbaum Associates.

Gopnik, A., & Graf, P. (1988). Knowing how you know: Young children's ability to identify and remember the sources of their beliefs. *Child Development, 59*, 1366–1371.

Jacoby, L. L., & Hay, J. F. (1998). Age-related deficits in memory: Theory and application. In M. A. Conway, S. E. Gathercole, & C. Cornoldi (Eds.), *Theories of memory: Vol. 2* (pp. 111–134). Hove, U.K.: Psychology Press.

Johnson, M. K., Hashtroudi, S. & Lindsay, D. S. (1993). Source monitoring. *Psychological Bulletin, 114*, 3–28.

Lindsay, D. S., & Johnson, M. K. (1987). Reality-monitoring and suggestibility: Children's ability to discriminate among memories from different sources. In S. J. Ceci, M. P. Toglia, & D. F. Ross (Eds.), *Children's eyewitness memory* (pp. 92–121). New York: Springer-Verlag.

Loftus, E. F. (1998). Imaginary memories. In M. A. Conway, S. E. Gathercole, & C. Cornoldi (Eds.). *Theories of memory: Vol. 2* (pp. 135–145). Hove, U.K.: Psychology Press.

O'Neill, D., & Gopnik, A. (1991). Young children's understanding of the sources of their beliefs. *Developmental Psychology, 27*, 390–397.

O'Neill, D. K., Astington, J. W., & Flavell, J. H. (1992). Young children's understanding of the role that sensory experiences play in knowledge acquisition. *Child Development, 63*, 474–490.

Parkin, A. J. (1997). The development of procedural and declarative memory. In N. Cowan (Ed.), *The Development of memory in childhood* (pp. 113–137). Hove, U.K.: Psychology Press.

Perner, J. (1991). *Understanding the representational mind.* London: MIT Press.

Perner, J. & Ruffman, T. (1995). Episodic memory and autonoetic consciousness: Developmental evidence and a theory of childhood amnesia. *Journal of Experimental Child Psychology, 59,* 516–548.

Pillow, B. H. (1993). Preschool children's understanding of the relationship between modality of perceptual access and knowledge of perceptual properties. *British Journal of Developmental Psychology, 11,* 371–389.

Qin, J., Quas, J. A., Redlich, A. D., & Goodman, G. S. (1997). Children's eyewitness testimony: Memory development in the legal context. In N. Cowan (Ed.), *The development of memory in childhood* (pp. 301–341). Hove, U.K.: Psychology Press.

Riggs, K., & Robinson, E. J. (1995). What people say and what they think: Children's judgments of false belief in relation to their recall of false messages. *British Journal of Developmental Psychology, 13,* 271–284.

Roazzi, A., & Bryant, P., (1998). The effects of symmetrical and asymmetrical social interaction on children's logical inferences. *British Journal of Developmental Psychology, 16,* 175–181.

Roberts, K. P., & Blades, M. (1995). Children's discrimination of memories for actual and pretend actions in a hiding task. *British Journal of Developmental Psychology, 13,* 321–333.

Roberts, K. P., & Blades, M. (1996). Children's eyewitness testimony for real-life and fantasy events. In N. K. Clark and G. M. Stephenson (Eds.), *Investigative and forensic decision making: Vol. 26* (pp. 52–57). Leicester, UK: British Psychological Society.

Robinson, E. J. (1994). What people say, what they think, and what is really the case: Children's understanding of utterances as sources of knowledge. In C. Lewis & P. Mitchell (Eds.), *Children's early understanding of mind: Origins and development* (pp. 355–381). Hillsdale, NJ: Lawrence Erlbaum Associates.

Robinson, E. J., Champion, H., & Mitchell, P. (1999). Children's ability to infer utterance veracity from speaker informedness. *Developmental Psychology, 35,* 535–546.

Robinson, E. J., Mitchell, P., & Nye, R. (1995). Young children's treating of utterances as unreliable sources of knowledge. *Journal of Child Language, 22,* 663–685.

Robinson, E. J., Thomas, G.V., Parton, A., & Nye, R. (1997). Children's overestimation of the knowledge to be gained from seeing. *British Journal of Developmental Psychology, 15,* 257–273.

Roediger, H. L., McDermott, K. B., & Robinson, K. J. (1998). The role of associative processes in creating false memories. In M. A. Conway, S. E. Gathercole, & C. Cornoldi (Eds.), *Theories of memory: Vol. 2* (pp. 187–258). Hove, UK: Psychology Press.

Russell, J. (1981). Dyadic interaction in a logical reasoning problem. *Child Development, 52,* 1,322–1,325.

Russell, J. (1982) Propositional attitudes. In M. Beveridge (Ed.), *Children thinking through language* (pp. 75–98). London: Edward Arnold.

Tulving, E. (1972). Episodic and semantic memory. In E. Tulving & W. Donaldson (Eds.), Organization of memory (pp. 381–403). New York: Academic Press.

Tulving, E. (1985). Memory and consciousness. Canadian Psychology, 26, 1–12.

Vosniadou, S., & Brewer, W. F. (1992). Mental models of the earth: A study of conceptual change in childhood. Cognitive Psychology, 24, 535–585.

Welch-Ross, M. K. (1995). Developmental changes in preschoolers' ability to distinguish memories of performed, pretended and imagined actions. Cognitive Development, 10, 421–441.

Welch-Ross, M. K. (1999, April). The development of knowing about knowing: Predicting the suggestibility of preschoolers. In M. K. Welch-Ross & L. Fasig, Chairs. Moderators of suggestibility and eyewitness memory in young children. Symposium held at the biennial meeting of the Society for Research in Child Development, Albuquerque, NM.

Welch-Ross, M. K., Diecidue, K., & Miller, S. A. (1997). Young children's understanding of conflicting mental representations predicts suggestibility. Developmental Psychology, 33, 43–53.

Whitcombe, E., & Robinson, E. J. (1999, April). Children's decisions about what to believe and their ability to report the source of their belief. Poster presented at the biennial meeting of the Society for Research in Child Development, Albuquerque, NM.

Wimmer, H., Hogrefe, G.-J., & Perner, J. (1988). Children's understanding of informational access as a source of knowledge. Child Development, 59, 386–396.

Zaitchik, D. (1991). Is only seeing really believing? Sources of the true belief in the false belief task. Cognitive Development, 6, 91–103.

4

Person Perspectives on Children's Memory and Learning: What Do Source-Monitoring Failures Reveal?

Hilary Horn Ratner
Wayne State University
Mary Ann Foley
Skidmore College
Nicole Gimpert
Wayne State University

Although a number of factors contribute to an individual's ability to identify the source of actions (e.g., Day, Howie, & Markham, 1998; Foley, Johnson, & Raye, 1983; Foley, Santini, & Sopasakis, 1989; Johnson, Foley, Suengas, & Raye, 1988; Johnson, Hashtroudi, & Lindsay, 1993; Johnson & Raye, 1981; Lindsay, Johnson, & Kwon, 1991; Raye & Johnson, 1980), involvement of what has been called "cognitive operations information" is critical to making source discriminations. The anticipation, initiation, and production of one's own actions, real or imagined, are mediated by cognitive operations (e.g., Foley et al., 1983; Raye, & Johnson, 1980). In the source-monitoring model, these operations are represented in memory and later serve to facilitate agent discrimination (e.g., self vs. other, subject vs. experimenter). Individuals may be able to identify their own actions, in part, because of the cognitive operations mediating their performance. For example, children and adults may anticipate how they would perform an action, anticipate the action's consequences, or reflect on the cognitive effort associated with the enactment itself. Remembering these operations would then influence source discrimination.

Indeed, when the cognitive operations involved in completing word tasks (e.g., searching for words in an associative task, solving problems such as anagrams, generating images) are more effortful, individuals are better able to discriminate their own productions from those of others on a subsequent surprise source-monitoring test (e.g., Durso & Johnson, 1980; Foley, Durso, Wilder, & Friedman, 1991; Johnson, Raye, Foley, & Foley, 1981). In contrast, when the cognitive operations mediating self-productions are more automatic and less attention-deploying (e.g., Foley et al., 1991), or when perceptual information rivals more cognitively-based information (e.g., Johnson, Foley, & Leach, 1988), source-monitoring errors increase for both children and adults. Thus, individuals' abilities to identify the source of their memories (e.g., the agents of actions) is affected by the nature of the cognitive processes or operations giving rise to the actions themselves.

In this chapter, we focus on particular kinds of cognitive-operations information, processes related to a person's goals, both individual and shared during an activity, and their relation to source-monitoring performance. We show that source-monitoring errors are sensitive to the presence of cognitive operations information, as predicted by the source-monitoring framework; however, we also show that errors vary, either in frequency or in form, with the goals invoked by an activity. Moreover, source-monitoring errors do not always reflect processes that are undesirable in some way.

The impact of goals on source-monitoring errors and the processes they index follows directly from a person-based perspective (e.g.,Foley & Ratner, in press; Ratner & Foley, 1994). From this perspective, cognitive-operations information is conceptualized as more than a marker for the occurrence of effortful processing. Cognitive-operations are seen instead as reflecting goal-directed processes which, in turn, promote complex modes of functioning, such as collaborative learning. Thus, source-monitoring errors can serve as indices of goal-related processes that are broadly related and beneficial to children's learning. In this chapter, we explore children's source-monitoring failures in the context of such a perspective and demonstrate a clear and surprising link between errors and learning. In some cases, errors actually predict better learning and indicate that a particularly important type of cognitive-operations information involves anticipation and planning of actions in an interconnected goal-directed sequence.

OVERVIEW OF THE PERSON-BASED PERSPECTIVE

Our person-based perspective shares a focus on activity, central to many theories of cognitive development (e.g., Nelson, 1986; Rogoff, 1990; Vygotsky, 1962; White, 1970). Memory for activity has been explored within a wide variety of domains, such as action concepts, autobiographical memory, event memory, eyewitness testimony, generation effects, motor-skill enhancement, and memory for script-based events, as well as source monitoring. Activity theories (e.g., Barsalou, 1991; Basov, 1991; Heckhausen & Beckmann, 1990; Heider, 1958; Leont'ev, 1978; Lewin, 1951; Nelson, 1986; Oppenheimer, 1991; Piaget, 1970; Rogoff, 1990; Schank & Abelson, 1977; von Cranach, Kalbermatten, Indermuhle, & Gugler, 1982) emphasize persons as goal-directed agents who carry out acts within the context of larger activities to bring about outcomes that satisfy some purpose. Goals function to organize activities, in part, by structuring: (a) action outcomes, (b) sequential relations among actions, (c) prospective processes (e.g., anticipation of effects or planning of actions), and (d) retrospective processes (e.g., activation of memories for similar or related past events, activation of conceptual or personal knowledge related to other action components). We suggest that these features influence processing during an activity and that activity memory is, at least in part, a by-product of these processes (Ratner & Foley, 1994). Thus, activity memory is thought to be influenced by action outcomes, the sequence of acts that produces an outcome, the plans that generate acts, and the retrospective activations of related and past episodes.

Performed actions in source-monitoring studies, however, are often not presented as goal-directed sequences, stripping them of their most important characteristics. In essence, these acts mimic surface features of actions, but do not reflect their goal-directed meanings. They become symbols of actions, rather than actions themselves. Thus, patterns of source monitoring previously reported in the literature may not have reflected the full range of goal-related processes. If source monitoring is sensitive to shifts in activity goals, then activity features should influence source monitoring, just as they do other activity domains (e.g., Bauer & Mandler, 1989; Fivush, Kuebli, & Clubb, 1992; Ratner, Foley, & Bukowski, 1999; Slackman, Hudson, & Fivush, 1986; Tomasello & Kruger, 1992).

For example, if goals activate prospective processes, such as planning or anticipating, and these processes in turn influence source monitoring, then the way in which children anticipate themselves executing actions should have consequences for source monitoring (Foley & Ratner, 1998a). In a recent study of the effects of anticipating, a type of prospective process, Foley and Ratner (1998b) asked 6-year-olds to imagine what it would feel like if they went through the motions involved in performing each action or to visualize themselves performing the actions. These two kinds of imagery instructions suggest the adoption of different perspectives when imagining the self. Kinesthetic instructions would lead to the adoption of a first-person perspective, which would emphasize the prospective processes (i.e., plans) underlying the actions. Visual instructions would lead to a third-person perspective, in which expressions of plans, such as the outcomes of actions, rather than the plans themselves, would be emphasized. If prospective processing cues contribute to children's confusion between memories for performed and imagined actions, then we would expect the presence of these kinds of cues in memory to falsely signal an imagined action was performed. This would produce a greater bias to report *performed* when an imagined action was recognized as old, especially among children who imagined what the actions would feel like to perform.

Children performed and imagined themselves performing actions (Foley & Ratner, 1998b). In one condition, when children imagined actions, they were asked to think about what they looked like when imagining the actions. In the other condition, when children imagined actions, they were asked to think of themselves going through the motions involved in performing the actions. In a surprise source-monitoring test three minutes later, the children were asked to decide whether each action was one they performed, one they imagined, or a new one.

Overall, children were more likely to claim that an imagined action was one they performed rather than the reverse, producing lower discrimination scores for imagined than performed actions. But this bias actually occurred only for the children who were instructed to think of themselves going through the motions of performing the actions. Children who visualized the actions were equally good at discriminating performed and imagined actions. These results point to the importance of prospective processes in children's source monitoring and indicate that errors are related to the goals underlying children's activities. Moreover, source errors indexed planning processes that would be potentially effective for other dimensions of performance in this or related tasks.

Of course, it is possible that the difference in error patterns was produced solely because of the difference in representational mode (visual vs. kinesthetic), independent of the link between mode and planning (i.e., in order to feel the actions, the movements producing the feelings had to be planned). Perhaps, for instance, kinesthetic encoding led to less elaborated representations of the actions, which in turn led to greater confusions between actions. If that were the case, however, greater confusions for both performed and imagined actions might have been expected in the kinesthetic condition. In addition, recognition memory for the actions was not influenced by representational mode. If a more general encoding failure were related to the effect for source monitoring, differences might have been expected in recognition memory as well. Finally, in another study (described later in the chapter) only kinesthetic instructions were used. Differences between two conditions were created by varying children's goals. If representational mode were the only factor critical to performance, then children's performance should have been the same in these conditions; however, in contrast to this prediction, differences in the errors that occurred were related to the goals.

The notion that source-monitoring errors can index cognitive processes that are beneficial in some way may seem somewhat discrepant with previous source-monitoring studies. Typically, source-monitoring accuracy is interpreted to reflect "effective" processes of some type—those that are more effortful or elaborated. In contrast, errors are usually interpreted as the consequence of cognitive operations that are "less" in some way—less deliberate, less demanding, or less desirable (e.g., Johnson, 1983, 1992; Johnson et al., 1993). Within this tradition, goals that might be seen as enhancing cognitive-operations information, making tasks more effortful or demanding, should lead to a decrease in source-monitoring errors. From a person-based perspective, however, a different prediction might follow.

Within this person-based perspective, sometimes preserving source information may be less relevant or helpful in the cognitive task an adult or child carries out, leading to an increase, rather than decrease, in source-monitoring errors, even in the context of cognitively effortful processing. These errors may then index cognitive operations that are highly adaptive, promoting more complex modes of functioning, rather than markers of processes that only result in poorer performance in some domain. If errors were greater following goal-directed activities, the support would be strong for the claim that the meaning of source-monitoring errors needs to be evaluated in relation to the meaning of source information in a person's goals and activities (Foley & Ratner, in press; Ratner & Foley, 1994).

ROLE OF PERSON GOALS IN SOURCE-MONITORING ERRORS

One convincing piece of evidence in support of our claim that source-monitoring judgments are sensitive to goals would be a demonstration that the purpose guiding self-activity has consequences for source monitoring even though the agent (here, the child) and the product of these activities are constant. Moreover, if errors actually increased rather than decreased in response to goal-related processes, support would be provided for the person-based perspective. In the first study reported here, preschoolers were asked to trace and to imagine tracing pictures arranged in a picture book. When tracing, children used a finger and when imagining, children placed their hands in their laps. For some children, the picture book was created to resemble a story book with text beneath the pictures. As children in the story condition listened to parts of the story unfold, the adult paused long enough for the child to trace (or imagine tracing) the pictures in the book, all of which were referred to in the story. Would children who traced and imagined tracing pictures in the context of a goal-directed, purposeful story perform differently than children who interacted with the same pictures, but not in a goal-directed way?

Description of the Study

Twenty-four children with a mean age of 4 years and 7 months participated in one of two conditions with boys and girls represented equally in each, as in the two studies that follow. Children were enrolled in a nursery school program at Skidmore College in Saratoga Springs.

Each child was presented a picture book, approximately 11 in. by 14 in. in size, containing 16 pages. On each page, a familiar object (e.g., squirrel, rabbit, strawberry, flower, kite) was depicted. In the Story condition, print appeared beneath each picture to increase the resemblance of the booklet to a story book. In the Standard condition, no print was presented beneath the pictures.

Each child was invited to play a picture game with the experimenter. Children were given either the story booklet or the standard booklet. They were told that sometimes they would be asked to trace a picture and sometimes to think of themselves tracing the picture. On imagination trials, children were asked to think about tracing the pictures with a finger. Specifically, children were asked to think about what it would feel like to trace over all the lines using their fingers. These instructions were similar to the kinesthetic instructions used in the study described earlier. In the Story condition, each picture was mentioned in the story and then traced or thought about. The story focused on a rabbit who took a walk with his friend, the squirrel. They ate strawberries, brought a flower home to Mother, and flew a kite.

After tracing or thinking about tracing each of the 16 pictures, children listened to music for two minutes. They were then surprised with a source-monitoring task. Children were read a list of 24 object names: Eight of the items were objects children had traced, eight were objects that children had thought about tracing, and eight were objects that were new. Children were asked to indicate whether they had traced the items, imagined tracing the items, or whether the items were new. The dependent variable was a source discrimination proportion in which the number of correct source identifications was divided by the number of total correct (i.e., hits).

Findings of the Study

Children in the Standard condition, who saw the pictures without the text, were more accurate ($M = 0.75$, $SD = 0.12$) than children in the Story condition ($M = 0.58$, SD = 0.24), $p < .05$. Although children were confused, producing relatively poor source-monitoring scores, there was no difference in source-monitoring accuracy for the pictures traced ($M = 0.68$, $M = 0.12$) or thought about ($M = 0.65$, $SD = 0.27$).

To test how well children remembered the pictures, the number of hits, or pictures identified accurately as seen before, was examined. Children in the Story condition ($M = 7.80$ out of 8, $SD = 0.70$) remembered more pictures accurately as seen before than children in the Standard condition ($M = 6.45$, $SD = 1.09$), $p < .01$. Children also remembered more pictures accurately that they had actually traced ($M = 7.30$, $SD = 0.93$) than only thought about tracing ($M = 6.90$, $SD = 1.29$), $p = 0.05$. We also examined the number of items children identified as seen before that were actually new (i.e., false positives). There were very few errors and no effects of condition or picture type.

How Do Person Goals Influence Source Monitoring?

Children who listened to a story about the pictures in the book while tracing and imagining tracing were subsequently more confused about what they did and what they imagined doing than were children who simply traced and imagined tracing the pictures in the absence of the goal-directed activity (listening to a story). This greater confusion was not a result of a failure to encode the pictures, an undesirable cognitive process; children who listened to the story actually remembered more pictures than children in the Standard condition. They were just more confused about which ones they had traced and which ones they had thought about tracing.

Although each group of children saw the same set of pictures, the goal-directed context of the story influenced how children encoded their interactions with the pictures. The goal-directed nature of their activity appeared to support memory for the pictures themselves, but to depress memory for source information and increase confusions. Thus, the errors children made reflected cognitive operations that were actually beneficial to their memory in some ways but not others, and the errors could not be understood without attention to the goals guiding the children's activity. The goals that children have clearly influence their memory for source information and therefore must be considered when assessing source-monitoring skills. Notably, the goal-directed nature of the activity, which led attention away from source information and increased source-monitoring errors, affected performance, consistent with our person-based perspective.

ROLE OF COLLABORATIVE GOALS
IN SOURCE-MONITORING ERRORS

Goals guide not only children's individual activity, but also their collaborations with other people. If a child's individual goals can influence source monitoring, children's goals when interacting with others should also affect performance. Our person-based theoretical framework suggests that as the nature of the child's goal changes, so should patterns in children's source monitoring. In our theoretical framework (Ratner & Foley, 1994), both the content of these processes (e.g., type of plan, focus of anticipation) and the context from which they arise (e.g., shared vs. solitary activities, goal directed vs. nonpurposeful) should influence cognitive operations and resulting source-monitoring errors. Moreover, error patterns should reveal goal-directed cognitive processes beneficial to performance in other domains.

In our previous studies (e.g., Foley, Ratner, & Passalacqua, 1993), 4-year-olds have made collages of a familiar animal, such as a bunny or a bear, with a female adult. The child and adult alternate taking turns placing the pieces of a collage on a poster board to make the animal. Children are then surprised by a source-monitoring task in which they are asked who placed each piece on the board, the child or the experimenter. Preschoolers consistently claim they contribute more to the collage than they actually did, committing more "I did it" errors than "You did it" errors. However, if young children help an adult complete a collage, but work on their own after the adult has started the collage, this bias is not observed. Thus, when the child shares a goal with an adult in a collaborative task, the bias in errors occurs; but when only the child's individual goal motivates performance, errors are low, and no error bias is present (Foley et al., 1993).

This bias to claim responsibility for more actions than were truly performed does not occur because of response biases or chance patterns of performance. In addition, encoding or access failures, reflecting ineffective cognitive processes, are also not responsible for the error pattern (Foley & Ratner, 1998a). Instead, children appear to recode the other person's actions, making them their own, and then subsequently take credit for the actions.

We propose that in the collage task children anticipate what the other person will do but imagine themselves carrying out the action. When a shared goal defines an activity, the participants need to anticipate the other person's actions and coordinate their own activity with the actions of their partner. Children appear to anticipate the other person's actions as if they themselves were the agent of their partner's actions, perhaps as a means of understanding the nature and purpose of the action more thoroughly. Why would the error bias reflect anticipation of another's actions by means of transformation of the source?

If children recode another person's actions as their own by becoming the agent, either in thought or deed, of the action the other person actually performs or is going to perform, then they should have difficulty identifying who did what as part of a collaborative task. Again, if children reconstruct another person's action as their own, they should be confused concerning who did what in the task. Specifically, they should claim more often that they performed the other person's actions than they should claim the other person performed their actions, saying more often "I did it" when the other person actually carried out the action than say "You did it" when they actually carried out the action. If children are recoding the other person's actions as their own actions, they should think they performed the action, leading them to mistakenly claim that they in fact carried it out. They recode themselves carrying out the action, then they think that they actually performed it. Thus, in our studies, we look for a bias in error patterns of more "I did it" errors than "You did it" errors.

The strongest evidence for this claim to date comes from a study in which we instructed children to create the anticipations that we believe they carry out spontaneously (Foley & Ratner, 1998a). For children in one group, the "Think about self" condition, children were told to think of themselves putting the experimenter's pieces on the collage. Children in this condition should be confused about who placed the piece and attribute it to themselves. Thus, we predicted the bias of more "I did it" than "You did it" errors. In another group, the "Think about other" condition, children were told to think of the experimenter putting her pieces on the collage. We predicted no bias in this condition because children would be unlikely to recode the experimenter's actions as their own. The results supported our predictions. In the "Think about self" condition, more "I did it" than "You did it" errors occurred; however, in the "Think about other" condition, the number of errors of each type did not differ.

Some researchers have found that similar sources are more likely to be confused than unique items (e.g., Lindsay, Johnson, & Kwon, 1991; chap. 6, this volume), and, at first glance, these findings might be thought to be the result of this more basic process. Specifically, there may be greater similarity between memories of self-performed actions and thinking about self-performed actions ("Think about self" condition) than between self-performed actions and thinking about someone else performing ("Think about other" condition). There are several reasons, however, that similarity cannot account for these results. First, the only performance differences between the two conditions was for memory of the other person's actions. "I did it" errors could only occur when remembering what the other person did. No differences occurred in remembering self-performed actions (i.e., the number of "You did it" errors). Second, similarity occurred as a by-product of anticipation. That is, to the extent that there may have been similarity between representations of actions that were self-performed and imagined actions that were other-performed, this similarity was created by the process of instructed anticipation. Similarity was not inherent in the actions themselves. Indeed, in many other studies, without instruction and without "similarity" a priori defining the relation between the performed actions, we have shown the same bias in errors. Related to this point is the fact that imagining was not a part of the source-monitoring judgment; it was only a part of the encoding conditions. The judgment was constant for the actions in the two conditions and it is unclear whether a bias would occur if the judgment involved imagination.

If these errors are indexing a recoding process related to coordinating and comprehending shared goals, then the errors may be related to other aspects of children's cognitive activity, such as learning. In most collaborative learning situations, young children interact with a more skilled learner (an adult or older child) to accomplish some goal together (e.g., planning a routine, solving a problem). When later working alone, these children show better learning on a related task than other children who initially encounter the tasks in a noncollaborative context. The appropriation (e.g., Rogoff, 1990) or internalization (e.g., Cox & Lightfoot, 1997; Lawrence & Valsiner, 1993; Tomasello, Kruger, & Ratner, 1993) of the partner's actions and strategies are seen as important in the process of learning from others. Although mechanisms of appropriation or internalization (i.e., recreating another person's knowledge or activity as one's own) are invoked to account for the advantage of collaborative learning, we do not know how appropriation occurs. How is it that children adopt the actions of another person in the context of shared exchanges, making the actions their own? The recoding process, initiated in an attempt to create or comprehend a shared goal in the collaboration, may contribute to internalization and learning.

We propose that an important operation in this process is a person's recoding of another individual's actions from the perspective of the self—just the sort of cognitive activity that is indexed by the "bias" in errors that occur in collaborative contexts, such as collage making. There are at least three potential advantages of self-recoding. First, the recoding of another's act as a self-act may help store and activate information for later use as a self-regulatory routine in new and individual contexts. Information encoded from the perspective of the self is often remembered better than information encoded from other sources (e.g., Keenan, Golding, & Brown, 1992; Rogers, Kuiper, & Kirker, 1977). Second, recoding actions as self-actions may create a more interconnected sequence because the source of the actions would be the same. Information encoded in the same way might promote better memory for the sequence (e.g., Ackerman, 1987; Tulving & Thompson, 1973). Finally, recreating the other person's actions as self-actions may contribute to understanding more completely why the actions were carried out by the other person. For example, when children attempt to explain why another person has reasoned as they have in conservation tasks, children learn the problems more effectively than if they explain their own reasoning (e.g., Siegler, 1995). Recoding could be accomplished in a variety of ways. For example, an individual could anticipate, imagine, or plan the actions of another as if he or she were performing or going to perform the actions himself or herself.

Although children's collaborative source-monitoring errors may reflect recoding processes, there is no evidence that these recodings may contribute to learning from other people as we have proposed. Establishing a connection among these errors (recoding another person's actions as a self-act) and learning was the aim of the second study reported in this chapter. If a connection were found, evidence would not only be provided that the recoding process we have described contributes to appropriation, but also that source-monitoring errors can reflect effortful and effective cognitive processes rather than just less effortful and less effective processes, as often demonstrated and described in the literature. Again, in order to understand the significance of errors and the processes they reflect, their relation to a person's goals must be considered.

If source-monitoring errors and learning are linked, an interesting prediction can be made. Children who show the misattribution error in remembering a collaborative task should perform better when later given the opportunity to carry out the task independently. This relation should occur if collaborative recodings are indexed by more "I did it" than "You did it" errors and reflect appropriation that in turn supports learning. In the context of these goal-directed activities, source-monitoring errors may index cognitive operations that are highly adaptive, promoting complex modes of functioning.

Description of the Study

Twenty-four kindergarten children, with a mean age of 5 years and 6 months, participated in one of two conditions (Collaboration or No Collaboration) in a categorization task (Freund, 1990). Children were enrolled in a public school in a working-class suburb of Detroit.

In both conditions, children were shown a doll house with 6 cubicles and 36 miniature replicas of common furniture items (e.g., couch, stove, sink, table, bed, toybox). Furniture was selected so that six items could be categorized as belonging in one of six rooms (i.e., living room, kitchen, bathroom, dining room, bedroom, or baby's room). During a delay period, children played with one of two puzzles depicting popular cartoon characters.

Categorization Task.   Children were invited to accompany one of two experimenters to a small, quiet room near their classroom. There were two tables and two chairs at each table in the room. The doll house and the furniture were placed on one of the tables. In the Collaboration condition, the furniture was lined up in front of the doll house. In the No Collaboration condition, three pieces of furniture appeared in each room of the house and the remaining furniture was placed in front of the doll house. A timer and the two puzzles were placed on the other table. Children in both conditions were invited to sit with the experimenter at the table with the doll house. The experimenter began by telling the child that they were going to move the furniture into the house. In both conditions, the experimenter pointed to and named each piece of furniture for the child.

In the Collaboration condition, children were then asked to choose a cubicle and identify what room they would like to make it. Next children were told to select a piece of furniture that would be a "good thing to put in" the room they had chosen. If the furniture item did not match their room selection or if children had difficulty finding an item, they were asked questions related to the item's function as hints (e.g., "What would be nice and soft to sit on in the living room?"). If after two or three questions, the child did not identify an item correctly, the experimenter told the child which item to select although experimenter-defined selections were infrequent.

When a match was made, the item was placed into the room. When it was the child's turn, he or she placed the item into the room. When it was the experimenter's turn, the experimenter placed the item into the room. Thus, children planned which pieces of furniture would be placed into the house for both themselves and the experimenter, but each person actually placed the item into the house when it was his or her turn. When a room was completed, the child was asked to select the name and location of the next room. The adult and child alternated turns, placing all 36 pieces of furniture appropriately into the six rooms.

In the No Collaboration condition, three furniture items were already placed into each room of the house when presented to the child. Children were told that the experimenter had already started moving the furniture into the house and that they were to move the other three items into each room. Each child in the No Collaboration condition was yoked to a child in the Collaboration condition. The three items that the experimenter had placed into a room for a child in the Collaboration condition were the items that appeared in the house and attributed to the experimenter for children in the No Collaboration condition. The items that the child had placed into each room of the house in the Collaboration condition were the same three items that the child in the No Collaboration condition had placed in the house. In the No Collaboration condition, the experimenter simply told children which items to move into the house and in which order. The order was the same as the child's Collaboration condition counterpart. Moreover, the location of each of the rooms and the sequence in which rooms were filled with furniture was the same as the child's Collaboration condition counterpart. Thus, only the child placed furniture in the house during categorization in this condition.

Children in both conditions, then, saw the correct solution to the categorization task, but only children in the Collaboration condition participated in the categorization decisions and plans. Moreover, it was only in the Collaboration condition that children had the direct opportunity to become the agent of the other person's action through their planning of the furniture placement. Other differences did occur between the two conditions and the possible effects of these differences are addressed in the next study.

Source-Monitoring Task.   After the categorization task was completed, children in both conditions were escorted to the other table in the room and were asked to play with the puzzles. The experimenter set a timer for seven minutes and then returned to the doll house, placing each piece of furniture into a box and then covering the box. When all of the pieces of furniture were in the box, the experimenter went back to the puzzle table and helped the child work with the puzzles until the timer chimed. The child was then escorted back to the table with the doll house to begin the surprise source-monitoring task. The experimenter took one piece of furniture randomly from the box and held it up in front of the child. Children were then asked who had placed the furniture item in the house, the adult or the child. The furniture item was then put into another box and the procedure repeated until the child had been asked about the placement of each piece of furniture.

Recategorization Task.   The furniture items were then taken out of the box and lined up in front of the doll house. Children were asked to put the items into the house "where they belonged" once again on their own.

Findings of the Study

More "I did it" errors than "You did it" errors were expected in the Collaboration condition. In the No Collaboration condition we expected no difference between the two types of errors. From the recategorization task, we expected children in the Collaboration condition to outperform children in the No Collaboration condition on all or some of the measures derived from the task. In addition, we expected the bias in errors ("I did it" errors minus "You did it" errors) to be positively correlated with recategorization performance within the two conditions. If the error bias reflects appropriation and appropriation supports learning, then children who commit the error bias to a greater extent would be expected to score better in the recategorization task.

Source-Monitoring Task.   From the source-monitoring task in which children were asked who had placed which item into the house, we identified the number of "I did it" and "You did it" errors. "I did it" errors were those in which the child mistakenly claimed to have placed a piece of furniture the adult actually placed. "You did it" errors were those in which the child mistakenly claimed that the adult had placed one of his or her pieces. In the Collaboration condition we also counted the number of times the child pointed, touched, or picked up the experimenter's furniture item during item selection. It is possible that source-monitoring errors could occur simply because children interacted with the experimenter's furniture piece.

Overall, children committed more "I did it" errors ($M = 4.08$, $SD = 4.33$) than "You did it" errors ($M = 1.54$, $SD = 1.69$), $p < .01$, and children in the Collaboration condition ($M = 9.58$, $SD = 3.94$) committed more errors than children in the No Collaboration condition ($M = 1.67$, $SD = 5.63$), $p < 0.0001$. The pattern of errors, however, differed in the two conditions. Collaboration children committed an average of 7.17 "I did it" errors, but only 2.42 "You did it" errors, $p < .01$. Children in the No Collaboration condition committed an equal number of "I did it" ($M = 1.00$, $SD = 1.04$) and "You did it" errors ($M = 0.67$, $SD = 0.78$), $p > .40$.

To assess whether more "I did it" than "You did it" errors occurred in the Collaboration condition because children interacted with the experimenter's furniture pieces during item selection, the number of times children pointed to, picked up, or touched experimenter items was identified. We then determined the percentage of these items that were incorrectly identified as a child placement during the source-monitoring task (i.e., "I did it" errors). If children attributed an item to themselves because of their earlier interaction with it, then the proportion of these items that were incorrect should be greater than a chance level of 0.50. The proportion of items that children had interacted with during the collaborative categorization task that were attributed to themselves during the source-monitoring task, however, was 0.49.

Recategorization Task. From the recategorization task, we counted the number of furniture items correctly placed and the number of rooms correctly defined. In order for a room to be considered correct, at least four of the items defined as belonging in the room had to be so placed. It was not necessary for children to label the room. Correct rooms were determined solely from the items placed into them. In addition, items were considered correct only if they were placed in a defined room. We also calculated an "organization score," which reflected the extent to which children placed all the items belonging to one room before going on to the next room. This measure was particularly important because planning was the activity around which the collaboration was co-constructed. To calculate this index, the number of item pairs within a defined room that were placed in sequence was summed. This number was then divided by the total number of correct items minus the number of rooms correctly defined. The organization score is similar to a clustering score and varied from 0 to 1; the higher the score the more organized and planned the placements appeared to be.

Although Collaboration children also placed more items correctly (M = 26.30, SD = 9.10) than No Collaboration children (M = 19.70, SD = 10.50) and created more correct rooms (M = 4.67, SD = 1.60) than No Collaboration children (M = 3.70, SD = 1.90), the differences were not statistically significant. Collaboration children (M = 0.78, SD = 0.23) did, however, have higher organization scores than No Collaboration children (M = 0.46, SD = 0.31), p < .05.

Although children as a group who committed the error bias (i.e., more "I did it" than "You did it" errors) also performed better in the recategorization task, it is not clear that individual children who committed the bias also scored better in the recategorization task. It is possible that collaboration with the adult led independently to the bias and to better learning. To assess the relation between source-monitoring errors and recategorization performance, partial correlations were calculated between the error bias and the number of items correct, the number of correct rooms, and the organization score, controlling for experimental condition (i.e., Collaboration or No Collaboration). The error bias was defined as the difference between the number of "I did it" errors and the number of "You did it" errors. The correlations between the error bias and the number of correct items (r = 0.30, p = 0.08) and the number of correct rooms (r = 0.32, p = 0.07) were positive, but only marginally significant. The correlation between the error bias and the organization score was not significant (r = 0.15, p = 0.24).

How Do Collaborative Goals Influence Source-Monitoring Errors?

The error bias observed in our earlier collage studies was repeated here when children carried out a collaborative categorization task with an adult. Again, similarly to the collage studies, when there was no collaboration and no shared goal in the task, errors were low and the bias in errors did not occur. Note that the confusions in source monitoring were clearly not related to the child's physical actions on the experimenter's items, but rather were related to the cognitive operations (i.e., the prospective processes) performed with respect to these items. Children were no more likely to be confused concerning who placed the experimenter's items if the child physically interacted with the item or not. In other studies of source monitoring, when children simply perform actions in alternation with adults and there is no shared goal, there is also no bias to claim they performed actions actually performed by the adults (e.g., Foley & Johnson, 1985). Thus, the frequency and form of the errors changed in relation to a change in children's goals. Moreover, more elaborated processing in the collaborative task was associated with greater errors and a bias in the errors that did occur. From past research, without reference to a person-based perspective, fewer errors might have been expected in the collaborative task because processing was more demanding. Apparently, the extent to which agent information is preserved or transformed in memory depends on the nature of the goals motivating the task.

When children assumed the decision-making role of their partner by planning the partner's actions in the presence of a shared goal, the partner's actions appeared to be recoded as self-actions. Items the partner placed into the house were confused with the items children actually did place into the house. Children in the Collaboration condition who had committed the misattribution bias also went on to organize the items more effectively on their own than the children in the No Collaboration condition, who as a group did not commit more "I did it" than "You did it" errors. Thus, the group of children who showed the bias in errors also learned more from the collaboration. This finding provides independent evidence that the cognitive operations indexed by more source-monitoring errors overall and a greater number of "I did it" errors in particular, were effortful, elaborated, and effective.

Next, we examined whether individual children who showed the error bias within the two conditions demonstrated greater learning during the recategorization task. Would children who were more likely to attribute the other person's actions to themselves also place more items correctly, define more rooms accurately, and organize the items more effectively when performing on their own? There was some evidence that the error bias did index learning-related processes for individual children. Positive correlations emerged between the error bias and the number of correct items and rooms children produced. Thus, children who made the most "I did it errors" relative to their "You did it" errors created more accurate categorizations than children for whom the error bias was lower. Nevertheless, these correlations were only marginally significant and no correlation emerged between the bias and the organization score. The small number of children included in this study may have interfered with our ability to observe a stronger relation between the measures. Moreover, it is possible that some other aspect of performance that we did not assess mediates the relation between the error bias and learning. Additional data will need to be collected in these conditions and the relations reassessed to evaluate whether the size of the error bias is related to individual differences in learning. Still, even a trend toward this relation with so few subjects hints that error patterns can index more complex modes of processing at an individual level.

Finally, these results, along with findings from our earlier collage studies, also point to intriguing ways in which internalization might occur. The misattribution bias suggests that children in the context of collaborative tasks recode agent information, transforming an act by representing the self as the agent of an action another person has or will perform. These recodings, in turn, appear to be related to children's learning, perhaps helping to encode and organize information. Action recoding seems to be activated typically within a shared activity, but may occur more generally whenever individuals create some sort of intersubjectivity with another person. This intersubjectivity may occur whether or not people actually interact with another person or perhaps more generally when observing someone else either live, through film, or through words (Rogoff, 1998).

DO SOURCE-MONITORING ERRORS INDEX RECODING PROCESSES?

Although the findings of the second study indicate that collaboration is related to the error bias, which in turn is related to learning, there are at least three other reasons that the error bias could have emerged in the Collaboration condition, but not in the No Collaboration condition. The Collaboration and No Collaboration conditions differed in the nature of the children's involvement in the task, whether planning occurred, whether the children and the adult did something together, taking turns, and whether the child watched the adult place items in the house. Thus, any one of these factors, other than the proposed recoding process, could have led to our findings. In Study 3, the aim was to clarify the nature of the relation between memory errors and children's learning, and determine more clearly whether appropriation does occur because of recoding another person's actions as one's own.

We hypothesized that children's planning of the other person's actions led to the recoding, but perhaps any action carried out by the child might have led to the same error. That is, children's involvement in the task varied between the two conditions. Perhaps if children had simply named the furniture item for the adult, rather than planned which item the adult was to put in the house, the same result might have occurred. Second, we hypothesized that the child's planning was important in recoding actions, but perhaps the availability of any person's plans would have led to the same result. Maybe if the child had been exposed to the experimenter's plans or even the experimenter's actions of placing the items into the house, the error bias would have occurred. Finally, children might have performed as they did not because of their planning, but because they took turns with the adult in the Collaboration condition, but not in the No Collaboration condition; if children alternated with the adult in the task, but had not planned for the experimenter, the same results might have been observed.

In this study, children participated in one of two conditions to examine these possibilities. In one condition, the experimenter planned which furniture pieces both the child and adult placed into the house. When it was the adult's turn, however, children named the furniture item (child names condition). In a second condition, the child and adult experimenter took turns planning and placing their own pieces (child plans condition): (a) If any cognitive operation, such as naming, is sufficient for the error bias to occur, then children should perform similarly to the Collaboration condition in Study 2. More "I did it" than "You did it" errors should be committed. On the other hand, if it is the child's planning of the experimenter's actions that is critical in recoding and appropriation, then no error bias should occur. Thus, by changing the nature of the child's involvement in the task we could determine what role involvement played in performance; (b) If the child's production of plans rather than plans for the experimenter is critical in coding and learning, then an error bias should emerge and learning should be the same as the Collaboration condition in the second experiment. Similarly, if (c) simply taking turns in a task; or (d) watching the experimenter place items in the house produces an error bias, then children in this condition should perform as those in the Collaboration condition. Recategorization performance should look similar as well.

Description of the Study

Thirty-two kindergarten children, with a mean age of 5 years and 7 months, participated in each of two conditions, Child Names and Child Plans, in a doll house categorization task. Children were enrolled in a public school in a working class suburb of Detroit. The same doll house and miniature furniture items used in Study 2 were used here. The room was set up similarly with the doll house and furniture on one table and puzzles, along with the timer, placed on another table.

In the Child Names condition, the experimenter selected the items that would be placed in the house by both the experimenter and the child. In the Child Plans condition the experimenter and the child planned their own furniture placements. The children in the Child Names condition were yoked to the children in the Child Plans condition. As in Study 2, the adult partner explained that they were going to move the furniture items into the house "where they belonged." Children in the Child Plans condition were given the choice of which room they wanted to make in which order and where they wished the room to be placed. Children in the Child Names condition were yoked to the order and placement of rooms chosen in the Child Plans condition.

The experimenter went first in each condition, selecting a furniture item and placing it into the doll house in the appropriate room. In the Child Names condition, children were then asked to name the item before the experimenter placed it into the house. The experimenter then selected the next item and gave it to the child to place into the room. In the Child Plans condition, children were asked to pick out an item for themselves and place it into the house. As in Study 2, hints were given if they chose an incorrect item or could not find an item. After two or three hints, an item was selected for the child, although this occurred infrequently. This procedure was followed in both conditions until all the items were placed into the house in their correct locations.

Children were then invited to sit at the puzzle table and the timer was set for seven minutes, as in the second experiment. The experimenter returned to the doll house to empty the furniture into a box. Once all the pieces were in the box and covered, the experimenter returned to the puzzle table until the delay period was over. The child and the experimenter then went back to the doll house to begin the surprise source-monitoring task. The source-monitoring task and the recategorization task procedures for children in both conditions followed those of the second experiment exactly. The same dependent measures were derived from the tasks as well.

Findings of the Study

Source-Monitoring Task. Children in the Child Names condition ($M = 7.50$, $SD = 4.12$) committed more errors overall than children in the Child Plans condition ($M = 3.83$, $SD = 3.90$), $p < .05$; however, there was no effect of error type, nor an interaction between condition and error type. Children in the Child Names condition committed an average of 4.13 ($SD = 3.40$) "I did it" errors and 3.47 ($SD = 2.17$) "You did it" errors. Children in the Child Plans condition committed an average of 2.50 ($SD = 3.78$) "I did it" errors and 1.33 ($SD = 1.07$) "You did it" errors. Thus, there was no error bias in the present study.

To compare source-monitoring performance in Studies 2 and 3, the number of errors from each was compared. The number of "I did it" errors in the Collaboration condition (Study 2) was greater than the number of "I did it" errors in the Child Names ($p < .05$) and Child Plans ($p < .01$) conditions; however, the number of "You did it" errors in the Child Names and the Child Plans ($ps > 0.10$) conditions did not differ from the errors committed in the Collaboration condition. Again, this indicates that the bias in errors only occurred in Study 2 and not in the present study. In addition, the number of "I did it" and "You did it" errors in the Child Plans condition did not differ from the number of errors committed in the No Collaboration condition ($.09 < ps < .20$), indicating that despite all the differences between the conditions, performance was the same. Although the number of "I did it" and "You did it" errors in the Child Names condition was greater than the number of errors committed in the No Collaboration condition ($ps < .01$), there were no differences between the number of "I did it" and "You did it" errors within the Child Names or Child Plans conditions. Once again, this shows that there was no bias in errors in the present study.

Recategorization Task. To assess performance in the recategorization task, the number of correct items, the number of rooms correctly defined, and the organization score were compared for the Child Names and Child Plans conditions. There were no significant differences between them ($.20 < p < .30$). Children in the Child Names condition organized their placements ($M = 0.56, SD = 0.29$), correctly placed furniture items ($M = 23.90, SD = 6.00$), and identified correct rooms ($M = 4.70, SD = 1.10$) as well as children in the Child Plans condition. Child Plans means were 0.56 ($SD = 0.30$), 24.40 ($SD = 10.70$), and 4.30 ($SD = 2.20$) for the organization score, number of correct items, and number of correct rooms, respectively. In comparing recategorization performance to that in Study 2, only the organization score differed among conditions. The Collaboration condition (Study 2) outperformed the Child Names condition ($p < .05$), which did not differ from the Child Plans condition or the No Collaboration condition (Study 2), $ps > 0.35$. This pattern indicates that children in the collaboration condition in Study 2 learned more from the collaboration than children in the present study.

Finally, the bias in errors (i.e., "I did it" errors minus "You did it" errors), controlling for experimental condition, was correlated with the three recategorization measures: number of furniture items correctly placed, number of rooms correctly defined, and the organization score. In contrast with Study 2, the error bias was negatively correlated with each measure, $rs(27) = -.31$ to $-.50$, $.01 < ps < .06$.

Further Evidence for Recoding Processes

Children in this study participated in two conditions that were designed to test whether differences between the Collaboration and No Collaboration conditions in Study 2, other than children's recoding of their partner's actions, could have contributed to the error bias and greater learning from the task. The findings demonstrate that neither the child's involvement in the task, the child's planning of any actions, exposure to experimenter plans or actions, turn taking, nor collaboration in itself led to the results of the second study. Performance in the Child Names and Child Plans conditions was identical. Neither condition led to an error bias and neither resulted in as much learning as occurred for children in the Collaboration condition in the first experiment. In addition, the error biases that did occur were negatively, rather than positively, correlated with the learning measures. Thus, children who were more confused in Study 3 did not perform as well in the recategorization task. We did not expect this outcome, but clearly the pattern of performance in these two conditions appeared to differ from the pattern in the second study.

Interestingly, children in the Child Names condition made more errors than children in the No Collaboration task. This finding suggests that cognitive operations carried out by the child in relation to the experimenter's actions do increase the overall number of errors; however, only operations that result in assuming agency of the other's actions leads to the error bias, and presumably recoding. It is possible that the different pattern of correlations in this experiment is related to the different cognitive operations that were carried out in relation to the experimenter's actions.

Our findings from this experiment indicate that source-monitoring performance serves as an index of how collaborative exchanges are encoded by young children and is related to how well children learn from these exchanges. When children become the cognitive agent of another person's actions in a joint task, the other's actions are encoded as if the child had performed them. These recodings in turn appear to support learning in the task. Collaboration children (Study 2) who recoded more of their partner's actions as self-actions organized the task better when given an opportunity to carry out the task on their own. Our findings also demonstrate that having people work together on a task does not necessarily ensure recoding and raises the question of what it means to be collaborative. Collaborative activity appears to depend on achieving intersubjectivity (e.g., Rogoff, 1990) and we speculate that recoding another's actions as one's own, which integrates the roles of actor and observer, is a reflection of intersubjectivity in an interaction. As yet, we have no assessment of how much children actually learned from the collaborative task because how much they knew before the task began was not measured. It is possible that by chance children in the Collaboration condition knew more about categorizing furniture in the doll house than children in the No Collaboration condition. It is also possible that children who knew more initially were more likely for some reason to show the error bias. Thus, prior knowledge may have influenced both source monitoring and recategorization performance. In an experiment now in progress, we are testing this possibility, assessing children's categorization knowledge on a pretest. Preliminary findings suggest that relations between source monitoring and learning cannot be attributed to children's previous knowledge (Ratner, Foley, & Gimpert, 1999).

CONCLUSIONS

From our theoretical perspective, cognitive-operations information figures prominently in children's activity memory; of crucial importance is the content of these processes (e.g., type of plan, focus of the anticipation) and the context from which they arise (e.g., shared vs. solitary activities, goal-directed vs. nonpurposeful). The studies reported in this chapter provide strong support for this person-based perspective. The goal guiding children's individual activity has consequences for source monitoring, leading to an increase in errors (Study 1). These consequences extend to collaborative contexts, and have implications for learning as well (Studies 2 and 3). What is critical in our approach is the relation between the consequences of reflection and the goal motivating the action or activity. The contribution reflective processes make to activity memory occurs not because of an additional or complex, conceptual code, but because of the relation between the information and the goal of the activity. For example, the pictures children interacted with in the first study were exactly the same in the two conditions. The only difference was that for some children they were a part of a goal-directed activity.

Our framework is not unique in its suggestion that reflection processes create entries in memory representations of events. We know that perceptual events, including action, trigger internally based ones (e.g., implicit associative responses) and these internally based events also give rise to memory representations that are sometimes mistaken as memories for actual events. Both words and implicit responses to words as well as symbolic actions (e.g., Deese, 1959) and inferences about instruments of actions (Paris & Lindauer, 1976) are thought to be represented in memory. Consider the resurrection of

Deese's paradigm for the study of implicit associative responses and false memories (Roediger & McDermott, 1995) as a case in point. More recent developmental memory models also share this point of view. For example, fuzzy-trace theory is consistent in its suggestion that events have multiple representations in memory—one version more generic in form and the other more specific in its relationship to the actual event (e.g., Reyna & Brainerd, 1995). Many factors determine which of these representations are accessed, including the purpose in remembering and the nature of the questions guiding the act of remembering (Reyna & Brainerd, 1995; Reyna & Kiernan, 1994, 1995). Moreover, as we have mentioned, Marcia Johnson and her colleagues have argued that the kind of operations giving rise to these reflective processes (e.g., relatively automatic vs. more effortful processing) are also represented in memory (Johnson, 1983, 1992; Johnson & Chalfonte, 1994; Johnson, Foley, & Leach, 1988; Johnson et al., 1993; Johnson & Raye, 1981; Johnson et al., 1981). According to the Multiple Entry Memory (MEM) model, reflective processing includes reflections about ongoing experiences (e.g., noticing commonalities between events) as well as reactivations of information not currently available to consciousness. In brief, these reflective processes may go beyond the immediate consequences of perception and include the processes mediating the manipulation of information, the anticipation of events, and the consideration of alternative perspectives about the interpretation of events. These reflective processes may vary from the relatively automatic activation of information to more deliberate acts, and are referred to as "supervisor" and "executive" functions. More than 15 years of research on source monitoring, or the ability to distinguish between the sources of memory (e.g., perception vs. imagination), confirm this aspect of Johnson's theoretical framework (Johnson, 1992; Johnson et al., 1993).

What is unique to our work is the emphasis on the perspective a person adopts during anticipation. A shift in perspective can affect source-monitoring judgments for both adults (Foley, Bouffard, Raag, & DiSanto-Rose, 1991) and children (Foley & Ratner, 1998a; 1998b). Moreover, these perspectives are linked to goals guiding children's activity in both individual (Study 1, this chapter) and collaborative contexts (Foley et al., 1993; Foley & Ratner, 1998b; Studies 2 & 3, this chapter) that have consequences for source monitoring. In addition, children's ability to remember the agent of actions occurring in a collaborative context appear to shed light on mechanisms of internalization. In this chapter, we examined children's source-monitoring failures in the context of collaborative learning and showed that in some cases source-monitoring errors reveal cognitive operations that benefit children's learning (Studies 2 and 3).

Until quite recently, most developmental studies of source monitoring have focused on actions representative of children's activities (e.g., such as play activities included in Simon-says games), but not organized into goal-directed sequences (Foley et al., 1983; Foley & Johnson, 1985; Lindsay et al., 1991), perhaps stripping them of their most important feature (Foley & Ratner, in press; Ratner & Foley, 1994). Exceptions include work reported by Parker (1995) and Roberts and Blades (1998) who studied monitoring for actions that were conceptualized as interactive or noninteractive. In Parker's study, performed and imagined actions occurred in vignettes each including four actions. These vignettes were essentially strings of four noninteractive or four sequential, interactive acts. Each interactive vignette (whether performed or imagined) was essentially defined by a goal-directed sequence (e.g., having a cookie party, taking pictures by arranging poses). After the two kinds of action sequences were performed or imagined, children were surprised with source-monitoring tests. In the Roberts and Blades study, all children interacted with an adult in a live event and then either interacted with or watched a videotaped event.

Parker reported superior source-monitoring performance for the interactive sequences, particularly after a longer retention interval. Thus, in her study, the goal-directed nature of the activities enhanced performance, whereas in our first experiment the goal-directed nature of the activities hindered performance. Notice, however, the focus of the judgments. In Parker's study, children made source-monitoring judgments about different sets of vignettes. In our first experiment, children's judgments were essentially confined to one goal-directed sequence. Thus, the presence of goals alone are not predictive of the frequency of source-monitoring errors. Indeed, Roberts and Blades found that children who interacted with the video confused actions from the video with the real-life event more than those who only watched the video. The meaning of the processes indexed by errors needs to be evaluated in relation to the meaning and characteristics of source information in a person's goals and activities. This indicates that a person-based component is a requisite for a source-monitoring model (e.g., Foley & Ratner, in press; Ratner & Foley, 1994).

The findings reported in this chapter point to the importance of a person-based perspective on source monitoring and emphasize the role of prospective processes in learning and memory. Source-monitoring errors may be worrisome in the context of eyewitness testimony (e.g., Ceci & Bruck 1993; Johnson & Foley, 1984; Poole & Lindsay,

1995; chaps. 7, 8, 9, and 10, this volume; Welch-Ross, 1995;) or when they index specific learning difficulties (chap. 5, this volume). However, their presence may well signal other kinds of enhancement effects in other contexts. For example, Poole and Lindsay (1995) reported that preschoolers are confused about the temporal features surrounding science demonstrations they learned about (e.g., pulley systems lifting weights, inflating balloons by mixing baking soda and vinegar). After watching Mr. Science demonstrate some phenomena and hearing their parents narrate episodes of Mr. Science demonstrating other phenomena, children were confused about what they saw directly and what they only heard. Clearly, there may well be occasions in which it is critically important to correctly represent the temporal ordering of episodes, distinguishing what was seen from what was experienced indirectly. But our studies point to the intriguing possibility that these source errors may be a by-product of children's internalization of the science demonstrations themselves. Perhaps young children who are most confused about what they saw and heard are those most likely to remember the demonstrations themselves. Indeed, many studies of source monitoring have shown a dissociation between source monitoring and recognition memory (e.g., Foley et al., 1993; Foley & Johnson, 1985; Roberts & Blades, 1995; chap. 5, this volume).

In summary, in order for the study of children's source monitoring to move forward we believe that there needs to be greater attention given to the goal-directed processes underlying the activities about which source discriminations are made. A person-based perspective on children's learning and memory suggests that the meaning of source-monitoring accuracy and errors cannot be adequately understood without reference to the individual and shared goals within an activity. Understanding the nature of the self-processes indexed by source-monitoring errors can also provide information about cognitive performance in other domains.

REFERENCES

Ackerman, B. (1987). Descriptions: A model for nonstrategic memory development. In H. W. Reese (Ed.), *Advances in child development and behavior: Vol. 20* (pp. 143–183). San Diego: Academic Press.

Barsalou, L. (1991). Deriving categories to achieve goals. In G. H. Bower (Ed.), *The psychology of learning and motivation: Advances in research and theory: Vol. 27* (pp. 1–64). New York: Academic Press.

Basov, M. (1991). The organization of processes of behavior. In J. Valsiner & R. van der Veer (Eds.), Structuring of conduct in activity settings: The forgotten contributions of Mikhail Basov, Part 1. *Soviet Psychology, 29*, 114–183.

Bauer, P., & Mandler, J. (1989). One thing follows another: Effects of temporal structure on 1- to 2-year-olds' recall of events. *Developmental Psychology, 25*, 197–206.

Ceci, S. J., & Bruck, M. (1993). The suggestibility of the child witness: A historical review and synthesis. *Psychological Bulletin, 113*, 403–439.

Cox, B., & Lightfoot, C. (Eds.). (1997). *Sociogenetic perspectives on internalization.* Mahwah, NJ: Lawrence Erlbaum Associates.

Day, K., Howie, P., & Markham, R. (1998). The role of similarity in developmental differences in reality monitoring. *British Journal of Developmental Psychology, 16*, 219–232.

Deese, J. (1959). On the prediction of occurrence of particular verbal intrusions in immediate recall. *Journal of Experimental Psychology, 58*, 17–22.

Durso, F. T., & Johnson, M. K. (1980). The effects of orienting tasks on recognition, recall and modality confusion of pictures and words. *Journal of Verbal Learning and Verbal Behavior, 19*, 416–429.

Fivush, R., Kuebli, J., & Clubb, P. (1992). The structure of events and event representations: A developmental analysis. *Child Development, 63*, 188–201.

Foley, M. A., Bouffard, V., Raag, T., & Disanto-Rose, M. (1991). The effects of type of imagery and type of movement on memory for dance. *Psychological Research, 53*, 251–259.

Foley, M. A., Durso, F. T., Wilder, A., & Friedman, R. (1991). Developmental comparisons of explicit versus implicit imagery and reality monitoring. *Journal of Experimental Child Psychology, 51*, 1–13.

Foley, M. A., & Johnson, M. K. (1985). Confusions between memories for performed and imagined actions: A developmental comparison. *Child Development, 56*, 1145–1155.

Foley, M. A., Johnson, M. K., & Raye, C. L. (1983). Age-related changes in confusion between memories for thoughts and memories for speech. *Child Development, 54*, 51–60.

Foley, M. A., & Ratner, H. H. (1998a). Children's recoding in memory for collaboration: A way of learning from others. *Cognitive Development, 13*, 91–108.

Foley, M. A., & Ratner, H. H. (1998b). Distinguishing between memories for thoughts and deeds: The role of prospective processing in children's source monitoring. *British Journal of Developmental Psychology, 16*, 465–484.

Foley, M. A., & Ratner, H. H. (in press). The role of action-based structures in activity memory. In H. Zimmer & R. Cohen (Eds.), *Memory for Actions.* New York: Oxford University Press.

Foley, M. A., Ratner, H. H., & Passalacqua, C. (1993). Appropriating the actions of another: Implications for children's memory and learning. *Cognitive Development, 8*, 146–169.

Foley, M. A., Santini, C., & Sopasakis, M. (1989). Discriminating between memories: Evidence for children's use of spontaneous elaborations. *Journal of Experimental Child Psychology, 48*, 146–169.

Freund, L. (1990). Maternal regulation of children's problem-solving behavior and its impact on children's performance. *Child Development, 61*, 113–126.

Heckhausen, H., & Beckmann, J. (1990). Intentional action and action slips. *Psychological Review, 97*, 36–48.

Heider, F. (1958). *The psychology of interpersonal relations*. New York: Wiley.

Johnson, M. K. (1983). A multiple-entry modular memory system. In G. Bower (Ed.), *Advances in the psychology of learning and motivation: Vol. 17* (pp. 81–123). New York: Academic Press.

Johnson, M. K. (1992). MEM: Mechanisms of recollection. *Journal of Cognitive Neuroscience, 4*, 268–280.

Johnson, M. K., & Chalfonte, B. L. (1994). Binding complex memories: The role of reactivation and the hippocampus. In D. L. Schacter & E. Tulving (Eds.), *Memory systems 1994* (pp. 311–350). Cambridge, MA: MIT Press.

Johnson, M. K., & Foley, M. A. (1984). Differentiating fact from fantasy: The reliability of children's memory. *Journal of Social Issues, 40*, 33–50.

Johnson, M. K., Foley, M. A., & Leach (1988). The consequences for memory of imagining in another person's voice. *Memory & Cognition, 16*, 337–342.

Johnson, M. K., Foley, M. A., Suengas, A. G., & Raye, C. L. (1988). Phenomenal characteristics for perceived and imagined autobiographical events. *Journal of Experimental Psychology: General, 117*, 371–376.

Johnson, M. K., Hastroudi, S., Lindsay, D. L. (1993). Source monitoring. *Psychological Bulletin, 114*, 3–28.

Johnson, M. K., & Raye, C. L. (1981). Reality monitoring. *Psychological Review, 88*, 67–85.

Johnson, M. K., Raye, C. L., Foley, H. J., & Foley, M. A. (1981). Cognitive operations and decision biases in reality monitoring. *American Journal of Psychology, 94*, 37–64.

Keenan, J. M., Golding, J. M., & Brown, P. (1992). Factors controlling the advantage of self-reference over other-reference. *Social Cognition, 10*, 79–94.

Lawrence, J., & Valsiner, J. (1993). Conceptual roots of internalization: From transmission to transformation. *Human Development, 36*, 150–167.

Leichtman, M. D., Morse, M. B., Dixon, A., & Spiegel, R. (this volume). Source monitoring and suggestibility: An individual differences approach. In K. P. Roberts & M. Blades (Eds.), *Children's source monitoring*. Mahwah, NJ: Lawrence Erlbaum Associates.

Lindsay, D. S., Johnson, M. K., & Kwon, P. (1991). Developmental changes in memory source monitoring. *Journal of Experimental Child Psychology, 52*, 297–318.

Leont'ev, A. N. (1978). *Activity, consciousness, and personality*. Englewood Cliffs, NJ: Prentice-Hall.

Lewin, K. (1951). *Field theory in social sciences*. New York: Harper.

Lorsbach, T. C. (this volume). Source monitoring as a framework for conceptualizing the nature of memory difficulties in children with learning disabilities. In K. P. Roberts & M. Blades (Eds.), *Children's source monitoring*. Mahwah, NJ: Lawrence Erlbaum Associates.

Nelson, K. (1986). *Event knowledge: Structure and function in development*. Hillsdale, NJ: Lawrence Erlbaum Associates.

Oppenheimer, L. (1991). The concept of action: A historical perspective. In L. Oppenheimer & J. Valsiner (Eds.), *The origins of action: Interdisciplinary and international perspectives* (pp. 1–35). New York: Springer-Verlag.

Paris, S., & Lindauer, B. (1976). The role of inference in children's comprehension and memory for sentences. *Cognitive Psychology, 8*, 217–227.

Parker, J. (1995). Age differences in source monitoring of performed and imagined actions on immediate and delayed tests. *Journal of Experimental Child Psychology, 60*, 84–101.

Piaget, J. (1970). Piaget's theory. In P. H. Mussen (Ed.). *Carmichael's manual of child psychology: Vol. 1* (pp. 703–732). New York: Wiley.

Poole, D. A., & Lindsay, D. S. (1995). Interviewing preschoolers: Effects of nonsuggestive techniques, parental coaching, and leading questions on reports of nonexperienced events. *Journal of Experimental Child Psychology, 60*, 129–154.

Quas, J. A., Schaaf, J. M., Alexander, K. W., & Goodman, G. S. (this volume). Do you *really* remember it happening or do you only remember being asked about it happening? Children's source monitoring in forensic contexts. In K. P. Roberts & M. Blades (Eds.), *Children's source monitoring.* Mahwah, NJ: Lawrence Erlbaum Associates.

Ratner, H. H., & Foley, M. A. (1994). A unifying framework for the development of children's activity memory. *Advances in Child Development and Behavior, 25*, 33–105.

Ratner, H. H., Foley, M. A., & Bukowski, P. (1999). *Outcomes and action cues in children's event memory.* Unpublished manuscript.

Ratner, H. H., Foley, M. A., & Gimpert, N. (1999). *The role of source monitoring in children's collaborative learning.* Manuscript submitted for publication.

Raye, C. L., & Johnson, M. K. (1980). Reality monitoring versus discriminating between external sources of memories. *Bulletin of the Psychonomic Society, 15*, 405–408.

Reyna, V. F., & Brainerd, C. J. (1995). Fuzzy-trace theory: An interim synthesis. *Individual Differences, 7*, 1–75.

Reyna, V. F., & Kiernan, B. (1994). Development of gist versus verbatim memory in sentence recognition: Effects of lexical familiarity, semantic content, encoding instructions, and retention interval. *Developmental Psychology, 30*, 178–191.

Reyna, V. F., & Kiernan, B. (1995). Children's memory and metaphorical interpretation. *Metaphor and Symbol, 10*, 309–331.

Roberts, K. P. & Blades, M. (1995). Children's discrimination of memories for actual and pretend actions in a hiding task. *British Journal of Developmental Psychology, 13*, 321–333.

Roberts, K. P., & Blades, M. (1998). The effects of interacting in repeated events on children's eyewitness memory and source monitoring. *Applied Cognitive Psychology, 12*, 489–503.

Rogers, T. B., Kuiper, N. A., & Kirker, W. S. (1977). Self-reference and the encoding of personal information. *Journal of Personality and Social Psychology, 35*, 677–688.

Roediger, H. L., III, & McDermott, K. B. (1995). Creating false memories: remembering words not presented in lists. *Journal of Experimental Psychology: Learning, Memory & Cognition, 21*, 803–814.

Rogoff, B. (1990). *Apprenticeship in thinking: Cognitive development in social context.* New York: Oxford University Press.

Rogoff, B. (1998). Cognition as a collaborative process. In D. Kuhn & R. Siegler (Eds.), Cognition, perception, and language. *Handbook of child psychology: Vol. 2*, (pp. 679–744).

Schank, R., & Abelson, R. (1977). *Scripts, plans, goals, and understanding.* Hillsdale, NJ: Lawrence Erlbaum Associates.

Siegler, R. (1995). How does change occur? A microgenetic study of number conservation. *Cognitive Psychology, 28*, 225–273.

Slackman, E., Hudson, J., & Fivush, R. (1986). Actions, actors, links, and goals: The structure of children's event representations. In K. Nelson (Ed.), *Event knowledge: Structure and function in development* (pp. 47–71). Hillsdale, NJ: Lawrence Erlbaum Associates.

Tomasello, M., & Kruger, A. C. (1992). Joint attention on actions: Acquiring verbs in ostensive and non-ostensive contexts. *Journal of Child Language, 19*, 311–333.

Tomasello, M., Kruger, A. C., Ratner, H. H. (1993). Cultural learning. *Behavioral and Brain Science, 16*, 495–552.

Tulving, E., & Thompson, D. M. (1973). Encoding specificity and retrieval processes in episodic memory. *Psychological Review, 80*, 352–373.

von Cranach, M., Kalbermatten, U., Indermuhle, K., & Gugler, B. (1982). *Goal-directed action.* New York: Academic Press.

Vygotsky, L. (1962). *Thought and language.* Cambridge, MA: MIT Press.

Welch-Ross, M. K. (1995). Developmental changes in preschoolers' ability to distinguish memories of performed, pretended and imagined actions. *Cognitive Development, 10*, 421–441.

White, S. (1970). The learning theory tradition and child psychology. In P. H. Mussen (Ed.), *Carmichael's manual of child psychology: Vol. 1* (pp. 657–701). New York: Wiley.

5

Source Monitoring as a Framework for Conceptualizing the Nature of Memory Difficulties in Children With Learning Disabilities

Thomas C. Lorsbach
University of Nebraska at Omaha

SOURCE MONITORING IN CHILDREN
WITH SPECIAL EDUCATIONAL NEEDS

The systematic investigation of source-monitoring difficulties provides a useful tool to theorists who are attempting to determine the nature of individual differences in memory. The source-monitoring framework has particular relevance for investigators who study the memory impairments of children who have special educational needs (e.g., mentally retarded, learning disabled, language impaired, etc.). Determining whether a particular handicapping condition is accompanied by either a global or a more specific deficit in source monitoring has theoretical as well as practical significance. At a theoretical level, identifying unique source-monitoring tendencies may serve to provide converging evidence and greater specificity to existing theories that address the cognitive impairments in children with a handicap. At a more applied level, the identification of a specific source-monitoring profile that is associated with a particular group of handicapped children would have diagnostic value, as well as implications for educators, clinicians, and other practitioners who are attempting to design appropriate interventions and accommodations for children within that handicapping condition. For example, knowing that children with a specific language disorder may tend to experience source confusions with verbal information, but not with activity memories, might provide the clinician with greater insight into the nature of a given language impairment.

Although a significant amount of research has examined the source-monitoring skills of "average" children who are developing without difficulty, relatively few studies have investigated the source-monitoring abilities of children who have special educational needs. In this chapter, I first review those studies that have examined the source monitoring of children with mental retardation, as well as children with autism. The remainder of the chapter gives particular attention to the source-monitoring abilities of children with learning disabilities.

Two studies have examined the source-monitoring abilities of children with developmental disabilities. Jens, Gordon, and Shaddock (1990) compared a group of 10-year-old mentally retarded children with a group of 6-year-old nonretarded children in terms of their ability to remember and discriminate previously performed and imagined activities (internal source monitoring). Each child was asked to either perform or imagine a series of simple tasks alone or together with the experimenter (e.g., "Put the hat on"). On completion of these tasks, a standardized memory test was administered, followed by an "interview" in which each child was asked an open-ended question ("Tell me everything we or you did or imagined doing while we were together"), followed by a more specific prompt ("What else did we or you do or imagine?"). For each activity that was recalled, the child was asked if he or she had performed or imagined the activity. Finally, for each unrecalled activity, the child was asked, "While you were with me did you or we ... ?", along with the additional source question, "Did we or you really do that, or did you imagine doing it?" About half of the children were interviewed a second time eight weeks later. Other than nonretarded children recalling more of the performed activities following "specific prompts" during the initial recall task, there were no group differences in recall performance. The source-monitoring performance is difficult to interpret because the error analyses included source errors for previously unrecalled activities and only descriptive statistics were provided. However, both mentally retarded and nonretarded children displayed similar patterns of responses, with source monitoring being generally more accurate for activities that were performed, as opposed to previously imagined.

Another study of children with mental retardation was subsequently performed by Gordon, Jens, Hollings, and Watson (1994) in what was designed to be a replication and extension of the previous study by Jens et al. (1990). Ten-year-old children with mental retardation, along with 6-year-old nonretarded children with the same mental ages as the older retarded children, were again asked to imagine or to perform a series of simple actions. Memory for these activities was then assessed during interviews that were conducted immediately and following a 6-week delay. The memory performance of mentally retarded and nonretarded children did not differ significantly when responding either to the open-ended or the more specific questions. Furthermore, the two groups of children did not differ in their memory for whether a remembered activity was previously imagined or performed. Included in the design of the experiment was a series of misleading questions, with some questions addressing previously performed actions (e.g., "I didn't touch your nose, did I?"), and other misleading questions dealing with actions that were not performed or imagined at all. A comparison of the correct responses of the two groups of children indicated that nonretarded children were somewhat more accurate than the retarded children in their performance during the immediate interview, but the two groups of children did not differ on the delayed interview. Both groups of children were more accurate with questions about activities that were actually performed, as opposed to those that were only imagined. Gordon et al. (1994, p. 248) indicated that these results "suggest that one can be optimistic about the abilities of children with mental retardation to provide accurate testimony at least at a level consistent with that of children with normal intelligence of the same mental age."

Source monitoring by children with autism has also been investigated. Bennetto, Pennington, and Rogers (1996) compared the memory performance of autistic and nonautistic adolescents on a battery of memory tasks that included both recall and recognition tasks. The autistic children committed more intrusion errors than the nonautistic children during the recall tasks. These intrusion errors consisted of recalling words that had been presented on a previously studied, but no longer to-be-remembered list, as well as recalling incorrect words that were semantically related to items in the to-be-remembered list. During recognition tasks, autistic children also made more false alarms to new items that were semantically related to items in the study list, but not to new, semantically unrelated items. Based on a comparison of the error patterns that were exhibited by the autistic and nonautistic children on recall and recognition tasks, Bennetto et al. (1996) concluded that the autistic children possessed a source-monitoring deficit. According to Bennetto et al. (1996, p. 1828), the error patterns suggest that the autistic children "failed to use the context of the current task to deselect inappropriate responses."

More recently, Farrant, Blades, and Boucher (1998) examined the reality-monitoring skills of autistic, mentally retarded, and nonhandicapped children. The 12-year-old autistic and the mentally retarded children were matched on mental ages and were compared to a younger group of 7-year-old nonhandicapped children. Each child was initially presented with a list of 28 words. As each word was presented, the child was instructed to either say the word aloud or listen to the experimenter say the word. Following the presentation of the list, each child was given a 42-item old–new recognition test. For each word that was judged as being "old," the child was asked to decide whether he or she had previously said the word aloud or had listened to the experimenter say the word. The analysis of recognition performance indicated that the mentally retarded children remembered fewer words than either the autistic children or the nonhandicapped children, with the latter groups of children showing comparable performance. The analysis of reality-monitoring performance did not reveal any group differences.

Because of the limited number of studies, it is difficult to make any conclusive statements about the source-monitoring skills of either mentally retarded or autistic children. However, it appears that children with mental retardation behave similarly to younger nonretarded children in their discrimination of memories for performed and imagined activities (Gordon et al., 1994; Jens et al., 1990). In addition, children with mental retardation do not seem to differ from nonretarded children in their ability to remember whether they had previously said or listened to a given word. Autistic children, on the other hand, may have difficulty using contextual information to retrieve memories from a particular learning episode (Bennetto et al., 1996), although it should be emphasized that this deficit was not replicated using a different task (Farrant et al., 1988). These errors may be due to a source-monitoring deficit or to difficulty inhibiting those memories that were acquired in a different context.

SOURCE MONITORING IN CHILDREN
WITH LEARNING DISABILITIES

The remaining discussion presents a detailed review of those studies that have examined the source-monitoring skills of children with learning disabilities. To provide some perspective for this research, the results of these studies are presented in relation to other memory research with learning disabled children to provide an overall perspective on their cognition. Although the number of source-monitoring studies is limited, the available evidence suggests that learning disabled children experience difficulty consciously remembering the source of memories containing verbal information. When considered within the context of other memory research with these children, these verbal source-monitoring difficulties do not simply reflect a more generalized memory deficit. Difficulty on tasks requiring the deliberate use of verbal source monitoring is, I argue, indicative of a fundamental problem in the use of those effortful memory processes that have been characterized by Johnson and her colleagues as "reflective" and "systematic" (Johnson, 1992; Johnson, Hashtroudi, & Lindsay, 1993; Johnson & Hirst, 1991).

Defining and Describing Learning Disabilities

The term *learning disabilities* is a general term that refers to a heterogeneous group of learning disorders that are manifested in children and adults with average or above average intelligence. In fact, a discrepancy between achievement and ability is typically used as a criterion when identifying children with learning disabilities. These learning disorders are presumed to be the result of some underlying problem within the central nervous system and are manifested in a variety of academic or nonacademic problems. The diversity of learning disorders within this population has presented a substantial challenge to those who have attempted to generate a widely accepted definition. Although a number of definitions have been proposed (e.g., Interagency Committee on Learning Disabilities, 1987; National Joint Committee on Learning Disabilities, 1997), perhaps the most influential definition is that which was included in Public-Law 94-142, Education for All Handicapped Children Act, in 1975 and is included in a subsequent update of this Act in 1997, Individuals with Disabilities Act (Public-Law 105-17):

> The term "specific learning disability" means a disorder in one or more of the basic psychological processes involved in understanding or in using language, spoken or written, which disorder may manifest itself in imperfect ability to listen, think, speak, read, write, spell, or to do mathematical calculations.... Such term includes such conditions as perceptual disabilities, brain injury, minimal brain dysfunction, dyslexia, and developmental aphasia.... Such term does not include a learning problem that is primarily the result of visual, hearing, or motor disabilities, of mental retardation, of emotional disturbance, or of environmental, cultural, or economic disadvantage. (Pub. L. No. 105-17, Sec. 602)

Learning disabilities are cross-cultural phenomena and appear throughout the world in countries with different written language systems (Lerner, 2000). Within the United States, children with learning disabilities represent 5.51% of all children between the ages of 6 and 17 (U.S. Department of Education, 1998). Of those school-aged children who are identified as learning disabled, 69.3% are males and 30.8% are females (U.S. Department of Education, 1998). This gender disparity may perhaps reflect some type of bias in the referral and testing of males for Special Education services (Hallahan, Kauffman, & Lloyd, 1999).

Memory Problems of Children With Learning Disabilities: An Overview

A considerable amount of research has been devoted to the examination of memory problems in children with learning disabilities. When compared with their nondisabled peers, children with learning disabilities remember significantly less information on a variety of both short- and long-term memory tasks (see reviews by Bauer, 1987; Cooney & Swanson, 1987; Swanson & Cooney, 1996; Swanson, Cooney, & O'Shaughnessy, 1998). O'Shaughnessy and Swanson (1998) recently conducted a meta-analysis of studies that have examined the immediate memory performance of children with learning disabilities. Included in the analysis were a wide range of studies that utilized both serial and free recall tasks with words or pictorial stimuli, as well as studies that were conducted with or without mnemonic instruction. The meta-analysis found that the immediate memory difficulties of children with learning disabilities appeared to be restricted to the use of verbal materials or nonlinguistic stimuli that may be labeled by the participant during the memory task. Furthermore, the differences between learning disabled and nondisabled children were evident on free recall tasks, and were yet greater with serial memory tasks. When visual–spatial stimuli are used that are not easily labeled (e.g., abstract shapes and nonsense figures), differences in memory performance between learning disabled and nondisabled children become small, and in many cases nonexistent. O'Shaughnessy and Swanson's (1998) analysis also revealed that, although the differences between learning disabled and nondisabled children were smaller with mnemonic instruction, the differences between the two populations remained sizable.

Both strategic and nonstrategic factors have been used by theorists in an attempt to explain the short-term or working memory difficulties of children with learning disabilities. According to many theorists, the memory difficulties of children with learning disabilities are due to an underlying deficit in the use of control processes (see discussions by Bauer, 1987; Borkowski, Johnston, & Reid, 1987; Cooney & Swanson, 1987; Stone & Conca, 1993; Swanson & Cooney, 1991). Using various laboratory measures, investigators have identified a number of strategic deficits in children with learning disabilities, including a failure to use rehearsal (e.g., Bauer, 1977a, b), organization (e.g., Bauer, 1979; Dallago & Moely, 1980; Gelzheiser, 1984), and semantic processing strategies (Baker, Ceci, & Herrmann, 1987; Ceci, 1982, 1983, 1984; Ceci & Baker, 1987; Ceci, Lea, & Ringstrom, 1980; Lorsbach & Gray, 1985). Other theorists have identified several nonstrategic factors that may account for the short-term and working memory problems of learning and reading disabled children. First, some theorists believe that the difficulties of learning and reading disabled children on short-term memory span tasks reflect an underlying deficit in the ability to encode temporal order information (Tallal, Galaburda, Llinas, & von Euler, 1993). Second, other investigators have observed a close link between language disorders and reading difficulties and have suggested that many children with learning disabilities have an underlying deficit in the use of phonetic codes that would allow them to store information in short-term memory (e.g., Mann & Liberman, 1984; Mann, Liberman, & Shankweiler, 1980; Vellutino, 1979; Vellutino, Steger, Moyer, Harding, & Niles, 1977). Finally, a number of other researchers have observed the longer naming latencies of children with learning and reading disabilities and have argued that their difficulties on short-term memory tasks may be due to a slower access to phonetic codes in long-term memory (Denckla & Rudel, 1976; Lorsbach & Gray, 1985; Spring & Capps, 1974; Torgesen & Houck, 1980). Slower access to phonetic information presumably reflects an impairment in the operational efficiency of short-term memory processes, and may impact the speed with which information is rehearsed in working memory (Case, Kurland, & Goldberg, 1982).

With respect to long-term memory tasks, the performance of children with learning disabilities has consistently been found to be inferior to that of nondisabled children. Brainerd, Kingma, and Howe (1986) have noted the variety of long-term memory tasks that have been used to compare learning-disabled and nondisabled children, including both free recall and cued recall of categorized word lists (Ceci et al., 1980; Howe, Brainerd, & Kingma, 1984; Wong, Wong, & Foth, 1977), single-trial recall and repeated free recall of unrelated word lists (Bauer, 1977b; Kail, Hale, & Leonard, 1983), free recall of lists of unrelated pictures (Howe et al., 1984), and free and cued recall of categorized lists of pictures (Ceci et al., 1980). In all cases, the memory performance of learning disabled children has been found to be significantly lower than their nondisabled peers. Performance analyses of children with learning disabilities on these long-term memory tasks have led investigators to conceptualize learning disabled children as inactive or passive learners who fail to spontaneously employ task-appropriate strategies (Hallahan & Kauffman, 1982; Torgesen, 1975, 1977). In support of this observation, investigators have found that when children with learning disabilities are explicitly instructed to use a given strategy, their memory difficulties are often reduced, or in some cases, eliminated, (e.g., Newman & Hagen, 1981; Tarver, Hallahan, Kauffman, & Ball, 1976; Torgesen, Murphy, & Ivey, 1979). Unfortunately, when learning disabled children are provided with appropriate strategy instruction, the benefits of training are often restricted to the specific training materials and the instructional benefits are not generalized to other learning and memory activities (e.g., Gelzheiser, 1984).

Rather than conceptualizing children with learning disabilities as passive learners, other investigators have argued that these children do employ strategies, but they do so inappropriately or inefficiently. Stone and Conca (1993) observe that there appear to be two types of strategy deficits in children with learning disabilities. First, children with learning disabilities seem to select simpler or less efficient strategies than nondisabled children. Second, children with learning disabilities often execute strategies in a novice, rather than in an expert manner. A number of theorists have argued that the strategic deficiencies of children with learning disabilities reflect a more fundamental problem in the area of metacognition (e.g., Borkowski et al., 1987; Wong, 1991). In this case, children with learning disabilities presumably lack awareness about their own cognitive processes or have difficulty regulating the use of their cognitive processes (e.g., planning, monitoring, revising, evaluating, etc.). This suggests that children with learning disabilities may also be impaired when making conscious source attributions.

Several investigators have noted that the memory difficulties of learning disabled children are not generalized, but appear to be restricted to those tasks where there is a conscious attempt to remember (but see Ackerman & Dykman, 1982; Sternberg & Wagner, 1982). Swanson and his colleagues (Cooney & Swanson, 1987; Swanson & Cooney, 1991; Swanson et al., 1998) have operated within a developmental perspective and have noted that the memory skills of learning disabled children parallel those of younger children. That is, similar to younger children, children with learning disabilities experience difficulties on tasks requiring cognitive effort and self-monitoring, but not on tasks that may be performed automatically. A similar observation was made by Bauer (1987), who noted that learning disabled and nondisabled children do not differ when memory performance is compared on tasks that do not require the use of control processes. This distinction between conscious and automatic forms of processing has been applied similarly in the analysis of the semantic processing abilities of children with learning disabilities. In this case, Ceci (1982, 1983, 1984) has provided evidence that children with learning disabilities are deficient in purposive (conscious), but not automatic forms of semantic processing. Most recently, children with learning disabilities have been found to differ from nondisabled children when presented with explicit tests of memory, but not when memory is tested implicitly (Lorsbach, Sodoro, & Brown, 1992; Lorsbach & Worman, 1989; 1990). As source-monitoring decisions can be automatic or effortful, children with learning disabilities may be especially impaired on source-monitoring tasks that require effortful decision making. We now review those studies that have formally examined the source-monitoring skills of children with learning disabilities.

Source-Monitoring Research With Learning Disabled Children

The results of two studies indicate that children with learning disabilities experience significantly greater difficulty than nondisabled children when attempting to remember the source of their verbal memories. Lorsbach, Melendez, and Carroll-Maher (1991) compared 48 learning disabled and 48 nondisabled children with respect to their reality monitoring and internal source-monitoring skills. The 48 children in each population consisted of twenty-four 8-year-olds (second grade) and twenty-four 12-year-olds (sixth grade). The learning disabled 8-year-olds had mean Verbal and Performance IQ scores of 92 and 102, respectively, and the learning disabled 12-year-olds had mean Verbal and Performance IQ scores of 94 and 109, respectively. The academic achievement of learning disabled children was well below average in the areas of reading and mathematics. Although the level of severity was not formally designated by school personnel, the extent of the learning disability for these children might be considered as mild–moderate in that all of the learning disabled children were attending general education classes all or most of each school day (none was enrolled in self-contained special education classes). Although no standardized test scores were available for the cognitive abilities of nondisabled children, they were considered to be in the average range of ability: Nondisabled children (a) had reading and math achievement test scores that were in the average range, (b) were not receiving remedial educational services, and (c) were not enrolled in educational programs for the gifted and talented. Children in each group were assigned to one of two conditions, "Say-Think" or "Say-Listen" that, respectively, were designed to assess internal source monitoring and reality monitoring. Each child was asked to listen to a series of 32 incomplete sentences that highly constrained a terminal noun (e.g., "Kermit is the name of a _____."; "We wear shoes on our _____."; "Jack and Jill went up the _____."). Children in the Say-Think condition were asked to generate the final word for each of the 32 sentences. In addition, children in the Say-Think condition were asked to "play a game" by either saying the word aloud or imagining themselves saying the word. For half of the sentences, the child was instructed to say the word aloud (Say items), and, for the remaining half, to imagine themselves saying the final word (Think items). Visual prompts to either say the word aloud or to imagine saying the word were provided with each sentence by the experimenter. Children who participated in the reality-monitoring condition were given the same sentences, but half of the sentences were missing the final word and the remaining half of the sentences were presented in their completed form. Children were cued as to whether they should either complete the sentence aloud (Say items) or listen to the final word in each sentence (Listen items). No mention was made of any subsequent memory or source-monitoring tasks. Following the presentation of the sentences, a 3-minute filler activity was presented, followed by a 64-item old or new recognition task. When children believed that a word had been used to complete one of the previous sentences (an "old" item), they were asked to remember whether they had originally said the word aloud or imagined themselves saying it (Say-Think condition) or whether they had said the word or listened to it (Say-Listen condition).

Overall, children with learning disabilities experienced greater difficulty than nondisabled children in the recognition of old and new nouns. Given that learning disabled children often fail to process information semantically (e.g., Baker et al., 1987; Ceci, 1982), it is possible that the poor recognition memory performance of learning disabled children was due to a failure to "spontaneously integrate terminal nouns with their respective sentence contexts" (Lorsbach et al., 1991). Such a failure to spontaneously encode or systematically retrieve the elaborative contextual information that was presented with terminal nouns may have adversely affected the recognition performance of learning disabled children.

The failure to adequately encode nouns within the context of their respective sentence frames may also have affected the amount of source information available to children with learning disabilities (see Fig. 5.1). Children with learning disabilities also experienced diffi-

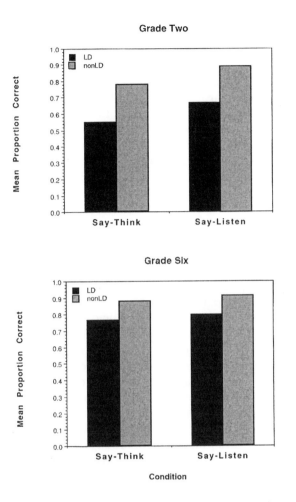

FIG. 5.1. Judgment of origin performance of second- and sixth-grade learning disabled and nondisabled children at each acquisition condition (Lorsbach, Melendez, & Carroll-Maher, 1991).

culty remembering the source of old words that had been correctly recognized (hits). The analysis of source-monitoring performance revealed that children with learning disabilities were significantly less accurate than nondisabled children in both the Say–Think (internal source monitoring) and the Say–Listen (reality monitoring) condition. Each of these source-monitoring conditions requires different memory characteristics and judgment processes (Johnson et al., 1993). According to Foley, Johnson, and Raye (1983), the Say–Think task involves discriminating between "unrealized ideas and ideas that have been realized or expressed in action (such as vocalization or other activities)" (p. 58). The Say-Think condition also requires that one have "memory for the presence or absence of kinesthetic information, or on memory for specific sensory information about voice quality" (Hashtroudi, Johnson, & Chrosniak, 1989, p. 111). On the other hand, the Say-Listen condition requires the discrimination between self-generated and externally derived verbal memories. In this case, source discriminations involve memory for cognitive operations (organizing, elaborating, retrieving, and identifying), as well as memory for sensory information (Johnson et al., 1993). The requirements of the Say-Think condition and the Say-Listen condition suggest that children with learning disabilities may have difficulty encoding or retrieving memories on the basis of their sensory attributes, as well as associated cognitive operations. Because learning disabled children experienced more source confusion than nondisabled children in both the Say-Think condition and the Say-Listen condition, learning disabled children appear to have a general impairment in monitoring the source of verbal information held in memory.

Despite the differences between learning disabled and nondisabled children, there were two similarities that were observed with the two populations. First, consistent with the source-monitoring framework, both groups of children were generally less accurate in the Say–Think condition than in the Say–Listen condition, and this is probably due to the fact that the characteristics of within-class memories are more similar than between-class memories (e.g., Foley & Johnson, 1985). Second, both learning disabled and nondisabled children demonstrated a similar bias to judge false positives in the Say–Listen condition as words they had listened to, as opposed to words that they had previously said. This bias perhaps reflects the metamemorial belief that self-generated memories are more memorable than memory representations that are based on information acquired from the environment. This metamemory assumption has been observed in previous research. Children (older than 9 years old) and adults tend to judge false positives as information that they had acquired from the environment, as opposed to information that they had previously generated (Foley et al., 1983; Johnson & Raye, 1981). According to Johnson and Raye (1981), this bias represents the belief that "'it-had-to-be-you' ('I'd remember it if it were me')" (p. 80).

The incomplete sentences that were used in the Lorsbach et al. (1991) study were adapted by Lorsbach and Ewing (1995) to examine external source monitoring (Listen-Listen condition) and reality monitoring (Think-Listen condition) in 12-year-old (sixth grade) learning disabled and nondisabled children. Thirty-eight children with learning disabilities and 36 nondisabled children participated in the study. The mean Verbal and Performance IQs of the learning disabled children were, respectively, 99 and 107. The learning disabled children exhibited difficulties in both reading and math achievement. Given that these children were attending general education classes and were receiving services from Resource Room teachers, the extent of their learning disability might be considered as mild–moderate. No standardized test scores were available that would provide a measure of the cognitive abilities of the nondisabled children. However, given that (a) their achievement scores were in the average range, (b) none were receiving special education services, and (c) none were enrolled in enrichment programs for the gifted, the nondisabled participants might be considered to have average ability.

Included in the design of this experiment was stimulus repetition, with critical nouns being presented once or twice. Rather than presenting sentences on an audiotape, Lorsbach and Ewing presented sentences through the use of a videotape. Each sentence frame was read aloud by an adult female and was completed aloud by one of two 10-year-old girls (Annie and Sarah) in the Listen-Listen condition. Participants were told that they would be viewing a videotape of a teacher as she reads incomplete sentences and calls on each of two girls to complete individual sentences. As participants viewed the videotape, they were asked to help the experimenter check whether or not each girl on the videotape was completing the sentence appropriately. Each child was asked to respond with a nod of the head as to whether they agreed or disagreed with the girl's response on the videotape. This cover task was used only to assure that each child listened to the words that were said aloud by each girl on the videotape.

Children assigned to the Think-Listen condition also viewed a videotape of the teacher. In this case, however, there was only one girl seated on one side of the teacher. On the other side of the teacher there was an empty chair. Participants were asked to play a game in which they imagined that they were seated in the empty chair next to the teacher. In this game, children were asked to further imagine that they were responding to incomplete sentences when the teacher called on them. Rather than saying the word aloud, however, each child was instructed to only imagine themselves saying the word on the videotape. Prompts to listen to the girl on the videotape or to imagine saying the word were provided by the teacher on the videotape as she pointed to the girl or to the empty chair. That is, through her nonverbal gestures, the teacher on the videotape cued the participant to either listen to the girl at the teacher's side or to think of (imagine) themselves saying a word.

After the sentences were presented, each child was presented with a 3-minute filler activity, followed by a 64-item old–new recognition task. Children were asked to judge the source of items that they believed were used to complete one of the preceding sentences. Children in the Think-Listen condition were asked to remember whether they had imagined saying the word or whether they had listened to the girl on the videotape say the word. Children in the Listen-Listen condition were presented with photographs of the two girls on the videotape and asked to point to the girl whom they believed used the word to complete a sentence.

Children with learning disabilities were significantly less accurate than nondisabled children in judging the source of their memories in both the Think-Listen condition and the Listen-Listen condition (see Fig. 5.2). Thus, children with learning disabilities were generally less accurate ($M = 0.79$) than nondisabled children ($M = 0.85$) in judging the source of their memories, $F(1, 67) = 4.23$, $p < .05$. Consistent with the previous findings of Lorsbach et al. (1991), the source discriminations of both learning disabled and nondisabled children were more accurate when source-monitoring judgments required between-class discriminations (Think-Listen) than within-class discriminations. In addition, both groups of children in the Think-Listen condition were more apt to attribute false positives to an external source (Listen) than to an internal source (Think). However, unlike

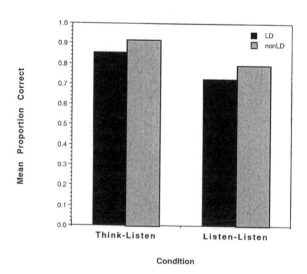

FIG. 5. 2. Judgment of origin performance of learning disabled and nondisabled children for each acquisition condition. (Lorsbach & Ewing, 1995).

the previous research of Lorsbach et al. (1991), the recognition memory performance of learning disabled children was comparable to that of nondisabled children. This dissociation between recognition memory and source monitoring suggests that the verbal source-monitoring difficulties of learning disabled children are not due solely to a more global deficit in memory.

Together, these two studies seem to suggest that children with learning disabilities may be generally impaired in their ability to accurately identify the source of their verbal memories. This general impairment appears to be manifested in difficulty discriminating between verbal memories that originate (a) within the same class of memories—either within self-generated memories (Say–Think) or within externally-derived memories (Listen-Listen), or (b) between classes of self-generated and externally-derived memories (Say–Listen or Think-Listen). This verbal source-monitoring deficit may also be expressed in terms of difficulties discriminating between (a) memory of thoughts from any other class of memories (Say–Think or Think-Listen), and (b) memory of verbalized thoughts from any other class of verbal memories (Say–Think or Say–Listen). Thus, unlike other populations such as nondisabled children (Foley & Johnson, 1985; Foley et al., 1983) and older adults (e.g., Hashtroudi et al., 1989; Schacter, Kaszniak, Kihlstrom, & Valdiserri, 1991) that have been found to be selectively impaired in some forms of source monitoring, children with learning disabilities appear to have a more general deficit with respect to monitoring the source of their verbal memories. Further research is needed to determine the pervasiveness of this deficit.

One other study suggests that the verbal source confusions of learning disabled children may be eliminated when different sources of information are made highly distinctive. In a study that was designed to examine dissociations of implicit and explicit memory in learning disabled and nondisabled children, Lorsbach et al. (1992) tested the effects of input modality upon repetition priming and recognition memory. Twenty-four learning disabled and 24 nondisabled 10-year-olds (fourth graders) participated in this study. The mean Verbal and Performance IQ scores of the children with learning disabilities was, respectively, 96 and 106. The children with learning disabilities were experiencing difficulties in the areas of both reading and mathematics. In addition, these learning disabled children were also manifesting spoken language difficulties. The fact that none of the learning disabled children were attending a self-contained special education classroom suggests that their learning disability might be in the mild-moderate range. The nondisabled participants exhibited average ability in both reading and math. None of the nondisabled children were receiving special education services or involved in programs for the gifted and talented.

Each child was initially presented with a series of stimuli that were presented either as a picture or as a spoken word. During a subsequent old–new recognition task, each child was presented with a series of pictures and asked to name each picture as rapidly as possible and to then decide whether the item had been presented on the preceding study list. In addition, each child was asked to decide if the remembered item had been originally presented as a picture or as a word (i.e., whether they "saw it" or "heard it"). Although the item recognition accuracy was lower in learning disabled than nondisabled children, the two groups did not differ in their memory for input modality. The relatively high performance of both groups suggested that ceiling effects may have been present. Despite being too easy to reveal group differences, the task nevertheless indicated that learning disabled children can differentiate source information if it is made highly salient or distinctive. The analysis of false positives indicated that both groups of children were more likely to attribute false positives to words, as opposed to pictures. This bias might reflect a belief that memories based on pictorial representations are more memorable than those that are based on auditory or verbal representations. Such a belief would be consistent with the common finding of a picture superiority effect where pictures are shown to be more memorable than words (e.g., Paivio & Csapo, 1973; Shepard, 1967).

Interpreting the Verbal Source-Monitoring Deficit of Children With Learning Disabilities Within the Source-Monitoring Framework

According to Johnson et al. (1993), "insofar as different source-monitoring tasks differentially draw on different characteristics of memories ... the pattern of deficits across source-monitoring tasks can help us identify which aspects of memories are not being encoded, reactivated, or weighted properly by populations with various source-monitoring deficits" (p. 7). Several factors may be contributing to the source-monitoring difficulties of learning disabled children. First, the ease and accuracy of source monitoring depends on the amount and quality of information that was initially recorded with a given event (Johnson et al., 1993). Quality here refers to information that is highly "differentiated" (Johnson et al., 1993). Differentiation is distinguished from concepts such as "strength" or "activation level" (Johnson, Kounios, & Reeder, 1994). Memory representations that are highly differentiated contain information that is rich in both perceptual and contextual detail and contain "phenomenal qualities such as color, form, spatial position, and so on" (Johnson et al., 1994). Tasks are presumed to vary in their differentiation requirements (Johnson et al., 1993). Tasks that depend on deliberate and conscious recollection (e.g., some types of source monitoring) require more highly differentiated information than tasks that may be performed with little or no conscious recollection (e.g., priming). Given the well-documented encoding difficulties of learning disabled children (e.g., Ceci, 1983, 1984), a failure to form more elaborate, highly differentiated memory representations may result in a reduction in the amount or the specificity of information that is available to learning disabled children about the source of various memories. The fact that learning disabled children have difficulty monitoring the source of information within sentence processing formats might further suggest that, relative to nondisabled children, the memory records of learning disabled children contain less differentiated information about the sounds of different voices, the contextualized semantic details of words, and the cognitive operations used during original learning (elaborating, retrieving, identifying). On the other hand, if different events are presented that contain unique, distinctive characteristics (e.g., pictures vs. spoken words), then memories are easier to discriminate and source discrimination becomes more accurate for learning disabled children.

The establishment of differentiated memory records is dependent on the use of reflective processes (Johnson, 1983; Johnson & Hirst, 1991; Johnson & Multhaup, 1992; Johnson et al., 1993). Reflective processes represent an important component of the Multiple-Entry Modular (MEM) memory framework (Johnson, 1992; Johnson & Hirst, 1991). Within the MEM framework, there are 16 component processes that are grouped into four functional subsystems, with two subsystems consisting of perceptual processes (P-1: Locating, resolving, extracting, and tracking; P-2: Placing, identifying, examining, and structuring), and two involving reflective processes (R-1: Reactivating, refreshing, shifting, and noting; R-2: Retrieving, rehearsing, initiating, and discovering). The characteristics of a given memory event represent the combined outcomes of both perceptual and reflective processes. Both P-2 and R-2 processes operate on more complex information than those processes used with the P-1 and R-1 subsystems. Thus, P-1 processes (e.g., locating) would be used with relatively undifferentiated information, whereas P-2 processes would be used when processing more differentiated stimulus information. R-1 processes might be devoted to processing activated information, whereas R-2 processes might be allocated to produce a change in a pattern of activation or to form new relationships. The two reflective subsystems (R-1 and R-2) include executive control and monitoring functions that are guided by various agendas. R-1 and R-2 processes generally map onto heuristic and systematic processing, respectively, with R-2 processes being more deliberate and controlled than R-1 processes. Agenda-driven reflective processes presumably affect the binding of central aspects of memory (content) with contextual information. Rehearsal processes may be particularly important for the binding of content with contextual information (Johnson, 1992).

Because both perceptual and reflective processes operate in combination to determine which characteristics of an experience are encoded, it is difficult to identify specific, individual processes that might be responsible for the verbal source-monitoring difficulties that have been observed with learning disabled children. However, given that the verbal source-monitoring tasks that have been used with learning disabled children have required the processing of more complex, differentiated information, it is likely that both P-2 and R-2 processes may be responsible for the lower performance of these children. In addition, it is likely that inefficient or impaired R-2 processes play a particularly important role in the poor verbal source-monitoring performance of these children. This hypothesis is based on Johnson et al.'s (1993) observation that R-2 processes are prototypical of systematic processes, and that systematic processes are more subject to disruption than heuristic processes. In addition, inefficient reflective processes may have a negative impact on the binding of central content information with its surrounding context.

Decision processes may represent another factor that contributes to the source-monitoring problems of learning disabled children. According to Johnson et al. (1993), source monitoring not only depends on the quality of information encoded, but also on the quality of decision-making processes. Johnson et al. (1993) invoke the concepts of "heuristic" and "systematic" to characterize two forms of judgment processes that are often used when making source decisions. By using heuristic judgment processes, some source-monitoring decisions may be made in a spontaneous manner. Heuristic judgments tend to be made rapidly, nondeliberately, and without any conscious awareness of the processes being used in the decision-making process. At other times, however, source-monitoring decisions must be made in a more systematic manner. In this case, judgments are analytic in nature and occur more slowly and with more deliberation than heuristic judgments. For example, when the characteristics of memories from two or more sources are very similar, source-monitoring decisions often require more deliberate judgment processes that evaluate the content of activated memories in relationship to other related memories or existing knowledge. Given that systematic processes are more subject to disruption (Johnson et al., 1993), it is possible that the source-monitoring difficulties of learning disabled children reflect difficulties in the use of more reflective, deliberate decision-making processes.

EXTENDING THE SOURCE-MONITORING FRAMEWORK TO OTHER MEMORY PHENOMENA: EXPLAINING MEMORY DISSOCIATIONS IN CHILDREN WITH LEARNING DISABILITIES

In this section, memory dissociations obtained with learning disabled children are discussed within the context of the source-monitoring framework. According to the source-monitoring framework, memory dissociations occur because differentiated information and decision processes (heuristic and systematic) are used differently in various memory tasks. For example, the facilitation that is displayed during implicit tests of memory (e.g., repetition priming) is presumably based on relatively undifferentiated information. In contrast, the conscious recollection of previously learned information that is required in explicit tests of memory depends on differentiated information and systematic decision processes. Based on the assumption that learning disabled children experience difficulty in the use of those reflective processes that form and utilize differentiated information, their performance may be expected to be impaired when a memory task requires access to differentiated information, but not when a task depends on the use of relatively undifferentiated information.

Dissociations Between Explicit and Implicit Tests of Memory

Explicit tests of memory are represented by tasks where a deliberate and conscious effort is made to bring memory records of past experiences back to mind. Implicit tests of memory, on the other hand, are obtained by asking participants to perform a simple task that makes no explicit reference to an earlier learning episode. Memory for the past is revealed implicitly through some facilitation in the form of greater speed or accuracy that accompanies the processing of old, relative to new, stimulus information.

The comparison of explicit and implicit memory in children with learning disabilities has been performed in three published studies using the preceding definition of learning disabilities. Lorsbach and Worman (1989) used the picture fragment-completion task to examine implicit and explicit memory in children with learning disabilities.

They initially presented children with a random series of pictures depicting exemplars from each of four categories (vehicles, carpenter's tools, animals, and clothing). Memory for the study-list items was tested explicitly (free recall task followed by a cued recall task) and implicitly with a picture fragment-completion task. The implicit memory task was not presented as a memory task, but rather as a "guessing game" in which the child was to simply provide the first word that came to mind when seeing the incomplete pictures. Nondisabled children recalled significantly more pictures than children with learning disabilities on both the free recall task and the cued task. In contrast, there were no group differences when memory was tested implicitly with the picture fragment-completion task.

Lorsbach et al. (1992) used primed picture-naming and item recognition as the implicit and explicit measures of memory, respectively. Learning disabled and nondisabled children initially viewed a series of 64 pictures and listened to the names of 64 common objects. Memory testing consisted of a picture naming and recognition task in which subjects were asked to name each of 64 pictures (32 old and 32 new) as fast as possible, followed by a recognition decision. The magnitude of facilitation associated with primed picture naming was found to be independent of conscious recognition for all subjects. Although the learning disabled children remembered significantly fewer pictures than nondisabled children, the learning disabled children exhibited significantly more priming than nondisabled children.

Finally, Lorsbach and Worman (1990) examined associative memory performance in learning disabled and nondisabled children. Each child was asked to study 16 noun pairs that were each presented in the context of a noun-verb-noun sentence frame (e.g., "The *mouse* hid the *grape*.") The noun pairs were presented randomly on each of two study trials. Each study trial was followed by cued recall task in which the verb served as the cue for the explicit retrieval of the corresponding subject and object noun pair. Memory for previously learned associations was tested implicitly on a separate item-recognition priming procedure that measured the amount of associative priming (McKoon & Ratcliff, 1980). Associative priming occurs when a stimulus is processed faster when it is preceded by an associatively related stimulus, as opposed to an unrelated stimulus. On the item-recognition priming task, each of 64 trials consisted of either a previously studied noun or a new noun. The list was constructed to include prime trials in which nouns from the same pair were presented successively (e.g., mouse, grape) and control trials in which nouns from different noun pairs followed each other. On hearing the noun, subjects were instructed to decide with the highest degree of speed and accuracy whether the noun had been included in the previous study list. Priming was measured by subtracting the response time on prime trials from that obtained on control trials. The priming reflects an implicit form of memory in that subjects are not asked to judge explicitly whether successive nouns were members of the same pair (Howard, 1988). Learning disabled children experienced greater difficulty than nondisabled children when they attempted to explicitly retrieve previously studied associations. However, these difficulties were absent when associative priming was used as an index of associative memory performance. The pattern of these results suggests that learning disabled children had indeed formed new associations, despite their difficulty in consciously bringing them to mind.

Each of the above studies has consistently found that, unlike implicit memory, explicit memory performance is impaired in children with learning disabilities. Because of the conscious and deliberate nature of explicit memory tasks, they rely heavily on reflective activities, such as rehearsing, retrieving, and discovering relationships (Johnson, 1983; Johnson & Hirst, 1991; Johnson et al., 1993). The use of reflective processes contributes to the formation of differentiated information that is critical for successful performance on explicit tests of memory, as well as on source-monitoring tasks. The observed deficits on both explicit tests of memory and source-monitoring tasks suggest that learning disabled children are specifically impaired in those reflective processes that are critical for the formation of differentiated information (e.g., perceptual information, semantic information, cognitive operations). The performance of learning disabled children is unimpaired on implicit tests of memory because performance on such tasks involves the processing of undifferentiated information where reflective processes, such as rehearsing information or initiating search strategies, are not required.

Dissociations Between Source Monitoring and Recognition Memory

Of the three studies that have tested source monitoring in children with learning disabilities, two have found that source monitoring and old–new recognition tasks dissociate the performance of learning disabled and nondisabled children. Lorsbach and Ewing (1995) found that the performance of learning disabled and nondisabled children did not differ on an old–new recognition task, but that the performance of learning disabled children was inferior to that of nondisabled children on a measure of source discrimination. In contrast, Lorsbach et al. (1992) found the opposite results. In this case, although the two populations differed on a measure of recognition memory, they did not differ on a measure of source discrimination. The third study (Lorsbach et al., 1991) did not find a dissociation and found that the performance of learning disabled children was lower than that of nondisabled children on measures of recognition accuracy and source monitoring.

Whether the performance of learning disabled children and nondisabled children is dissociated in a particular experiment may depend on the type of information and the decision processes that are used in the source-monitoring task and the old–new recognition task. According to the source-monitoring framework, source monitoring and recognition memory may draw on the same information and utilize similar decision processes. In a given study, the type of informational input and decision processes that are used in a source discrimination task may be similar or different to an old–new recognition task. In general, however, when compared with old–new recognition tasks, source discrimination tasks tend to rely more on differentiated information and systematic decision processes. Thus, the apparent inconsistencies of the dissociations found in three studies of learning disabled children has to do with the type of memory information and decision processes used in different tasks within a given experiment. With respect to the Lorsbach and Ewing (1995) study, both learning disabled and nondisabled children were comparable in their discrimination of old and new words on the recognition task. However, when making their source decisions, the nondisabled children were able to reflect on their memory records and retrieve yet more information than learning disabled children. Apparently, the opposite was true in the Lorsbach et al. (1992) study. In this case, although the recognition decisions may have required the use of reflective processes, the discriminations on the source-monitoring task were sufficiently easy for both populations to rely on relatively undifferentiated memory information and heuristic decision processes.

ALTERNATE THEORETICAL ACCOUNTS OF DISRUPTED SOURCE MONITORING IN CHILDREN WITH LEARNING DISABILITIES

The source-monitoring difficulties of learning disabled children may also be interpreted within the context of a number of other theoretical memory perspectives. There are two frameworks that are particularly useful in conceptualizing source-monitoring problems of learning disabled children. The first is the Constructive Memory Framework (CMF) of Schacter, Norman, and Koustaal (1998). According to the CMF, encoding processes bind distributed features of an episode together into a "coherent" representation, as well as to separate patterns of similar episodes. The source-monitoring errors that have been observed with learning disabled children may be the result of a failure to bind features of a given memory episode. According to Schacter et al. (1998) a disruption in feature binding may lead one to retrieve fragmentary information from an experience in the absence of any accompanying information about how or when those fragments were acquired. Alternatively, such retrieval processes may be unimpaired in learning disabled children, but source-monitoring difficulties might arise because they initially fail to include sufficient information in the bound representation of the memory episode. Also, poor source monitoring in learning disabled children may occur because they have difficulties with pattern separation processes that would allow them to keep bound memory episodes separate from one another. "If episodes overlap extensively with one another, individuals may recall the general similarities (Hintzman & Curran, 1984) or gist (Reyna & Brainerd, 1995) common to many episodes, but fail to remember distinctive, item-specific information that distinguishes one episode from another" (Schacter et al., 1998, p. 291).

Alternatively, the CMF suggests that the source-monitoring problems of learning disabled children may also be attributed to retrieval problems. Within the CMF, the retrieval of previous experiences involves a process that is referred to as "pattern completion" where "a subset of the features comprising a particular past experience are reactivated, and activation spreads to the rest of the constituent features of that experience" (Schacter et al., 1998, p. 291). The source-monitoring difficulties of learning disabled children may be due to a failure to put forth the necessary effort in reactivating specific features of a prior memory event. Alternatively, specific information may be retrieved, but such information is simply not used.

A second framework that is helpful when interpreting the source-monitoring problem of learning disabled children is fuzzy-trace theory (Reyna & Brainerd, 1995). An overview of fuzzy-trace theory, and a comparison with source-monitoring theory, are presented elsewhere in this volume (see Thierry, Spence, & Memon, this volume), so a detailed discussion will not be presented here. Fuzzy-trace theory makes relatively few assumptions about those factors that might affect memory for source information. First, fuzzy-trace theory is based on the assumption that both verbatim and gist representations of a memory episode are stored separately and in parallel, and may be retrieved independently of one another. Second, verbatim representations are considered to be more fragile than gist representations. Relative to gist representations, verbatim representations are less durable, become inaccessible more rapidly, and are more sensitive to the effects of interference. Experiments that examine memory for source information, such as those that are described previously, typically test memory for verbatim or surface details of a previous memory episode (Reyna & Lloyd, 1997). A failure to remember source information occurs because the verbatim details of an event were not encoded, the verbatim representations were forgotten, or the wrong verbatim detail was retrieved. This suggests that the verbal source-monitoring difficulties of learning disabled children may be due either to a failure to encode surface, verbatim details, or to greater forgetting of verbatim representations that were previously stored in memory.

IMPLICATIONS OF THE SOURCE-MONITORING FRAMEWORK FOR RESEARCH WITH LEARNING DISABLED CHILDREN

First, much of the current discussion has been based on only a few studies that have examined source monitoring in learning disabled children. Obviously, much more research is needed in order to specify the exact nature and extent of these source-monitoring problems. In light of the fact that the memory problems of learning disabled children appear to be limited to the use of verbal information or nonlinguistic materials that may be labeled (e.g., O'Shaughnessy & Swanson, 1998; Vellutino, 1979; Vellutino et al., 1977), it may be that the verbal source-monitoring problems that have been found are restricted to a specific subtype of learning disabilities in which language impairments are observed. Although Foley et al. (1983) and Foley and Johnson (1985) found similar source-monitoring patterns in young children using words and actions, many learning disabled and language- or reading-disabled children experience phonological processing difficulties, and so it is possible that a phonological deficit may play a central role in the verbal source-monitoring difficulties of these children. If some form of language impairment plays a role in source-monitoring difficulties of learning disabled children, source-monitoring problems should be absent when nonverbal materials or activities are used, or when other forms of learning disabilities are examined that do not involve a language disorder. Roberts and Blades (1995) found that very young children showed good source monitoring when given a behavioral test, but did poorly with a verbal test. If children with learning disabilities have a similar cognitive profile to young children (as suggested earlier), this may also add support to the hypothesis for a verbal source-monitoring deficit.

Second, as Johnson et al. (1993, p. 19) have noted, it is important to embed discussions of source monitoring within the context of a specific processing model. Using several alternate theoretical models, a number of hypotheses were generated in this chapter about those cognitive processes that may be responsible for the verbal source-monitoring difficulties of learning disabled children. For example, depending on the theoretical assumptions that are made, the inefficient or impaired processes that underlie the source-monitoring problems of learning disabled children may involve a failure to use reflective processes (MEM framework), a failure to bind or separate the features of various learning episodes (CMF framework), or a failure to process the verbatim details of memory episodes (fuzzy-trace model). The use of these theoretical frameworks will enable investigators to generate hypotheses about specific cognitive mechanisms that are responsible for the disrupted source monitoring in learning disabled children.

Third, the source-monitoring framework is valuable in that it provides a useful way of integrating unrelated research and otherwise disparate findings with learning disabled children. In addition, the source-monitoring framework leads to a number of interesting hypotheses about the cognitive and behavioral tendencies of these children. For example, the finding that children with learning disabilities have difficulty making accurate source decisions has important implications for their ability to oppose the unconscious influences of prior unrelated experiences. As a result of such a source-monitoring deficit, the learning disabled child may, at times, find it impossible to escape the unconscious influences of prior verbal events. For example, in the absence of sufficient source information, language-disabled or learning disabled children might lack awareness of how they have come to know what they know and how prior experiences have influenced their current performance. Consequently, when participating in group discussions in the classroom, language-disabled or learning disabled children might unknowingly repeat the ideas that have been expressed recently by another student (or perhaps even their own ideas) merely because those ideas come to mind easily. As another example, the learning disabled child may accept as true statements that have been presented from an unreliable source. Thus, during a quiz, children with learning disabilities may inadvertently respond with the incorrect solution to a problem that was previously generated by themselves or another student, simply because that solution comes to mind easily.

Finally, although the analysis of source misattributions may be used as a tool for examining related memory difficulties, the systematic study of source-monitoring errors may also be useful in identifying those memory mechanisms that are being used appropriately in certain learning environments. For example, through the careful examination of children's source misattributions, Foley and Ratner recently have obtained valuable information about those mechanisms that children use during a collaborative learning activity (see Ratner, Foley, & Gimpert, this volume). By analyzing source misattributions, Foley and Ratner (e.g., Foley & Ratner, 1998) were able to determine that younger children (4-year-olds) recode the actions of adults as their own during a collaborative activity. Foley and Ratner's approach would be useful in studying how children with learning disabilities learn in a collaborative learning setting. For example, if research determines that learning disabled children recode the actions of others, classroom teachers may want to make a special effort to incorporate collaborative learning activities with these children, and thus harness their source-monitoring behavior toward a productive goal.

REFERENCES

Ackerman, P. T., & Dykman, R. A. (1982). Automatic and effortful information-processing deficits in children with learning and attention disorders. *Topics in Learning & Learning Disabilities, 2,* 12–22.

Baker, J. G., Ceci, S. J., & Herrmann, D. (1987). Semantic structure and processing: Implications for the learning disabled child. In H. L. Swanson (Ed.), *Advances in learning and behavioral disabilities: Memory and learning disabilities: Supplement 2* (pp. 83–109). Greenwich, CT: JAI.

Bauer, R. H. (1977a). Short-term memory in learning disabled and nondisabled children. *Bulletin of the Psychonomic Society, 10,* 128–130.

Bauer, R. H. (1977b). Memory processes in children with learning disabilities: Evidence for deficient rehearsal. *Journal of Experimental Child Psychology, 24,* 415–430.

Bauer, R. H. (1979). Memory, acquisition, and category clustering in learning-disabled children. *Journal of Experimental Child Psychology, 27,* 365–383.

Bauer, R. H. (1987). Control processes as a way of understanding, diagnosing, and remediating learning disabilities. In H. L. Swanson (Ed.), *Advances in learning and behavioral disabilities: Memory and learning disabilities: Supplement 2* (pp. 41–81). Greenwich, CT: JAI.

Bennetto, L., Pennington, B. F., & Rogers, S. J. (1996). Intact and impaired memory functions in autism. *Child Development, 67,* 1816–1835.

Borkowski, J. G., Johnston, M. B., & Reid, M. K. (1987). Metacognition, motivation, and controlled performance. In S. J. Ceci (Ed.), *Handbook of cognitive, social, and neuropsychological aspects of learning disabilities*: Vol. 2 (pp. 147–173). Hillsdale, NJ: Lawrence Erlbaum Associates.

Brainerd, C. J., Kingma, J., & Howe, M. L. (1986). Long-term memory development and learning disability: Storage and retrieval loci of disabled/nondisabled differences. In S. J. Ceci (Ed.), *Handbook of cognitive,* social, and neuropsychological aspects of learning disabilities: Vol. 1 (pp. 161–184). Hillsdale, NJ: Lawrence Erlbaum Associates.

Case, R., Kurland, D. M., & Goldberg, J. (1982). Operational efficiency and the growth of short-term memory span. Journal of Experimental Child Psychology, 33, 386–403.

Ceci, S. J. (1982). Extracting meaning from stimuli: Automatic and purposive processing of the language-based learning disabled. Topics in Learning & Learning Disabilities, 2, 46–53.

Ceci, S. J. (1983). Automatic and purposive semantic processing characteristics of normal and language/learning disabled (L/LD) children. Developmental Psychology, 19, 427–439.

Ceci, S. J. (1984). A developmental study of learning disabilities and memory. Journal of Experimental Psychology, 38, 352–371.

Ceci, S. J., & Baker, J. G. (1987). How shall we conceptualize the language problems of learning disabled children? In S. J. Ceci (Ed.), Handbook of cognitive, social, and neuropsychological aspects of learning disabilities: Vol. 2 (pp. 103–112). Hillsdale, NJ: Lawrence Erlbaum Associates.

Ceci, S. J., Lea, S. E. G., & Ringstrom, M. (1980). Coding characteristics of normal and learning disabled 10-year-olds: Modality-specific pathways to the cognitive system. Journal of Experimental Psychology: Human Learning and Memory, 6, 685–697.

Cooney, J. B., & Swanson, H. L. (1987). Memory and learning disabilities: An overview. In H. L. Swanson (Ed.), Advances in learning and behavioral disabilities: Memory and learning disabilities: Supplement 2 (pp. 2–40). Greenwich, CT: JAI.

Dallago, M. L. L., & Moely, B. E. (1980). Free recall in boys of normal and poor reading levels as a function of task manipulations. Journal of Experimental Child Psychology, 30, 62–78.

Denckla, M. B., & Rudel, R. G. (1976). Rapid "automatized" naming (R.A.N.): Dyslexia differentiated from other learning disabilities. Neuropsychologia, 14, 471–479.

Farrant, A., Blades, M., & Boucher, J. (1998). Source monitoring by children with autism. Journal of Autism and Developmental Disorders, 28, 43–50.

Foley, M. A., & Johnson, M. K. (1985). Confusions between memories for performed and imagined actions: A developmental comparison. Child Development, 56, 1145–1155.

Foley, M. A., Johnson, M. K., & Raye, C. L. (1983). Age-related changes in confusion between memories for thought and memories for speech. Child Development, 54, 51–60.

Foley, M. A., & Ratner, H. H. (1998). Children's recoding in memory for collaboration: A way of learning from others. Cognitive Development, 13, 91–108.

Gelzheiser, L. M. (1984). Generalization from categorical memory tasks to prose by learning disabled adolescents. Journal of Educational Psychology, 76, 1128–1138.

Gordon, B. N., Jens, K. G., Hollings, R., & Watson, T. E. (1994). Remembering activities performed versus those imagined: Implications for testimony of children with mental retardation. Journal of Clinical Child Psychology, 23, 239–248.

Hallahan, D. P., & Kauffman, J. M. (1982). *Exceptional children*. Englewood Cliffs, NJ: Prentice-Hall.

Hallahan, D. P., Kauffman, J. M., & Lloyd, J.W. (1999). *Introduction to learning disabilities*. Boston: Allyn and Bacon.

Hashtroudi, S., Johnson, M. K., & Chrosniak, L. D. (1989). Aging and source monitoring. *Psychology and Aging, 4*, 106–112.

Hintzman, D. L., & Curran, T. (1994). Retrieval dynamics of recognition and frequency judgments: Evidence for separate processes of familiarity and recall. *Journal of Memory and Language, 33*, 1–18.

Howe, M. L., Brainerd, C. J., & Kingma, J. (1984). *Storage-retrieval processes of normal and learning-disabled children: A stages analysis of picture-word effects*. Research Report, Department of Psychology, University of Victoria.

Howard, D. V. (1988). Implicit and explicit assessment of cognitive aging. In M. L. Howe & C. J. Brainerd (Eds.), *Cognitive development in adulthood: Progress in cognitive development research* (pp. 3–37). NY: Springer-Verlag.

Interagency Committee on Learning Disabilities. (1987). *Learning disabilities: A report to the U.S. Congress*. Bethesda, MD: National Institutes of Health.

Jens, K. G., Gordon, B. N., & Shaddock, A. J. (1990). Remembering activities performed versus imagined: A comparison of children with mental retardation and children with normal intelligence. *International Journal of Disability, Development and Education, 37*, 201–213.

Johnson, M. K. (1983). A multiple-entry, modular memory system. In G. H. Bower (Ed.), *The psychology of learning and motivation: Vol. 17* (pp. 81–123). San Diego, CA: Academic Press.

Johnson, M. K. (1992). MEM: Mechanisms of recollection. *Journal of Cognitive Neuroscience, 4*, 268–280.

Johnson, M. K., Hashtroudi, S., & Lindsay, D. S. (1993). Source monitoring. *Psychological Bulletin, 114*, 3–28.

Johnson, M. K., & Hirst, W. (1991). Processing subsystems of memory. In R. G. Lister & H. J. Weingartner (Eds.), *Perspectives on cognitive neuroscience* (pp. 197–217). New York: Oxford University Press.

Johnson, M. K., Kounios, J., & Reeder, J. A. (1994). Time-course studies of reality monitoring and recognition. *Journal of Experimental Psychology: Learning, Memory, and Cognition, 20*, 1409–1419.

Johnson, M. K., & Multhaup, K. S. (1992). Emotion and MEM. In S. A. Christianson (Ed.). *The handbook of emotion and memory: Current research and theory* (pp. 33–66). Hillsdale, NJ: Lawrence Erlbaum Associates.

Johnson, M. K., & Raye, C. L. (1981). Reality monitoring. *Psychological Review, 88*, 67–85.

Kail, R. V., Jr., Hale, C. A., & Leonard, L. B. (1983). *Lexical storage and retrieval in language-impaired children*. Research Report, Department of Psychological Sciences, Purdue University.

Lerner, J. W. (2000). *Learning disabilities: Theories, diagnosis, & teaching strategies*. Boston: Houghton Mifflin.

Lorsbach, T. C., & Ewing, R. H. (1995). Source monitoring in children with learning disabilities. *International Journal of Disability, Development and Education, 42*, 241–257.

Lorsbach, T. C., & Gray, J. W (1985). The development of encoding processes in learning disabled children. *Journal of Learning Disabilities, 18,* 222–227.

Lorsbach, T. C., Melendez, D. M., & Carroll-Maher, A. (1991). Memory for source information in children with learning disabilities. *Learning and Individual Differences, 3,* 135–147.

Lorsbach, T. C., Sodoro, J., & Brown, J. S. (1992). The dissociation of repetition priming and recognition memory in language/learning-disabled children. *Journal of Experimental Child Psychology, 54,* 121–146.

Lorsbach, T. C., & Worman, L. J. (1989). The development of explicit and implicit forms of memory in learning disabled and nondisabled children. *Contemporary Educational Psychology, 14,* 67–76.

Lorsbach, T. C., & Worman, L. J. (1990). Episodic priming in children with learning disabilities. *Contemporary Educational Psychology, 15,* 93–102.

Mann, V. A., & Liberman, I. Y. (1984). Phonological awareness and verbal short-term memory: Can they presage early reading success? *Journal of Learning Disabilities, 17,* 592–598.

Mann, V. A., & Liberman, I. Y., & Shankweiler, D. (1980). Children's memory for sentences and word strings in relation to reading ability. *Memory & Cognition, 8,* 329–335.

McKoon, G., & Ratcliff, R. (1980). Priming in item recognition: The organization of propositions in memory for text. *Journal of Verbal Learning and Verbal Behavior, 19,* 369–386.

National Joint Committee on Learning Disabilities. (1997). Operationalizing the NJCLD definition of learning disabilities for ongoing assessment in schools. *Perspectives: The International Dyslexia Association, 23,* 29–33.

Newman, R. S., & Hagen, J. W. (1981). Memory strategies in children with learning disabilities. *Journal of Applied Developmental Psychology, 1,* 297–312.

O'Shaughnessy, T. E., & Swanson, H. L. (1998). Do immediate memory deficits in students with learning disabilities in reading reflect a developmental lag or deficit? A selective meta-analysis of the literature. *Learning Disability Quarterly, 21,* 123–148.

Paivio, A., & Csapo, K. (1973). Picture superiority in free recall: Imagery or dual coding? *Cognitive Psychology, 5,* 176–206.

PL 105–17 (1997). The Individuals with Disabilities Education Act of 1997.

Ratner, H. H., Foley, M. A., & Gimpert, N. (this volume). Person perspectives on children's memory and learning: What do source-monitoring failures reveal? In K.P. Roberts & M. Blades (Eds.), Children's source monitoring. Mahwah, NJ: Lawrence Erlbaum Associates.

Reyna, V. F., & Brainerd, C. J. (1995). Fuzzy-trace theory: An interim synthesis. *Learning and Individual Differences, 7,* 1–75.

Reyna, V. F., & Lloyd, F. (1997). Theories of false memory in children and adults. *Learning and Individual Differences, 9,* 95–124.

Roberts, K. P., & Blades, M. (1995). Children's discrimination of memories for actual and pretend actions in a hiding place. *British Journal of Developmental Psychology, 13,* 321–333.

Schacter, D. L., Kaszniak, A. W., Kihlstrom, J. F., & Valdiserri, M. (1991). The relation between source memory and aging. *Psychology and Aging, 6*, 559–568.

Schacter, D. L., Norman, K. A., & Koutstaal, W. (1998). The cognitive neuroscience of constructive memory. *Annual Review of Psychology, 49*, 289–318.

PL 105–17 (1997). The Individuals with Disabilities Education Act of 1997.

Shepard, R. N. (1967). Recognition memory for words, sentences, and pictures. *Journal of Verbal Learning and Verbal Behavior, 6*, 156–163.

Spring, C., & Capps, C. (1974). Encoding speed, rehearsal, and probed recall in dyslexic boys. *Journal of Educational Psychology, 66*, 780–786.

Sternberg, R. J., & Wagner, R. K. (1982). Automatization failure in learning disabilities. *Topics in Learning & Learning Disabilities, 2*, 1–11.

Stone, C.A., & Conca, L. (1993). The origin of strategy deficits in children with learning disabilities: A social constructivist perspective. In L. J. Meltzer (Ed.), *Strategy assessment and instruction for students with learning disabilities* (pp. 23–59). Austin, TX: Pro-ed.

Swanson, H. L., & Cooney, J. B. (1991). Learning disabilities and memory. In B. Y. L. Wong (Ed.), *Learning about learning disabilities* (pp. 104–127). NY: Academic Press.

Swanson, H. L., & Cooney, J. B. (1996). Learning disabilities and memory. In D. D. Reid, W. P. Hresko, & H. L. Swanson (Eds.), *Cognitive approaches to learning disabilities* (pp. 287–314). Austin, TX: pro-ed.

Swanson, H. L., Cooney, J. B., & O'Shaughnessy, T. E. (1998). Learning disabilities and memory. In B. Y. L. Wong (Ed.), *Learning about learning disabilities* (pp. 107–162). NY: Academic Press.

Tallal, P. Galaburda, A. M., Llinas, R. R., & von Euler, C. (1993). Temporal information processing in the nervous system: Special reference to dyslexia and dysphasia. *Annals of the New York Academy of Science, 682*, ix.

Tarver, S. G., Hallahan, D. P., Kauffman, J. M., & Ball, D. W. (1976). Verbal rehearsal and selective attention in children with learning disabilities: A developmental lag. *Journal of Experimental Child Psychology, 22*, 375–385.

Torgesen, J. K. (1975). Problems and prospects in the study of learning disabilities. In E. M. Hetherington (Ed.), *Review of Child Development Research: Vol. 5* (pp. 385–440). Chicago: University of Chicago Press.

Torgesen, J. K. (1977). The role of nonspecific factors in the task performance of learning disabled children: A theoretical assessment. *Journal of Learning Disabilities, 10*, 27–34.

Torgesen, J. K., & Houck, D. G. (1980). Processing deficiencies in children who perform poorly on the digit span test. *Journal of Educational Psychology, 72*, 141–160.

Torgesen, J. K., Murphy, H. A., & Ivey, C. (1979). The effects of orienting task on the memory performance of reading disabled children. *Journal of Learning Disabilities, 12*, 396–401.

U.S. Department of Education. (1998). *To assure the free appropriate public education of all children with disabilities.* Twentieth Annual report to Congress on the Implementation of the Individuals with Disabilities Education Act. Washington, DC: U.S. Government Printing Office.

Vellutino, F. R., Steger, J. A., Moyer, B. M., Harding, S. C., & Niles, C. J. (1977). Has the perceptual deficit hypothesis led us astray? *Journal of Learning Disabilities, 10,* 54–64.

Wong, B., Wong, R., & Foth, D. (1977). Recall and clustering and verbal materials among normal and poor readers. *Bulletin of the Psychonomic Society, 10,* 375–378.

Wong, B. Y. L. (1991). The relevance of metacognition to learning disabilities. In B. Y. L. Wong (Ed.), *Learning about learning disabilities* (pp. 231–258). NY: Academic Press.

6

Discriminating Between Memories of Television and Real Life

Kim P. Roberts
*National Institute of Child Health
and Human Development*
Mark Blades
University of Sheffield, UK

Children learn about the world from many different sources including peers, books, personal experiences, parents, teachers, or other adults. On many occasions, the information provided by these sources is useful or entertaining for children. On other occasions, however, the information may be fictitious (see chaps. 7, 8, and 10, this volume), incomplete (chap. 4, this volume), or ambiguous (chap. 3, this volume). It is clearly important to know how exposure to multiple sources of information can affect children's knowledge of, and consequently their behavior in, the world in which they live. If children can integrate information gleaned from multiple, credible sources, then they can effectively build up a coherent knowledge base. When children are exposed to inaccurate, inconsistent, or incoherent information, however, their resulting knowledge base may be quite different. One way that children would be protected from such "contamination" is if they can judge the credibility of the source that provided the information and discount information from those that are noncredible, and interested readers are referred to the research discussed by Robinson (chap. 3, this volume) and Welch-Ross (chap. 9, this volume) on this issue.

In contrast to the research on the potential contamination of memory of an actual, real-life event with fictitious or incomplete information, the focus of this chapter is on children's discriminations of different events that have actually occurred. One way in which children's knowledge or memories can be protected is through being able to accurately distinguish between memories from the different sources that provided the information. This is necessary even when children can competently judge the credibility of a source. If a child knows that everything that Aunt Val says is accurate, and everything that Uncle David says is inaccurate, memories and beliefs can still be contaminated if the child cannot later distinguish which of the two speakers provided the information. It is this latter process, that of *source monitoring* (Johnson, Hashtroudi, & Lindsay, 1993), that is the focus of this chapter.

In the preceding list of potential sources to which children are exposed, we failed to mention one source (although the chapter title gives it away) that has a dominant presence in most children's lives—television. In the U.S., children spend an estimated 3 to 4 hours watching television each day, with approximately 25% of children watching from 4 to 11 hours daily (Jason & Hanaway, 1997). One researcher has suggested that "most children spend more time engaged in television viewing than in any other single activity besides school" (Van Evra, 1998, p.181). The prevalence of television in children's lives means that it is one of their major sources of information, education, and entertainment (see Clifford, Gunter, & McAleer, 1995; Gunter & McAleer, 1997). Many commentators have voiced concern over children's exposure to television because of the alleged poor quality of much of the available programming. For example, Jason and Hanaway (1997) argued that children's knowledge of the world sometimes comes from distorted information such as that embodied in the race and gender stereotypes that are often portrayed on television. It is obviously of practical importance, then, to understand what happens to the information that children are exposed to through television. Can children distinguish memories of information presented in a television program from memories from other sources of information?

Investigating children's memories of televised and real-life events also offers a useful paradigm for understanding how children's memories of complex, real-life events are modified by exposure to other sources. Children who confuse memories of what they have actually experienced and memories of other events may encounter difficulties interacting with others, for example, when sharing memories with caregivers (Hudson, 1990b). In situations where the child is an eyewitness, it is important to know whether the information they report is based on memory of an actual live event or whether the information has been provided by some other source such as a suggestive interviewer

(Ceci, Huffman, Smith, & Loftus, 1994a; Ceci, Loftus, Leichtman, & Bruck, 1994b; chap. 8, this volume), or a peer. Sometimes social workers and law enforcement personnel suspect sexual abuse has occurred when a child has a degree of sexual knowledge unusual for their age. One way in which children could glean such information is from television, and so it is useful to examine whether children are likely to confuse memories of incidents viewed on television with real life occurrences and report the televised events as if they were witnessed in real life. Investigating source monitoring for televised and real-life events, therefore, is of practical importance for our understanding of children's source monitoring for complex events.

As well as practical significance, investigations of source monitoring for televised and live events has important theoretical contributions to make. As discussed earlier (chap. 2, this volume), one way in which people carry out source-monitoring decisions is by examining the characteristics of their memories and making an attribution about the source of those memories based on knowledge of which characteristics are typical of certain kinds of memories (see Johnson et al., 1993). For example, a memory of an actually perceived event will contain perceptual and contextual details from the time of the event, whereas a memory of an imagined event will not contain the same perceptual information (because the event was not, in fact, perceived) but will contain details of the cognitive operations information that took place at the time of the event (e.g., imagery, search, generation). Memories of television and real-life events, however, are particularly intriguing with regard to examining the characteristics of memories. Although not derived from experienced, actual, real-life events, memories of television are likely to contain details typical of actually perceived events such as perceptual information like colors and sounds. In addition, as children and adults view television events, they are likely to encode the same kinds of affective reactions that real-life events may elicit. This means that memories of real-life may be more likely to be confused with memories of television than they would with, say, memories of information gleaned through print (books, newspapers, etc.). Accurate source monitoring for memories of real life versus televised events, therefore, must rely on decision making using other types of comparisons. In the remainder of this chapter, we present some results from our ongoing program of research to illustrate some of the factors that may affect those comparisons.

The methodology we have developed is portable and can be used with a wide range of ages. We can easily manipulate a variety of important variables using this method. From the work we have conducted thus far, we are beginning to understand that the deceptively simple question "Do children confuse memories of television and real life?" does not have a yes or no answer. Rather, we have found that, in accordance with source-monitoring theory (Johnson et al., 1993), the types of cues that are available for children to use in their source-monitoring decisions greatly influence the extent to which children confuse their memories. When memories of television and real-life contain similar characteristics, children sometimes have difficulty knowing which details were viewed in which events. This chapter demonstrates some of the factors that affect the similarity of memory characteristics, including the degree of involvement in the events, the time interval between presentation of the events, and the gist of the events. We describe how these variables affect the cues available to children and, hence, how they affect their source monitoring. We also show that our perception of children's abilities is affected by the measures used to examine children's source monitoring. These findings are of particular significance when applied to children's education and eyewitness performance, two fields with a strong focus on extracting information from children.

THE PARADIGM

In our studies, we investigate whether children confuse memories of events they have seen on television with memories of events they have witnessed in real life. In these studies, children watch a live staged event, and (on another occasion) a video of an event that is related to the live event. The videos include "formal features," which are special effects unique to television (e.g., zooming in, panning across the screen, scene changes) to ensure that they have the same format as everyday television. The children are later questioned to see whether they confuse memories of the two events. Children are questioned about one event at a time, although the questioning is identical for each event. A variety of questioning techniques can be used, such as free recall, so that the child chooses what information to report (e.g., "Tell me everything that happened"), focused questions that probe more specific details such as colors, specific actions, and verbalizations (e.g., "What color was her dress?"), yes/no questions (e.g., "She broke the plate, didn't she?") or misleading questions, in which inaccurate information is suggested to have been present during the event.

Using variations of this procedure, we have investigated source monitoring by children aged 4 through 10 years. By changing aspects of the events, the interview, or the procedure (such as the time delay between viewing the two events), we are beginning to construct a picture of how television can affect children's knowledge and event memory. We now turn to the research to demonstrate what factors affect children's source monitoring for real-life and televised events.

THE CONTENT OF THE EVENTS

Lindsay, Johnson, and Kwon (1991) showed that children find source monitoring difficult when the sources are similar. In one experiment, children listened to two speakers who said a list of words out loud. When the speakers were of the same gender, the children were more confused as to who said which word than when the speakers were of different genders. In another experiment, children who watched two stories on two separate videos were more confused when the story items were common than unique to the two videos.

Lindsay et al.'s experiments showed that children were most likely to confuse memories of words and acts when the sources were similar (e.g., female voices). It is not clear, however, whether we can generalize these results to memories of complex events that are richer, more detailed, and contextually embedded in children's everyday lives. To explore this issue, we investigated children's source monitoring using complex events that varied in the degree of similarity between them.

Are Children Confused Between Memories of Similar, Complex Events?

To compare children's source monitoring for complex events that were similar to each other with children's source monitoring for events that were different from each other, 4- and 10-year-olds individually watched two 12-minute events—a live staged event, and a video of an event (Roberts & Blades, 1999, Experiment 1). As research on source monitoring has some relevance for reports by eyewitnesses (see Ceci et al., 1994b; Lindsay & Johnson, 1989; Roberts, 1996), the events were chosen so that we could ask questions about activities that might be probed in an investigation of sexual abuse, for example, instances of touching, dressing and undressing, and taking photographs. All children watched a live, staged event called "Children's Hospital" and an experimenter dressed as a nurse looked after a baby doll with an injured leg. The experimenter removed the doll's clothing to see where she was injured, saw that the doll's knee was bleeding, washed the knee, gave the doll an injection in her knee, bandaged it, replaced the doll's clothing, and put the doll to bed. Half of the participants (similar condition) also watched a similar film called "Birthday Party" that involved the same experimenter preparing a girl (mannequin) to go to a party. The events in the similar film were carefully matched to parallel those of the live event, for example, the mannequin was undressed, her hands and face were washed (to parallel washing the doll's knee in the live event), she was dressed again, and her ears were pierced with a needle (to parallel the injection in the doll's knee in the live event). The remaining participants (different condition) saw a film that was dissimilar to the live event called "Baking Cakes" and involved the same experimenter who was disguised (e.g., wearing a wig that was a different color to her natural hair color) and who baked some cakes with the help of a girl (mannequin). The events were different from the live event, but were chosen so that the same questions could be asked in the interview, for example, washing the kitchen utensils used to make the cakes (in contrast to washing parts of a doll in the live event and similar video), and the doll crying because she touched the hot mixing bowl (in contrast to the doll crying because of the pain from the needle, as viewed in the live event and similar video).

Each participant watched the live event and the (similar or different) video individually in a room with the experimenter with a delay of two days between presentation of the events. The order in which the events were viewed was counterbalanced in each condition. A week after viewing the second event, each participant was individually interviewed about both of the events. The same interview script was used for both events, but memory for each event was probed separately, such that the child was asked all of the questions about one event, and then the same questions would be asked about the other event. The order in which the events were probed was also counterbalanced.

We first probed the children's memory of the events using free recall prompts (e.g., "Tell me everything that happened on the television," followed by an "Anything else?" prompt). Each detail recalled was coded as *accurate* (if it actually happened in the event being probed), *inaccurate* (if the description was distorted), or *source confusion* (if the item occurred in the event *not* being probed). For example, in the live event, the adult washed the doll's leg; in the similar film, the adult washed the doll's face. If the participant said "he washed her face" when describing the live event, this would be coded as two accurate items (*washed, her*), one inaccurate item (*he*) as there was no male present in the live event, and one source confusion (*face*) because the adult washed the doll's face in the similar film and not in the live event.

Although the actual differences between conditions were small (possibly because children are generally accurate at free recall tasks [e.g., Dent & Stephenson, 1979; Goodman & Reed, 1986]), we found that the children in the similar condition made slightly more source confusions than those in the different condition (Means = 1.06, 0.10, respectively; $p < .05$). As described later in the chapter, this was replicated with a group of same-age children in a subsequent experiment using the same events (Roberts & Blades, 1999, Experiment 2). In this experiment, we again found that children were most confused when they had watched events that were similar to each other (Means = 0.93, 0.16, for the source confusions made in the similar and different conditions, respectively; $p < .05$).

After the free recall probes, we also asked a set of 20 focused questions like "What did I wash?" and "Where was the needle?" When children freely recall memories of events, they are free to choose which information to report. It is likely, therefore, that they report the information that is most salient to them and that they are most confident occurred. When they are probed for specific information, however, they are under more pressure to provide the interviewer with an answer. It is possible, then, that children may relax their source-monitoring criterion in this instance so that they can provide the adult with an answer to their question and consequently do not check the source of that information as stringently. For example, if they are asked "What did I break [in the live event]?" and they remember that in one of the events the confederate broke a plate, they may report this without attributing memory of this detail to the video event from which it came. If this is the case, then children should make more source confusions in response to direct questions than in response to open-ended, free recall prompts that do not pressure the child. When we analyzed the accuracy of the responses to the focused questions, there was a clear difference: Children in the similar condition imported details from the video event into their reports of the live event more than twice as many times as did those in the different condition (Means = 3.16, 1.45, respectively; $p < .02$). The increased confusion of children in the similar condition compared to those in the different condition was clearly more evident when children were pressured to provide specific details.

In summary, children who watched similar events were more confused between the events when memory was later probed than children who had watched events that were different from each other. A small effect was seen in the freely recalled reports, but the source confusions were more prevalent in response to the direct questions.

Increasing the Similarity of Events

In the studies described previously, we varied the similarity of events by manipulating particular details within the event, such as colors, people, and actions, but the events differed in their context (e.g., one was set in a hospital, and one in a kitchen) and overall gist (e.g., one involved giving medical treatment, and one involved getting ready for a party). We went on to investigate children's source monitoring for televised and real-life events that were similar on many more dimensions (Roberts & Blades, 1998). In this experiment, 4- , 6-, and 9-year-old children watched two events—one live and one televised—in which an experimenter made a puppet. There were small differences between the live event and the video, for example, the puppet was called "Joe" and wore green clothes in the live event, and was called "Daisy" and wore red clothes in the video event, but the action sequences, verbalizations, temporal organization, actor, gist, and so on, were identical. The events were viewed the day after each other and the children were interviewed a week later about what happened in the live event.

This time, when the events were virtually identical, there was a greater prevalence of source-monitoring errors in the children's free recall than in the two previous experiments. In the first two experiments, on average, 4–5% of the information in the free recall reports from the 4-year-olds and 2% of those from the 10-year-olds in the similar condition were made up of source confusions; in the puppet study, 8%, 5%, and 9% of the information in the reports of the 4-, 6-, and 9-year-olds were source confusions. Although most researchers of children's source monitoring report a developmental *decrease* in source-monitoring errors (e.g., Foley, Harris, & Hermann, 1994; Foley & Johnson, 1985; Foley, Johnson, & Raye, 1983; Lindsay et al., 1991; Roberts & Blades, 1995), we found that the highest number of spontaneous source confusions came from the older children. One reason for this unusual finding could be the type of measurement chosen—none of the source-monitoring studies cited previously elicited a free narrative of a complex event as a measure of source monitoring as we did in this study. It has been shown repeatedly that the amount of information reported in free recall increases with age (Gee & Pipe, 1995; Goodman & Reed, 1986; Marin, Holmes, Guth, & Kovac, 1979; Rudy & Goodman, 1991), and as the 9-year-olds in this study also reported more of each type of information (accurate, inaccurate, source confusion), we calculated proportional scores (e.g., number of source confusions divided by the total amount of details reported), but there were no age differences in the source confusion proportions. In other words, when the amount of information was held constant, the rate of source confusions was equivalent across age groups. We recommend that researchers use a variety of measures to gain a more complete picture of children's source confusions.

Although it is well established that young children have difficulty distinguishing between events that are highly similar in structure and gist (e.g., Farrar & Goodman, 1990; Price & Goodman, 1990), or actual and fictitious events that have been suggested to them (e.g., Ackil & Zaragoza, 1995; Ceci et al., 1994a, 1994b; Poole & Lindsay, 1995), our results suggest that memories of two actually perceived, similar events can be confused after mere exposure to those events, in the absence of suggestive influences, when presented in different media, and even when they have different gist. The results confirm that the effects of similarity found by Lindsay et al. (1991) using lists of words and actions can be replicated in experiments with more complex events, and the effect extends to events that may differ in their gist and context.

When the results of the three experiments reported in Roberts and Blades (1998, 1999) are considered together, it is clear that the degree of confusion between the events is proportional to the degree of similarity between them. When the events were very similar along a number of dimensions (gist, actor, actions, etc.) as in the puppet study (Roberts & Blades, 1998), we saw more confusion than when just the context and gist of the events were different (Roberts & Blades, 1999). It is important to be able to systematically understand what constitutes "similarity" of sources. Further research could shed light on this issue by varying the similarity of different types of information (e.g., context, actors, story lines) and determining the probability that children spontaneously confuse the sources when the similarity is varied along different dimensions. Clearly, the more similar the events, the more confusion is to be expected. Extending this further, we believe that any factor that makes memory characteristics less distinctive will have an adverse effect on children's source monitoring.

INVOLVEMENT IN THE EVENTS

There are several reasons why it is important to investigate how the degree of involvement with the events children experience affects their source monitoring for those events. In some eyewitness situations, children are passive bystanders, such as when they witness a traffic accident. In other cases, such as sexual abuse, they are more actively involved in the events and are forced to interact with the perpetrator(s). A basic Piagetian principle is that children learn through their direct interaction with the environment (Piaget, 1952/1936) and educators have long preferred using methods of instruction that actively involve the child, suggesting that the degree of learning is proportional to the degree of interaction by the child (see Ratner, Foley, & Gimpert, this volume, for an analysis of source monitoring in a collaborative learning context). Finally, with the growing popularity of interactive technology such as video games, computer games, and the Internet, there is public concern that children may be more susceptible to confusing the boundaries of fantasy and reality (Jason & Hanaway, 1997; Van Evra, 1998). One way in which this potential confusion may be mediated is through confusion regarding where information was obtained—in real life or via electronic media.

Theoretically, it is important to investigate this question because of how the degree of involvement can affect the quality of the memories retained (see section "Interaction with the Sources", chap. 2, this volume). It was discussed earlier that comparing the characteristics of memories of televised and real-life events is interesting because television contains some of the same information that is processed during a real-life experience (e.g., perceptual and affective information). In some real-life experiences, children may be actively involved, and so memories of these events may also contain kinesthetic cues, visible consequences, and goal-related information (see Ratner et al., this volume, for a more extended discussion of the goal-related nature of activities) that may later be used for source monitoring. Foley, Aman, and Gutch (1987) asked children to trace pictures with a finger, a pencil, or a stylus (pencil without lead). When later asked to say which tool they had used to draw each picture, Foley et al. found that the children were most accurate when distinguishing whether they had a used a finger versus a pencil. They concluded that the kinesthetic feedback and the visible consequences of using the pencil aided discrimination when compared with tools that provided little kinesthetic feedback (i.e., a finger) and no visible consequences (i.e., the stylus). When distinguishing between memories of real-life events in which they have been actively involved and television events that they have merely watched, children may use the kinesthetic feedback and visible consequences from their involvement in real-life events when source monitoring. If, however, children interact with television and other electronic media, then kinesthetic cues and visible consequences cease to be unique to real-life events, thus leaving fewer criteria that can be used to distinguish the events and, consequently, resulting in later source confusions.

Few researchers have investigated how interaction affects memory for *multiple* events, although Murachver, Pipe, Gordon, Owens, and Fivush (1996; repeated experience condition) found that children who interacted in an event three times produced more organized and accurate reports than those who had heard a story three times. The TV–real-life methodology that we have developed enables us to explore the effects of interaction on memory for specific details of the events, as well as to look at potential source confusions after interacting with video events.

In the study reported by Roberts and Blades (1998) and mentioned previously, we also explored how interacting in the video affected children's memory and source monitoring for the live event. All children interacted in the live event in which the experimenter made a puppet. Half of the children also interacted in a video version of the live event (interactive condition), and half watched the video version without interacting (watch condition). The children were asked to interact on 14 occasions by pointing to items, answering questions about items, and pretending to perform some actions. The interactions from the live event were also used in the video in the interactive condition. For example, after putting the hair on the puppet, the confederate in the video said to the children, "Can you say what color the puppet's hair is?" and the camera would then focus on the puppet's head for three seconds (i.e., the children were interacting with the video and not with a live person). In the video in the watch condition, all 14 instructions from the female experimenter were edited out so that (apart from the video being three minutes shorter because of the editing) the children watched exactly the same film as children in the interactive condition, thus controlling exposure to stimulus materials.

Although we argued that interacting in both the live and video events may be detrimental to source monitoring because the kinesthetic and cognitive characteristics of memories of those events may be similar, there are several reasons why interacting may improve memory, and this may enhance source monitoring. Rudy and Goodman (1991) found that interacting in a single event improved memory for that event and argued that this was because the interaction increased attention, reliance on self-schemas, level of arousal, and made the event more interesting. Also, children can benefit from the effects of context reinstatement (Geiselman, 1988) and mental rehearsal (Keeney, Canizzo, & Flavell, 1967) each time they experience an event. In the present study, if the memory traces are strong and contain a substantial amount of information, the children are likely to have access to more cues that can be used to make an accurate source attribution. Children in the interactive condition, therefore, may pay more attention to the events, and physically and mentally reinstate context during the second event so that they more readily rehearse the first event, leading to improved memory and source monitoring.

We found that, when asked 16 nonmisleading questions about the live event (e.g., "What color was the puppet's hair?"), children in the interactive group responded with more source confusions (i.e., claiming that a detail from the video occurred in the live event) than did children in the watch condition (Means = 3.87, 3.13, respectively, $p <$ .05). Accurate source monitoring was reduced, therefore, when distinguishing between memories of two events in which the children had been actively involved, and this did not interact with age. In contrast to these results, Parker (1995) found that interacting improved source monitoring for some children. In her study, 5- to 6-year-olds and 9- to 10-year-olds interacted in short vignettes with a confederate. Parker found that the older, and not the younger, children were more accurate at distinguishing between actions that they had actually carried out versus actions that they had only imagined performing. There are two reasons why the present pattern of results may differ from Parker's results. First, the events used in the current study each comprised a complex sequence of actions directed at the end goal of making a puppet. The children's actions did not affect the puppet-making goal, but the children were aware of the end goal. Although the vignettes in Parker's (1995) study individually contained a more interconnected sequence than early investigations of source monitoring (e.g., Foley & Johnson, 1985), the goal of the whole exercise may not have been apparent to the children. Ratner et al. (chap. 4, this volume) show how the goal-related nature of tasks and children's planning processes affect source-monitoring accuracy in important ways. Specifically, they have shown that children can anticipate and plan actions in a goal-directed sequence and, although this appears to benefit learning from the activity, this decreases the accuracy of source monitoring. In the present study, then, children would have found it quite easy to plan and anticipate the sequence of events in the puppet-making activity because they experienced the same event on multiple occasions. Indeed, this was the pattern of results because even the youngest children showed the same decrease in source-monitoring accuracy as the older children, consistent with Ratner and Foley's studies. Second, Parker (1995) found that interaction benefitted source monitoring only for the imagined, and not the performed, actions. In the present study, all of the interactions comprised actually performed actions (saying, pointing, etc.) and so this may also account for the difference in results.

As children who interacted in our study were more confused between the live and video events than those who did not interact with the video, we argued that it was not merely the amount of cues that were available for source-monitoring decisions, but the differences in cues that enhanced source judgments (see Suengas & Johnson, 1988). Although children in the interactive condition probably had more cues to use in making source attributions (e.g., kinesthetic cues, cognitive operations) than did children in the watch condition, source monitoring may have suffered because the cues in each memory were not qualitatively distinct for each event. A prediction that follows from this is that accurate source monitoring is possible even with decayed memories, provided that the qualitative difference in cues in individual memories is sufficient to enable a distinction between memories of different events. The effects of similarity seen in our first two studies, therefore, extends to the kinesthetic and cognitive cues in memories.

Another possibility for why the children in the interactive condition were more confused between the events than children in the watch condition is related to another type of cue that children may use when making source judgments, particularly regarding video events. Producers signal salient aspects of television programs through the use of "formal features," such as scene changes, zooms, and pans (Van Evra, 1998). These formal features are unique to television and can signal that the event is staged. The children who interacted with the video may have made more source confusions because the engagement of self in the video activities reduced their attention to peripheral aspects of the video, such as the formal features. Possibly, the children who interacted in the video did not encode the formal features, and thus they were not available for use as cues in their later source monitoring, thereby leading to confusion between the video and the real-life event. It is difficult to research how the encoding of "formal features" affects source monitoring because the inclusion of "formal features" makes the event more interesting, provides a strategy for the regulation of attention, and aids comprehension (Van Evra, 1998) thus creating a confound between the presence of formal features and attention to the event.

PRESENTATION INTERVALS

So far we have shown that source monitoring is adversely affected when the characteristics of those memories are similar. Specifically, we showed that when the content of two events are similar, or when cues laid down from physical and cognitive involvement in the events are similar, children can become confused between televised and real-life events. It is likely, then, that children can also become confused when other characteristics that are used in source judgments are similar. One other characteristic that can differ between memories and, hence, be used in source-monitoring judgments, is temporal information associated with individual events, and so in our final section we show how the amount of time between presentation of the events affects memory and source monitoring.

Memory may be more accurate if two events are viewed shortly after each other because of rehearsal (Keeney et al., 1967), "consolidation" (Poole & White, 1993), "redintegration" (Brainerd, Reyna, Howe, & Kingma, 1990), and strengthening of the memory trace (Pezdel & Roe, 1995) of the original event. For example, if a child sees an action carried out in the first event performed in the second event, it may remind them of the first event leading them to review their memory of that event. Accordingly, we might expect that this reinstatement effect is stronger for children who view similar than dissimilar events because there will be more overlap between features of both events and, hence, more opportunity for rehearsal and reactivation of memory of the original event.

As shown in Roberts and Blades' (1998) study, however, the amount or strength of information in memory may not be as important as the qualitative differences in those memories during source monitoring. If events are presented with a long interval between them, this temporal information can later be used as a source-specifying cue. Therefore, we would predict that children who watch two events shortly after each other will be more confused than children who watch those events with a longer delay between them. If events are presented close together, however, then the temporal information that is associated with them may not be distinctive enough to enable an accurate source comparison based on temporal information alone. This may not matter when memories for the events contain other characteristics that differ between the events such as dissimilar content (see Powell & Thomson, 1997), and it is more likely anyway that multiple criteria are jointly considered when making source discriminations (Suengas & Johnson, 1988). Source discriminations between events viewed close together are likely to be more difficult in situations where other source-specifying cues are not available, such as when children watch two similar events. We would predict, then, that children who view similar events shortly after each other will be more confused than children who view dissimilar events shortly after each other.

In the first study we described in the section "The Content of the Events" (Roberts & Blades, 1999, Experiment 1), we compared memories and source monitoring for similar versus dissimilar events. Recall that children aged 4 and 10 years watched a live event ("Children's Hospital") and either a video that was similar ("Birthday Party") or different ("Baking Cakes") to the live event. There was a gap of two days between presentation of the events in this study. In our replication (Roberts & Blades, 1999, Experiment 2), we shortened the delay to just one day and, as the same procedure and free recall prompts were used in both experiments, we were able to directly compare the children's reports to see what effects presentation interval had on the children's reports. We expected that the children who viewed the events a day after each other (short delay condition; Roberts & Blades, Experiment 2) would be more inaccurate and report more source confusions than those who viewed the second event two days after the first (long delay condition; Roberts & Blades, Experiment 1).

In terms of memory for the events, children in the short delay condition reported more inaccurate details (distorted or new items than were not in either event) than children in the long delay condition (Means = 2.00, 0.67, respectively, p = .05). As reports from children in the long delay condition were longer than reports from children in the short delay condition, we calculated the proportion of information that was recalled that was accurate and found that children in the long delay group remained more accurate than those who had viewed the events a day after each other (long delay, 96% accurate; short delay, 91% accurate, p < .05), after controlling for the amount of information reported. There was no difference, however, in the number of source confusions made by children in the different delay conditions, regardless of the degree of similarity between the events they viewed. In other words, there seemed to be a global, negative effect of viewing the events shortly after one another because reports were overall less accurate than when there was a longer delay between presentation of the events.

There may have been no effect of delay on source confusions because the intervals chosen were not sufficiently different to show an effect. Also, recall that earlier we showed how source confusions were more prevalent in response to direct, focused prompts than to free recall measures. It could be that the children were confused but that the free recall measures were not sensitive enough to illuminate the source confusions. It is interesting to note, however, that a similar, global effect was reported in a recent study using free recall, direct prompts, and suggestive questions. Roberts, Lamb, and Sternberg (1999) staged an event with preschoolers and exposed them to a misleading postevent narrative a day or a month after the event. When interviewed five weeks after the event, there was no difference between the conditions in the number of times that the misleading details were incorporated into the reports of the event, although children who heard the misleading information soon after the event reported fewer accurate details than those in the longer delay group. It seems, then, that when memories for the events are difficult to distinguish, for example, when they are presented close together in time and therefore lack distinctive temporal information, the accuracy of children's memory suffers, even if children do not specifically confuse details from the two events.

ALTERNATIVE THEORETICAL INTERPRETATIONS

Schema-based models have been used to explain why children confuse memories of different events (Nelson, 1986). As children become more familiar with an event, they form a general event representation that helps to organize their memory of the events, and increases the amount of information that they recall. This process sometimes leads to increased confusion of details from the separate occurrences (Hudson, 1990a; Fivush, Kuebli, & Clubb, 1992) because as the common features are abstracted, it becomes more difficult to remember an individual occurrence. In the present studies, therefore, the children who made source misattributions may have been confused because they formed a schema of typical events (e.g., making the puppet), making it difficult to retrieve specific instantiations of the details. It is difficult to interpret the results of Studies 1 and 2 according to schema theory, however. The events used in the similar and different conditions did not resemble each other as closely as the types of events used in schema development research (e.g., Farrar & Goodman, 1990; Price & Goodman, 1990) because, although there were parallels between the items and actions, even the similar events differed in gist and context. It is unlikely, therefore, that a single script was developed for the events used in the present studies, although previous scripts (e.g., a baking script) may have been instantiated. It is possible that the children began to form a script of "what happens when [the experimenter] visits" but each visit was quite different (the experimenter carrying out a staged event vs. watching television with the child). It is more likely that the degree of confusion in these first two studies was related to the degree of similarity between the events such that the greater the number of dimensions on which the events were similar (e.g., gist, structure, actions, sequence), the more confusion there was between memories of the events.

According to fuzzy-trace theory (e.g., Brainerd et al., 1990), some confusions can result from processing the gist of the events rather than focusing on an examination of the verbatim details that differ across events (Reyna, 1995). In a series of experiments on children's story recall, more source errors were made when children engaged in gist-based reasoning than when they focused on memory for the verbatim details of the story (Ackerman, 1992, 1995). Although fuzzy-trace theory can succinctly explain the age differences we found in our studies (see Roberts & Blades, 1999), it provides a less parsimonious account of the other effects we reported. The events used in the first two studies differed with regard to gist, and so in this situation, accessing the gist representations of the events would probably have been informative for source attributions, at least for those in the different condition. Also, when the verbatim details were cued in the focused questions, and, hence, when accurate source discrimination was optimized, between 15 and 20% of the questions were responded to with a source error. Some of these errors may have occurred because the wrong verbatim representation was retrieved (Reyna, 1995), for example, retrieving a detail from the live event when talking about the video, but fuzzy-trace theory at present is not clear on what factors would influence which detail was retrieved. These studies were not designed, however, to distinguish between source monitoring and fuzzy-trace accounts of source confusions, and interested readers are referred to Thierry et al.'s chapter (this volume) for a more thorough, theoretical comparison.

CONCLUSIONS

We have shown that in certain circumstances, children can confuse memories of real-life and televised events that they have witnessed. This is clearly a concern if children are exposed to information through television programs that give an inaccurate or distorted view of the world. It may be no surprise that television can greatly influence children's knowledge about the world, but the work we have described specifies one mechanism through which this can happen. Specifically, if children cannot attribute their knowledge and memories to the actual source from which it came, then they can report information acquired through watching television programs as if they had actually seen it happen in a real-life event. The present experiments do not shed light on the important question of whether children are more likely to misattribute a detail viewed on television to a memory of a real-life event, or vice versa, because the content of the events was not counterbalanced across medium.

We can conclude that factors that increase the similarity of the characteristics in memories of televised and actual events will lead to greater confusion, and we identified several such factors. Lindsay et al. (1991) argued that children are more confused when the events to be remembered and their sources are similar, and we did find that when the events were similar in content, the children were more confused than when they watched events that were less similar. The results of the present research program show, however, that it is not only similarity of the events themselves that leads to confusion. We also demonstrated negative effects on memory and source monitoring when other dimensions of similarity were manipulated, specifically, how much the child participated in the events and when they were presented. Even though some of these factors, such as increased attention because of their involvement in the events, may have actually improved memory, if that information is not later distinctive (e.g., if the child has been equally involved in two events) some source confusions are to be expected. It is likely that there are other ways in which the similarity of the viewing experience, memories of the events, and consequently the characteristics available when later source monitoring, affect children's knowledge in the world. The results reported in this chapter demonstrate that source monitoring is more accurate with the availability of distinctive cues (Johnson et al., 1993), any factor that makes the characteristics of memories of two events similar will adversely affect source monitoring. Furthermore, as children may use more than one characteristic in conjunction when source monitoring (e.g., kinesthetic cues, perceptual information, cognitive information), the greater the number of dimensions that share similar characteristics, the greater the number of expected source confusions.

Our results have implications for several applied areas. With regard to education, it is clear that children can incorporate information from television programs into their knowledge of real life, and this may be beneficial when children are exposed to high-quality educational programming. Attention to television is schema driven (Huston & Wright, 1998), and so relevant information can be incorporated into a child's developing knowledge base. It may even be that, as suggested by Ratner et al. (this volume), children who make more source-monitoring errors stand to gain most from learning interactions. In their studies, Ratner and Foley have found that children who confused self-performed actions with those performed by an adult during a collaborative learning exercise, showed greater recall and superior organization of their knowledge than children who did not make source-monitoring errors. Applied to our television research, if a child confuses what they learn from television with what they learn in the traditional classroom, they may integrate and synthesize that knowledge more effectively than if they did not confuse the two sources (if in a collaborative context). On the other hand, negative outcomes are to be expected when children are exposed to distorted versions of reality in television programs, for example, when only white, middle-class males are portrayed in positions of authority or there is an exaggeration of the number of individuals from ethnic minorities who are portrayed as criminals. Even if children recognize that television programs distort reality, they may still come to believe that all people from a particular ethnic group really are criminals if they mistakenly believe that they learned this information in real life from a more credible source, such as a school teacher.

Second, these results have some implications for investigative interviewing. Obviously, the events, situations, and dynamics of the experiments reported here were very different from the kinds of personal and situational factors that may affect children who are interviewed by police and other authorities. Extreme caution must be taken before generalizing to these situations, and readers are referred elsewhere for examples of the use of source-monitoring research to study reports of actual sexual abuse allegations (see Roberts, Lamb, Zale, & Randall, 1998). With these limitations in mind, we believe that there are two important findings that can be applied to the real world of criminal investigations in which children may be witnesses. Confusing memories of television and real life is one way in which children's eyewitness reports may be contaminated (for other contaminating influences, see chaps. 8, 9, and 10, this volume). In some situations, it may be helpful for investigators to explore whether any information reported by children could have been gleaned from television programs, and to make an effort to corroborate the details in the child's account. This is also an issue in those situations in which sexual abuse is suspected because the child has displayed knowledge of sexual acts, and this knowledge is believed to be unusual in someone of their age; it may be possible that some of this information was learned through television instead of, or in addition to, a real-life experience. The second finding of relevance concerns the level of source confusions observed with our different measures. In all of our studies, we have found that the number of source confusions made in response to open-ended recall questions was low and always less than that seen when children were more thoroughly probed to provide specific details of the events. This is consistent with other research (see chap. 3, this volume). That the number was low does not, of course, mean that there are no serious consequences of confusions reported in response to free recall prompts—ten confusions about details peripheral to the investigation may be less harmful than one confusion in which an innocent bystander is accused of being the perpetrator. Nevertheless, the finding remains that the chances of the children reporting details imported from memories of events other than the incident under investigation is greatly reduced when open-ended probes are used. Furthermore, when children were successfully misled that what happened in one event happened in the other (e.g., that a detail from the live event was included in the video when it was actually absent), they gave accurate reports when they were subsequently given the opportunity to freely recall the events (Roberts, Zale, Sirrine, Marein-Efron, & Dunne, 1999). As suggested earlier, one possible explanation for the differences in the number of source confusions focuses on the motivation to adopt strict criteria for source monitoring coupled with confidence of the source of that memory. Specifically, in situations of free recall probing, children may report information that they are confident occurred in the target event; when they are pressured to answer a specific probe, however, they may adopt a "familiarity criterion" (Johnson et al., 1993) and report information that is familiar without a thorough examination of its source.

In summary, children may incidentally confuse memories of details viewed on television with memories of real-life events. The extent of this confusion is dependent on factors that increase or decrease the similarity of the characteristics of memories of those events and the measures used to assess source monitoring. Specifically, we have shown that the content of the events and the level of participation across the events can increase source confusions if these factors are constant across viewing. If the events are presented close together, children's reports are also more inaccurate. When memories contain distinctive information, children are not coerced to report one event in favor of the other, and children are allowed to spontaneously report what they remember, the number of source confusions evidenced will be few. We have cautiously argued that these results have implications for both education and forensic investigations, although there is a need for further research with greater ecological validity in this area (e.g., Quas et al., this volume; Roberts et al., 1998).

REFERENCES

Ackerman, B. P. (1992). The sources of children's source errors in judging causal inferences. *Journal of Experimental Child Psychology, 54*, 90-119.

Ackerman, B. P. (1995). Fuzzy-trace theory: A grand theory. *Learning and Individual Differences, 7*, 77-81.

Ackil, J. K., & Zaragoza, M. S. (1995). Developmental differences in eyewitness suggestibility and memory for source. *Journal of Experimental Child Psychology, 60*, 57-83.

Brainerd, C. J., Reyna, V. F., Howe, M. L., & Kingma, J. (1990). The development of forgetting and reminiscence. *Monographs of the Society for Research in Child Development, 55*, 1–111.

Ceci, S. J., Huffman, M. L. C., Smith, E., & Loftus, E. F. (1994a). Repeatedly thinking about a non-event: Source misattributions among preschoolers. *Consciousness and Cognition, 3*, 388–407.

Ceci, S. J., Loftus, E. F., Leichtman, M. D., & Bruck, M. (1994b). The possible role of source misattributions in the creation of false beliefs among preschoolers. *International Journal of Clinical and Experimental Hypnosis, 42*, 304–320.

Clifford, B. R., Gunter, B., & McAleer, J. L. (1995). *Television and children: Programme, evaluation, comprehension and impact.* Mahwah, NJ: Lawrence Erlbaum Associates.

Dent, H. R., & Stephenson, G. M. (1979). An experimental study of the effectiveness of different techniques of questioning child witnesses. *British Journal of Social and Clinical Psychology, 18*, 41–51.

Farrar, M. J., & Goodman, G. S. (1990). Developmental differences in the relation between scripts and episodic memory: Do they exist? In R. Fivush &

J. A. Hudson (Eds.). *Knowing and remembering in young children* (pp. 30–64). New York: Cambridge University Press.

Fivush, R., Kuebli, J., & Clubb, P. A. (1992). The structure of events and event representations: A developmental analysis. *Child Development, 63,* 188–201.

Foley, M. A., Aman, C., & Gutch, D. (1987). Discriminating between action memories: Children's use of kinesthetic cues and visible consequences. *Journal of Experimental Child Psychology, 44,* 335–347.

Foley, M. A., Harris, J. F., & Hermann, S. (1994). Developmental comparisons of the ability to discriminate between memories of symbolic play enactments. *Developmental Psychology, 30,* 206–217.

Foley, M. A., & Johnson, M. K. (1985). Confusions between memories for performed and imagined actions: A developmental comparison. *Child Development, 56,* 1145–1155.

Foley, M. A., Johnson, M. K., & Raye, C. L. (1983). Age-related changes in confusion between memories for thoughts and memories for speech. *Child Development, 54,* 51–60.

Gee, S., & Pipe, M. (1995). Helping children to remember: The influence of object cues on children' accounts of a real event. *Developmental Psychology, 31,* 746–758.

Geiselman, R. E. (1988). Improving eyewitness memory through mental reinstatement of context. In G. M. Davies & D. M. Thomson (Eds.), *Memory in context: Context in memory* (pp. 245–266. Great Britain: Wiley.

Goodman, G. S., & Reed, R. S. (1986). Age differences in eyewitness testimony. *Law and Human Behavior, 10,* 317–332.

Gunter, B., & McAleer, J. L. (1997). *Children and television.* London: Routledge.

Hudson, J. A. (1990a). Constructive processing in children's event memory. *Developmental Psychology, 26,* 180–187.

Hudson, J. A. (1990b). The emergence of autobiographical memory in mother-child conversation. In Fivush & J. A. Hudson (Eds.), *Knowing and remembering in young children* (pp. 166–196) Cambridge: Cambridge University Press.

Huston, A. C., & Wright, J. C. (1998). Mass media and children's development. In I. E. Sigel, & A. Renninger (Eds.). *Child psychology in practice* (pp. 999–1058). New York: Wiley.

Jason, L. A., Hanaway, L. K. (1997). *Remote control: A sensible approach to kids, TV, and the new electronic media.* Sarasota, FL: Professional Resource Press.

Johnson, M. K., Hashtroudi, S., & Lindsay, D. S. (1993). Source monitoring. *Psychological Bulletin, 114* 3–28.

Keeney, T. J., Canizzo, S. R., & Flavell, J. H. (1967). Spontaneous and induced verbal rehearsal in a recall task. *Child Development, 38,* 953–966.

Lindsay, D. S., & Johnson, M. K. (1989). The eyewitness suggestibility effect and memory for source. *Memory and Cognition, 17,* 349–358.

Lindsay, D. S., Johnson, M. K., & Kwon, P. (1991). Developmental changes in memory source monitoring. *Journal of Experimental Child Psychology, 52,* 297–318.

Marin, B. V., Holmes, D. L., Guth, M., & Kovac, P. (1979). The potential of children as eyewitnesses. *Law and Human Behavior, 3,* 295–306.

Murachver, T., Pipe, M. E., Gordon, R., Owens, J. L., & Fivush, R. (1996). Do, show and tell: Children's event memories acquired through direct experience, observation, and stories. *Child Development, 67*, 3029–3044.

Nelson, K. (1986). *Event knowledge: Structure and function in development*. Hillsdale, NJ: Lawrence Erlbaum Associates.

Parker, J. F. (1995). Age differences in source monitoring of performed and imagined actions on immediate and delayed tests. *Journal of Experimental Child Psychology, 60*, 84–101.

Pezdek, K., & Roe, C. (1995). The effect of memory trace strength on suggestibility. *Journal of Experimental Child Psychology, 60*, 116–128.

Piaget (1952/1936). *The origins of intelligence in children*. New York: International Universities Press.

Poole, D. A., & Lindsay, D. S. (1995). Interviewing preschoolers: Effects of nonsuggestive techniques, parental coaching, and leading questions on reports of nonexperienced events. *Journal of Experimental Child Psychology, 60*, 129–154.

Poole, D. A., & White, L. T. (1993). Two years later: Effects of question repetition and retention interval on the eyewitness testimony of children and adults. *Developmental Psychology, 29*, 844–853.

Powell, M. B., & Thomson, D. M. (1997). Contrasting memory for temporal-source and memory for content in children's discrimination of repeated events. *Applied Cognitive Psychology, 11*, 339–360.

Price, D. W. W., & Goodman, G. (1990). Visiting the wizard: Children's memory for a recurring event. *Child Development, 61*, 664–680.

Reyna, V. F. (1995). Interference effects in memory and reasoning: A fuzzy trace theory analysis. In F. N. Dempster & C. J. Brainerd (Eds.), *Interference and inhibition in cognition*, (pp. 29–59). San Diego, CA: Academic Press.

Roberts, K. P. (1996). How research on source monitoring can inform cognitive interview techniques: Commentary on Memon and Stevenage (1996). *Psycoloquy. 7* (44) witness-memory.15.roberts.

Roberts, K. P., & Blades, M. (1995). Children's discrimination of memories for actual and pretend actions in a hiding task. *British Journal of Developmental Psychology, 13*, 321–333.

Roberts, K. P., & Blades, M. (1998). The effects of interacting with events on children's eyewitness memory and source monitoring. *Applied Cognitive Psychology, 12*, 489–503.

Roberts, K. P., & Blades, M. (1999). Children's memory and source monitoring for real-life and television events. *Journal of Applied Developmental Psychology, 20*,575–596.

Roberts, K. P., Lamb, M. E., Zale, J. L. & Randall, D. W. (1998, March). Qualitative differences in children's accounts of confirmed and unconfirmed incidents of sexual abuse. In A Crossman & M. Scullin (1998), Chairs. *Avenues for assessing the reliability of children's statements: A panoply of approaches*. Symposium presented at the biennial meeting of the American Psychology-Law Society of the American Psychological Association, Redondo Beach, CA.

Roberts, K. P., Lamb, M. E., & Sternberg, K. J. (1999). Effects of the timing of postevent information on preschoolers' memories of an event. *Applied Cognitive Psychology, 13*, 541–559.

Roberts, K. P., Zale, J. L., Sirrine, N., Marein-Efron, G., & Dunne, J. E. (1999, April). The effects of focused questions on children's spontaneous recall. In M. K. Welch-Ross, & L. Fasig, Chairs. *Moderators of suggestibility and eyewitness memory in young children*. Symposium presented at the biennial meeting of the Society for Research in Child Development, Albuquerque, NM.

Rudy, L., & Goodman, G. S. (1991). Effects of participation on children's reports: Implications for children's testimony. *Developmental Psychology, 27*, 527–538.

Suengas, A. G. & Johnson, M. K. (1988). Qualitative effects of rehearsal on memories for perceived and imagined complex events. *Journal of Experimental Psychology: General, 117*, 377–389.

Van Evra, J. P. (1998). *Television and child development* (2nd Ed.). Mahwah, NJ: Lawrence Erlbaum Associates.

7

A Comparison Between Fuzzy-Trace Theory and Source-Monitoring Theory: Evidence From an Eyewitness Suggestibility Study

Karen L. Thierry
Melanie J. Spence
University of Texas at Dallas
Amina Memon
University of Aberdeen, Scotland

In this chapter, we compare fuzzy-trace theory and source-monitoring theory, two approaches that have posited mechanisms explaining the role of source information for memory tasks. Fuzzy-trace theory proposes a memory system consisting of two kinds of representations: Gist and verbatim. We discuss how fuzzy-trace theory explains source confusions by way of interactions thought to occur between gist and verbatim representations. In doing so, ways that fuzzy-trace theory differs from the source-monitoring framework are highlighted and discussed. General findings from the eyewitness suggestibility literature, as well as a specific study, are used as a base from which to discuss differences between the two theories.

OVERVIEW OF FUZZY-TRACE THEORY AND SOURCE-MONITORING THEORY

Fuzzy-trace theory (Brainerd & Reyna, 1990; Reyna & Brainerd, 1995) differs from the source-monitoring framework (Johnson,

Hashtroudi, & Lindsay, 1993) regarding how one accesses source information from memory. As previously discussed (Roberts, & Blades, this volume), the source-monitoring framework asserts that source is attributed through a decision-making process. One way that people attribute source involves an examination of the qualitative characteristics of activated memories (Johnson et al., 1993). For example, one might "correctly attribute a memory of a conversation to imagination on the basis of knowledge that one is not acquainted with that person" (Johnson et al., 1993, p. 4). In addition to the quality of memory characteristics, source-monitoring judgments are also influenced by such factors as metamemory and one's current goals and agendas (Johnson et al., 1993). In terms of metamemory, one's knowledge that experienced events are accompanied by clear memories with rich perceptual detail will prevent one from accepting imagined memories (which are not as clear and perceptually rich) as something that was actually experienced. Additionally, source-monitoring judgments may involve more effortful strategic processes, depending on the goal or agenda when reporting an event. For example, in formal situations, such as testifying in court, one may reflect seriously on memories before making source attributions. In less formal situations, such as social gatherings with friends, less deliberate processes may be used when making source attributions.

Fuzzy-trace theory, on the other hand, asserts that source information is laid down as an actual representation in memory, which can be directly accessed when this information is cued. Specifically, source is considered a type of "verbatim" trace or a "well-defined, ornate representation that preserves the content of recently encoded data with exactitude" (Brainerd & Reyna, 1990, p. 9). Verbatim representations are distinct from a second kind of memory representation discussed by Brainerd and Reyna (1990), that of "gist" or "fuzzy" representations. Gist or fuzzy traces are "vague, degenerate representations that conserve only the sense or pattern of recently encoded data" (Brainerd & Reyna, 1990, p. 9). Developmentally, persons of all ages tend to process gist or fuzzy traces more readily than verbatim traces. However, gist processing develops slowly and is not refined until early adulthood (Reyna & Brainerd, 1995). Verbatim memory, on the other hand, develops quickly and is completed by early school age (Reyna & Brainerd, 1995).

A primary tenet of fuzzy-trace theory is that gist and verbatim representations are independent (Brainerd & Gordon, 1994; Reyna & Kiernan, 1994; Titcomb & Reyna, 1995). That is, gist and verbatim traces are stored in parallel, and depending on such factors as the type of question used to probe a gist or verbatim representation and the delay between encoding of gist or verbatim traces and testing, either representation can be accessed at any point in time. However, verbatim traces decay at a faster rate than gist traces (Reyna & Brainerd, 1995) and may no longer be accessible after a delay. In terms of delay, for example, people are "more likely to rely on verbatim representations immediately after original information is presented, but shift to gist after a delay" (Titcomb & Reyna, 1995, p. 285).

FUZZY-TRACE THEORY AND EYEWITNESS SUGGESTIBILITY STUDIES

Fuzzy-trace theory makes certain predictions concerning the accuracy of children's and adults' memory for a witnessed event, particularly when they are asked suggestive questions that mislead them about what actually occurred in the event. These predictions are based on interference processes thought to occur between verbatim and gist representations. As previously mentioned, gist and verbatim traces are laid down in parallel and are considered to be independent of each other (Brainerd & Gordon, 1994; Reyna & Kiernan, 1994; Titcomb & Reyna, 1995); however, it is possible that one kind of trace may interfere with the other. One type of interference process is gist interference with verbatim memory (Titcomb & Reyna, 1995). Both children and adults should be relatively accurate in response to misleading questions immediately after witnessing an event because they should be relying on their accessible verbatim representations of the event. After a delay, however, they should rely on gist representations, because the verbatim representations will have decayed. If they are relying on gist, such representations may be consistent with the information presented in misleading questions. For example, in the standard misinformation paradigm (Loftus, 1979), subjects witness an original event, such as observing someone steal a screwdriver. After the original event, they are presented with misinformation concerning aspects of the event, such as an inaccurate description of the tool as a wrench. At delayed testing, subjects may have accurate memories that a tool of some sort was associated with the original event, but may not remember what kind of tool was actually presented in the original event. Errors at delayed recognition testing could occur if subjects accept "wrench" as the tool presented in the original event (Titcomb & Reyna, 1995). In this instance, subjects may be remembering aspects of events that were merely suggested to them in a previous interview session and may subsequently accept the misleading information as accurate. Unrefined gist thereby interferes with retrieval of less accessible verbatim representations of the original event.

Source-monitoring theory would explain the misinformation effect as a failure to accurately identify the source of the misleading information; subjects misattribute the suggested information as something that was present in the original event. Had subjects sufficiently evaluated the characteristics of their memories of the suggested information, they might have realized that these memories (e.g., that a wrench was stolen) lacked perceptual information associated with actually seeing a "wrench" stolen. They might then realize that a wrench was something they must have only heard about and further realize that a screwdriver was actually stolen, remembering information about the color or form of the screwdriver. According to source-monitoring theory, such a decision-making process should lead subjects to choose the correct item.

Fuzzy-trace theory and the source-monitoring approach differ, then, in their conceptualization of how "source" information is derived. The source-monitoring framework asserts that the discrimination of source involves an attributional process based on qualitative characteristics of memories of an experienced event as well as memories of suggested information, or by using heuristic devices. According to fuzzy-trace theory, however, because source information is laid down as a verbatim trace, this attributional process is not needed. Source can be directly accessed, if these verbatim traces are still well integrated in memory. If not, gist representations may be used to answer questions regarding an event, which, as previously discussed, can result in incorrect responses.

Developmental Differences in Source Memory

Fuzzy-trace theory asserts that younger children are less likely than older children and adults to dissociate gist from verbatim memory, especially at delayed testing (Reyna, 1995). This assertion can account for study results indicating that younger children produce more source errors than older children and adults. For example, Ackil and Zaragoza (1995) found that 6-year-olds, as compared with 10-year-olds and adults, were more likely to claim seeing suggested information in a witnessed event. In addition, the source errors produced by 6-, 8-, and 10-year-olds increased significantly at a one-week delayed source-monitoring test as compared with an immediate source-monitoring test. Poole and Lindsay (1995) also found that 4-year-olds were inaccurate on a source-monitoring test in which they were required to distinguish an experienced event from events only suggested to have occurred. Fuzzy-trace theory asserts that children's poorer source memory may be specifically due to gist interference with verbatim memory. At delayed testing, especially, young children may only access their gist representations of the event and may fail to access verbatim source information. Accessing source information could prevent reporting of misinformation (Reyna, 1995).

Developmental Differences in Two Eyewitness Suggestibility Paradigms: A Gist Interference With Verbatim Memory Explanation

In explaining children's suggestibility due to gist–verbatim interference, two lines of eyewitness research are illustrative. In one line of research, the misinformation paradigm, children view an original event and are later presented with misinformation concerning what happened in the event. This misinformation can consist of distracters of items or actions that did not occur in the target event. For example, Ceci, Ross, and Toglia (1987) asked 3- to 4-, 5- to 6-, 7- to 9-, and 10- to 12-year-olds to observe a target event. They were then told information about certain items, or distracters, that never occurred in the target event, for example, that the girl ate "eggs" for breakfast, whereas in the actual story, the girl ate cereal. Results from such studies revealed that at delayed testing, the 3- and 4-year-olds more often erroneously recognized the misinformation as something that actually occurred in the original event, as compared with the older children and adults. This effect can be described as a failure to consider or access verbatim source information. At delayed testing, children may remember the gist of the event, for example, that a breakfast food of some sort was eaten, but may not remember the specific kind of food eaten. When presented with misinformation (e.g., eggs) which may be familiar due to recency, subjects may accept this item as correct because it is consistent with their gist representation of the event. Had they remembered that "eggs" was only suggested by the interviewer (source information), then they might produce fewer incorrect responses.

In a second line of research investigating eyewitness suggestibility, children watch events presented from two actual sources—live and on video. They are then asked questions that mislead them about details that occurred live and on video (see Roberts & Blades, this volume, for a full outline of the methodology). For instance, in Roberts and Blades' (1996) study, 4-, 10-year-olds, and adults watched a live and a videotaped event. The children and adults then answered misleading questions concerning the events such as, "Did I (female experimenter) eat a rice krispie cake in real life?" when, in fact, the female experimenter ate a sandwich in real life and a rice krispie cake on video. This type of question can be thought of as a misleading-detail question because certain details of one event are suggested to have occurred in another event. Roberts and Blades (1996) found that the 4-year-olds produced more incorrect responses to these misleading-detail questions than the 10-year-olds and adults. There was no difference between the number of incorrect responses produced by the 10-year-olds and adults. Again, this finding may be a result of developmental differences in the failure or inability to access source information and a tendency to rely on gist representations of events. Children may remember that the experimenter ate something in both events, but may fail to remember specific source information, that is, that the experimenter ate a sandwich in the live event and a rice krispie cake on the video.

PURPOSE OF THIS STUDY

If the disintegration of children's verbatim representations for source are responsible for the preceding findings concerning suggestibility, then a manipulation designed to prevent this disintegration of source may decrease children's suggestibility. As Reyna and Lloyd assert (1997), "explicit source monitoring could improve memory performance because it provides retrieval cues from verbatim memories, and allows subjects to redintegrate original event information with source information (i.e., to re-integrate verbatim memories), or both" (p. 116). In the present study, therefore, we tested whether a group of children who received repeated rehearsal of source information would display a reduction in suggestibility (i.e., produce fewer incorrect responses to misleading questions) as compared with a control group of children that did not receive source rehearsal but only yes–no recognition questions.

Source-monitoring theory also predicts that paying attention to source reduces confusion (Lindsay, 1990; Lindsay & Johnson, 1989; Zaragoza & Koshmider, 1989). For example, Lindsay and Johnson (1989) found that adults who received a source-monitoring test, in which they were required to discriminate witnessed events from events only heard about, produced fewer source misattributions than a group of adults administered only a yes–no recognition test, in which they were required to indicate simply whether or not a given item occurred in the witnessed event.

Overview

We investigated children's susceptibility to misinformation from the following sources: (a) information seen in real life versus information seen on a video (similar to Roberts & Blades, 1996, 1998, in press) and (b) information seen in target events versus information only suggested to have occurred (similar to Ceci et al., 1987). In order to investigate developmental differences in the effectiveness of directing children's attention to source as a way to decrease suggestibility, two age groups participated: 3- to 4- and 5- to 6-year-olds (Thierry, Spence, & Memon, 1999). After witnessing live and video events, half of the children in each age group received source questions concerning the events and half received recognition questions. Immediately afterward, all children were asked two types of misleading questions: 1) misleading detail and 2) misleading distracter. One week later, children were again administered source or recognition questions according to their condition at the immediate interview, followed by the same set of misleading questions. Seventy-five children participated in the study. There were thirty-nine 3- to 4-year-old children (17 females, 22 males), with a mean age of 4.37 years ($SD = 0.42$), and thirty-six 5- to 6-year-olds (16 females, 20 males), with a mean age of 5.61 years ($SD = 0.38$). Children in each age group were randomly assigned to either the source-directed or the control condition described as follows.

The target events consisted of science demonstrations (Wilkes, 1990) performed by "Mrs. Science" (similar to Poole & Lindsay, 1995). One event was a live demonstration of three experiments, such as floating or sinking objects in a glass jar and charging balloons with static electricity. A second event consisted of another set of three similar science demonstrations performed again by the same Mrs. Science, but on a video, which the children viewed immediately after the live demonstration. The type of presentation of each set of events was counterbalanced so that the events seen live by half the children were seen on video by the other half of the children. Additionally, the order of presentation of live and video events was counterbalanced across children.

Children were randomly assigned to one of two groups. These groups were defined as a function of the type of questions presented to the children during the first phase of the interview. One group, the source-directed (SD) group, was asked a set of 20 questions that required them to distinguish where (i.e., live, on video, or not at all) they saw Mrs. Science performing the named experiment. The second group, the control group, was asked a set of 20 yes or no recognition questions. Two randomized orders of the SD and recognition questions were constructed, and question order was counterbalanced.

The second phase of the interview, which was administered immediately after the first phase (SD or recognition questions), consisted of misleading questions, which all subjects received. Children were ad-

ministered the first and second phases of the interview at an immediate and 1-week delay.

Procedure

Groups of 3 to 4 children were escorted by Mrs. Science to a quiet
room in the school and presented with the live or videotaped demonstrations. Immediately following this activity, the children then viewed
the other set of experiments, presented via the alternate medium.
Children observed the video and live demonstrations in the same
room.

Immediate Interview

Phase 1: Source or Recognition Questions.   Following the filler activity, the first phase of the interview began (see Table 7.1 for summary
of experimental manipulations). Each child was questioned individually by the second experimenter and asked either source questions
(source-directed condition) or recognition questions (control condition) that did not cue the child to the source of the previously observed
target events. The source test consisted of 20 questions about target
experiments as well as distracter items about experiments that never
occurred (including the same distracter items mentioned in misleading-distracter questions). Pilot testing revealed that children had difficulty remembering the different response options (live, video, not at
all). As a result, children were shown three pictures that corresponded to the three response options. One picture was a snapshot of
"Mrs. Science." Children were instructed to point to this picture if the

TABLE 7.1
Summary of Experimental Manipulations

Condition	Target Events	Interview Session	
		Phase 1**	Phase 2
Source-directed	Live/Video	Source questions	Misleading questions
Control	Live/Video	Yes/no Recognition questions	Misleading questions

Note. Interview Session administered immediately and 1 week after target events.
**Phase 1 constitutes only difference between treatment of source-directed and control
groups.

experimenter named an item that Mrs. Science did "in real life." A second picture was a snapshot of the television on which the video experiments were viewed. Children pointed to this picture if the experimenter named an item that Mrs. Science did on TV (or video). The third picture was used to depict distracter items that Mrs. Science did not do at all. This picture was essentially a snapshot of white light, representing the idea that the distracter item was "nothing" Mrs. Science had done. For example, one question was "Where did Mrs. Science tap a spoon on glass bottles?" and children pointed to the picture indicating whether this happened live, on video, or not at all. An example of a question about a distracter experiment was "Where did Mrs. Science make a volcano?"

The control group received 20 yes or no recognition questions. At the start of questioning for this group, the children were simply reminded that Mrs. Science had performed experiments in real life and on video. Like the source-directed group, they were shown the pictures corresponding to the real-life and video events. However, unlike the source-directed group, the control group was not instructed to point to the pictures when answering the recognition questions. Children simply answered the questions with yes or no or gestured by nodding their head for "yes" or shaking their head for "no." The content of these recognition questions was identical to the source questions, except the control group only had to reply whether or not they saw Mrs. Science performing the named experiment, for example, "Did Mrs. Science tap a spoon on glass bottles?" and "Did Mrs. Science make a volcano?"

Phase 2: Misleading Questions. After receiving source or recognition questions (Phase 1), the child was accompanied to another room in the school where a third experimenter, also not present during the target event, administered the second phase of the interview—the misleading questions. All children were asked a set of 10 misleading questions concerning the target events. Before asking the misleading questions, the third experimenter warned children in both groups that some of the information in the questions might be incorrect. They were encouraged to inform the experimenter of any incorrect information in the questions. In addition, the experimenter gave all children the option of saying "don't know" in response to the misleading questions.

The misleading questions consisted of a set of 10 prescribed questions read by the experimenter to the child. There were two types of misleading questions. One type consisted of six *misleading-detail* questions. These questions misled children about details that occurred in individual live and video experiments. For example, one question asked "Mrs. Science made songs using glass bottles filled with colored water. What did Mrs. Science do when she dropped a key chain into the bottles of colored water?" In fact, Mrs. Science did "make songs using glass bottles filled with colored water." However, she did not drop a key chain into the bottles. A key chain was dropped into a jar in the "floaters and sinkers" experiment, which was shown to them via the source (e.g., video) that differed from the source of the bottles and songs experiment (e.g., live). "Key chain" is therefore the misleading detail. The second type of misleading questions consisted of four *misleading-distracter* questions. These questions probed children about distracter items, included within the source–recognition tests, performed in neither the live nor video experiments. For example, one question asked, "How did Mrs. Science make a volcano?" when, in fact, a volcano was never made. The order of misleading questions was randomized, resulting in two versions of the questions. One-half of the children in each condition received Version 1, and one-half received Version 2. All interview sessions were audiotaped.

Delayed Interview

After a 1-week delay, the children were again tested at the school by the second and third experimenters who had questioned the children at the immediate test. The children underwent the identical memory testing procedure used in the immediate session. The second experimenter told each child that she wanted to see how much the child could remember about the live and video events observed a week ago, and then immediately administered the source–recognition questions. The third experimenter also told each child that she wanted to see how much the child could remember about the live and video events observed a week ago, and then administered the misleading questions. As in the immediate session, all children were again warned that some information in the questions might be incorrect. Children were also reminded of the *don't know* response option.

RESULTS

Phase 1: Source Test

In order to ensure that children in the source-directed group were correctly accessing source information, discrimination scores representing their ability to correctly discriminate the live and video events were computed. We also calculated false positive scores on distracter items within the source test, to ensure that source-directed group children were correctly rejecting these items as not occurring in the live and video events.

Discrimination Scores. For the live events, the discrimination score was calculated by dividing the number of live events called "live" by the number of live events called either "live" or "video." For the TV events, the discrimination score was found by dividing the number of video events called "video" by the number of video events called either "video" or "live." A 2 (Age: 3- to 4-year-olds, 5- to 6-year-olds) × 2 (Source: live, video) × 2 (Delay: immediate, one week) repeated measures analysis of variance (ANOVA) was performed on these discrimination scores. Results indicated a main effect of source, $F(1, 34) = 10.46, p < .01$, such that children's discrimination scores for the live event (immediate test: $M = 87.92, SD = 20.47$; delayed test: $M = 88.89, SD = 19.50$) were higher than their discrimination scores for the video event (immediate test: $M = 76.17, SD = 26.78$; delayed test: $M = 66.58, SD = 36.62$). No effects of age or delay were evidenced. Despite this effect of source, 5- to 6-year-olds' discrimination of the live and video events at immediate and delayed testing was significantly greater than chance (50%), $ps < .05$ (see Table 7.2). The 3- to 4-year-old children's discrimination of the live and video events at immediate testing and their discrimination of the live events at delayed testing were greater than chance, however, their discrimination of the video events at the delay did not differ significantly from chance, $t(18) = 1.42, p = 0.17$.

False Positives. Children's false positives, their tendency to accept distracter items as events that actually occurred, were measured by dividing the number of distracter items labeled "live" or "video" by the total number of distracter items. A 2 (Age) × 2 (Delay) repeated

TABLE 7.2

Discrimination Scores of Source-Directed Group
(Standard Deviations in Parentheses)

Age	Live		Video	
	Immediate	Delay	Immediate	Delay
3- to 4-year-olds	82.63 (23.06)	86.32 (19.14)	72.47 (27.00)	62.63 (38.81)
5- to 6-year-olds	93.82 (15.76)	91.76 (20.07)	80.29 (26.72)	71.00 (34.63)

measures ANOVA was performed on these false positive percentages. No effects of age or delay were evidenced. Children in both age groups rarely accepted distracter items as occurring in the live or video events. False positive percentages remained quite low at both immediate ($M = 8.06, SD = 19.25$) and delayed ($M = 10.83, SD = 21.56$) testing sessions.

Phase 2: Misleading Questions

The percentages of correct, incorrect, and don't know responses to each type of misleading question (misleading detail, misleading distracter) were entered into separate 2 (Age) × 2 (Group) × 2 (Delay) repeated measures ANOVAs. For the misleading detail questions, the percentages were computed by dividing the number of each response type by the total number of misleading detail questions. The percentages were computed in the same way for the misleading distracter questions. Percentages were computed because for some children in the immediate (source directed = 9, control = 9) and delayed sessions (source directed = 9, control = 9), we could not code all of their responses to misleading questions due to unintelligibility of their responses or experimenter error.

Misleading Detail Questions. (Questions that misled subjects about the source, i.e., live or video, of details in witnessed events). The percentage of misleading detail questions correctly answered by each child was entered into a 2 (Age) × 2 (Group) × 2 (Delay) ANOVA. We found a main effect of age, $F(1, 71) = 9.27$, $p = 0.003$. Five- to 6-year-olds ($M = 57.18$, $SD = 25.31$) produced more correct responses than the 3- to 4-year-olds ($M = 40.83$, $SD = 28.59$), but there were no effects for condition.

For incorrect responses, an Age × Group interaction, $F (1, 71) = 7.67, p = .007$, emerged (see Table 7.3). Simple effects analyses, $F(1, 71) = 7.02, p < .025$, indicated that 3- to 4-year-olds in the control group ($M = 48.75$, $SD = 23.70$) produced more incorrect responses to these questions than 3- to 4-year-olds in the source-directed group ($M = 31.85$, $SD = 22.80$). In addition, 3- to 4-year-olds in the control group produced more incorrect responses than 5- to 6-year-olds in the control group ($M = 29.48$, $SD = 23.36$), $F(1, 71) = 9.13, p < .01$. There was no difference in the incorrect responses produced by 5- to 6-year-olds in the source-directed and control groups.

For *don't know* responses, a main effect of age, $F(1, 71) = 4.47, p = .038$, was found (see Table 7.3). Three- to 4-year-olds ($M = 18.21, SD = 24.66$) produced more don't know responses than 5- to 6-year-olds ($M = 9.40, SD = 15.02$). An Age × Group interaction approached statistical significance, $F (1, 71) = 3.76, p = 0.057$, with the pattern of

TABLE 7.3
Percentages for Each Response Type to Misleading Questions
(Standard Deviations in Parentheses)

Group	Correct		Incorrect		Don't Know	
	Immediate	Delay	Immediate	Delay	Immediate	Delay
Misleading-Detail Questions						
3- to 4-year-olds						
SD	46.68 (25.31)	41.58 (29.57)	33.74 (19.39)	29.95 (26.21)	18.74 (23.43)	28.42 (34.77)
Control	37.85 (21.96)	37.55 (29.00)	49.25 (23.40)	48.25 (24.00)	12.05 (18.52)	14.15 (22.38)
5- to 6-year-olds						
SD	51.76 (29.30)	60.76 (22.99)	42.12 (27.31)	34.06 (22.08)	7.06 (12.01)	5.18 (8.29)
Control	63.32 (18.39)	52.68 (30.72)	27.11 (19.58)	31.84 (27.14)	9.68 (12.76)	15.00 (26.00)
Misleading-Distracter Questions						
3- to 4-year-olds						
SD	75.00 (35.35)	60.53 (39.77)	9.21 (19.02)	6.58 (23.34)	15.79 (31.41)	32.89 (36.81)
Control	77.05 (35.17)	49.15 (43.84)	15.85 (33.02)	32.90 (41.40)	7.10 (18.65)	17.90 (28.38)
5- to 6-year-olds						
SD	88.24 (25.18)	91.18 (24.91)	8.82 (24.91)	5.88 (24.25)	2.94 (8.30)	2.94 (8.30)
Control	85.53 (31.53)	84.21 (26.63)	6.12 (16.70)	3.95 (12.54)	8.32 (24.04)	11.84 (19.31)

Note. SD = Source-directed group.

means suggesting that 3- to 4-year-olds in the source-directed group (M = 23.58, SD = 29.1) produced more "don't know" responses than both 3- to 4-year-olds in the control group (M = 13.1, SD = 20.45) and 5- to 6-year-olds in the source-directed (M = 6.12, SD = 10.15) and control (M = 12.34, SD = 19.38) groups.

Misleading Distracter Questions. (Questions about distracter items not performed). With percentage of correct responses to misleading distracter questions as the dependent measure, we found a main effect of age, $F(1, 71)$ = 9.22, p = .003. On average, 5- to 6-year-olds (M = 87.16, SD = 27.18) produced more correct responses than 3- to 4-year-olds (M = 67.00, SD = 38.56). In addition, an Age × Delay interaction was evidenced, $F(1, 71)$ = 13.58, p = 0.0004. Simple effects analyses, $F(1, 71)$ = 29.65, p < .01, indicated that the 3- and 4-year-olds produced fewer correct responses at delayed (M = 54.69, SD = 41.86) as compared with immediate (M = 76.05, SD = 35.26) testing. No difference in the immediate (M = 86.00, SD = 28.53) and delayed (M = 88.00, SD = 25.82) performance of the 5- to 6-year-olds was found, and there were no differences for condition.

With percentage of incorrect responses to misleading distracter questions as the dependent measure, a Group × Delay interaction, $F(1, 71)$ = 6.24, p = .015, was revealed. Simple effects analyses, $F(1, 71)$ = 7.69, p < .01, revealed that children in the control groups produced more incorrect responses at delayed as compared with immediate testing. There was no difference in the immediate and delayed performance of the source-directed group (see Table 7.3). This interaction, however, was qualified by an Age × Group × Delay interaction, $F(1, 71)$ = 5.38, p = 0.02. The means indicated that 3- to 4-year-olds in the control group produced more incorrect responses to misleading distracter questions at delayed (M = 32.90, SD = 41.40) as compared with immediate (M = 15.85, SD = 33.02) testing. The means also suggested no difference in the immediate and delayed performance of 3- to 4-year-olds in the source-directed group or 5- to 6-year-olds in the source-directed and control groups.

Finally, with percentage of *don't know* responses as the dependent measure, a main effect of age, $F(1, 71)$ = 5.83, p = .018, was again revealed (see Table 7.3). On average, 3- to 4-year-olds (M = 18.27, SD = 28.68) produced more "don't know" responses than 5- to 6-year-olds (M = 6.71, SD = 15.36). The Age × Group interaction again approached statistical significance, $F(1, 71)$ = 3.70, p = 0.058. The means suggested that 3- to 4-year-olds in the source-directed group

($M = 24.34, SD = 34.11$) produced more "don't know" responses than both 3- to 4-year-olds in the control group ($M = 12.50, SD = 23.52$) and 5- to 6-year-olds in the source-directed ($M = 2.94, SD = 8.30$) and control ($M = 10.08, SD = 21.68$) groups.

To sum up the findings (see Table 7.4), there was evidence that orienting to source decreased the 3- to 4-year-olds' suggestibility, that is, production of incorrect responses to both misleading detail and misleading distracter questions. For the misleading distracter questions only, the 3- to 4-year-olds in the control group produced more incorrect responses at delayed as compared with immediate testing. No differences in the immediate and delayed responses of the 3- to 4-year-olds in the source-directed group and 5- to 6-year-olds in the source-directed and control groups were evidenced. Although reinforcing the source decreased 3- to 4-year-olds' suggestibility, the pattern of means did not reveal similar effects in the 5- to 6-year-olds' responses. There was no difference between the correct and incorrect responses to misleading distracter and misleading detail questions given by the 5- to 6-year-olds in the source-directed and control groups.

A second major finding was that although 3- to 4-year-olds in the source-directed group produced fewer incorrect responses than their agemates in the control group, they did not produce more correct responses. Rather, the data suggested that the 3- to 4-year-olds in the source-directed group made less errors due to their greater utilization (although not statistically significant) of the "don't know" response option. This effect was indicated in children's responses to both the misleading detail and misleading distracter questions.

Finally, as found in other studies of children's suggestibility (e.g., Ceci et al., 1987), we found clear developmental differences because the 5- to 6-year-olds in the source-directed and control groups produced fewer incorrect responses to misleading detail and misleading distracter questions than 3- to 4-year-olds in the control group.

EFFECT OF SOURCE-DIRECTED QUESTIONS ON RESPONSES TO MISLEADING QUESTIONS

Misleading-Detail Questions

For the misleading detail questions, 3- to 4-year-olds in the control group produced more incorrect responses than all other groups, although no effect of delay was found. These age differences in incorrect responses to questions that confused the details from live and video events is consistent with that found by Roberts and Blades (1996).

TABLE 7.4

Significant Effects for Each Response Type to Misleading Questions

Misleading-Distracter Questions		Misleading-Detail Questions	
Analysis and Effect	F-test	Analysis and Effect	F-test
Age x Group x Delay		Age x Group x Delay	
Correct			
Age	$F(1, 71) = 9.22, p = 0.003$	Age	$F(1, 71) = 9.27, p = 0.003$
Age x Delay	$F(1, 71) = 13.58, p = 0.0004$		
Incorrect			
Group x Delay	$F(1, 71) = 6.24, p = 0.015$	Age x Group	$F(1, 71) = 7.67, p = 0.007$
Age x Group x Delay	$F(1, 71) = 5.38, p = 0.02$		
Don't Know			
Age	$F(1, 71) = 5.83, p = 0.018$	Age	$F(1, 71) = 4.47, p = 0.038$
Age x Group	$F(1, 71) = 3.70, p = 0.058*$	Age x Group	$F(1, 71) = 3.76, p = 0.057*$

* Borderline significant

The children in the source-directed groups may have accessed source information more often than 3- to 4-year-olds in the control group. If this latter group were relying on their gist representations of the event, then the misleading detail questions would have been consistent with these gist representations. For example, one question asked, "Mrs. Science tested a magnet to see if it would work through glass. What happened when she dropped a spoon into the glass?" In this question, the incorrect detail is "spoon" because, in fact, a spoon was never used in this magnet–glass experiment to which the question refers. A metal spoon was used in another experiment that the children viewed from a different source. The item "spoon" is, however, consistent with the gist of what happened in the magnet–glass experiment because a metal object (paper clip) was dropped into the glass. If the 3- to 4-year-olds in the control group accessed their gist representations that a metal object of some sort was used in the magnet–glass experiment, then they would agree (incorrectly) to the idea that a spoon (metal object) was dropped into the glass. Because of the rehearsal of source information by children in the source-directed group, they may have realized that the spoon was used in another science demonstration that was presented from a different source. However, the discrimination scores of the 3- to 4-year-olds in the source-directed group do not support this assertion. At the delayed source test, their discrimination of the video events did not differ significantly from chance (see Table 7.2). It is possible, therefore, that the 3- to 4-year-olds in the source-directed group were more confused about the live and video event details at the delay. This finding is actually consistent with the fact that the 3- to 4-year-olds in the source-directed group gave fewer incorrect responses to misleading-detail questions than their agemates in the control group because of their greater utilization of the "don't know" response option (not necessarily because they were more correct). These findings are consistent with fuzzy-trace theory. The verbatim source representations of the 3- to 4-year-olds in the source-directed group may not have been available to them when responding to the misleading-detail questions.

If the children were truly confusing the live and video event details, however, then why did they not give more incorrect responses to the misleading-detail questions, as opposed to saying *don't know*? A hypothesis consistent with source-monitoring theory can be offered as an explanation for these findings. Source monitoring is a kind of self-regulatory process, that requires one to make judgments concerning existing memories. Although some source decisions are made automatically (see Johnson et al., 1993), some source monitoring entails a form of metacognitive awareness because one must systematically evaluate memories of events in order to make source decisions. Consistent with the results presented by Robinson (this volume), young children, such as 3- to 4-year-olds, are less likely than older children and adults to engage in metacognitive (Bjorklund & Douglas, 1997; Justice, 1989; Schneider & Pressley, 1997) processes. From the perspective of source-monitoring theory, the source task explicitly required children to engage in a metacognitive process; hence, the 3- to 4-year-olds in the source-directed group may have acquired a heightened sense of awareness that some of the information in the misleading questions was incorrect, but, due to the delay, may have been unsure as to exactly why the questions were misleading. As a result, they may have resorted to the *don't know* response option as a sign of their unsureness. These younger children might have benefitted from explicit instructions that they should consider the previously monitored source information when answering the misleading questions. Also note that Leichtman, Morse, Dixon, and Spiegel (this volume) found that reinforcing source decreased the suggestibility of young children, but no more so than reinforcing memory of the content of the events.

Misleading Distracter Questions

For the misleading distracter questions, 3 to 4-year-olds in the control group produced more incorrect responses at delayed testing than their agemates in the source-directed group and the 5- to 6-year-olds in the source-directed and control groups. This effect is similar to that found in other studies revealing developmental differences in suggestibility (Ceci et al., 1987; Leichtman & Ceci, 1995; Memon & Vartoukian, 1996; Poole & White, 1991, 1993). There was no difference between the incorrect responses produced by children in the source-directed and control groups at immediate testing. These findings are consistent with the description of gist interference with verbatim memory outlined in fuzzy-trace theory. At the immediate test, children in both the source-directed and control groups were likely relying on their verbatim representations, including source, of the target events. After a one-week delay, however, the verbatim source representations of children in the control group may have disintegrated. As a result, this group, particularly the 3- to 4-year-olds, may have accessed only their gist representations of the target events. The misleading-distracter questions were consistent with the gist of the events. Similar to the target events, these questions probed children about science-related activities, for example, "using a fire to heat up water" and "making a volcano." Children in the source-directed group, due to rehearsal of source information (i.e., events that occurred live, on video, or not at all), were less likely to rely on gist. Source information may have remained well integrated with the target events (due to immediate and delayed source rehearsal). For example, when presented with the misleading distracter question "How did Mrs. Science make a volcano?" children in the source-directed group may have realized that this event occurred neither in real life nor on video and was something that they never saw Mrs. Science do. This assertion is supported by the ability of children in both of the source-directed groups to reject these distracter items (e.g., making a volcano) presented in the source test, as indicated by their low false positive scores.

However, upon inspection of the correct responses to misleading distracter questions at delayed testing by children in the source-directed groups, the assertion that children recognized the events as not occurring holds for 5- to 6-year-olds, but not for 3- to 4-year-olds. At the 1-week delay, 3- to 4-year-olds in the source-directed group performed similarly to their agemates in the control group in terms of their correct responses to misleading distracter questions. What made the younger children in the source-directed group less incorrect than their agemates in the control group was their greater utilization of the "don't know" response option. Given, however, that both age groups were able to reject the distracter items during the source test, it is puzzling why the younger children failed to produce as many correct responses to the misleading distracter questions as the older children. Because children in the source-directed group performed quite well when discriminating the distracter items on the source test, both fuzzy-trace theory and source-monitoring theory would predict that they should produce more correct responses to misleading questions than the control group. However, this was not the case for the 3- to 4-year-olds. Fuzzy-trace theory does not adequately address why 3- to 4-year-olds in the source-directed group did not use their recently rehearsed verbatim source representations when responding to specific misleading questions. Because the source test results indicate that these children did indeed know that the distracter experiments did not happen at all, even at delayed testing, they should have been more likely to also reject these distracter items when responding to the misleading questions (that were presented immediately after the source test).

Two alternative explanations can be offered for these findings. One explanation involves the social demands associated with the misleading question task. As previous studies have found (Ceci, Ross, & Toglia, 1987; Davis & Bottoms, in press; Zaragoza, Dahlgren, &

Muench, 1992), young children seem reticent to object to false suggestions proposed by an adult interviewer. We did attempt to minimize the demand characteristics of the misleading question task by warning the children that the questions might contain incorrect information. Maybe the 3- to 4-year-old children in the source-directed group heeded these warnings to some extent by saying "don't know," as opposed to overtly contradicting the interviewer. Because the questions were repeated, their increase in "don't know" responses may have been evidence of their sensitivity to the demand characteristics of the task. Immediately upon hearing the questions once, the children may have not had problems correcting the interviewer (see Table 7.3). However, when the questions were repeated at the delayed session, though the 3- to 4-year-olds in the source-directed group knew that the distracter events did not actually occur, they may have been uncomfortable correcting the interviewer a second time. Evidence for such effects of repeated questioning has been found in eyewitness studies (Poole & White, 1991, 1993).

A second explanation for the increased usage of "don't know" by the 3- to 4-year-olds in the source-directed group is again related to source-monitoring theory. Three- to 4-year-olds in the source-directed group may have had some sense that the questions were incorrect (due to engaging in the metacognitive process of source monitoring), and as a sign of this uncertainty regarding the accuracy of the questions, utilized the "don't know" response option. As with the misleading detail questions, these younger children might have benefited from explicit instructions that they should consider the previously monitored source information when answering the misleading distracter questions.

Developmental Differences in the Effect of Source-Directed Questions

One additional finding concerns our failure to find a difference in the responses produced by 5- to 6-year-olds in the source-directed and control groups. These two groups were similarly correct and incorrect when responding to both the misleading detail and misleading distracter questions. There was no difference between the number of correct and incorrect responses to misleading questions produced by the 5- to 6-year-olds in the source-directed and control groups. Both fuzzy-trace theory and the source-monitoring framework could explain these findings. In terms of fuzzy-trace theory, the older children may have maintained their verbatim representations for source better than the younger children. Fuzzy-trace theory does in fact predict age trends in children's ability to encode and retrieve verbatim traces. Evidence from the 5- to 6-year-olds' recognition tests are noteworthy here. Upon inspection of the recognition responses by children in the control group, we found that although they were simply asked whether or not a given event occurred, over half of the 5- to 6-year-olds provided spontaneous reports that they accessed source information at this time. For example, when asked, "Did Mrs. Science tap a spoon on glass bottles?" a number of 5- to 6-year-olds would respond, "Yeah, she did that in real life." We found evidence that 10 (53%) 5- to 6-year-olds in the control group spontaneously reported source information when responding to recognition questions, and only 5 (25%) 3- to 4-year-olds in the control group spontaneously reported source. This finding can explain the similar response pattern to misleading questions evidenced by 5- to 6-year-olds in the source-directed and control groups. If 5- to 6-year-olds in the control group were actually rehearsing source, then they would have had accessible verbatim source representations that could have prevented them from relying on gist, especially at delayed testing, just like the source-directed group.

What caused or allowed the older children in the control group to spontaneously access or consider source information? The development of children's spontaneous use of strategies may answer this question. Older children are more likely than younger children to spontaneously use strategies without being explicitly cued (Bjorklund & Douglas, 1997). They are more metacognitively aware of the need to engage in some process that might enhance their memory of events. Because source monitoring is one kind of metacognitive process, perhaps the older children were more aware of the need to engage in this process when answering random yes or no questions about what happened in the witnessed events. As source-monitoring theory would predict, these children should thus be less prone to confusing details that occurred in live events with details that occurred in video events, and vice versa.

CONCLUSIONS

The present findings are explained from the perspective of fuzzy-trace theory in terms of a failure to access source information, due to gist interference with verbatim memory. In addition, these findings are consistent with predictions from the source-monitoring framework. The source-monitoring perspective can interpret the finding of fewer incorrect responses to misleading questions by children in the source-directed group than those in the control group as resulting from the attributional process in which source-directed children engaged when deciding on source. The younger children in the source-directed group, however, were not necessarily more correct than their agemates in the control group when responding to misleading-detail and misleading-distracter questions. One explanation for this effect would support fuzzy-trace theory. That is, for the misleading-detail questions, the 3- to 4-year-olds in the source-directed group may *not* have had accurate verbatim source representations (as suggested by their source test discrimination performance) regarding the live and video events. As a result, they were not able to provide correct responses to the misleading-detail questions and so said "don't know" more frequently. But, given the unavailability of source representations regarding the live and video events, it would seem that they would provide more incorrect responses, as opposed to responding more often with "don't know." For the misleading-distracter questions, the 3- to 4-year-olds in the source-directed group may have known the correct answer (as suggested by the false positive data) but due to demand characteristics, said "don't know" more frequently.

A second explanation for the don't know response tendency by the 3-to 4-year-olds in the source-directed group would be consistent with the source-monitoring framework. Children may have been metacognitively aware that the information in the questions was incorrect as a result of engaging in source monitoring, but uncertain as to why the questions were incorrect and so said "don't know." The tendency of the 3- to 4-year-olds in the source-directed group to use more "don't know" responses when answering the misleading detail and misleading distracter questions may have been evidence of their heightened metacognitive awareness that resulted from source monitoring. If children were simply accessing a verbatim trace for source, then this simple retrieval of source should not have necessarily engaged any metacognitive processes. At present, the role of such variables as metamemory and strategy use are not factored into fuzzy-trace theory. Rather, memory phenomena are explained by basic cognitive mechanisms associated with gist and verbatim representations (Bjorklund, 1995; Miller & Bjorklund, 1998).

Although we have suggested ways that each theory might more adequately explain certain findings, we do not have conclusive evidence that this is the case. The design of this study did not afford directly testing the validity of the two theories. However, from these findings and the predictions offered by both theories, some directions for future research can be suggested. A strength of the source-monitoring framework consists of its extensive account of when source decisions may be more or less difficult. This account is based on the "discriminability principle" (see Reyna & Lloyd, 1997). When sources are highly similar, source decisions should be more difficult as compared with sources that are highly dissimilar. Because discriminability was not specifically manipulated in this study, it would be interesting to note the effects of source monitoring on suggestibility, given conditions of information presented from similar versus dissimilar sources. Specific predictions could be made in this instance from the source-monitoring perspective. For example, children who view events under conditions of low source discriminability should benefit more from source monitoring than children who view events under conditions of high source discriminability.

Fuzzy-trace theory, on the other hand, does not make specific predictions about the accuracy of source memory, given variations in source discriminability. If source is encoded as a verbatim representation, then it would seem that this tag could be accessed to the same degree of accuracy regardless of variations in the similarity of sources. Hence, given that the source-monitoring framework does provide evidence that source decisions vary by the degree of similarity between sources (Johnson, Raye, Foley, & Foley, 1981; Lindsay, 1990; Lindsay, Johnson, & Kwon, 1991), it is important for fuzzy-trace theory to offer an account of how these differential effects could occur, if source is indeed laid down as a verbatim trace.

Another limitation associated with fuzzy-trace theory is that the kinds of stimuli on which much of the theory is based do not directly map onto the kinds of stimuli inherent in the eyewitness suggestibility literature. Many of the experimental paradigms that have been used to test fuzzy-trace theory use tasks in which distinctions between gist and verbatim information are easy to recognize. For example, in transitive inference tasks, subjects are presented with a set of sentences, such as "The cocoa is hotter than the tea. The tea is hotter than the coffee." If one accessed gist representations concerning these sentences, then one would accept the statement at test that the "coffee is cooler than the cocoa." However, if one relied on verbatim representations when deciphering the accuracy of this test statement, then the statement would be considered inaccurate or false.

The information in eyewitness events and subjects' responses cannot be so neatly classified into this gist–verbatim distinction. The to-be-remembered stimuli are not just auditorally presented, as in much of the fuzzy-trace theory research, but are often both visually and auditorally presented. For example, in Poole and White's (1991) study, children witnessed an ambiguous interaction between a male and a female. The male questioned the female about a pen he thinks she has and briefly tapped her on her shoulder as he angrily left the room. In the test session, children freely recalled the event and were then asked repeated and leading questions. Information in this event that can be classified as verbatim details includes the appearance of the persons involved, such as that the man was wearing a red shirt, and any objects involved, such as the pen. Gist information might be a general memory of an exchange between two persons without remembering exactly which person did or said something, or remembering that a writing utensil of some kind was also involved without recalling that the utensil was a pen. However, given variations in subjects' responses, it is difficult to determine if certain information should be considered as gist or verbatim representations. For example, if subjects responded that a "pen" as opposed to simply a "writing utensil" was involved in the witnessed event, "pen" would seem to be a verbatim trace. However, other subjects might remember there being a "ball point pen" or a "felt tip pen." This latter information would indicate representations of even more detailed verbatim information. Would "pen" in the former response be considered a lower level of verbatim traces or a higher level of gist traces? Such difficulties in making these gist–verbatim distinctions are not sufficiently addressed by fuzzy-trace theory at present. One cannot define a priori what information is gist and what information is verbatim. The theory does allow for a "hierarchy of gist" (Brainerd & Reyna, 1990) or a fuzzy-to-verbatim continuum (Reyna, 1995); however, as the previous example reveals, distinguishing between gist and verbatim representations presents a challenge for research using eyewitness paradigms.

In summary, both theories represent important contributions to our understanding of how source can affect children's susceptibility to misleading questions and how differential access to source information might interact with age to produce developmental differences in suggestibility. What is now needed is a way to distinguish between fuzzy-trace and source-monitoring explanations of suggestibility effects. In making source attributions, the source-monitoring framework suggests that variables such as one's use of strategies and metamemory can influence the accuracy of these source judgments. Fuzzy-trace theory, on the other hand, does not contain the influence of these variables in the theory. Source confusions are simply explained by way of gist–verbatim interactions (e.g., gist interference with verbatim memory). This difference between the two theories can be tested by designing an experiment such that the effects of strategy use on source monitoring can be observed. For example, if strategy usage has no effect on source-monitoring performance, then such a finding would support fuzzy-trace theory. If, however, strategy usage does differentially affect source monitoring, then this finding would support source-monitoring theory. This kind of experimental work can have important theoretical implications as well as practical implications, such as examining specific variables found to influence source monitoring in child witnesses.

REFERENCES

Ackil, J. K., & Zaragoza, M. S. (1995). Developmental differences in eyewitness suggestibility and memory for source. *Journal of Experimental Child Psychology, 60*, 57–83.

Bjorklund, D. F. (1995). *Children's Thinking: Developmental Function and Individual Differences*. New York: Brooks/Cole Publishing Company.

Bjorklund, D. F., & Douglas, R. N. (1997). The development of memory strategies. In N. Cowan (Ed.), *The development of memory in childhood*. Hove East Sussex, U.K.: Psychology Press.

Brainerd, C. J., & Gordon, L. L. (1994). Development of verbatim and gist memory for numbers. *Developmental Psychology, 30*, 163–177.

Brainerd, C. J., & Reyna, V. F. (1990). Gist is the grist: Fuzzy-trace theory and the new intuitionism. *Developmental Review, 10*, 3–47.

Ceci, S. J., Ross, D. F., & Toglia, M. P. (1987). Suggestibility of children's memory: Psycholegal implications. *Journal of Experimental Psychology: General, 116*, 38–49.

Davis, S. L., & Bottoms, B. L. (in press). The effects of social support on the accuracy of children's reports: Implications for the forensic interview. In M. L. Eisen, G. S. Goodman, & J. A. Quas (Eds.), *Memory and suggestibility in the forensic interview*. Mahwah, NJ: Lawrence Erlbaum Associates.

Johnson, M. K., Raye, C. L., Foley, H. J., & Foley, M. A. (1981). Cognitive operations and decision bias in reality monitoring. *American Journal of Psychology, 94*, 37–64.

Johnson, M. K., Hashtroudi, S., & Lindsay, D. S. (1993). Source monitoring. *Psychological Bulletin, 114*, 3–28.

Justice, E. M. (1989). Preschoolers' knowledge and use of behaviors varying in strategic effectiveness. *Merrill-Palmer Quarterly, 35*, 363–377.

Leichtman, M. D., & Ceci, S. J. (1995). The effects of stereotypes and suggestion on preschoolers' reports. *Developmental Psychology, 31*, 568–578.

Lindsay, D. S. (1990). Misleading suggestions can impair eyewitness' ability to remember event details. *Journal of Experimental Psychology: Learning, Memory, and Cognition, 16*, 1077–1083.

Lindsay, D. S., & Johnson, M. K. (1989). The eyewitness suggestibility effect and memory for source. *Memory & Cognition, 17*, 349–358.

Lindsay, D. S., Johnson, M. K., & Kwon, P. (1991). Developmental changes in memory source monitoring. *Journal of Experimental Child Psychology, 52*, 297–318.

Loftus, E. F. (1979). *Eyewitness Testimony*. Cambridge, MA: Harvard University Press.

Memon, A., & Vartoukian, R. (1996). The effects of repeated questioning on young children's eyewitness testimony. *British Journal of Psychology, 87*, 403–415.

Miller, P., & Bjorklund, D. F. (1998). Contemplating fuzzy-trace theory: The gist of it. *Journal of Experimental Child Psychology, 71*, 184–193.

Poole, D. A., & Lindsay, D. S. (1995). Interviewing preschoolers: Effects of nonsuggestive techniques, parental coaching and leading questions on reports of nonexperienced events. *Journal of Experimental Child Psychology, 60*, 129–154.

Poole, D. A., & White, L. T. (1991). Effects of question repetition on the eyewitness testimony of children and adults. *Developmental Psychology, 27*, 975–986.

Poole, D. A., & White, L. T. (1993). Two years later: Effects of question repetition and retention interval on the eyewitness testimony of children and adults. *Developmental Psychology, 29*, 844–853.

Reyna, V. F. (1995). Interference effects in memory and reasoning: A fuzzy-trace theory analysis. In F. Dempster & C. Brainerd (Eds.), *Interference and inhibition in cognition* (pp. 29–59). San Diego: Academic Press.

Reyna, V. F., & Brainerd, C. J. (1995). Fuzzy-trace theory: An interim synthesis. *Learning and Individual Differences, 7*, 1–75.

Reyna, V. F., & Kiernan, B. (1994). The development of gist versus verbatim memory in sentence recognition: Effects of lexical familiarity, semantic content, encoding instructions, and retention interval. *Developmental Psychology, 30*, 178–191.

Reyna, V. F., & Lloyd, F. (1997). Theories of false memory in children and adults. *Learning and Individual Differences, 9*, 95–123.

Roberts, K. P., & Blades, M. (1996). Do children confuse memories of events seen on television and events witnessed in real life? In N. K. Clark & G.M. Stephenson (Eds.), *Investigative and forensic decision making* (pp.52–57). Leicester, UK: British Psychological Society.

Roberts, K. P. & Blades, M. (1998). The effects of interacting in repeated events on children's eyewitness memory and source monitoring. *Applied Cognitive Psychology, 12*, 489–503.

Roberts, K. P., & Blades, M. (in press). Children's memory and source monitoring for real-life and television events. *Journal of Applied Developmental Psychology.*

Schneider, W., & Pressley, M. (1997). *Memory development between two and twenty* (2nd ed.). Mahwah, NJ: Lawrence Erlbaum Associates.

Titcomb, A. L., & Reyna, V. F. (1995). Memory interference and misinformation effects. In F. Dempster & C. Brainerd (Eds.). *Interference and inhibition in cognition* (pp. 263–294). San Diego: Academic Press.

Wilkes, A. (1990). *My First Science Book*. New York: Alfred A. Knopf.

Zaragoza, M. S., Dahlgren, D., & Muench, J. (1992). The role of memory impairment in children's suggestibility. In M. L. Howe, C. J. Brainerd, & V. F. Reyna (Eds.). *Development of long-term retention* (pp. 184–216). New York: Springer-Verlag.

Zaragoza, M. S., & Koshmider, J. W. (1989). Misled subjects may know more than their performance implies. *Journal of Experimental Psychology: Learning, Memory, and Cognition, 15*, 246–255.

8

Do You *Really* Remember It Happening or Do You Only Remember Being Asked About It Happening? Children's Source Monitoring in Forensic Contexts

Jodi A. Quas
University of California, Berkeley
Jennifer M. Schaaf
Kristen Weede Alexander
Gail S. Goodman
University of California, Davis

Nowhere have concerns about children's mnemonic capabilities and limitations been greater than in the legal arena. Concerns have focused primarily on whether children can be led to report false information and whether children can not only claim but actually *believe* the false information. When children come into contact with the legal system, they are most often questioned about alleged events that they personally experienced; events that involved some form of body contact, as in the case of sexual or physical abuse; and events for which physical evidence of the alleged wrongdoings is minimal (e.g., Goodman, Quas, Bulkley, & Shapiro, in press). In these situations, the words of a child can have great impact on the progression and outcome of a legal case. As such, it is imperative to ensure that the information children provide is as accurate and error free as possible.

During the past decade, there has been a virtual outpouring of research on children's memory and suggestibility, and this research has brought important insight into individual, situational, and social factors that affect the accuracy and completeness of children's memory and children's susceptibility to false suggestions. It is not the intent of our chapter to review this large and growing body of literature (see Ceci & Bruck, 1998; Poole & Lamb, 1998; Saywitz & Goodman, 1996, for more complete reviews). Rather, our goal is to highlight experiential and situational factors often evident in forensic interviews that may affect children's source-monitoring capabilities, specifically, children's ability to distinguish between memories of an event gleaned from actually experiencing the event and memories of an event gleaned from some other source (e.g., an interviewer's questions, imagining the event occurring). We begin the chapter with a brief discussion of contextual factors often associated with forensic interviews that may affect children's source monitoring. Next, we review research on children's source-monitoring capabilities in relation to experienced, witnessed, and imagined events, and follow this with a review of research on how question type, timing, and repetition and characteristics of interviewers may influence children's ability to identify the source of their memory reports. We then turn our attention to false-memory studies and outline how source-monitoring failures may play a role in the creation of children's false-event reports. Finally, we discuss ongoing research in our laboratory in which we have investigated children's source-monitoring capabilities for true and false events in repeated interview situations.

CONTEXT OF FORENSIC INTERVIEWS

Obviously all child witnesses' legal experiences are not identical, and considerable variability exists in the progression of a legal case and in a child's own involvement in a particular case. Nonetheless, there are also some similarities, particularly in the context of forensic interviews. Similarities often include repeated interviews, questions about events that occurred and events that did not occur, lengthy time delays, and interacting with multiple adults differing in status (e.g., Goodman, Taub, et al., 1992). As will be highlighted throughout the chapter, these factors can affect children's source monitoring. Because children most often come into contact with the legal system as the result of some form of alleged child abuse (Goodman et al., in press), our description of children's legal experiences focuses on their involvement following an allegation of child maltreatment. However, children do enter the legal system as witnesses in many types of cases, including domestic violence and even murder (e.g.,

Eth & Pynoos, 1994; Fantuzzo, Boruch, Beriama, & Atkins, 1997; Pynoos & Eth, 1984). To the extent that many witnesses can be subjected to repeated interviews, leading questions, and lengthy delays, the points raised regarding children's capabilities when questioned about alleged abuse are relevant to child witnesses questioned about other types of crimes as well.

When an allegation of abuse arises, a child may be questioned by a social worker, a police officer, or another professional about what happened. If a child discloses abuse, follow-up interviews may be conducted to gather additional evidence (young children's memory reports are often skeletal or incomplete, necessitating subsequent interviews and focused or direct questions). If a child does not disclose abuse but there is some reason to suspect abuse has occurred (e.g., a sibling disclosed abuse), follow-up interviews may still be conducted to determine whether the child failed to disclose initially because of fear or failure to understand the earlier interview questions or because no such abuse occurred (see Hewitt, 1999). Throughout a legal case, a child may be interviewed by police officers, social workers, investigators, attorneys, guardian ad litems, and judges about the alleged incidents to review what happened and obtain additional information. Note that these simply constitute formal interviews. There may also be informal conversations with parents, siblings, therapists, and anyone else in contact with the child during the legal proceedings. Each subsequent interview, formal and informal, has the potential to influence the child's memory and suggestibility (e.g., Ceci, Loftus, Leichtman, & Bruck, 1994; Poole & Lindsay, 1995). Further, as the number of interviews increases, the child may become confused as to whether information he or she provided stems from an actual memory representation or from knowledge obtained in earlier interviews.

Another typical feature of legal cases is lengthy delays. Children sometimes do not disclose abuse until months or even years after its occurrence, leading to long delays between the to-be-remembered event and an initial interview (e.g., Faller, 1989; Kellogg & Huston, 1995; see Kendall-Tackett, Williams, & Finkelhor, 1993). Long delays may then ensue between interviews, and between interviews and formal hearings, such as a trial. Like adults' memories, children's memories tend to fade after lengthy delays (Brainerd, Reyna, Howe, & Kingma, 1990; Ebbinghaus, 1913), which could include forgetting of details relevant to the source of the memory. Additionally, as we discuss later, the combination of lengthy delays and repeated interviews may have particularly negative consequences on children's ability to identify the source of their event memories.

When children are questioned about an alleged crime, interviewers typically are not aware of the objective facts of the event. Even if interviewers have some indication that a crime did occur (e.g., a child who has made an allegation of sexual abuse is diagnosed with a venereal disease), specific information must still be gathered from the child (e.g., the identity of the perpetrator). Young children often have difficulty providing detailed, complete narratives when questioned about their experiences (e.g., Dent & Stephenson, 1979; Fivush & Haden, 1997), which can lead to the necessity of asking direct or more focused questions to gather additional information about the alleged event. Children may be instructed to visualize an event occurring or imagine what would have happened, again, with the goal of gathering more detailed information about the alleged event (Ceci & Bruck, 1998). Regardless of the technique employed, in attempting to conduct a thorough interview, it is likely that the interviewer will ask about some events that did not occur or provide distorted descriptions of events originally experienced by the child (Roberts & Lamb, 1999). Even if the interviewer does not ask these questions in a leading or suggestive manner or does not ask a child to imagine an event occurring, there remain concerns as to whether merely questioning the child about a false event creates inaccuracies in the child's reports (e.g., Brainerd & Reyna, 1996). Of particular relevance to this chapter, concerns are also raised as to whether the child can later distinguish an experienced event from an event only asked about in the interview.

Although perhaps more subtle than the other aspects of forensic interviews we have discussed, the social context of the interview may also have implications for children's memory, suggestibility, and source-monitoring accuracy. Children learn early in life that authority figures, such as police officers, should be trusted and obeyed (Clayton, Cattarallo, Day, & Walden, 1991; Moran, 1994; Wright, Huston, Truglio, Fitch, Smith, & Piemyat, 1995). Such knowledge could make children especially careful about the accuracy of their reports when questioned by police. Alternatively, children may be intimidated by police officers, especially those who maintain a stoic rather than friendly attitude, or children may believe that a police officer's presence signals a wrongdoing was committed, both of which could increase children's willingness to acquiesce to an officer's suggestions (Smith & Ellsworth, 1987; Tobey & Goodman, 1992). Finally, children may trust and believe police officers' suggestions because of their perceived authority status and subsequently report suggested information as having occurred. In contrast, children may perceive counselors and social workers as less authoritarian. These perceptions may foster trust and support, which could enhance children's ability to resist false suggestions. Because the status and demeanor of the interviewer may influence children's reporting of their experiences, although not necessarily their original memory, it is of interest to determine whether children are willing and able to identify the correct source of a memory report following an error.

Clearly, forensic interviews contain complex factors that have the potential to influence children's memory and suggestibility. Indeed, several of the previously mentioned factors have been the focus of intense research efforts to determine their precise effects on the accuracy of children's accounts (e.g., Briere, Berliner, Bulkley, Jenny, & Reid, 1996; Ceci & Bruck, 1998; Quas, Eisen, & Goodman, in press). Those factors that affect children's memory accuracy and suggestibility can also influence children's ability to identify the source of their memories. If a child makes an error in a forensic interview and incorrectly alleges an event he or she only learned about during an interview, a natural follow-up question is whether the child could, if probed, identify the correct source of her or his memory. In the remainder of this chapter, we turn to this question and review situational factors that decrease (or increase) children's source-monitoring capabilities, and highlight how these factors relate to forensic interview contexts. Clearly, situational factors are not the only influences on children's source monitoring; rather, important individual characteristics also contribute to the likelihood of accurate source identification and Leichtman, Morse, Dixon, and Spiegel (this volume) and Welch-Ross (this volume) review research on individual differences in source monitoring. It will be important in the future to investigate how individual differences and situational factors interact to affect children's emerging source-monitoring abilities.

SITUATIONAL INFLUENCES ON CHILDREN S
SOURCE-MONITORING CAPABILITIES

In studies of children's event memory, researchers have interviewed children about a variety of personally experienced events, including those in which children actively participated (e.g., Rudy & Goodman, 1991; Roberts, Lamb, & Sternberg, in press), those children witnessed (e.g., Bugental, Blue, Cortez, Fleck, & Rodriguez, 1992; Flin, Boon, Knox, & Bull, 1992), and those children neither experienced nor witnessed, that is, false events (e.g., Bruck, Ceci, & Melnyck, 1997; Quas, Goodman, & Schaaf, 1999). Children have been questioned about these events once or on repeated occasions (e.g., Bjorklund, Bjorklund, Brown, & Cassel, 1998; Poole & Lindsay, 1995); interview formats have included very general open-ended questions, direct (e.g., yes or no) questions, leading or suggestive questions (e.g., Gee, Gregory, & Pipe, 1999), and instructions to visualize or imagine the events occurring (e.g., Brown, 1998; Ceci, Huffman, Smith, & Loftus, 1994); finally, delays between the to-be-remembered event and the memory interview have ranged from a few minutes to several months (e.g., Carter, Bottoms, & Levine, 1996; Goodman, Hirschman, Hepps, & Rudy, 1991). Each of these variations can affect the accuracy with which children can identify the sources of their event memories.

Experienced, Witnessed, and Imagined Events

Classic source-monitoring studies concerned individuals' ability to discriminate memories (or knowledge and beliefs) about experienced events from memories of imagined, fictitious events (see Roberts, this volume, for more detail). If a witness is asked to imagine what happened during an alleged event (perhaps to elicit additional information), source-monitoring capabilities can be an important factor contributing to the accuracy (or inaccuracy) of the witness' account (Ceci & Bruck, 1998).

In the relevant source-monitoring studies, conducted with both children and adults, participants are asked to perform a task (e.g., saying a word) or imagine performing the task. Participants are then asked to recall the task and to identify whether they had actually performed or merely imagined performing it (e.g., Foley & Johnson, 1985; Foley, Johnson, & Raye, 1983; Foley, Santini, & Sopasakis, 1989; Johnson & Raye, 1981; Lindsay, Johnson, & Kwon, 1991). Variations on this paradigm have included asking participants to imagine or witness another person perform the task (e.g., Markham, 1991), increasing the complexity of the task (e.g., Foley, Durso, Wilder, & Friedman, 1991), or using age-appropriate tasks and nonverbal testing techniques (e.g., Roberts & Blades, 1995). Across studies, both age and similarity of sources have emerged as two of the most consistent predictors of children's ability to discriminate experienced versus imagined events.

It is perhaps not surprising that the most robust finding involves age differences. With age, individuals' ability to distinguish among sources of event information, including internal (e.g., imagined) and external (e.g., performed, watched) sources, improves considerably (e.g., Foley & Johnson, 1985; Lindsay et al., 1991; Markham, 1991; Parker, 1995; Roberts & Blades, 1998; Welch-Ross, 1995; but see Johnson, Raye, Hasher, & Chromiak, 1979). For example, Foley et al. (1991) asked 7-year-olds, 10-year-olds, and adults to say a word or imagine themselves or someone else saying a word. Shortly after, participants were given a recall and a discrimination test. For the recall test, participants were asked to remember as many words as possible. For the discrimination test, participants were given the original words plus new words and asked to indicate whether each one was a word they said, a word they imagined themselves or another person saying, or a new word. The 7-year-olds were significantly poorer than the 10-year-olds and adults at discriminating between the spoken and imagined words. Age-related increases in source-monitoring capabilities are even larger when particularly young children (e.g., preschoolers) have been included in samples (e.g., Foley, Harris, & Hermann, 1994), leading some researchers to argue that the biggest source-monitoring developments take place between the ages of 3 and 8 years (chaps. 2, 3, and 9, this volume).

Similarity of sources has also been shown to affect the degree to which children (and adults) are able to identify the correct sources of their memories (see also chapter 2, this volume). Lindsay et al. (1991) compared preschoolers, school-age children, and adults across a series of experiments in which source similarity was manipulated. In one study, participants experienced two of the following: watched a video of an adult performing a specific action (e.g., touching her nose), watched a video of an adult while imagining her perform the action (e.g., imagine the woman touching her nose), performed the action themselves (e.g., touched their own nose), or imagined performing the action themselves. Child participants performed significantly worse than adult participants when discriminating actual versus imagined actions, but only when the action involved the same actor. When the actor changed across the actual and imagined actions, children's and adults' performance did not differ.

Other research suggests that, although similarity can affect children's source-monitoring accuracy, children are not generally poor at discriminating similar sources. Rather, children's deficits may be specific to discriminating between real and imagined events when both actions involve themselves (see Lindsay & Johnson, 1987). Foley et al. (1983) found that 6-year-olds were more likely than 9-year-olds to confuse sources when asked whether they had performed or imagined an action. Similar age differences were not evident when children were asked whether another person had performed or imagined an action. More recently, Roberts and Blades (1998) found that 4-year-olds were better at distinguishing among actions someone else performed than among actions they performed, which is consistent with the interpretation that children have difficulty discriminating sources involving themselves. However, the reverse was found for 6-

and 9-year-olds, who demonstrated improved source-monitoring capabilities when they, rather than someone else, performed the actions. These findings indicate that age may interact with involvement of the self to affect children's ability to discriminate sources.

Not all results, however, implicate the involvement of the self as a special source-monitoring hurdle for younger children. Day and colleagues (Day, Howie, & Markham, 1998) compared the abilities of 6-year-olds with those of 11- to 12-year-olds in a study manipulating similarity of person, involvement of the self, and similarity of action. There was a substantial main effect of similarity of action such that children had a more difficult time discriminating actions as their similarity increased. Interestingly, no significant effect was observed for similarity of person or whether the self was involved.

Together, findings indicate that, although source similarity does negatively affect children's (and often adults') source-monitoring capabilities, whether the effects of similarity are influenced by children's personal involvement remains, in part, an unresolved question. Research by Foley and Ratner (e.g., Foley & Ratner, 1998; chap. 4, this volume) indicates that the perspective children adopt may affect whether similar sources are confused. Furthermore, as May suggested in chapter 6, this volume, the similarity or dissimilarity of sources can differ across several dimensions. Nonetheless, given that, in forensic interviews, children are typically questioned about events in which they were the victim, understanding more precisely the relations among self involvement, similarity, and source monitoring is an important direction for future research.

In summary, investigations of children's source-monitoring studies have revealed that children sometimes have difficulty identifying whether information they possess is from an actually experienced event or from another source, such as visualizing the event. Such source-monitoring difficulties may be particularly robust in young children, when children are asked to imagine themselves engaging in an event as opposed to actually engaging in the event, and when the to-be-remembered event is highly similar to other, experienced events. Implications for forensic interview situations are apparent: Insofar as children are asked to imagine themselves experiencing an event, particularly an event highly similar to other events they have experienced, they might be expected to confuse sources of event information. In contrast, when no instructions to imagine an event are provided and when children have not experienced similar events, they may be better able to distinguish different sources of event information.

The Interview Context

Several characteristics associated with the format and context of a memory interview can affect children's ability to identify the source of their memories. These include the suggestiveness of the interview, the delay between the to-be-remembered event and memory interview, the number of interviews conducted, and characteristics of the person conducting the interview.

Suggestive Interviews. When children are asked to recount a personal experience, the format of the interview can vary considerably. It is beyond the scope of this chapter to discuss all questioning formats that influence children's memory and suggestibility. Instead, we focus on two particular types of interview strategies: (a) misleading questions, and (b) visualization instructions. These two strategies have implications for children's ability to discriminate between knowledge derived from experiencing the event and knowledge derived from the interview itself.

In memory interviews, misleading questions typically either suggest an incorrect answer in the question (e.g., "The man's shirt was red, wasn't it?" when the man's shirt was blue) or indirectly imply incorrect information through the phrasing of the question (e.g., "What color was the man's hat?" when the man was not wearing a hat). Young children (e.g., preschoolers) are especially vulnerable to errors following misleading questions (e.g., Goodman, Bottoms, Schwartz-Kenney, & Rudy, 1991; Leichtman & Ceci, 1995). Additionally, once children fall prey to misleading suggestions, they may report the suggested information when subsequently questioned (e.g., Ackil & Zaragoza, 1995; Leichtman & Ceci, 1995; Poole & Lindsay, 1995). Moreover, some research suggests that a subset of children who err come to believe that the false suggestions, which can include entirely fictitious events, occurred. In a study of children's memories for a stranger's visit to their classroom, Leichtman and Ceci (1995) repeatedly interviewed 3- to 6-year-olds in a suggestive or neutral manner about what happened. The suggestions concerned whether the visitor had ruined some items at the preschool during his visit. Children interviewed in the suggestive manner were more likely to claim that the visitor had ruined the items than were children interviewed in the neutral manner. Interestingly, although children's errors decreased when they were asked whether they actually witnessed the visitor performing the suggested actions that ruined the items, a few children maintained their reports when asked if they "really saw the events with their own eyes," indicating that source failures may have played a role in these children's errors. Ackil and Zaragoza (1995) more directly tested whether children came to believe suggested information. Six- to 7-, 8- to 9-, and 10- to 11-year-olds, and adult participants watched a video. They were then read a summary of the video that included misleading information about the contents. Finally, an unfamiliar experimenter explained that the summary contained some errors and asked participants to indicate which items they (a) saw in the video, (b) heard about in the summary, and (c) both saw and heard. Six- to 7-year-olds were significantly more likely than the older children and adults to report they had seen in the video items about which they had been misled in the story. Of note, although these findings reveal limitations in young children's ability to answer source-monitoring questions, in the research reviewed in chapter 3 (this volume), children seem to err more often in the direction of claiming they actually "saw" events they only heard about than vice versa (i.e., claiming they heard about events they only saw). Thus, children's source errors may also reflect response bias toward claiming their knowledge derived from actual experience (e.g., visual input), regardless of the true source of that knowledge (see also Gopnik & Graf, 1988; Markham, Howie, & Hlavacek, 1999). As suggested by Ratner et al. (this volume), these source errors may actually function to enhance children's learning; however, these source errors clearly have negative consequences for the accuracy of event memory and eyewitness testimony.

Visualization instructions given during a forensic interview may also be problematic in terms of source monitoring. During interviews, children may be urged to think hard about events to help them remember, or they may be encouraged to imagine what would have happened. Such instructions could create event images rich in sensory detail—one of the characteristics used to distinguish experienced from imagined actions (Johnson & Raye, 1981). When children are encouraged to imagine an event repeatedly, their visualizations may gradually become more elaborate, incorporating information from previous visualizations into subsequent reports, thus increasing the perceptual detail associated with the images. This, in turn, will increase the likelihood of source errors (Ceci et al., 1994, Roberts, 1996). Ceci and colleagues (Ceci, Huffman, et al., 1994) questioned 3- to 6-year-olds on 12 separate occasions about fictitious events. Instructions included telling children that their mother confirmed the events' occurrence, that they are playing a "picture-in-the-head game," and that they should "think real hard" about the events. Across the interviews, more than one third of the children erroneously reported that at least one false event had actually occurred. The researchers concluded that some of the children who falsely assented to the never-experienced events came to believe their false claims, because they resisted parents' and researchers' debriefing attempts at the end of the study. Rather than acknowledge that the visualized events had not occurred when told so by their parents, these children steadfastly maintained that they remembered the events.

As with source-monitoring errors following misleading questions, source errors following visualization instructions may be caused by factors other than actual failure in identification of source, such as response biases or acquiescence. For example, when children are instructed to imagine events during an interview, they may believe they are playing a game. Children may then continue to play the game when asked source questions (e.g., Ceci, Huffman et al., 1994). Alternatively, children who claim to have experienced imagined events may maintain their reports during debriefing so that their responses are consistent or because they do not want to admit that they hadn't really experienced the event (Goodman, Quas, & Redlich, 1998). Finally, response biases, such as answering in the affirmative (e.g., "Yes, I really remember"), may also contribute to inaccuracies in children's reports and source-monitoring performance (e.g., McBrien & Dagenbach, 1998; Poole & Lindsay, 1995).

Delay Between the Event and Interview.   After a crime occurs, children may be interviewed at delays ranging from minutes to years. Shortly after the crime, children's (like adults') memory may be rich in perceptual detail (e.g., a verbatim memory trace). With time, however, the memory trace may fade and become gist-like, that is, only contain the general idea and important features at the expense of the detail (Brainerd & Reyna, 1990; Reyna & Brainerd, 1998), perhaps including loss of detail concerning the source of the memory (Reyna, 1997). Whether source information is maintained as a component of or separate from a memory trace continues to be debated (see Johnson & Raye, 1981; Thierry, Spence, & Memon, this volume). However, insofar as memory fades and perceptual detail is lost, source confusions are likely to increase.

By comparing children of different ages, and using a variety of delays, researchers often find age and delay differences in memory and source-monitoring performance (Ackil & Zaragoza, 1995; Gee & Pipe, 1995; Ornstein, Gordon, & Larus, 1992; Parker, 1995). Across most studies, as delay increases, memory and source accuracy decrease. Furthermore, although children of all ages often show decrements over time, younger children are particularly susceptible to memory and source errors relative to older children and adults (Ackil & Zaragoza, 1995; Bornstein & LeCompte, 1995; Parker, 1995; Powell

& Thomson, 1997a). Gopnik and Graf (1988), for example, asked children about the sources of recently acquired knowledge immediately after learning the information and again after a brief delay. Even when 3-year-olds had correctly identified the source of their knowledge moments after acquiring it, they were often unable to remember the source a short while later, this despite maintaining an accurate memory for the acquired knowledge. Powell and Thomson (1997a) exposed 4- to 8-year-olds to an event six times, with target items differing each time. After 1 or 6 weeks, children were asked to recall the items, and, as a source-monitoring test, to indicate which item was presented during the final occurrence of the event. The recall task ensured that memory failure was not an underlying cause of limitations in children's ability to identify the order of item presentation. Results demonstrated that, regardless of memory for the items, children's ability to identify the item order declined as delay increased.

Studies generally suggest that children's memory and source-monitoring accuracy deteriorates with time, and the amount of deterioration may be greater for younger than older children. Findings also indicate that source information may be stored separately and hence dissociable from other information about a particular event. Importantly, results of a few recent studies indicate that delay may not be as strongly associated with decreases in children's long-term memory for highly distressing personal experiences, such as medical procedures, accidents, and injuries, compared with their memory for more neutral events (e.g., Peterson & Bell, 1996; Quas Goodman, Bidrose, Pipe, Craw, & Ablin, 1999; but see Goodman, Bottoms et al., 1991). In future research, it will be necessary to investigate the combined influence of delay and emotional valence on children's source-monitoring capabilities.

Interview Repetition.   Another factor of critical importance in forensic interviews is the repetition of questions and interviews. Repeated interviews cause concern because children may incorporate information obtained in one interview into their report given in a subsequent interview, and such errors might lead to false criminal charges. Several researchers have examined children's memory accuracy and suggestibility across repeated interviews (e.g., Bjorklund et al., 1998; Brown, 1998; Goodman, Hirschman, et al., 1991). Only a few studies, however, have also tested children's source-monitoring performance (e.g., Poole & Lindsay, 1995; Powell & Thomson, 1997a, 1997b).

There are several reasons why repeated interviews could lead to considerable source-monitoring errors. For one, questioning children multiple times about an event may cause them to rehearse and elaborate on the event. Such mental elaboration, whether the event occurred or not, may well increase the amount of information associated with the event representation as well as the familiarity of the event. Because sensory detail is a major factor used to distinguish experienced versus nonexperienced (e.g., imagined) events, any increases in this detail would increase the likelihood of source confusions (Johnson, Hashtroudi, & Lindsay, 1993). If children are questioned about false information within an experienced event, with repetition, false information may actually become incorporated into the original event representation, leading to inaccurate claims about the source of the false information. Finally, unless otherwise instructed, individuals tend to use lax criteria when judging the sources of memories (Johnson & Raye, 1981). And, when lax criteria are employed, an event may be judged to have occurred because it has high familiarity, which may be the case after repeated interviews.

Interestingly, it could be argued that merely asking source-monitoring questions within the context of repeated interviews could cause children to use stringent rather than lax criteria when making source judgments. Specifically, questions, such as "Did you really see that happen or did someone just tell you that it happened?" may highlight the potential for source errors, which could improve children's performance. Poole and Lindsay (1999) reported a beneficial effect for older (e.g., 6- to 8-year-old) children of preinterview source-monitoring training on their performance in response to questions about what really happened during a science demonstration versus what they had learned about the interaction from a story their parents had read. Three- to 8-year-olds participated in a series of laboratory events with an unfamiliar man, Mr. Science. Immediately afterward, children were questioned about what happened. Approximately three months later, parents read brief, personalized stories to their children that included descriptions of events that had and had not occurred during children's interaction with Mr. Science, including a description of nonexperienced body touch (the man wiping children's faces with a wet wipe that tasted yucky), an event that bears some limited relevance to events about which children may be questioned in forensic situations. The day after the third story reading, children were interviewed about their encounter with Mr. Science. Before the interview, some children received training in discriminating experienced and heard-about events. At the end of the interview, all children were asked to state how they knew about the laboratory events (whether they experienced the events, heard about the events in the story their parent read, or both). It may be that the pre-interview training heightened the older children's awareness of the potential for source confusions and led them to use more stringent criteria when judging an event as one they experienced as opposed to one they only heard about.

A final reason for negative effects of repeated interviews on source-monitoring capabilities stems from demand characteristics. Repeated questions within or across interviews (Poole & White, 1991; Warren & Lane, 1995) may signal to children that their earlier answers were incorrect and should be altered. If children succumb to social pressure and change their answers, they may feel reticent to recant those answers later and instead claim to "really" remember the event when asked source questions. Social pressure may also lead to source confusions: It is possible that after repeated interviews children may become confused about their original event memories and their previous reports of the events, despite initial errors being based on demand characteristics rather than on memory failures.

Interviewer Characteristics. Several studies indicate that both the status and demeanor of an interviewer can influence children's memory accuracy and susceptibility to false suggestions (Carter et al., 1996; Ceci, Ross, & Toglia, 1987; Goodman, Bottoms et al., 1991). Although relatively few studies have investigated the influence of interviewer status and demeanor on children's source-monitoring capabilities, because these factors can affect children's reporting of their experiences, they may also affect children's performance when answering source questions.

For adults as well as children, susceptibility to misleading information is affected by the credibility of the source of the information and the authority of the interviewer (Ceci et al., 1987; Dodd & Bradshaw, 1980; Smith & Ellsworth, 1987; Templeton & Hunt, 1997). Lampinen and Smith (1995), for example, explored preschool children's memory for a book that was read to them. After hearing the story, misinformation was presented to the children by another child, a discredited adult, or a credible adult. Only misinformation from the credible adult had a deleterious effect on children's later recall, indicating that children were affected not just by the adult status of the information source, but also by the adult's perceived credibility. In forensic settings, the authority status of the interviewer (e.g., a police officer) may be especially salient, increasing the likelihood that children will report information suggested by the interviewer, if for no other reason than because the interviewer is thought to be a highly credible source. Unfortunately, little is known as to whether similar negative effects would be evident in children's ability to identify the source of their memories following misleading questions asked by a high versus low credibility interviewer. However, it is likely that children could be negatively affected because children differentially use source information depending on whether the information is coming from a more or less knowledgeable adult (chaps. 3, and 9, this volume).

The personal demeanor of the interviewer, which includes such factors as openness, approachability, and familiarity, may also influence children's memory and suggestibility, and possibly source-monitoring capabilities. Although findings have been somewhat mixed, results seem to indicate that children are more accurate and less suggestible when questioned by a familiar or warm and friendly adult than when questioned by an unfamiliar or cold and professional adult (Carter et al., 1996; Goodman, Bottoms et al., 1991; Goodman, Sharma, Thomas, & Consodine, 1995). Douglas and colleagues (1997) interviewed 5- and 7-year-old children and adults on two occasions about a video of a theft. The first interview included misleading questions about details that did not occur during the video. The second interview was conducted either by the same interviewer or by a new interviewer. Children's but not adults' accuracy increased when the second interview was conducted by the same person who conducted the first interview. This finding emerged despite the same interviewer being the person who had previously provided misleading information. Carter et al. (1996) reported that children were more accurate and less suggestible when interviewed by a supportive as opposed to a nonsupportive (cold, intimidating) adult about a play session. We speculate that children's level of comfort and familiarity with the interviewer may have affected their willingness to contradict the interviewer's suggestions. Also, children may have felt more confident in their abilities when questioned by a supportive rather than a nonsupportive interviewer, leading to an increased resistance to misleading questions (Davis & Bottoms, in press). Although in none of the preceding studies were children asked about the sources of their memories, it seems reasonable to suppose that similar beneficial effects of a warm versus cold interviewer would emerge. Children may be comfortable revealing a lack of actual memory when questioned by a familiar interviewer, whereas children may be intimidated by an unfamiliar or cold interviewer and may not be comfortable identifying the interviewer as the source of event information. Alternatively, if an interviewer asks misleading questions in an initial interview, children may come to perceive the interviewer as being less knowledgeable or credible than they would if they did not talk with the interviewer previously. Decreased credibility of the interviewer may then facilitate children's ability to separate the two sources of event information: the interviewer and the original experience. In our laboratory, we have recently conducted a study designed to investigate directly the effects of interviewer familiarity on children's source-monitoring accuracy. We turn to this research shortly.

To summarize, research reveals that children sometimes have difficulty making accurate source-monitoring discriminations after lengthy delays. This may be due to a variety of factors associated with the content and context of the interview itself. Source-monitoring difficulties may be particularly apparent when an unfamiliar interviewer asks children suggestive questions or instructs children to visualize an event occurring. Source errors may also increase when children are questioned repeatedly about events that occurred a long time in the past. In general, as the level of sensory detail of an event representation fades and the level of sensory detail provided by other sources of event information increases, source confusions become more likely. Importantly, as has been stressed throughout this section, at least some of children's apparent source failures may reflect factors other than source confusion, such as response biases or demand characteristics. Continued research is needed to specify more clearly the underlying mechanisms that contribute to poor performance when children are asked about the source of their memories under various interview conditions.

Children s False Memories

Children's source monitoring has recently been investigated in relation to their false event memories, that is, their memories of entire events that never actually took place. Although false memories typically represent a form of suggestibility, we discuss false memories separately because their occurrence has grave implications for legal cases and because the interview formats used to elicit false event reports implicate source failures as at the root of false reports. In false memory studies, children are questioned about never-experienced events in highly suggestive manners, often repeatedly (e.g., Brown, 1998; Ceci et al., 1994). Interview strategies have included explicitly telling children they experienced false events, having children visualize false events, or having children pretend the events occurred. Across studies and interview techniques, between 20% and 75% of the participants, including children as young as 3 years and adults of all ages, have asserted that never-experienced events occurred (e.g., Brown, 1998; Hyman, Husband, & Billings, 1995; Loftus & Pickrell, 1995; Pezdek, Hodge, & Finger, 1997; Quas et al., 1999). Several researchers have argued that source failures, or incorrectly claiming imagined or visualized events actually occurred, underlie children's (and adults') false reports (e.g.,

Ceci et al., 1995; Schacter, Kagan, & Leichtman, 1994; but see Quas et al., 1999, and McBrien & Dagenbach, 1998).

As discussed earlier (see section on "Suggestive Interviews"), in one of the first published false event studies, Ceci, Huffman, et al. (1994) repeatedly queried 3- to 6-year-olds about fictitious events using a variety of suggestive tactics including instructions to imagine the events. Across interviews, approximately one third of the children reported that at least one false event had occurred. Ceci, Huffman, et al. speculated that children confused their memories of the events gleaned from imagining what would have happened with actual event memories and hence incorrectly reported the imagined events as true. This interpretation is consistent with source-monitoring studies in which young children appear to have difficulty distinguishing their memory for actions they actually performed from actions they only imagined performing (e.g., Foley & Johnson, 1985; Gopnik & Graf, 1988; Parker, 1995).

Also described earlier (see section on "Interview Repetition"), Poole and Lindsay (1995) tested whether source-monitoring failures accounted for children's false reports in their Mr. Science study. When children's memory was tested immediately after the interaction, even the 3-year-olds gave highly accurate reports. However, at the 3-month follow-up, children typically reported events they only heard about in a story read to them as having taken place during the original event. This was especially evident when the 3- to 4-year-olds were tested with source-monitoring questions. As discussed previously, young children in particular are poor at source monitoring when sources are highly similar (e.g., Lindsay et al., 1991; Roberts & Blades, this volume). Although the sources per se in Poole and Lindsay's study (experiencing science demonstrations in a laboratory, hearing a story at home) were not similar, the content of the two sources was similar: both involved the children and Mr. Science performing science demonstrations, which likely contributed to source confusions. As an aside, children's source accuracy was significantly better when children had to respond "yes" than "no," which may indicate a tendency to acquiesce. However, children were able to reject correctly events they neither heard about nor experienced, indicating that there was not an overarching "yes" response bias, but rather, the bias was confined to questions about events for which children had some knowledge from either the original event, the story, or both. These results again stress the importance of separating errors due to source-monitoring failures from errors due to other social factors, such as response biases or effects of credibility (see also Lindsay, Gonzales, & Eso, 1995).

OUR CURRENT RESEARCH

Recently, we conducted a study of young children's source-monitoring capabilities following a series of repeated interviews about either a true or false play interaction (Quas et al., 1999). The to-be-remembered event involved children interacting with a man, being touched by the man on their bodies (i.e., the nose, neck, arm, and waist), and the man "doing something yucky." This particular to-be-remembered event was chosen because of its potential relevance to forensic settings involving child witnesses. As mentioned, children are typically questioned in forensic interviews about personally experienced events involving their own bodies (Goodman et al., in press), and children are often interviewed on multiple occasions about their experiences (Gray, 1993). It was thus important to determine not only how well children remembered a true or false event involving body touch across repeated interviews, but also how well children could identify the source of their memory of the true or false event.

In the study, 3- and 5-year-olds participated in a semistructured play session. For some children, this involved playing with an adult male confederate and being touched on their noses, necks, arms, and waists. For other children, this involved playing with the man but not being touched. And for still other children, this involved them playing alone and never seeing the man (see Table 8.1). Children were then interviewed on three separate occasions about what occurred with the man, including about whether the man touched their noses, necks, arms, and waists (which happened for one-third of the children) and about whether the man did something yucky (which never happened for any of the children). In the final interview, children were also asked

TABLE 8.1

Three Play Session Conditions in the Study

	Play Session Conditions		
	Interaction— Touched	Interaction— Not Touched	No Interaction
Child played with the man	Yes	Yes	No
Child was touched on nose, neck, waist, and arm	Yes	No	No
Child experienced something yucky	No	No	No

about the source of their memory for being touched and the man do-ing something yucky. Half of the children were questioned by the same person during each interview, and half of the children were questioned by a new, unfamiliar person in the final interview. In the latter case, a photograph of the previous interviewer was presented in conjunction with the source-monitoring questions.

The play-session manipulation allowed us to gain valuable insight into how well children could identify the source of their memory for being touched when (a) the touching had actually occurred, (b) the touching had not occurred but was plausible given that children had interacted with the man (e.g., Loftus & Pickrell, 1995; Pezdek, Finger, & Hodge, 1997), and (c) the touching had not occurred and was implausible given that children had not interacted with the man (Pezdek, Finger et al., 1997). By manipulating children's familiarity with the interviewer, we were able to identify whether interviewer familiarity improved children's source-monitoring performance. Although prior research indicates that children often are more accurate and less suggestible when questioned by a supportive interviewer or an interviewer with whom they are familiar (Carter et al., 1996; Douglas et al., 1997), it was unknown whether similar benefits would be evident in children's identification of the source of their memories.

Our first question concerned children's ability to answer the yes/no questions about having been touched or the man doing something yucky after children had been subjected to two prior interviews that contained misleading questions about what happened with the man. Several studies indicate that repeated interviews can lead children to report erroneous information, including information of relevance to abuse allegations, such as being touched or something yucky happening (e.g., Bruck et al., 1997; Poole & Lindsay, 1995). When proportion correct responses to the yes/no questions were examined, younger children, $M = 0.64$, were less accurate than older children, $M = 0.76$. Also, children who actually had been touched by the man, $M = 0.46$, were considerably less accurate than children who had not been touched, regardless of whether they played with the man, $M = 0.80$, or not, $M = 0.84$. Thus, despite children having been questioned repeatedly about being touched and the man doing something yucky, children generally did not report these events as having occurred. Because one-third of the children had in fact been touched during their play session, these results suggest that denial of true touch was much more pervasive than false claims of being touched.

Given that children who had not experienced any touching were fairly accurate in responding to questions about being touched and the man doing something yucky, we next sought to determine whether they would also be accurate in reporting that they had been asked about these details in prior interviews. In other words, we were interested in whether they could identify the prior interview as a source of event information after claiming that the event did not occur. At the same time, we were interested in whether the minority of children who falsely claimed to have been touched or that the man did something yucky could accurately state whether they "really" remembered these events happening or remembered having been asked about them previously. In the latter case, we investigated whether the children could identify the correct source of the information in their memory report. Researchers have found that, in repeated interview situations, children at times report information they only heard about as having occurred (e.g., Ackil & Zaragoza, 1995; Poole & Lindsay, 1995), leading us to speculate that similar effects would be evident in our study when the event-in-question concerned a personal experience involving children's own bodies.

Children's source accuracy when they denied they had been touched or the man did something yucky reflects their ability to state that they had been asked in previous interviews about these play session events. Unlike children's performance in response to the yes/no questions, all children, regardless of play session experience, had considerable difficulty indicating that they had been asked about the play session events previously (mean proportion source accuracy: 0.43 for children who were touched; 0.33 for children who played with the man but were not touched; 0.37 for children who played alone). Overall, older children ($M = 0.50$) were more likely than younger children ($M = 0.25$) to accurately report that they had been questioned previously about the events. Similarly, children questioned by a familiar interviewer ($M = 0.48$) were more likely than children questioned by an unfamiliar interviewer ($M = 0.28$) to indicate that they had been asked about the events previously. However, as can be seen in Fig. 8.1, the effects of age and interviewer familiarity were primarily due to beneficial effects of familiarity for 5-year-olds, who performed better than all other children in response to the source questions. In general, children claimed not to have been questioned previously about the man touching them or doing something yucky, this despite children having been asked about the events twice previously.

A compelling issue in forensic situations concerns how well children can identify the source of their memory for an event when they claim the event occurred but they have also been repeatedly questioned about it. To extrapolate to our study, when children assented that the man had touched them or had done something yucky, could they identify whether they "really and truly" remembered him performing the alleged actions or whether they only remembered having

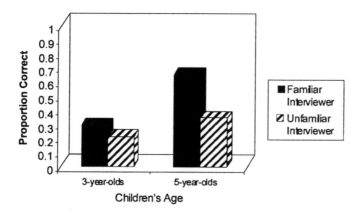

FIG. 8.1. Children's ability to indicate that they have been asked about the play session events in prior interviews when they denied the play session events occurred by their age and their familiarity with the interviewer.

been interviewed previously about such events? Among children who actually had been touched, more than one half said yes to one or more of the yes/no questions about whether they were touched or whether the man did something yucky (i.e., 16 of 24 children; nine 3-year-olds and seven 5-year-olds), and their source-monitoring proportion accuracy was 0.63 (0.56 for 3-year-olds, and 0.71 for 5-year-olds). Although less than one half of the children who were not touched when they played with the man incorrectly reported that at least one of the play session events occurred in response to yes/no questions (9 of 24 children; five 3-year-olds and four 5-year-olds), when asked about the source of their memories, all of these children claimed to have "really and truly" experienced the events. Finally, five of the 3-year-olds who played alone incorrectly responded "yes" that at least one of the play session events occurred, and these children's proportion source accuracy was 0.20. (None of the 5-year-olds who played alone incorrectly claimed that they had been touched or the man did something yucky, hence, they do not have source-accuracy scores on this measure.) These results suggest that children who were touched when they played with the man performed much better than the other children, although the 3-year-olds in the former group still performed near chance in their responses. However, across play-session conditions, children who claimed the events occurred responded that they really remembered events occurring as opposed to only remembering being asked about the events previously. Because children who were touched could in fact accurately remember some of the events occurring, their proportion source accuracy was naturally higher. Importantly, as was evident in children's source performance when they denied the play session events occurred, children tended *not* to identify the prior interviews as a source of play-session information.

These findings suggest that children were able to deny, often correctly, that they had been touched or that the man did something yucky. At the same time, however, children generally were not able to report that they had been asked about these events in prior interviews. Rather, children who claimed the events occurred typically claimed to have really experienced the events as opposed to learning about the events in prior interviews. Children who claimed the events did not occur typically claimed that they had not been asked about the events in prior interviews. As a group, children who seemed most able to identify accurately the prior interviews as a source of event information was the older children questioned by a familiar person.

It is possible that children's poor performance in identifying an interview as a source of event information was because they simply did not remember the previous interviews, which led to their typical denial of having been asked previously about the play-session events. However, at the outset of the interviews, children indicated that they remembered the former sessions. It is thus more likely that children either did not remember specifically what had been discussed in the interviews or that children did not understand the source questions and simply repeated the response they had just given to the memory question, leading to a response bias following the yes/no questions (cf. Peterson & Biggs, 1997; Poole & Lindsay, 1995).

Other researchers have found evidence that young children have particular difficulty identifying an interviewer or interview as a source of event information (e.g., Gopnik & Graf, 1988; Robinson, this volume; Taylor, Esbensen, & Bennett, 1994). For example, Gopnik and Graf either showed children the location of a hidden object, provided a clue that allowed children to infer its location, or explicitly told children the location. Three-year-olds were significantly less accurate in identifying the source of their knowledge when they were told the object's location than when they saw or inferred where it was. Similarly, Taylor et al. (1994) found that children tended to report that they had known for a long time facts they had learned about from an interviewer that day. Together, these findings suggest that children may have difficulty identifying an interview as a source of information. Although studies indicate that children who falsely assent to never-experienced events generally maintain their false assents when asked source-monitoring questions or when pressured about whether they actually experienced the events (e.g., Leichtman & Ceci, 1995; Poole &

Lindsay, 1995), at least some of children's errors may simply be due to a lack of understanding of source-monitoring questions or an inability to identify an interview as a source of event information. A final possibility is that children did not want to admit they erred or "lied" in their earlier claims of a false report and instead maintained their answer to save face (see Goodman et al., 1998). Clearly additional research is needed to determine more precisely why children appear to have such difficulty identifying an interview (or interviewer) as a source of event information.

In a more positive light, our current results reveal that there are ways of facilitating children's source-monitoring performance, or at least 5-year-olds' performance. Namely, having the same interviewer ask children source-monitoring questions who had also interviewed children previously improved 5-year-olds' ability to report that they had been asked about the play session events in previous interviews. Interviewer familiarity and support have both been found to improve children's memory accuracy and resistance to false suggestions (e.g., Carter et al., 1996; Douglas et al., 1997; Goodman et al., 1995). Familiarity may similarly make children more comfortable indicating how they know event information, again leading to improved performance. Familiarity may also serve as a memory cue, reminding children of what the interviewer had said and reduce the need to conduct a memory search to remember the former interviews, all of which are likely to facilitate memory (Kail, 1990). Alternatively, children at this age may be able to reason appropriately about the knowledge possessed by a familiar interviewer (see chap. 9, this volume). Finally, children questioned by a new person were shown a photograph of the previous interviewer. These children thus had to remember who the previous interviewer was, what was discussed, and then compare this with what happened in the play session, making the source-monitoring task more cognitively demanding and thus perhaps more difficult (Case, 1992).

CONCLUSIONS

In this chapter, we reviewed several factors that are relevant to both forensic-interview settings and children's source-monitoring capabilities. Indeed, some factors that can decrease children's performance when they are asked to identify the sources of their memories include young age; similar memory sources, especially those involving the self; lengthy delays; repeated questions and interviews; and intimidating or unfamiliar interviewers. An important next step is to determine the extent to which children's errors are due to actual failure to remember the source, confusion between sources, or such factors as social acquiescence, forgetting, or lack of understanding of source questions. Whether children's errors reflect source failures per se or some form of response bias has important implications for forensic interviewing with children: if the latter, there may be interview techniques that decrease social influences and, in effect, improve children's eyewitness source-monitoring capabilities. Yet, there also seem to be several situations in which children should be able to perform quite well in responding to source questions, such as when children are questioned on a single occasion, when there are short delays between to-be-remembered events and source questions, and when a warm, friendly interviewer questions children, although further research is needed to confirm these ideas. As was evident in our study, when repeated interviews are necessary, which may be the case in forensic interview situations, maintaining a familiar interviewer may improve at least older preschoolers' ability to separate event information provided by the interviewer from event information derived from the actual event experience.

In closing, throughout the chapter, we have attempted to highlight several areas in need of future research, some of which we are currently pursuing in our laboratory. Our hope is that, with continued efforts to understand experiential and situational influences on children's source-monitoring abilities, this growing body of research can contribute much-needed answers to theoretical questions about source-monitoring development and to applied questions about children's eyewitness capabilities.

REFERENCES

Ackil, J. K., & Zaragoza, M. S. (1995). Developmental differences in eyewitness suggestibility and memory for source. *Journal of Experimental Child Psychology, 60,* 57–83.

Bjorklund, D. F., Bjorklund, B. R., Brown, R. D., & Cassel, W. S. (1998). Children's susceptibility to repeated questions: How misinformation changes children's answers and their minds. *Applied Developmental Science, 2,* 99–111.

Bornstein, B. H., & LeCompte, D. C. (1995). A comparison of item and source forgetting. *Psychonomic Bulletin and Review, 2,* 254–259.

Brainerd, C. J., & Reyna, V. F. (1990). Gist is the grist: Fuzzy-trace theory and the new intuitionism. *Developmental Review, 10,* 3–47.

Brainerd, C. J., & Reyna, V. F. (1996). Mere memory testing creates false memories in children. *Developmental Psychology, 32,* 467–478.

Brainerd, C. J., Reyna, V. F., Howe, M. L., & Kingma, J. (1990). The development of forgetting and reminiscence. *Monographs of the Society for Research in Child Development, 55.*

Briere, J., Berliner, L., Bulkley, J. A., Jenny, C., & Reid, T. (Eds.). (1996). *The APSAC handbook on child maltreatment*. Thousand Oaks, CA: Sage.

Brown, R. D. (1998, June). *Children's false memory creation for emotional and physical events: Individual differences in inhibitory and mental imagery abilities*. Paper presented at the 6th National Colloquium of the American Professional Society on the Abuse of Children, Chicago, IL.

Bruck, M., Ceci, S. J., & Melnyk, L. (1997). External and internal sources of variation in the creation of false reports in children. *Learning & Individual Differences, 9*, 289–316.

Bugental, D. B., Blue, J., Cortez, V., Fleck, K., & Rodriguez, A. (1992). Influences of witnessed affect on information processing in children. *Child Development, 63*, 774–786.

Carter, C. A., Bottoms, B. L., & Levine, M. (1996). Linguistic and socioemotional influences on the accuracy of children's reports. *Law & Human Behavior, 20*, 335–358.

Case, R. (1992). *The mind's staircase: Exploring the conceptual underpinnings of children's thought and knowledge*. Hillsdale, NJ: Lawrence Erlbaum Associates.

Ceci, S. J., & Bruck, M. (1998). Children's testimony: Applied and basic issues. In W. Damon, I. E. Sigel, & K. A. Renninger (Eds.), *Handbook of child psychology: Vol. 4* (5th ed., pp. 713–773). New York: Wiley.

Ceci, S. J., Huffman, M. L. C., Smith, E., & Loftus, E. F. (1994). Repeatedly thinking about a non-event: Source misattributions among preschoolers. *Consciousness and Cognition, 3*, 388–407.

Ceci, S. J., Loftus, E. F., Leichtman, M. D., & Bruck, M. (1994). The possible role of source misattributions in the creation of false beliefs among preschoolers. *International Journal of Clinical & Experimental Hypnosis, 42*, 304–320.

Ceci, S. J., Ross, D. F., & Toglia, M. P. (1987). Suggestibility of children's memory: Psycholegal implications. *Journal of Experimental Psychology: General, 116*, 38–49.

Clayton, R. R., Cattarello, A., Day, L. E., & Walden, K. P. (1991). Persuasive communication and drug prevention: An evaluation of the DARE program. In L. Donohew & H. W. Sypher (Eds.), *Persuasive communication and drug abuse prevention* (pp. 295–313). Hillsdale, NJ: Lawrence Erlbaum Associates.

Davis, S., & Bottoms, B. B. (in press). The effects of social support on the accuracy of children's reports: Implications for the forensic interview. In J. A. Quas, M. Eisen, & G. S. Goodman (Eds.), *Memory and suggestibility in the forensic interview*. Mahwah, NJ: Lawrence Erlbaum Associates.

Day, K., Howie, P., & Markham, R. (1998). The role of similarity in developmental differences in source monitoring. *British Journal of Developmental Psychology, 16*, 219–232.

Dent, H. R., & Stephenson, G. M. (1979). An experimental study of the effectiveness of different techniques of questioning child witnesses. *British Journal of Social and Clinical Psychology, 18*, 41–51.

Dodd, D. H., & Bradshaw, J. M. (1980). Leading questions and memory: Pragmatic constraints. *Journal of Verbal Learning and Verbal Behavior, 21*, 207–219.

Douglas, R., Park, C., Bjorklund, B., Ganhe, J., Sanders, L., Nelson, L., Cassel, W., & Bjorklund, D. F. (1997, April). *Social demand characteris-*

tics in children's eyewitness memory and suggestibility: The effects of different interviewers. Poster presented at the biennial meetings of the Society for Research in Child Development, Washington, DC.

Ebbinghaus, H. (1913). Memory (H. Ruyer & C. E. Bussenius, Trans.). Columbia, NY: New York Teachers College. (Original work published 1885)

Eth, S., & Pynoos, R. S. (1994). Children who witness the homicide of a parent. Psychiatry: Interpersonal & Biological Processes, 57, 287–306.

Faller, K. C. (1989). The role relationship between victim and perpetrator as a predictor of characteristics of intrafamilial sexual abuse. Child & Adolescent Social Work Journal, 6, 217–229.

Fantuzzo, J., Boruch, R., Beriama, A., & Atkins, M. (1997). Domestic violence and children: Prevalence and risk in five major U.S. cities. Journal of the American Academy of Child & Adolescent Psychiatry, 36, 116–122.

Fivush, R., & Haden, C. A. (1997). Narrating and representing experience: Preschoolers' developing autobiographical accounts. In P. W. van den Broek, P. J. Bauer, & T. Bourg (Eds.), Developmental spans in event comprehension and representation: Bridging fictional and actual events (pp. 169–198). Mahwah, NJ: Lawrence Erlbaum Associates.

Flin, R., Boon, J., Knox, A., & Bull, R. (1992). The effect of a five month delay on children's and adults' eyewitness memory. British Journal of Psychology, 83, 323–336.

Foley, M. A., Durso, F. T., Wilder, A., & Friedman, R. (1991). Developmental comparisons of explicit versus implicit imagery and reality monitoring. Journal of Experimental Child Psychology, 51, 1–13.

Foley, M. A., Harris, J. F., & Hermann, S. (1994). Developmental comparisons of the ability to discriminate between memories for symbolic play enactments. Developmental Psychology, 30, 206–217.

Foley, M. A., & Johnson, M. K. (1985). Confusions between memories for performed and imagined actions: A developmental comparison. Child Development, 56, 1145–1155.

Foley, M. A., Johnson, M. K., & Raye, C. L. (1983). Age-related changes in confusion between memories for thoughts and memories for speech. Child Development, 54, 51–60.

Foley, M. A., & Ratner, H. H. (1998). Distinguishing between memories for thoughts and deeds: The role of prospective processing in children's source monitoring. British Journal of Developmental Psychology, 16, 465–484.

Foley, M. A., Santini, C., & Sopasakis, M. (1989). Discriminating between memories: Evidence for children's spontaneous elaborations. Journal of Experimental Child Psychology, 48, 146–169.

Gee, S., & Pipe, M. -E. (1995). Helping children to remember: The influence of object cues on children's accounts of a real event. Developmental Psychology, 31, 746–758.

Gee, S., Gregory, M., & Pipe, M. -E. (1999). "What colour is your pet dinosaur?" The impact of pre-interview training and question type on children's answers. Legal and Criminological Psychology, 4, 111–128.

Goodman, G. S., Bottoms, B. L., Schwartz-Kenney, B. M., & Rudy, L. (1991). Children's testimony about a stressful event: Improving children's reports. Journal of Narrative and Life History, 1, 69–99.

Goodman, G. S, Hirschman, J. E, Hepps, D., & Rudy, L. (1991). Children's memory for stressful events. Merrill-Palmer Quarterly, 37, 109–157.

Goodman, G. S., Quas, J. A., Bulkley, J., & Shapiro, C. (in press). Innovations for child witnesses: A national survey. *Psychology, Public Policy, and Law.*

Goodman, G. S., Quas, J. A., & Redlich, A. D. (1998). The ethics of conducting 'false memory' research with children: A reply to Herrmann and Yoder. *Applied Cognitive Psychology, 12,* 207–217.

Goodman, G. S., Sharma, A., Thomas, S. F., & Considine, M. G. (1995). Mother knows best: Effects of relationship status and interviewer bias on children's memory. *Journal of Experimental Child Psychology, 60,* 195–228.

Goodman, G. S, Taub, E. P., Jones, D. P., England, P., Port, L. K., Rudy, L., & Prado, L. (1992). Testifying in criminal court: Emotional effects on child sexual assault victims. *Monographs of the Society for Research in Child Development, 57*(5, Serial No. 229).

Gopnik, A., & Graf, P. (1988). Knowing how you know: Young children's ability to identify and remember the sources of their beliefs. *Child Development, 59,* 1366–1371.

Gray, E. (1993). *Unequal justice: The prosecution of child sexual abuse.* New York: Free Press.

Hewitt, S. K. (1999). *Assessing allegations of sexual abuse in preschool children: Understanding small voices.* Thousand Oaks, CA: Sage.

Hyman, I. E., Husband, T. H., & Billings, F. J. (1995). False memories of childhood experiences. *Applied Cognitive Psychology, 9,* 181–197.

Johnson, M. K., Hashtroudi, S., & Lindsay, D. S. (1993). Source monitoring. *Psychological Bulletin, 114,* 3–28.

Johnson, M. K., & Raye, C. L. (1981). Reality monitoring. *Psychological Review, 88,* 67–85.

Johnson, M. K., Raye, C. L., Hasher, L., & Chromiak, W. (1979). Are there developmental differences in reality monitoring? *Journal of Experimental Child Psychology, 27,* 120–128.

Kail, R. (1990). *The development of memory in children.* New York: W. H. Freeman & Co.

Kellogg, N.D., & Huston, R. L. (1995). Unwanted sexual experiences in adolescents: Patterns of disclosure. *Clinical Pediatrics, 34,* 306–312.

Kendall-Tackett, K. A., Williams, L. M., & Finkelhor, D. (1993). Impact of sexual abuse on children: A review and synthesis of recent empirical studies. *Psychological Bulletin, 113,* 164–180.

Lampinen, J. M., & Smith, V. L. (1995). The incredible (and sometimes incredulous) child witness: Child eyewitnesses' sensitivity to source credibility cues. *Journal of Applied Psychology, 80,* 621–627.

Leichtman, M. D., & Ceci, S. J. (1995). The effects of stereotypes and suggestions on preschoolers' reports. *Developmental Psychology, 31,* 568–578.

Lindsay, D. S., Gonzales, V., & Eso, K. (1995). Aware and unaware uses of memories of postevent suggestions. In M. S. Zaragoza, J. R. Graham, G. C. N. Hall, R. Hirschman, & Y. S. Ben-Porath (Eds.), *Memory and testimony in the child witness* (pp. 86–108). Thousand Oaks, CA: Sage.

Lindsay, D. S., & Johnson, M. K. (1987). Reality monitoring and suggestibility: Children's ability to discriminate among memories from different sources. In S. J. Ceci, M. P. Toglia, & D. F. Ross (Eds.), *Children's eyewitness memory* (pp. 92–121). New York: Springer-Verlag.

Lindsay, D. S., Johnson, M. K., & Kwon, P. (1991). Developmental changes in memory source monitoring. *Journal of Experimental Child Psychology*, 52, 297–318.

Loftus, E. F., & Pickrell, J. E. (1995). The formation of false memories. *Psychiatric Annals*, 25, 720–725.

Markham, R. (1991). Development of reality monitoring for performed and imagined actions. *Perceptual and Motor Skills*, 72, 1347–1354.

Markham, R., Howie, P., & Hlavacek, S. (1999). Reality monitoring in auditory and visual modalities: Developmental trends and effects of cross-modal imagery. *Journal of Experimental Child Psychology*, 72, 51–70.

McBrien, C. M., & Dagenbach, D. (1998). The contributions of source misattributions, acquiescence, and response bias to children's false memories. *American Journal of Psychology*, 111, 509–528.

Moran, R. A. (1994). Stages of emotion: An adult adoptee's postreunion perspective. *Child Welfare*, 73, 249–260.

Ornstein, P. A., Gordon, B. N., & Larus, D. M. (1992). Children's memory for a personally experienced event: Implications for testimony. *Applied Cognitive Psychology*, 6, 49–60.

Parker, J. F. (1995). Age differences in source monitoring of performed and imagined actions on immediate and delayed tests. *Journal of Experimental Child Psychology*, 60, 84–101.

Peterson, C., & Bell, M. (1996). Children's memory for traumatic injury. *Child Development*, 67, 3045–3070.

Peterson, C., & Biggs, M. (1997). Interviewing children about trauma: Problems with "specific" questions. *Journal of Traumatic Stress*, 10, 279–290.

Pezdek, K., Finger, K., & Hodge, D. (1997). Planting false childhood memories: The role of event plausibility. *Psychological Science*, 8, 437–441.

Pezdek, K., Hodge, D., & Finger, K. (1997, April). *Planting false childhood memories for familiar versus unfamiliar events.* Paper presented at the biennial meeting of the Society for Research in Child Development, Washington DC.

Pezdek, K., & Roe, C. (1995). The effect of memory trace strength on suggestibility. *Journal of Experimental Child Psychology*, 60, 116–128.

Poole, D. A., & Lamb, M. E. (1998). *Investigative interviews of children: A guide for helping professionals.* Washington, DC: American Psychological Association.

Poole, D. A., & Lindsay, D. S. (1995). Interviewing preschoolers: Effects of nonsuggestive techniques, parental coaching, and leading questions on reports of nonexperienced events. *Journal of Experimental Psychology*, 60, 129–154.

Poole, D. A., & Lindsay, D. S. (1999, April). *Counteracting the effects of contamination on children's eyewitness reports.* Poster presented at the biennial meetings of the Society for Research in Child Development, Albuquerque NM.

Poole, D. A., & White, L. T. (1991). Effects of question repetition on the eyewitness testimony of children and adults. *Developmental Psychology*, 27, 975–986.

Powell, M. B., & Thomson, D. M. (1997a). Contrasting memory for temporal source and memory for content in children's discrimination of repeated events. *Applied Cognitive Psychology*, 11, 339–360.

Powell, M. B., & Thomson, D. M. (1997b). The effect of an intervening interview on children's ability to remember one occurrence of a repeated event. *Legal and Criminological Psychology, 2*, 247–262.

Pynoos, R. S., & Eth, S. (1984). The child as witness to homicide. *Journal of Social Issues, 40*, 87–108.

Quas, J. A., Eisen, M., & Goodman, G. S. (in press) (Eds.), *Memory and suggestibility in the forensic interview.* Mahwah, NJ: Lawrence Erlbaum Associates.

Quas, J. A., Goodman, G. S., Bidrose, S., Pipe, M. -E, Craw, S., & Ablin, D. (1999). Emotion and memory: Children's long-term remembering, forgetting, and suggestibility. *Journal of Experimental Child Psychology, 72*, 235–270.

Quas, J. A., Goodman, G. S., & Schaaf, J. M. (1999). *Children's memories of experienced and nonexperienced events across repeated interviews.* Unpublished manuscript.

Reyna, V. F. (1997). Conceptions of memory development with implications for reasoning and decision making. In R. Vasta (Ed.), *Annals of child development: A research annual: Vol. 12, 1996* (pp. 87–118). London, England: Jessica Kingsley Publishers, Ltd.

Reyna, V. F., & Brainerd, C. J. (1998). Fuzzy-trace theory and false memory: New frontiers. *Journal of Experimental Child Psychology, 71*, 194–209.

Roberts, K. P. (1996). How research on source monitoring can inform cognitive interview techniques: Commentary on Memon and Stevenage (1996). *Psycoloquy, 7(44) witness-memory,.15.roberts*

Roberts, K. P., & Blades, M. (1995). Children's discrimination of memories for actual and pretend actions in a hiding task. *British Journal of Developmental Psychology, 13*, 321–333.

Roberts, K. P., & Blades, M. (1998). The effects of interacting in repeated events on children's eyewitness memory and source monitoring. *Applied Cognitive Psychology, 12*, 489–503.

Roberts, K. P., & Blades, M. (in press). Children's memory and source monitoring for real-life and television events. *Journal of Applied Developmental Psychology.*

Roberts, K. P., & Lamb, M. E. (1999). Children's responses when interviewers distort details during investigative interviews. *Legal and Criminological Psychology, 4*, 23–31.

Roberts, K. P., Lamb, M. E., & Sternberg, K. J. (in press). Effects of the timing of postevent information on preschoolers' memories of an event. *Applied Cognitive Psychology.*

Rudy, L., & Goodman, G. S. (1991). Effects of participation on children's reports: Implications for children's testimony. *Developmental Psychology, 27*, 527–538.

Saywitz, K. J., & Goodman, G. S. (1996). Interviewing children in and out of court: Current research and practice implications. In J. Briere, L. Berliner, J. A. Bulkley, C. Jenny, & T. Reid (Eds.), *The APSAC handbook on child maltreatment* (pp. 297–318). Thousand Oaks, CA: Sage.

Schacter, D. L., Kagan, J., & Leichtman, M. D. (1995). True and false memories in children and adults: A cognitive neuroscience perspective. *Psychology, Public Policy, & Law, 1*, 411–428.

Smith, V. L., & Ellsworth, P. C. (1987). The social psychology of eyewitness accuracy: Misleading questions and communicator expertise. *Journal of Applied Psychology, 72(2),* 294–300.

Speaker, C. J., & Myers, N. A. (1997, April). *Four-year olds remember an event from age 2: Are event repetition timing effects still observed?* Poster presented at the Biennial meetings of the Society for Research in Child Development, Washington, DC.

Taylor, M., Esbensen, B. M., & Bennett, R. T. (1994). Children's understanding of knowledge acquisition: The tendency for children to report that they have always known what they have just learned. *Child Development, 65,* 1581–1604.

Templeton, L. M., & Hunt, V. H. (1997, April). *The effects of misleading information and level of authority of interviewer on children's eyewitness memory.* Poster presented at the biennial meetings of the Society for Research in Child Development, Washington, DC.

Tobey, A. E., & Goodman, G. S. (1992). Children's eyewitness memory: Effects of participation and forensic context. *Child Abuse and Neglect, 16,* 779–796.

Warren, A. R., & Lane, P. (1995). Effects of timing and type of questioning on eyewitness accuracy and suggestibility. In M.S. Zaragoza, J. R. Graham, G. C. N. Hall, R. Hirschman, & Y. S. Ben-Porath, (Eds.), *Memory and testimony in the child witness* (pp. 44–60). Thousand Oaks, CA: Sage.

Welch-Ross, M. K. (1995). Developmental changes in preschoolers' ability to distinguish memories of performed, pretended, and imagined actions. *Cognitive Development, 10,* 421–441.

Wright, J. C., Huston, A. C., Truglio, R., Fitch, M., Smith, E., & Piemyat, S. (1995). Occupational portrayals on television: Children's role schemata, career aspirations, and perceptions of reality. *Child Development, 66,* 1706–1718.

9

A Mental-State Reasoning Model of Suggestibility and Memory Source Monitoring

Melissa Welch-Ross
Georgia State University

Preschoolers can report memories of personal experience accurately in many circumstances (Fivush, 1997). However, the reality of forensic interviewing practices is that individuals must often provide eyewitness accounts after others have suggested inaccurate information (e.g., Ceci & Bruck, 1995). These suggestions seem to reduce the accuracy of preschoolers' reports more than the reports of older children and adults. For example, 3- and 4-year-olds acquiesce immediately to an interviewer's suggestions more often than older children do (Goodman, Quas, Batterman-Faunce, Riddlesberger, & Kuhn, 1994; Goodman, Rudy, Bottoms, & Aman, 1990; for a review, see Ceci & Bruck, 1993). In addition, research on misinformation effects shows that the reports of both adults and children are typically less accurate for details when they are misled than when they are not (Ceci, Ross, & Toglia, 1987; Loftus, Hoffman, & Wagenaar, 1992; Loftus, Miller & Burns, 1978; McCloskey & Zaragoza, 1985; Toglia, Ross, Ceci, & Hembrooke 1992; Zaragoza, McCloskey, & Jamis, 1987); however, this effect is especially strong for 3- and 4-year-olds (Ceci et al., 1987; Toglia et al., 1992, but see Zaragoza, Dahlgren, & Muench, 1992, for a failure to replicate).

Many factors may contribute to these age differences in misinformation effects. For example, social factors, such as the friendliness of the interviewer and the interviewer's age, which could affect perceptions of credibility, seem to affect the reports of younger and older children differently. Also, age differences in basic memory processes may cause younger children to make "source errors" in which they report suggested information instead of their personal experience. Older children encode information better than younger children do, perhaps because they have more knowledge or better processing capacities (Howe, 1991; Howe & Brainerd, 1989; Marche & Howe, 1995). In addition, younger children forget information more quickly than older children do, after controlling for developmental differences in encoding (Brainerd, Reyna, Howe, & Kingma, 1990; Howe, 1991; Howe & Brainerd, 1989).

However, younger children sometimes report both their original experience and suggested details (Ackil & Zaragoza, 1995; Marche & Howe, 1995), indicating they encoded and retrieved both items, and became confused about the sources of their memories. According to source-monitoring models, qualitative differences in the phenomenal experiences of remembering information acquired from different sources help us determine the origin of a single memory, or distinguish between sources of two conflicting memories (for further detail, see Johnson, Hashtroudi, & Lindsay, 1993; Lindsay & Johnson, 1987; chap. 2, this volume). If young children fail to encode source information or effectively retrieve source cues as well as older children and adults do, they may experience more frequent source misattributions in which they confuse episodes they saw with episodes they know about from a different source (Ackil & Zaragoza, 1995; Lindsay & Johnson, 1987).

An integrative approach that focuses on both the social and information-processing components of children's thinking during a social exchange with an interviewer may help us understand developmental differences in source errors and source misattributions when misled. For example, when an interviewer offers a detail that conflicts with the child's experience, the child must reason about a contradiction between the interviewer's apparent perspective and her own perspective about the episode. Do developmental changes in the ability to reason effectively about conflicting mental perspectives in this context affect how children process information when they are misled, and affect their source errors later?

In addition, does the child's ability to engage in other kinds of mental-state reasoning, such as the ability to reflect on the relation between what one knows and the experience that led to that knowledge, affect the child's source errors and source misattributions? This chapter presents a conceptual, working model that addresses questions concerning how the development of reasoning about mental states affects the processing of information when an interviewer offers information that conflicts with the child's personal experience.

First, research on the development of three aspects of mental-state reasoning is reviewed. The sections that follow outline the mental-state reasoning model of suggestibility and review studies that address predictions of the model. The conclusion highlights several practical implications of the model for understanding the types of questions and contexts that can produce or minimize suggestibility, depending on the child's level of mental-state reasoning, and offers directions for future research.

THE DEVELOPMENT OF REASONING ABOUT MENTAL STATES

Children begin developing an organized understanding about mental processes during the preschool years. This "theory of mind" is a set of principles that structures our understanding about how individuals represent and interpret experience, and it provides a conceptual basis for comprehending, explaining, and predicting human behavior (see Astington, 1993; Flavell & Miller, 1998; Perner, 1991; Taylor, 1996; Wellman, 1990). This chapter focuses on three aspects of reasoning about knowledge states (see also Flavell, Miller, & Miller, 1993) and their relation to memory source monitoring in the context of eyewitness memory and suggestibility. These include: (a) recognizing that an informative experience is associated with the mental state of knowing, (b) becoming explicitly aware that knowledge states originate with specific types of experiences, and (c) reasoning about conflicting and counterfactual representations of a single reality.

The Experience Knowing Connection

First, between ages 3 and 4, children show an explicit understanding that the mental state of knowing depends on experiencing. For example, they begin to recognize that someone who looks inside a container knows its contents, whereas someone who does not look does not know what is inside (Pillow, 1989; Pratt & Bryant, 1990; Robinson, this volume; Ruffman & Olson, 1989; Wimmer, Hogrefe, & Perner, 1988). Yet, many 4-year-olds do not fully appreciate the connection between an informative experience and the mental state of knowing. Most children, until age 5 or 6, will attribute knowledge on the basis of a person's desire to know a piece of information (Montgomery & Miller, 1997), a person's lucky guess, or the successful performance of a goal-directed action taken in the absence of knowledge (Moore, Bryant, & Furrow, 1989; Miscione, Marvin, O'Brien, & Greenberg,

1978; Perner, 1991). Also, 5- and 6-year-olds understand that access to complete, unambiguous, and relevant information is required for knowing (e.g., Chandler & Helm, 1984; Sodian, 1988, 1990; Taylor, 1988; but see Perner & Davies, 1991 and Ruffman, Olson, & Astington, 1991 for evidence that children understand ambiguity at about age 4).

Linking Knowledge to Specific Experiences

Although many 4-year-olds associate an informative experience with knowing, they still seem to lack an explicit awareness that a person's current knowledge is linked with a specific informative experience, such as seeing, feeling, hearing, inferring, and so on. For example, O'Neill and Gopnik (1991) allowed 3- to 5-year-olds to discover the contents of a drawer across several trials by looking inside, hearing what was inside, or inferring the contents using a clue the researcher provided. In an immediate test, all children could name the object inside the drawer. However, when asked to state explicitly how they knew what was inside, only 5-year-olds were able to determine the origin of their knowledge more often than would be expected from guessing (see also Gopnik & Graf, 1988). The same finding holds when children must specify the source of another person's knowledge (Wimmer & Perner, 1983), and when children are faced with conflicting sources of information (Robinson, this volume).

In other research, children understood that someone who looked inside a container would know its contents whereas someone who did not look would not know. However, they were unable to state explicitly why the person did or did not know what was inside (i.e., because she looked, or because she did not look; Wimmer et al., 1988; see also Perner & Ruffman, 1995). Clearly, children recognize a connection between experiencing and knowing before they seem explicitly aware that current knowledge is linked to a specific informative experience.

Counterfactual and Conflicting Representations

Four- and 5-year-olds are also beginning to understand that mental processes involve representations that do not necessarily correspond with actual circumstances. They are becoming able to reason effectively about counterfactual mental states concerning a single real-world circumstance, and to understand that conflicting mental representations can result from having access to different information (e.g., Gopnik & Astington, 1988; Flavell, 1988; Riggs, Peterson, Robinson, & Mitchell, 1998). For example, in a "mistaken location" version of the false-belief task, a child watches as a researcher enacts a scenario with dolls (Wimmer & Perner, 1983). In the scenario, a character puts an object in one location and exits. A second character then enters and moves the object to a different location. The first character returns and the researcher asks the child where this character will look for the object. Most 3-year-olds state that the character will look where the object really is, whereas most 5-year-olds understand that the character holds a false belief and will look for the object where he or she placed it originally (see Astington, 1993, for a review).

The "mistaken contents" version of the false-belief task shows a similar developmental transition relating to reasoning about one's own mental representations (e.g., Gopnik & Astington, 1988; Perner, Leekam, & Wimmer, 1987). In this task, the researcher presents a container, such as a crayon box. After the child states the belief that crayons are inside, she looks to discover candles inside the box. When the box is closed, most 3-year-olds, but few 5-year-olds, report they had believed candles were inside. When asked what another person who has not looked inside the box would believe to be inside, most 3-year-olds, but few 5-year-olds report that the person would believe candles to be inside, as in the mistaken location task.

Similarly, in the mistaken identity version (also, appearance–reality tasks), children see a sponge painted to look like a rock (Flavell, Green, & Flavell, 1986). After stating the object is a rock, they are allowed to squeeze it. Then, while only looking at the sponge, children must report what the object is really and what it looks like to their eyes. Three-year-olds typically report it is really a sponge and it looks like a sponge. Most children seem unable to consider simultaneously a representation of the object itself and a representation of what the object appears to be until about age 5. In summary, younger children appear to update their original representation to maintain a single, consistent view of the world, and thus they seem unable to reason about contradictory representations of events that result from different informative experiences (although see chap. 3, this volume).

THE MENTAL-STATE REASONING MODEL OF SUGGESTIBILITY

Why should reasoning about knowledge states affect suggestibility? The model depicted in Fig. 9.1 outlines a set of conceptual relations between the development of reasoning about knowledge states and suggestibility that serves as the organizing framework for the research presented in this chapter. The proposal is that each of the three pathways—a, b, and c—contributes uniquely to a decrease in suggestibility, and suggestibility should decrease incrementally as each type of understanding about knowledge states develops.

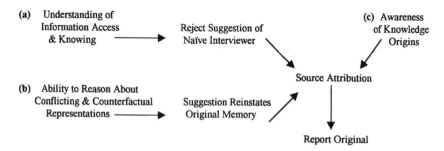

FIG. 9.1. A mentat-state reasoning model of suggestibility.

First, children who recognize the relation between access to information and knowing can determine that a naïve interviewer (who did not experience the event) cannot know about the event. Consequently, these children will reject the suggestions of the naïve interviewer (for relevant research on knowledge states see Mitchell, Robinson, Nye, & Isaacs, 1997; Perner & Davies, 1991; Robinson, 1994; Robinson & Mitchell, 1992; chap. 3, this volume). However, children without an understanding of this experiencing–knowing connection would not have a clear basis for rejecting the naïve interviewer's suggestions.

Yet, children who understand the relation between experiencing and knowing still may update their original memories with conflicting information in some circumstances, as they do in the mistaken contents task, if they cannot reason about conflicting and counterfactual representations (CMRs) that result from different informative experiences. When hearing information that directly conflicts with their experiences, children who cannot reason about CMRs would update their representation of the event to be consistent with the suggestion, as they do in the "mistaken contents" task.

However, even questions that are misleading may help children who *can* reason about CMRs to report events accurately. Consider that research on memory reinstatement effects shows that an interviewer's questions reinstate memories of original experience under some conditions, even if the question suggests information that conflicts with the child's experience (Marche & Howe, 1995). This reinstatement effect seems specific to details targeted in the interview and does not spread to other items.

According to a mental-state reasoning perspective on suggestibility, misleading questions could reinstate memories of original details, increasing the chance that these details will be recalled accurately later, but only for children who can reason about CMRs of events. Whereas children who cannot reason about CMRs update their original representations with new, conflicting information, children who can reason about CMRs are able to consider simultaneously the conflicting information and their memory of the original item, as they do in the mistaken contents task. Reinstating the original memory together with rejecting the naïve interviewer's suggestions when initially misled results in a greater chance of reactivating the original memory later compared with the suggested detail. Thus, the reports of children who can reason effectively about the experiencing and knowing connection and about CMRs may not be compromised after hearing misleading information, as would the reports of other children.

Children still may produce source errors or source misattributions when asked later to report only those episodes they actually saw, if they are unable to retrieve source cues. Lindsay and Johnson (1987) suggest that some kind of metacognitive awareness may be necessary for source monitoring, but the specific nature of this awareness has not been studied. According to the mental-state reasoning model, an explicit awareness that knowledge originates with specific experiences should help children report events they actually experienced instead of suggested information (see also Zaragoza et al., 1992). This awareness should motivate the retrieval of source cues that enable children to make these source distinctions.

Several types of source attributions may reduce suggestibility. Perhaps at a minimum, children must make simple see–not see judgments and determine which details in a larger set of episodes they actually saw and those they did not see. Later, children may be able to answer more precise source questions in which, for example, they identify which details they saw and which were told to them (e.g., Foley & Johnson, 1985; Foley, Johnson, & Raye, 1983; Lindsay, Johnson, & Kwon, 1991). Yet, the former judgment may be sufficient for resisting much information that did not originate with the child's firsthand experience. According to the model, children who are unaware that current knowledge is linked with a specific experiential origin may not be able to reflect on or efficiently access source information relevant to making reliable see–not see judgments that will prevent source errors. Indeed, these children may not even comprehend an interviewer's request to report only those experiences they saw firsthand and not the details they know from another source.

TESTING THE CLAIMS OF THE MODEL

The following section describes several studies that tested initial predictions that follow from the model. These predictions are:

1. Each type of mental-state reasoning is associated with re-duced suggestibility.

2. Exposure to suggested information reinstates original memo-ries among children who can reason about conflicting and counterfactual mental representations.

3. Children who reason about conflicting and counterfactual men-tal representations are more likely than other children to consider conflicting memories at retrieval, particularly if these children have good memories and thus are likely to remember the suggested item. Support for this claim would demonstrate that reasoning about con-flicting and counterfactual mental representations affects children's information processing, enabling them to represent both the original and suggested detail in memory, whereas other children update their original memory and later consider only one representation of the suggested detail.

4. Reasoning about conflicting, counterfactual information *spe-cific to conflicting knowledge states* affects suggestibility independ-ent of closely related cognitive achievements. These include reasoning about multiple pieces of information simultaneously, reasoning about conflicting mental states that do not involve counterfactual claims, and reasoning about conflicting information regardless of whether or not the conflict involves reasoning about knowledge states (for related discussions see Welch-Ross, 1999a, 1999b; Welch-Ross, Diecidue, & Miller, 1997).

5. An explicit awareness that knowledge is linked to a specific ori-gin leads to retrieving information necessary for making accurate source judgments; therefore, this understanding emerges prior to, but is related to, a decrease in source errors and source misattribu-tions after being misled.

CMR Reasoning and Suggestibility (Prediction 1)

Reasoning about CMRs predicts reporting events accurately after be-ing misled. In one study (Welch-Ross et al., 1997), 3-, 4-, and 5-year-olds listened to a researcher read a story accompanied by pictures. Af-ter a 4-minute delay, a second researcher entered the room and asked "straightforward" questions about half of the target details in the story (e.g., "Did Sally feed a pet fish?"). Half of the straightforward ques-tions contained accurate information and required a "yes" response, and half contained inaccurate information and required a "no" re-sponse. The interviewer asked misleading tag questions for the re-maining half of the target details, (e.g., "Sally ate cereal for breakfast, didn't she?"). One week later, a third researcher asked children straightforward, yes–no questions ("Did Sally feed her pet fish?", "Did Sally eat cereal for breakfast?"), which referred to the original episodes and suggested items. Following the interview, children completed a set of theory of mind tasks, including appearance–reality and false-belief tasks. A composite index of the ability to reason about CMRs was computed.

A regression performed on responses to the initial interview showed that the number of items children remembered correctly when not misled predicted the number of misleading questions answered correctly, after controlling for age. CMR scores did not predict suggestibility after controlling for the number of questions answered correctly when not misled. However, a regression performed on responses to the recognition test one week later showed that suggestibility (i.e., the number of questions children answered incorrectly at the second session relating to episodes about which they had been misled) decreased with an increase in conflicting mental representation scores. This relation remained significant after controlling for age, memory at the second session for items about which children had not been misled, and the number of questions children answered correctly at the initial interview when they were not misled. Thus, in support of the model, children who were able to reason about CMRs confirmed original information and rejected suggested information more often than other children.

Mental-State Reasoning, Memory Reinstatement, and Conflicting Memories at Retrieval (Predictions 1, 2, and 3)

Another study (Welch-Ross, 1999a) was conducted to test whether each type of mental-state reasoning predicts reduced suggestibility (Prediction 1), whether an interviewer's suggestions reinstate memories of original details for children who can reason about CMRs (Prediction 2), and whether reasoning about CMRs predicts considering multiple memories at retrieval (Prediction 3).

Fifty-seven preschoolers listened to a 27-episode story. Pictures accompanied 24 target episodes and were displayed on the screen of a computer. Each detail was displayed for 7 seconds, while the researcher read the associated text. Following the story, a second researcher entered the room, stated she had not read the story, and interviewed children about the details. As in the previous study, half the questions were straightforward yes–no questions and half were tag questions that presented misleading information that conflicted with the original items.

Approximately one week later, children completed a computerized recognition test. Pairs of pictures were displayed on a computer screen according to three conditions that required choosing between: (a) the original detail and a novel item that corresponded to targets about which interviewers had asked straightforward questions, (b) the original detail and the suggested item (Loftus et al., 1978; Loftus et al., 1992), and (c) the original detail and a new item, which corresponded to targets about which children had been misled (McCloskey & Zaragoza, 1985). Children were instructed, "As fast as you can, punch the button that goes with the story" (see Welch-Ross, 1999a, for complete details of the procedure). Accuracy and response times of children in the two test conditions for items about which they had been misled showed similar patterns for all analyses and are reported together here.

After the recognition test, children completed a set of tasks described previously to measure understanding of the relation between experiencing and knowing (Pillow, 1989, Ruffman & Olson, 1989, and Wimmer, Hogrefe, & Perner, 1988), tasks that measured an explicit awareness that current knowledge originates with a specific experience, such as seeing or hearing (O'Neill & Gopnik, 1991), and a set of appearance–reality (Flavell et al., 1986) and false-belief tasks (Gopnik & Astington, 1988) to measure reasoning about CMRs.

Response times were collected to determine whether reasoning about CMRs predicts the ability to consider multiple memories at retrieval (Prediction 3). The rationale for studying response times was that children who can reason about CMR should respond more slowly on the recognition test than other children after they are misled because these children spend cognitive resources processing memories of both original and conflicting information. Children who cannot reason about CMRs should select items more quickly because they updated their original memory when the interviewer suggested the conflicting item. Therefore, they consider only the suggested item at the recognition test and should not spend cognitive resources processing multiple representations. Children who can reason about CMRs, and who also have very good memories, as indicated by their memory for details when not misled, should be especially likely to consider memories of original and suggested information at the test, and make their responses more slowly than other children.

First, partial correlations showed that each measure of reasoning about mental states was negatively related to suggestibility, after controlling for chronological age (Prediction 1). However, contrary to the previous study (Welch-Ross et al., 1997), memory when not misled moderated this relation between reasoning about mental states and suggestibility. Regression analyses showed that the negative relation between mental-state reasoning and suggestibility was nonsignificant among children who had good story memory, as indicated by remembering details correctly when not misled at a level greater than chance. However, mental-state reasoning predicted a reduction in suggestibility for children who had poorer story memory, which was defined as accuracy that was equal to or less than chance when not misled. The relation was significant after controlling for age.

Why did reasoning about mental states predict accurate memory reports for children with poorer memories? These data do not provide a basis for making specific hypotheses because the ratio of variables to participants required summing responses to mental state tasks to compute a composite index of mental-state reasoning for the regression. One possibility is that reasoning about mental states related to knowing allows children with poorer memories to evaluate the potential validity of the information the naïve interviewer suggests. Although the suggested item may not reinstate memories of original details, children who recognize the experiencing–knowing connection may reject the suggested item and fail to encode the item in memory. In summary, children with poorer memories who can reason about knowledge states may be less suggestible because they do not accept suggestions from naïve interviewers simply because they are unsure about their own memories. An alternative possibility, consistent with the proposed reinstatement mechanism is that the interviewer's suggestions reinstate original memories for children who can reason about CMRs, and this process is particularly beneficial for children who have weaker memories of the original details. Reactivating original memories, together with rejecting a naïve interviewer's suggestions at the initial interview, may help children select the original detail.

In support of Prediction 2, children who spontaneously produced at least one original detail when misled at the initial interview had greater scores on CMR tasks than children who did not offer a single original detail when first misled. This result is consistent with the claim that misleading suggestions reinstate original memories for children who can reason about conflicting, counterfactual mental representations.

Finally, multiple regression showed a positive relation between the ability to reason about conflicting mental representations and response times when children were misled (Prediction 3). Unexpectedly, the positive relation between CMR scores and response times was specific to children's incorrect choices when they were misled. That is, reasoning about CMRs did not predict response times for correct choices concerning items about which they were misled. As expected, CMR scores did not predict response times for incorrect choices when children were *not* misled because all children should possess a single representation of the original detail in this case. Importantly, the positive relation between CMR scores and response times for incorrect choices when misled was independent of age and performance on tasks measuring the two other types of reasoning about knowledge states. These results confirm that selecting the incorrect item slowly after being misled was associated specifically with performance on the only mental-state reasoning task that required considering conflicting representations.

Next, additional partial correlations confirmed that the relation between reasoning about conflicting mental representations and making incorrect choices slowly was attributable primarily to children whose memory performance was significantly above chance when they were not misled (Prediction 3).

These findings support the claim that children who can reason about CMRs are more likely than other children to consider memories of both the original and suggested items at the recognition test. A possible explanation for the unexpected finding that this relation was evident only when these children made incorrect choices is that children who could reason about CMRs experienced source confusion, and therefore responded more slowly only when the confusion was significant enough to make errors. Consistent with this explanation, this relation was attributable primarily to children who could reason about CMRs and who also had good memories and thus were likely to remember both the original and suggested items. These children may be especially likely to become confused about which of the two items they actually saw.

In further support of this interpretation, consider that researchers speculate that the speed with which a person makes incorrect choices after being misled indicates how firmly the person believes the inaccurate memory (Loftus, Donders, Hoffman, & Schooler, 1989). In this study, low CMR scores were associated with making incorrect choices relatively quickly when misled. Thus, children who could not reason about CMRs appeared more confident, or less confused about, their incorrect choices. This interpretation is consistent with the claim that these children updated their original memory when misled and therefore used processing resources to consider only a single memory of the suggested item at the recognition test. However, children who could reason about CMRs, particularly those with good memories, appeared to consider both the original and suggested item at the recognition test and to experience source confusion, and thus they made their incorrect choices more slowly.

In summary, the results showed that mental-state reasoning predicted a reduction in suggestibility independent of age (Prediction 1), especially among children with poorer memories. In addition, children who spontaneously recalled original memories when initially misled had greater CMR scores than other children. This finding is consistent with the proposal that exposure to misleading information may reinstate original memories for these children (Prediction 2). Finally, children who can reason about CMRs made choices on the recognition test more slowly than other children, indicating that they consider representations of both original and suggested information after they are misled (Prediction 3). This finding confirms that developmental changes in the ability to reason about CMRs is associated with how children process information when misled.

That children who could reason about CMRs responded more slowly than other children did only when they selected the suggested item was not a predicted result, but it is consistent with the model and with a source misattribution interpretation. Children who could reason about CMRs recalled both the original and suggested information at the test, especially if they also had very good memories, and they experienced source confusion, made source misattributions, leading to the positive relation between CMR scores and slower response times when children made incorrect choices. Consistent with the model, children who could not reason about CMRs made source errors in the sense that they selected the incorrect item because they updated their original representations, considered only their memory of the suggested item at the test, and made their incorrect choices quickly and with confidence.

Reasoning Specific to Knowledge States (Prediction 4)

Many cognitive, linguistic, social, and neurological changes undoubtedly contribute to an understanding of mental states and to reductions in suggestibility. In addition, the ability to perform well on any task designed to target a specific kind of understanding, such as a false-belief task, requires a variety of skills. However, a fundamental claim of the model is that the relation between performance on false-belief tasks and suggestibility is a function of reasoning specifically about knowledge states (Prediction 4).

This claim was tested in a third study by exposing children to a context that required reasoning about knowledge states (Welch-Ross, 1999b). Specifically, a naïve interviewer and a knowledgeable interviewer took turns interviewing and misleading children about the details of a story. The expectation was that the knowledge of the interviewer would affect the suggestibility of children who passed false-belief tasks, which involve reasoning about conflicting knowledge states, but the knowledge of the interviewer would not affect the suggestibility of children who failed false-belief tasks. According to the model, children who pass false-belief tasks should be less suggestible when the interviewer is naïve than when the interviewer is knowledgeable, but naïve and knowledgeable interviewers should mislead children who fail false-belief tasks equally often.

Both suggestibility research and theory of mind research indicate that the interviewer's knowledge and the ability to reason about knowledge states should moderate suggestibility in this way. For example, in a study of suggestibility, 4- and 8-year-olds were misled more often when a more knowledgeable person suggested information than when a less knowledgeable person did (Toglia et al., 1992), although children's understanding of the mental state of knowledge was not measured independently (see also Lampinen & Smith, 1995; Smith & Ellsworth, 1987). Studies on children's understanding of mind show that 4- and 5-year-olds, but not 3-year-olds, can judge whether a person would accept or reject information on the basis of that person's access and the informant's access to relevant information (Mitchell et al., 1997; Perner & Davies, 1991; Robinson, 1994, this volume; Robinson & Mitchell, 1992). For example, in one study, children listened to stories in which a character who was either naïve or knowledgeable about the contents of a box received from another character either true or false information about its contents (Perner & Davies, 1991). Four- and 5-year-olds, but not 3-year-olds, realized that the character who looked inside the box would be more likely to reject a false description of the contents than the character who did not look.

In the current study (Welch-Ross, 1999b), 51 preschoolers listened to a researcher read the same 27-episode story used in previous research, which consisted of 24 target episodes shown in pictures presented on a computer screen. In a within-subjects design, each interviewer asked children six straightforward, yes-no questions about half the items and six tag questions that presented conflicting information about half the items. Whether the naïve interviewer or the knowledgeable interviewer asked questions first was counterbalanced between participants.

One week later, children completed a verbal recognition test to measure story memory in which they chose between the original detail and a suggested item. A researcher asked, for example, "Did John wrap a stuffed teddy bear for Amy on her birthday, or did John wrap a stuffed elephant for Amy on her birthday?" Then, children completed a set of tasks that required reasoning about the relation between seeing and knowing (Pillow, 1989; Pratt & Bryant, 1990; Ruffman & Olson, 1989), and a set of false-belief tasks (mistaken contents, mistaken identity) (Gopnik & Astington, 1988) that required reasoning about conflicting, counterfactual mental representations that result from different informative experiences.

Responses to the initial interview replicated the findings of Welch-Ross et al. (1997). Mental-state reasoning was not associated with reduced suggestibility at the initial interview. Instead, all children were correct more often in response to straightforward questions than misleading questions, regardless of their mental-state reasoning.

Responses to the recognition test also replicated previous research relating to Prediction 1 (Welch-Ross et al., 1997; Welch-Ross, 1999a) although suggestibility was measured differently. In the suggestibility literature, a misinformation effect is evident if memory for misleading items is poorer than memory for items when not misled (Loftus et al., 1992; Toglia et al., 1992; Zaragoza et al., 1992). In this study, mean comparisons showed that children who passed false-belief tasks did not show a misinformation effect when a naïve interviewer misled them, whereas children who failed false-belief tasks did. Therefore, consistent with previous studies, performance on false-belief tasks was associated with resisting suggestion.

Next, the results showed a significant 3-way interaction (Interviewer: knowledgeable, naïve x False-Belief Task Performance: pass, fail x Item: misled, not misled), which supported Prediction 4. Although children who passed false-belief tasks did not show a misinformation effect when the interviewer was naïve, these children did show a misinformation effect when the interviewer was knowledgeable. However, for children who failed theory of mind tasks, the magnitude of the misinformation effect did not differ significantly as a function of interviewer knowledge. Considering responses only to items about which children had been misled, children who passed false-belief tasks remembered items less accurately when misled by a knowledgeable interviewer than when misled by a naïve interviewer; however knowledgeable and naïve interviewers misled children who failed false-belief tasks equally often.

Finally, individual differences in memory ability would help children resist suggestion and to distinguish between memories of details suggested by two different interviewers. Therefore, a regression analysis controlled for the relation between individual differences in memory and relative suggestibility between interviewers. The measure of memory was the number of straightforward questions answered correctly at the initial interview and the number of recognition questions answered correctly when not misled. The dependent measure of relative suggestibility between interviewers was a ratio score in which the number of items correct when misled by the knowledgeable interviewer was divided by the number of items correct when misled by the naïve interviewer. Therefore, lower scores indicated that children were less accurate when a knowledgeable interviewer misled them than when a naïve interviewer did. False-belief scores predicted the tendency to be misled more often by a knowledgeable interviewer than by a naïve interviewer, after controlling for age and memory when not misled.

In summary, performance on false-belief tasks moderated whether or not the knowledge state of the interviewer affected suggestibility. These findings provide compelling evidence that performance on false-belief tasks predicts suggestibility effects among preschoolers, at least in part, because they require children to reason specifically about conflicting knowledge states (see Welch-Ross, 1999a, 1999b, for additional discussion).

Source Monitoring and Awareness of Links Between Knowledge and its Specific Origins (Prediction 5)

According to the mental-state reasoning model of suggestibility, an explicit awareness that knowledge originates with particular experiences motivates the encoding and retrieval of source cues, which improves the accuracy of memory after being misled. However, another possibility is that developmental improvements in memory source monitoring help children to become aware that a variety of specific experiences cause the mental state of knowing. Alternatively, source monitoring and an awareness of origins of knowledge may affect one another indirectly or simply emerge simultaneously as a function of related cognitive, social, linguistic, or neurological changes.

Data from two studies address whether or not an explicit awareness of knowledge origins emerges prior to, and is related to, a decrease in source errors and source misattributions (Prediction 5). First, unpublished data from a sample of eighteen 4½- to 6-year-olds, originally collected for a different purpose, address the claim that an awareness of knowledge origins develops prior to the ability to distinguish actually experienced episodes from pretended or imagined ones. Following the procedure reported in Welch-Ross (1995), children engaged in seven pretend actions with objects, seven imagined actions without objects, and actually performed seven actions with real objects. After a 5-minute delay, children answered 28 general recognition questions (e.g., "Did we talk about smelling flowers?") that contained the 21 old items and 7 new items. If a child reported recognizing an action, then a specific source-monitoring question followed immediately (e.g., "Did you pretend to smell a flower, did you imagine smelling a flower, or did you smell a flower for real?").

One week later children completed a "how-know" task to measure the awareness that knowledge originates with specific informative experiences (O'Neill & Gopnik, 1991). Children discovered the contents of a bag by either looking inside or being told about the contents. Each child received two "look" and two "tell" trials. For each trial, children were asked, "What is inside the bag?" and then the test question, "How do you know what's inside?" All children answered the four "how-know" questions correctly, indicating a perfect awareness of origins of knowledge.

Considering source attributions for the new actions first, children rarely reported performing actions that were new. Five children (27%) reported recognizing a new action, and of these children, only one (5%) reported actually performing two of the new actions. Two children (11%) reported imagining a total of three new actions and three children (16%) reported pretending a total of four of the new actions. Average source attribution errors for old actions recognized, however, were 46%, 18%, and 5% for imagined, pretended, and performed actions, respectively. Regarding the origin of the three kinds of actions, 14 (77%), six (33%), and two (11%) children did not identify, respectively, the source of imagined, pretended, and performed actions more accurately than would be expected from guessing. Few of these errors involved reports of performing imagined actions. Five (27%) children reported performing at least one of the actions they had only imagined. Three children (16%) reported performing one imagined action, one child (5%) reported performing four imagined actions, and one child (5%) reported performing five imagined actions.

Thus, children were explicitly aware that current knowledge is linked to a specific experiential origin before they distinguished the sources of their memories reliably. However, confusions between performed and imagined actions were few, as would be expected from children who passed awareness of knowledge origins tasks. Also, the ability to identify sources of memories does not guarantee that children or adults will always retrieve source cues spontaneously or effectively. They may neglect to do so for a variety of reasons that may be either developmental (e.g., newly acquired strategies for remembering are too effortful to execute consistently) or contextual (e.g., support is not available for directing attention to sources). For example, we know that adults who receive explicit source questions that focus attention on the experiential origin of their memories experience fewer source confusions between experienced details and conflicting, post-event information than adults who receive recognition questions that require choosing between the original and suggested details (Lindsay, 1990; Lindsay & Johnson, 1989). This result is consistent across laboratory and forensic contexts (e.g., Morton, 1994), and several contributors to this volume have indicated that orienting young children to source before a memory interview decreases their suggestibility (see chap. 7, and 10, this volume).

Therefore, in a recent study following a procedure similar to the one used by Lindsay and Johnson (1989) with adults, children were misled and then answered recognition questions in which they chose between the original detail and a suggested item. This was followed by a set of direct source-monitoring questions (Welch-Ross, 1999c). One goal was to determine if an awareness of knowledge origins predicts a decrease in suggestibility across questions of different types. A second goal was to determine if an awareness of knowledge origins is necessary for explicit source monitoring. In this case, direct source questions may not reduce reports of suggested information for children who lack an awareness of knowledge origins. Therefore, these children should answer recognition questions better than direct source questions, whereas children who are aware of knowledge origins should answer direct source questions more accurately than recognition questions, as adults do.

Alternatively, children who lack an awareness of knowledge origins may be capable of source monitoring, but require additional contextual support to recall source information spontaneously or effectively. In this case, children who lack an awareness of knowledge origins may answer direct source questions as accurately as recognition questions, and as accurately as children who show an awareness of knowledge origins do.

As in previous studies, sixty 3- to 6-year-olds listened to a researcher read a 27-episode story consisting of 24 target episodes that were displayed each for seven seconds on a computer screen. After a 4-minute delay, a second researcher named Kristin entered and asked 12 straightforward, yes–no questions and 12 misleading tag questions. After a delay of 5 to 7 days, a third researcher asked recognition questions for half of the target items (e.g., "Did John wear Big Bird pajamas or did John wear Mickey Mouse pajamas?") and direct source questions for half the items (e.g., "Did you see Sally fall from the jungle-gym or did Kristin tell you Sally fell from the jungle-gym?"). Children had been asked straightforward questions for half of the items and misleading questions for the other items within each interview condition.

Then, children completed tasks to assess their awareness that current knowledge is linked to a specific experiential origin. They completed four "how-know" task trials (O'Neill & Gopnik, 1991), as described earlier, and four trials of a "why-know" task (adapted from Wimmer et al., 1988). In the "why-know" task, the child and a puppet named "Kermit" took turns looking into a box for four trials. After each trial, the researcher asked "Do you know what's inside the box?" and "Does Kermit know what's inside the box?" If children answered the pair correctly they were asked to state explicitly why Kermit did or did not know the contents of the box. The correlation between "how-know" and "why-know" tasks was strong and significant after controlling for age; however, the tasks showed different patterns of relations to memory measures. Therefore, each was considered separately in the analyses.

Responses to the initial interview showed that all children showed a misinformation effect regardless of their awareness of knowledge origins. Children answered more straightforward questions correctly than misleading questions.

Focusing next on responses to the recognition test, multiple regression showed that performance on the "why-know" task predicted the number of items correct on the recognition test when children were misled, independent of age and the number of straightforward questions answered correctly. In contrast to the pattern of results for "why-know" scores, "how-know" scores did not predict the number of items correct on the recognition test. Therefore, results involving the "why-know" task supported Prediction 5.

Recall that a misinformation effect exists if memory is worse when misled than when not misled. Therefore, a ratio score of suggestibility was computed for the recognition text. The number of errors when misled was divided by the total number of errors. Thus, higher scores indicated a misinformation effect. Children whose "why-know" scores were accurate at a level greater than chance had lower ratio scores than other children, after controlling for age. This difference remained significant after controlling for the number of straightforward questions answered correctly at the initial interview. The same pattern of findings was obtained for children whose responses to "how-know" scores were accurate at a level exceeding chance, after controlling for age. However, this difference was only marginally significant after controlling for the number of straightforward questions answered correctly at the initial interview. In summary, results concerning the relative accuracy of memory when misled compared with when not misled also supported Prediction 5, particularly when an awareness of knowledge origins was measured using the "why-know" task.

Results for direct source questions showed that neither of the awareness-of-knowledge-origins tasks predicted accurate responses to direct source questions, which required that children report not seeing or only hearing about suggested details. Also, awareness-of-knowledge-origins tasks did not predict reports of seeing the original episode after they were misled. Therefore, regression analyses involving direct source questions did not support the predicted relation between understanding knowledge origins and reduced suggestibility.

In order to address the second goal of the study, the final set of analyses compared responses to recognition questions with responses to direct source questions between children who performed above chance level on origin-of-knowledge-tasks and children who did not. All children answered recognition questions more accurately than direct source questions, regardless of their awareness of knowledge origins. More specifically, fewer children selected the suggested item on the recognition test than reported seeing the suggested item in response to direct source questions. Therefore, at least with respect to this particular measure, even preschoolers with an awareness of knowledge origins did not benefit from direct source questions. Instead, children resisted suggestions more often if given a choice between two alternatives, even if one of these was the suggested item.

However, main effects involving origin of knowledge scores showed that children who passed the "why-know" task (i.e., who were correct at a level exceeding chance) both selected the original item on the recognition test and reported not seeing and only hearing about suggested items on the direct source test more often than children who failed "why-know" tasks. This result was significant after controlling for age and memory at the initial interview. Thus, consistent with the model, children with an awareness of knowledge origins were more accurate on recognition and direct source questions than were children who lacked awareness of knowledge origins.

In summary, this study showed partial support for hypotheses relating to the model. As expected, an awareness of knowledge origins was associated with fewer source errors on the recognition test. Consistent with the model, children who were aware of knowledge origins answered direct source questions correctly more often than other children did. However, the findings did not show that only those children who are aware of knowledge origins remembered information better when asked direct source questions than recognition questions, as adults do. Neither did the results support the notion that children who lack an awareness of knowledge can remember the sources of their memories as well as other children, however, if asked direct source questions that seem to focus attention on source cues, as for adults. Instead, children with an awareness of knowledge origins answered both recognition and direct source questions more accurately than children who lacked an awareness of knowledge origins. These results are consistent with the model in that an awareness of knowledge origins was associated with fewer source errors across different types of questions; however, additional research is needed to clarify the developmental relation between source monitoring and the awareness of knowledge origins.

PRACTICAL IMPLICATIONS AND DIRECTIONS FOR FUTURE RESEARCH

The "events" in these studies, and the procedure for the final "interview" in one study (Welch-Ross, in press), involved stories and pictures presented on paper or on a computer screen. Also, children listened passively to these stories rather than participating in an actual event. Researchers conducted interviews about a relatively neutral event in a familiar school environment. The interviews were conducted only twice, rather than repeatedly, following a brief delay of only a few days. These and other differences between the procedures reported here and real-world circumstances undoubtedly qualify their immediate application. Yet, several themes and intriguing results that emerged from these studies are relevant for understanding the contexts that affect the eyewitness reports of children who differ in their ability to reason about mental states. The practical implications that follow, as well as others, will be important to pursue in field research.

First, interviewers in all of the studies asserted very specific details about the stories. These specific suggestions certainly would convey that the interviewers knew a great deal about the story firsthand, although they had not been present when the story was presented. This aspect of the procedure has a certain ecological validity in that forensic interviewers are often well informed, or have specific theories, about an event before interviewing children about their personal experiences. Yet, each study confirms that children who possess specific kinds of understandings about mental states resist this kind of suggestion better than other children do.

Consider specifically the procedure that involved a knowledgeable interviewer and a naïve interviewer, who not only was absent during the story, but confirmed verbally to children that she had never read the story or seen the pictures (Welch-Ross, 1999a). Children who passed false-belief tasks did not show a misinformation effect when the interviewer was naïve, whereas children who failed false-belief tasks did. Moreover, whether or not the interviewer had access to relevant information affected the suggestibility of children who passed false-belief tasks, but the interviewer's access to information did not affect the suggestibility of children who failed false-belief tasks. Clearly, children who passed false-belief tasks were better able than other children were to determine that information access is more important for attributing knowledge than is behavior extremely consistent with knowing. In summary, preschoolers who can reason about conflicting knowledge states may be capable of reporting memories accurately in some circumstances after being misled by someone who did not have firsthand experience with the event, even when that person's verbal behavior strongly indicates knowledge.

Second, the pattern across studies shows that, although children who can reason about mental states may acquiesce initially to strongly misleading questions, they can resist suggestion better than other children (Welch-Ross, 1999a; Welch-Ross, 1999c; Welch-Ross et al., 1997) and can report details later that are as accurate when they are misled as when they are not (Welch-Ross, 1999b). That is, all children conformed initially to social pressure to agree with the interviewer; yet, those children who could reason about mental states resisted suggestion later. A variety of CMR tasks and origin of knowledge tasks predicted reporting events accurately after a delay (Welch-Ross, 1999a; Welch-Ross, 1999c; Welch-Ross et al., 1997) and children who passed false-belief tasks did not show a misinformation effect (Welch-Ross, 1999b). This resistance to suggestion is quite robust given that the recognition questions are leading because they offered the suggested item as a viable option. Applied, field investigations of real-world events are needed to confirm whether individual differences in reasoning about mental states predicts answering leading questions correctly after a delay, even when children acquiesce initially to strongly suggestive questions.

Third, these studies offer a foundation for predicting how preschoolers' perceptions of the interviewer's knowledge state affect their information processing when misled. Much basic and field research is needed to specify the steps of online processing that influence preschoolers' eyewitness reports in particular real-world interpersonal contexts; however, the studies reviewed here offer a starting point for these investigations. For example, consider that Welch-Ross (1999a) showed that children who passed false-belief tasks showed a misinformation effect when the interviewer was knowledgeable, but they did not when the interviewer was naïve. How did children reach this judgment? After a delay, do children who can reason about knowledge states intentionally select the misleading suggestions of a knowledgeable person, and intentionally reject the suggestions of a naïve interviewer?

Additional data that were not reported earlier showed that children did not select the item on the recognition test that the knowledgeable person suggested more often than would be expected from guessing (see Welch-Ross, 1999b). Instead, they selected the original and suggested items equally often when misled by a knowledgeable person, but still selected the suggested item more often than when not misled (hence, the misinformation effect). This finding indicates that children who can reason about knowledge states do not necessarily endorse intentionally the episode that a knowledgeable person suggested earlier. Rather, a more implicit process may account for this result.

For example, perhaps children do not expect a knowledgeable person to propose inaccurate details. This violated expectation, or a tendency to consider whether or not the item could be true because a knowledgeable person suggested it, may lead to more elaborated processing of the interviewer's suggestion. However, children would not be surprised that a naïve person could offer inaccurate information, and would reject it, failing to process it further. As a result, children may judge when presented with both alternatives after a delay that the suggested item is more familiar when a knowledgeable interviewer suggests it than when a naïve interviewer does. Thus, when the interviewer is knowledgeable, children select the suggested detail as often as the original item. Alternative explanations can account for this result (see Welch-Ross, 1999b, for additional discussion). A valuable direction for future research will be to specify how the development of mental-state reasoning affects the online processing of information when misled.

Finally, the last study indicates that asking young preschoolers direct source questions—even those who have an awareness of knowledge origins—may not improve the accuracy of memory beyond the accuracy obtained with other questions. Although direct source questions improve the memory reports of adults (Lindsay & Johnson, 1989), the study reported last showed that children were as accurate on recognition questions as they were on direct source questions (Welch-Ross, 1999b). This finding is particularly striking because the recognition questions were leading in that they contained the suggested information. Consistent with predictions, children with an awareness of knowledge origins were more accurate on both types of questions than were other children.

These results and future studies that focus on the relation between suggestibility and the developing awareness of knowledge origins will have implications for identifying the types of questions that affect the accuracy of memory reports of young preschoolers who differ in their understanding of knowledge states. For example, one possibility is that training children to focus attention on sources of knowledge will benefit the reports of some children who are beginning to become aware of knowledge origins but lack a firm understanding. Given that performance on origin of knowledge tasks was associated with answering direct source and recognition questions accurately, the benefits of such training may not be limited to direct source questions. Instead, it may generalize to other types of questions that can be answered more reliably with an understanding of knowledge origins.

In addition to investigating the claims of the model in field research to advance the practical application of the findings, research is needed to address basic questions that follow naturally from the model. For example, all of the studies reported here offer information that conflicts directly with the child's experience. Does mental-state reasoning predict resistance to other kinds of misleading suggestions? Also, would these results generalize to other interview formats that did not include misleading tag questions, and to other situations such as real-world experiences in which the child participates rather than observes? Moreover, the model may become more differentiated by examining other aspects of mental-state reasoning, closely related to the ones discussed here, that develop during the preschool years. For example, between the ages of 3 and 5, children begin to understand that specific types of experiences (e.g., seeing) lead to knowing about particular attributes (e.g., color) but not others (e.g., texture; O'Neill, Astington, & Flavell, 1992; Pillow, 1993). How might this understanding affect children's source memory in some contexts?

In addition, the model may be extended to include transitions in mental-state reasoning that emerge across childhood. For example, the framework presented here focuses on the development of a seeing=knowing understanding of knowledge states. However, children gradually begin to understand that other processes, such as inference, lead to knowing (e.g., Keenan, Ruffman, & Olson, 1994; O'Neill & Gopnik, 1991; Sodian & Wimmer, 1987). Later a more complex understanding of subjectivity develops, in which children recognize that individuals exposed to the same information will interpret it differently depending on their idiosyncratic histories of experience (e.g., Carpendale & Chandler, 1996; Pillow & Henrichon, 1996). How might these transitions in children's understanding of knowledge affect their perception of what they and the interviewer can know, and thus their tendency to report later an interviewer's suggestion rather than their personal experience?

As children begin to understand that knowledge originates with a variety of experiences and mental processes, such as inference, how does this understanding affect the retrieval of source cues? For example, as a general rule, the mental-state reasoning model would predict that training or direct source questioning may be effective initially with particular types of source distinctions and not others because children understand that some experiences lead to knowing before understanding that others do.

In sum, many factors such as exposure to related events (e.g., Quas, Schaaf, Alexander, & Goodman, this volume; Roberts & Blades, this volume; Thierry et al., this volume) and various individual differences (e.g., Leichtman et al., this volume) affect the accuracy of children's memory reports. The work reviewed in this chapter shows that children make sense of and remember their experiences using the social and cognitive skills available to them at the time. A reasonable expectation is that specific kinds of social-cognitive skills, such as mental-state reasoning, influence how children interpret and process information during social exchanges, such as forensic interviews. This chapter offered an initial framework for conceptualizing these relationships and documented empirical tests that laid a foundation for thinking further about the various ways that developmental changes in reasoning about mental states could affect source errors in the context of suggestibility and eyewitness testimony. Working toward a more detailed and extended model of how transitions in mental-state reasoning affect information processing in situations related to forensic interviewing should enhance our ability to understand and predict developmental and individual differences in the memory reports of children.

REFERENCES

Ackil, J. K., & Zaragoza, M. S. (1995). Developmental differences in eyewitness suggestibility and memory for source. *Journal of Experimental Child Psychology, 60*, 57–83.

Astington, J. W. (1993). *The child's discovery of the mind.* Cambridge, MA: Harvard University Press.

Brainerd, C. J., Reyna, V. F., Howe, M. L., & Kingma, J. (1990). The development of forgetting and reminiscence. *Monographs of the Society for Research in Child Development, 55*, (Serial No. 222).

Carpendale, J. I., & Chandler, M. J. (1996). On the distinction between false belief understanding and subscribing to an interpretative theory of mind. *Child Development, 67*, 1686–1706.

Ceci, S. J., & Bruck, M. (1993). Suggestibility of the child witness: A historical review and synthesis. *Psychological Bulletin, 113*, 403–439.

Ceci, S. J., & Bruck, M. (1995). *Jeopardy in the courtroom: A scientific analysis of children's testimony.* Washington, DC.: American Psychological Association.

Ceci, S. J., Ross, D. F., & Toglia, M. P. (1987). Age differences in suggestibility: Psycholegal implications. *Journal of Experimental Psychology: General, 116,* 38–49.

Chandler, M., & Helm, D. (1984). Developmental changes in the contributions of shared experience to social role-taking competence. *International Journal of Behavioral Development, 7,* 145–156.

Fivush, R. (1997). Event memory in early childhood. In N. Cowan (Ed.), *The development of memory in childhood: Studies in developmental psychology.* (pp. 139–161). Hove, UK: Psychology Press.

Flavell, J. H. (1988). The development of children's knowledge about the mind: From cognitive connections to mental representations. In J. W. Astington, P. L. Harris, & D. R. Olson (Eds.), *Developing theories of mind* (pp. 244–270). New York. Cambridge University Press.

Flavell, J. H., & Miller, P. H. (1998). Social Cognition. In W. Damon (Series Ed.), D. Kuhn & R.S. Siegler (Vol. Eds.). *Handbook of child psychology: Vol. 3. Cognition, perception, and language* (5th ed., pp. 851–898). New York: Wiley.

Flavell, J. H., Miller, P. H., & Miller, S. A. (1993). *Cognitive Development (3rd ed.).* Englewood Cliffs, NJ: Prentice-Hall.

Flavell, J. H., & Green, F. L., & Flavell, E. R. (1986). Development of knowledge about the appearance-reality distinction. *Monograph of the Society for Research in Child Development, 60,* 201–213.

Foley, M. A., & Johnson, M. K. (1985). Confusions between memories for performed and imagined actions. *Child Development, 56,* 1145–1155.

Foley, M. A., Johnson, M. K., & Raye, C. L. (1983). Age-related confusion between memories for thoughts and memories for speech. *Child Development, 54,* 51–60.

Goodman, G. S., Quas, J. A., Batterman-Faunce, J. M., Riddlesberger, M. M., & Kuhn, J. (1994). Predictors of accurate and inaccurate memories of traumatic events experienced in childhood. *Consciousness and Cognition, 3,* 269–294.

Goodman, G. S., Rudy, L., Bottoms, B., & Aman, C. (1990). Children's concerns and memory: Issues of ecological validity in the study of children's eyewitness testimony. In R. Fivush & J. A. Hudson (Eds.), *Knowing and remembering in young children* (pp. 249–284). New York: Cambridge University Press.

Gopnik, A., & Astington, J. W. (1988). Children's understanding of representational change and its relation to the understanding of false belief and the appearance-reality distinction. *Child Development, 59,* 26–37.

Gopnik, A., & Graf, P. (1988). Knowing how you know: Young children's ability to identify and remember the sources of their beliefs. *Child Development, 59,* 1366–1371.

Howe, M. L. (1991). Misleading children's story recall: Forgetting and reminiscence of the facts. *Developmental Psychology, 27,* 746–762.

Howe, M. L., & Brainerd, C. J. (1989). Development of children's long-term retention. *Developmental Review, 9,* 301–340.

Johnson, M. K., Hashtroudi, S., & Lindsay, D. S. (1993). Source monitoring. *Psychological Bulletin, 114,* 3–28.

Keenan, T., Ruffman, T., & Olson, D. R. (1994). When do children begin to understand logical inference as a source of knowledge? *Cognitive Development, 9*, 331–353.

Lampinen, J. M., & Smith, V. L. (1995). The incredible (and sometimes incredulous) child witness: Child eyewitnesses' sensitivity to source credibility cues. *Journal of Applied Psychology, 80*, 621–627.

Lindsay, D.S. (1990). Misleading suggestions can impair eyewitnesses' ability to remember event details. *Journal of Experimental Psychology: Learning, Memory, and Cognition, 16*, 1077–1083.

Lindsay, D. S., & Johnson, M. K. (1987). Reality monitoring and suggestibility: Children's ability to discriminate among memories from different sources. In S. J. Ceci, M. P. Toglia, & D. F. Ross (Eds.), *Children's eyewitness memory* (pp. 92–121). New York: Springer-Verlag.

Lindsay, D. S., & Johnson, M. K. (1989). The eyewitness suggestibility effect and memory for source. *Memory and Cognition, 17*, 349–358.

Lindsay, D. S., Johnson, M. K., & Kwon, P. (1991). Developmental changes in memory source monitoring. *Journal of Experimental Child Psychology, 52*, 297–318.

Loftus, E. F., Donders, K., Hoffman, H. G., & Schooler, J. W. (1989). Creating new memories that are quickly accessed and confidently held. *Memory & Cognition, 17*, 607–616.

Loftus, E. F., Hoffman, H. G., & Wagenaar, W. A. (1992). The misinformation effect: Transformations in memory induced by postevent information. In M. L. Howe, C. J. Brainerd, & V. F. Reyna (Eds.), *Development of long-term retention*. New York: Springer-Verlag.

Loftus, E. F., Miller, D. G., & Burns, H. J. (1978). Semantic integration of verbal information into a visual memory. *Journal of Experimental Psychology: Human Learning and Memory, 4*, 19–31.

Marche, T. A., & Howe, M. L. (1995). Preschoolers report misinformation despite accurate memory. *Developmental Psychology, 31*, 554–567.

McCloskey, M., & Zaragoza, M. (1985). Misleading postevent information and memory for events: Arguments and evidence against memory impairment hypotheses. *Journal of Experimental Psychology: General, 114*, 1–16.

Miscione, J. L., Marvin, R. S., O'Brien, R. G., & Greenberg, M. T. (1978). A developmental study of preschool children's understanding of the words "know" and "guess." *Child Development, 49*, 1107–1113.

Mitchell, P., Robinson, E. J., Nye, R. M., & Isaacs, J. E. (1997). When speech conflicts with seeing: Young children's understanding of informational priority. *Journal of Experimental Child Psychology, 64*, 276–294.

Montgomery, D. E., & Miller, S. A. (1997). Young children's attributions of knowledge when speaker-desire and listener-access conflict. *British Journal of Developmental Psychology, 15*, 159–175.

Moore, C., Bryant, C., & Furrow, D. (1989). Mental terms and the development of certainty. *Child Development, 60*, 167–171.

Morton, J. (1994). Cognitive perspectives on memory recovery. *Applied Cognitive Psychology, 4*, 389–398.

O'Neill, D. K., Astington, J. W., & Flavell, J. H. (1992). Young children's understanding of the role that sensory experiences play in knowledge acquisition. *Child Development, 63*, 474–490.

O'Neill, D. K., & Gopnik, A. (1991). Young children's ability to identify the sources of their beliefs. *Developmental Psychology, 27*, 390–397.

Perner, J. (1991). *Understanding the representational mind*. Cambridge, MA: MIT Press.

Perner, J., & Davies, G. (1991). Understanding the mind as an active information processor: Do young children have a "copy theory of mind"? *Cognition, 39*, 51–69.

Perner, J., Leekam, S., & Wimmer, H. (1987). Three-year-olds difficulty with false belief: The case for a conceptual deficit. *British Journal of Developmental Psychology, 5*, 125–137.

Perner, J., & Ruffman, T. (1995). Episodic memory an autonoetic consciousness: Developmental evidence and a theory of childhood amnesia. *Journal of Experimental Child Psychology, 59*, 516–548.

Pillow, B. H. (1989). Early understanding of perception as a source of knowledge. *Journal of Experimental Child Psychology, 47*, 116–129.

Pillow, B. H. (1993). Preschool children's understanding of the relationship between modality of perceptual access and knowledge of perceptual properties. *British Journal of Developmental Psychology, 11*, 371–389.

Pillow, B. H., & Henrichon, A. J. (1996). There's more to the picture than meets the eye: Young children's difficulty understanding biased interpretation. *Child Development, 67*, 803–819.

Pratt, C., & Bryant, P. (1990). Young children understand that looking leads to knowing (so long as they are looking in a single barrel). *Child Development, 61*, 973–982.

Riggs, K. J., Peterson, D. M., Robinson, E. J., & Mitchell, P. (1998). Are errors in false belief tasks symptomatic of a broader difficulty with counterfactuality? *Cognitive Development, 13*, 73–90.

Robinson, E. J. (1994). What people say, what they think, and what is really the case: Children's understanding of utterances as sources of knowledge. In C. Lewis & P. Mitchell (Eds.), *Children's early understanding of mind: Origins and development* (pp. 355–384). Hillsdale, NJ: Lawrence Erlbaum Associates.

Robinson, E. J., & Mitchell, P. (1992). Children's interpretation of messages from a speaker with a false belief. *Child Development, 63*, 639–652.

Ruffman, T. K., & Olson, D. R., (1989). Children's ascriptions of knowledge to others. *Developmental Psychology, 25*, 601–606.

Ruffman, T. K., Olson, D. R., & Astington, J. W. (1991). Children's understanding of visual ambiguity. *British Journal of Developmental Psychology, 9*, 89–103.

Smith, V. C., & Ellsworth, P. C. (1987). The social psychology of eyewitness accuracy: Misleading questions and communicator expertise. *Journal of Applied Psychology, 72*, 294–300.

Sodian, B. (1988). Children's attributions of knowledge to the listener in a referential communication task. *Child Development, 5*, 378–385.

Sodian, B. (1990). Understanding verbal communication: Children's ability to deliberately manipulate ambiguity in referential messages. *Cognitive Development, 5*, 209–222.

Sodian, B., & Wimmer, H. (1987). Children's understanding of inference as a source of knowledge. *Child Development, 58*, 424–433.

Taylor, M. (1988). Conceptual perspective taking: Children's ability to distinguish what they know from what they see. *Child Development, 59*, 703–718.

Taylor, M. (1996). A theory of mind perspective on social cognitive development. In R. Gelman & T. K-F. Au (Eds.), *Perceptual and cognitive development* (pp. 283–329). San Diego, CA: Academic Press.

Toglia, M. P., Ross, D. F., Ceci, S. J., & Hembrooke, H. (1992). The suggestibility of children's memory: A social-psychological and cognitive interpretation. In M. L. Howe, C. J. Brainerd, & V. F. Reyna (Eds.), *Development of long term retention,* (pp. 217–244). New York: Springer-Verlag.

Welch-Ross, M. K. (1995). Developmental changes in preschoolers' ability to distinguish memories of performed, pretended, and imagined actions. *Cognitive Development, 10,* 421–441.

Welch-Ross, M. K. (1999a). Preschoolers' understanding of mind: Implications for suggestibility. *Cognitive Development, 14,* 101–131.

Welch-Ross, M. K. (1999b). *Interviewer knowledge and preschoolers' reasoning about knowledge states moderate suggestibility.* Cognitive Development, 14, 1–20.

Welch-Ross, M. K. (1999c). *Preschoolers' awareness of knowledge origins, memory source monitoring, and suggestibility.* Manuscript in preparation.

Welch-Ross, M. K., Diecidue, K., & Miller, S. A. (1997). Children's understanding of conflicting mental representation predicts suggestibility. *Developmental Psychology, 33,* 43–53.

Wellman, H. M. (1990). *The child's theory of mind.* Cambridge, MA: MIT Press.

Wimmer, H., Hogrefe, A., & Perner, J. (1988). Children's understanding of informational access as a source of knowledge. *Child Development, 59,* 386–396.

Wimmer, H., & Perner, J. (1983). Beliefs about beliefs: Representation and constraining function of wrong beliefs in young children's understanding of deception. *Cognition, 13,* 103–128.

Zaragoza, M., Dahlgren, D., & Muench, J. (1992). The role of memory impairment in children's suggestibility. In M. L. Howe, C. J. Brainerd, & V. F. Reyna (Eds.), *Development of long term retention* (pp. 184–216). New York: Springer-Verlag.

Zaragoza, M. S., McCloskey, M. K., & Jamis, M. (1987). Misleading postevent information and recall of the original event: Further evidence against the memory impairment hypothesis. *Journal of Experimental Psychology: Learning, Memory, & Cognition, 13,* 36–44.

10

Source Monitoring and Suggestibility: An Individual Differences Approach

Michelle D. Leichtman
Marjorie B. Morse
Harvard University
Angela Dixon
University of Sydney
Rainer Spiegel
Cambridge University

For several decades, research on how people remember events has offered growing evidence that memories are often less accurate than people believe them to be. The reconstructive nature of memory, first delineated by Bartlett (1932/1954) and confirmed by much contemporary literature, leaves mental traces of past experience vulnerable to distortion (Loftus & Palmer, 1974; Neisser & Harsch, 1992; Schacter, 1995; Wright, 1993).

From a developmental perspective, the myriad influences that shape event memory are particularly rich ground for consideration. Many studies currently attest to a developmental trend whereby children's suggestibility declines with age. The central phenomenon of interest is the vulnerability of children's memory reports to distortion from influences outside the original memory trace. Although adults are also prone to memory distortion (Loftus, 1991; Schacter, 1995), young children's recollections show a particular vulnerability to the effects of misleading information (Ceci & Bruck, 1993, 1995; Lepore & Sesco, 1994). Over the past 15 years, a burgeoning literature has emerged concerning the questions of why and under what circumstances children's memories are affected by suggestion (Ackil &

Zaragoza, 1995; Ceci & Bruck, 1993; Leichtman & Ceci, 1995). In this chapter, we offer a theoretical perspective on the mechanism behind children's suggestibility that is supported by research on individual differences in children's source-monitoring abilities. Before describing three studies that illustrate the connection between source monitoring and suggestibility, we briefly explain the suggestibility phenomenon and the theoretical groundwork for our empirical approach.

Typically, investigators have examined children's suggestibility using misinformation paradigms, in which children experience a story or event, and subsequently receive misleading information concerning the details of what they witnessed. For example, in a seminal study, 3- to 12-year-old children heard a story about events in the life of a protagonist (Ceci, Ross, & Toglia, 1987). Subsequently, a researcher asked participants questions about the story. She included subtle misinformation in questions to experimental participants, and included only correct information in questions to children in a control group. Later, another researcher gave all participants forced-choice recognition tasks, asking children to choose between items present in the original story and suggested items. The results indicated that control participants of all ages were very accurate in recognizing the original items. In contrast, there was a sharp age trend in the experimental group, due to younger children's incorrect selection of suggested items, or false alarms. Three- to 4-year-olds made the most errors, followed by 5- to 6-year-olds, and older children, respectively (see chap. 7, this volume, for further description of these data).

Subsequent investigations have uncovered similar age effects using more naturalistic paradigms and a variety of misinformation inductions and types of interviews (e.g., Leichtman & Ceci, 1995; Poole & Lindsay, 1995; chap. 8, this volume, for further examples.) Across widely varying circumstances, preschoolers have shown disproportionate vulnerability to suggestion, leading in extreme cases to false memories of past events. Developmentalists have naturally been intrigued by this phenomenon, and have proposed a number of mechanisms that might account for young children's relatively high levels of suggestibility (e.g., Ackil & Zaragoza, 1995; Reyna & Lloyd, 1997; Schacter, Kagan, & Leichtman, 1995; Welch-Ross, Diecidue, & Miller, 1997). Certainly, under some questioning conditions, social factors play a role. Young children, for example, may consciously bow to the suggestions of adult authority figures or mentally question the accuracy of their own recollections in the face of alternative suggestions from powerful adults (Ceci & Bruck, 1993). However, although these social factors may give rise to or enhance children's report distortion, research findings also suggest that exposure to misleading information can affect fundamental cognitive aspects of young children's memory. For example, as in Ceci et al.'s (1987) study, in a typical misinformation paradigm researchers present children at test with a forced choice between the correct item they originally experienced and an item that was suggested during intervening sessions. However, in a twist on this paradigm, researchers instead have asked children at test to identify the original item when given a choice between the original item and a novel item they have never seen before. Studies using this method have indicated that participants sometimes have difficulty identifying the original item once they have been exposed to misleading suggestions, whether or not the suggestion is included in the choices at test (Ceci et al., 1987; McCloskey & Zaragoza, 1985; Payne, Toglia, & Anastasi, 1994). Studies that have induced similar misinformation effects in adults have indicated that participants often come to believe that they actually remember seeing the suggested details they report (Loftus, Hoffman, & Wagenaar, 1992; Zaragoza & Lane, 1994).

Further evidence of memory distortion comes from a number of studies showing that repeated leading questions, strong stereotypes, or visualizations of events that did not occur can induce young children to produce extensive false narratives (Ceci & Bruck, 1993, 1995). As Schacter et al. (1995) have noted, the misinformed narratives some children produce bear a strong resemblance in several qualitative ways to the reports of adult amnesiacs who are confabulating as a result of damage to the prefrontal regions of the brain. For example, children's narratives are often full of vivid detail and have an "automatic" quality; questioning seems to elicit them reflexively. Such narratives also seem autobiographical, in that they sometimes incorporate verbatim conversations and the child's own online reactions to an event that did not happen. Further, just as confabulating patients do, children often insist on their misled versions of events in the face of either disconfirming evidence, social pressures to reverse their reports, or challenges to their credibility (Ceci, Huffman, Smith & Loftus, 1994; Leichtman & Ceci, 1995; White, Leichtman, & Ceci, 1997). Thus, whether the incorporation of misleading information into a memory report was originally social or not, after committing to a particular version of an event, it appears that some young children are quite likely to believe that this version represents a memory of an actual event.

A series of studies in which children were encouraged to imagine events that in reality did not occur further illustrates this phenomenon (Ceci, Huffman et al., 1994; Ceci, Loftus, Leichtman, & Bruck, 1994). Participants in these experiments were 3- to 6-years-old. In the illustrative original study, once each week for 10 weeks children participated in an interview in which they were asked to draw from the same group of cards. Half of the cards described real events that occurred in the children's classrooms, whereas the other half referenced events that never happened in the children's lives (Ceci, Huffman, et al., 1994). During each one-on-one session with a researcher, the children drew one card at a time until all of the cards had been drawn. After the children drew each card, the researcher read the event described on the card aloud, and asked, "think real hard, and tell me—did that ever happen to you?" After children answered this question with a "yes" or "no," they moved on to the next card. In the eleventh and final week, a new interviewer queried the children, asking a similar question for each card. In this session, however, the interviewer also asked them to elaborate. If children said that events on the cards had happened to them, the researcher asked them to tell her about these events. Further, the researcher asked detailed follow-up questions after each open-ended question.

The results indicated that by the final interview, more than one-third of the children reported remembering an event that never actually occurred; in most cases, events they originally denied remembering. Moreover, the children's inaccurate reports were internally consistent, full of vivid detail, and accompanied by a confident attitude. When condition-blind adult raters were asked to discriminate between the children's accurate and inaccurate memories, they were unable to do so at a level above chance. Subsequent experiments using even stronger manipulations, such as asking children to visualize events that did not occur, have induced very high levels of inaccuracy by the final interview (e.g., Ceci, Loftus et al., 1994).

These studies suggest that as children repeatedly think about an event that did not actually happen, they may begin to confuse the source of their information about that event. In the simplest example of this, children may confuse facts or pictures they were given after an event with those that were part of the event. In suggestibility paradigms involving only verbal instructions, repeated misleading questions or instructions to visualize events may induce children to create mental images of nonevents while answering the questions. During subsequent interviews (e.g., during the later sessions in the 11-interview card-drawing paradigm), children may call to mind the images inspired during past interviews. When they do so, preschool children may have difficulty identifying the origins of these images. Importantly, they may confuse the mental images they generated internally in response to past questioning with images of the actual events they experienced.

This explanation for children's performance leads to the possibility that poor source-monitoring abilities—or children's difficulties in identifying the origins of their mental images— are at the root of the suggestibility effect. Along with other authors, we have suggested that preschool children's relatively impoverished source-monitoring skills may account to a large extent for their suggestibility (Ceci & Bruck, 1993, 1995; Leichtman & Ceci, 1995; Lindsay & Johnson, 1987; Poole & Lindsay, 1995; Roberts & Blades, 1996; Schacter et al., 1995). In this chapter, we present three experiments directed at examining the relationship between source-monitoring abilities and suggestibility in a preschool population.

As described in chapter 1, this volume, source monitoring refers to the ability to identify the origin of one's own knowledge, beliefs and memories (Johnson, Hashtroudi, & Lindsay, 1993). Across a number of experimental paradigms, young children show particular difficulty with some kinds of source monitoring, making source misattribution errors. For example, in one paradigm, participants were asked to either perform or imagine performing a number of actions (e.g., standing up, touching their noses). After doing so, younger children were more likely than older children to make source misattributions; they claimed to have performed actions that they only imagined, and vice versa (e.g., Foley & Johnson, 1985; Roberts & Blades, 1995; Welch-Ross, 1995). Similarly, young children have difficulty remembering the circumstances under which they have acquired new information. Taylor, Esbensen and Bennett (1994) conducted a series of studies exploring this phenomenon. They found that after learning novel facts, 4-year-olds incorrectly stated, and acted as though they believed, that they had always known facts they had learned just minutes earlier. Thus, across tasks requiring source monitoring, young children are often unable to specify the original context in which they encountered information, even when they accurately recall the information itself.

Studies of both source monitoring and suggestibility show substantial individual differences among children. On both types of tasks, even the performance of children in the most error-prone preschool age group varies widely. Although, in general, young participants make a substantial numbers of errors, in every experiment there are individual children who resist suggestions and do not appear to confuse actual from imagined events.

This subset of young children who resist misleading information are apparently capable of correctly identifying the origins of their beliefs on specific suggestibility tasks. However, it is not clear from extant data whether this ability is particular to a certain suggestibility task, or whether it reflects a traitlike ability with source-monitoring that generalizes across a variety of traditional source-monitoring and suggestibility tasks.

As we have noted, Schacter et al. (1995) suggested that children's source-monitoring problems and memory suggestibility were similar to the source amnesia and high rates of false recognition found among adults with frontal lobe damage. Given this parallel, the authors proposed that both the phenomena of suggestibility and source misattributions might be caused by immature frontal lobe development in preschoolers. Individual differences between children on both types of tasks could then be explained by differential maturity of prefrontal cortex.

In a subsequent attempt to directly evaluate the relationship between children's frontal lobe functioning and source-monitoring skills, Drummey and Newcombe (1999) gave seventy 4-year-old children a source memory task that had been developed by Schacter, Harbluk, and McLachlan (1984) for use with older participants. Children learned novel facts and were tested after a 1-week delay on these facts as well as other simple facts they had learned elsewhere, and were also asked in each case to identify the source of their knowledge. In addition, the researchers gave participants a series of behavioral measures designed to assess prefrontal function. As expected, children showed significant levels of source amnesia, or a complete inability to identify the source of their knowledge, very much like older patients with frontal lobe damage. Among children, such problems with source information were significantly correlated with some, but not all of the putative prefrontal measures the researchers looked at, although all of the correlations were in the predicted direction. Notably, the ability to answer source questions was significantly correlated with categories completed on the Wisconsin Card-Sorting Task, a test of goal directed activity and impulsive responding often used to diagnose frontal patients. It is possible that young children, like older children with learning difficulties, require more contextual support with these kinds of cognitive tasks than mature individuals (see chap. 5, this volume).

Thus, there is good reason to suspect that significant variation in young children's performance on misleading information tasks and other suggestibility paradigms may be due to global individual differences in their source-monitoring abilities. However, support for this provocative suggestion requires evidence of a direct relationship between source monitoring and suggestibility performance in a group of young children. We conducted Experiments 1 and 2 to examine this relationship, bringing together tasks inspired by two traditionally unconnected literatures (Leichtman & Morse, 1997). In these studies, children were given classic source-monitoring tasks and tasks measuring the suggestibility of memory. By including several diverse forms of both types of task, we were able to observe whether different kinds of source-monitoring tasks correlated with each other, whether different kinds of suggestibility tasks correlated with each other, and how the two kinds of tasks were interconnected. In these studies we predicted significant positive correlations between diverse source-monitoring tasks and between diverse suggestibility tasks. We predicted negative correlations between source-monitoring tasks and suggestibility tasks, a pattern that would indicate that among young children, generally poor source-monitoring skills predict vulnerability to suggestion.

EXPERIMENT 1: INDIVIDUAL DIFFERENCES IN SOURCE MONITORING AND SUGGESTIBILITY

Outline of Study

Twenty-four 4-year-old children (M = 55 months) participated. Two source-monitoring tasks and one suggestibility task were administered to each child, as described in the following section.[1] An additional sixteen 4-year-olds participated in the source-monitoring tasks during pilot testing; thus their responses are included in the source-monitoring results.

Source-Monitoring Tasks. An experimenter met individually with participants and administered two different source-monitoring tasks on the same day. The first task was a version of Gopnik and Graf's (1988) "drawer task." During the learning phase of the task, the experimenter showed the child a small set of six drawers, each of which held a toy or object (e.g., a plastic egg, a crayon, a toy car). Children learned the contents of two of the drawers by opening them up and seeing what was inside (e.g., "What's inside this drawer? Let's open it up and see"). They learned the contents of two of the drawers by the experimenter's instruction (e.g., "We can't open up this drawer, but I'll tell you what's inside"). They learned the contents of the final two drawers by inference from an easy "clue" (e.g., "We can't open this drawer up, but I can give you a clue about what's inside"). After learn-

---

[1]Children also took part in a task measuring visual imagery. The data did not show significant correlations with source-monitoring performance. Details of these data are out of the scope of the present discussion.

ing the name of the object in each drawer, children were asked immediately to recall how they learned this information in a forced-choice format (i.e., "How do you know what's inside this drawer? Did you see it, did I tell you, or did you guess it with a clue?"). Children's answers to this question served as the "immediate" source-monitoring measure. After the children had learned the contents of all the drawers and had been asked for their immediate recall of the source of this knowledge, the experimenter repeated the object and source recall tasks once again for each drawer. All of the source questions were presented in a forced choice format, and the order of items was counterbalanced. Children's answers to this second source question served as a measure of "delayed" source monitoring.

The second source-monitoring task was adapted from Foley and Johnson's (1985) procedure, in which children either performed or imagined performing actions such as body movements (e.g., touch your nose) or facial expressions (e.g., smile). In Foley and Johnson's original procedure, participants watched others perform actions in addition to imagining and carrying out actions themselves. In our adaptation, we eliminated the condition in which subjects watched others perform actions and used only 12 of the 36 original body movements and expressions.

The experimenter first provided the child with an explanation and an example (modeled by the experimenter) of what it means to "do something" in contrast to what it means to "just imagine" doing something. The child was then told that he or she would play a game, in which the researcher would provide a list of actions, and would ask her or him to either do or imagine each one. After completing the entire list of actions, either performing or imagining each in turn, the child was immediately asked to recall all of the actions that he or she remembered doing and imagining. Finally, the researcher went through this list of all of the actions asking the child to distinguish whether he or she did or imagined doing each one. The order in which children did or imagined doing the actions was systematically varied, so that half the children did a particular action and half imagined doing it.

Suggestibility Task. The suggestibility data were originally collected by Bruck and colleagues as part of another study (see Bruck, Hembrooke, & Ceci, 1997). Measures of suggestibility were taken over a 5-week period. Once a week, the same researcher met individually with each child and probed four salient events. Two of the events were "true events" that all of the children had actually experienced and two were "false events" that none of the children had experienced, according to reports from parents and teachers. For example, one of the true events, which had previously been staged by the researchers, focused on the children helping a lady who had tripped and hurt her ankle.

For each event, the child was asked during the first week of the procedure whether the event had ever happened to her or him. If the child assented, he or she was asked to report all the details he or she remembered about the event (i.e., "Please tell me everything you remember about that"). This first interview provided a measure of participants' baseline levels of acquiescence.

For the next three weeks, the experimenter began each session by asking the child again whether the events had happened and eliciting a free narrative if the child assented. Unlike the first interview, however, the second and third interviews included a combination of suggestive techniques such as peer pressure, visualization, and the selective reinforcement of some items of information, all encouraging the child to acquiesce that each of the events had occurred. During these interviews, the experimenter asked the child scripted questions about the details of each of the events, encouraging the child to generate concrete images of different event details. If the child initially denied that an event had happened, the experimenter asked the child to pretend that it did and answer the scripted questions. (The fourth interview differed from the others in that the experimenter interviewed the children through a puppet and did not use the same array of suggestive techniques; see Bruck et al., 1997, for details.)

During the fifth interview, a new experimenter met individually with the child. This experimenter told the child that she had heard some things and then asked whether or not each of the events had happened. If the child assented, she was asked for a free narrative of the details that she remembered about the event. Thus, in the final analysis, each participant had five opportunities to either deny or assent to the occurrence of each of the four events. Interviews were recorded on audiotape and free narratives were transcribed.

Results and Discussion

Source-Monitoring Tasks. Thirty-eight children completed the source-monitoring tasks and the results indicated that there was considerable variation in children's performance on each task. On the drawer task, children were close to 100% accurate when asked to identify the objects in each drawer. However, they were often inaccurate in their immediate source answers after learning each object. Only 24% of the children correctly answered all immediate source questions, and only 42% correctly answered half or more. Children were equally inaccurate on the delayed source task. Only 13% correctly answered all of the source questions, and only 54 % correctly answered half or more. This pattern of results differed from Gopnik and Graf's (1988) findings in which children performed close to ceiling on the immediate source task and only showed source memory problems in the delay condition. Overall, children in our sample showed more source confusion than Gopnik and Graf's (1988) participants of the same age. Children's immediate and delayed source memory performance was highly correlated ($r = 0.56, p < .01$). This is discussed further in the conclusion.

In the do–imagine task, children recalled an average of four performed and imagined actions in free recall. When children were asked to tell whether they had performed or imagined each of the 12 actions, 64% of their answers were correct ($M = 7.70$ correct out of 12 possible). Thus, unsurprisingly the 4-year-olds in this sample demonstrated performance that was below that of Foley and Johnson's (1985) original sample of 6- and 9-year olds, who achieved 82% and 91% correct, respectively.

The correlations between source-monitoring measures supported predictions. The two tasks were quite different on a number of dimensions. Notably, the do–imagine task involved the child's own actions and the drawer task did not, and the source in the do–imagine task was mental images versus actual performance and the source in the drawer task was the way the interviewer conveyed information. Nonetheless, the correlation between children's immediate source scores on the drawer task and their scores on the do–imagine task showed a trend in the predicted direction ($r = 0.41$, p < .10), and delayed source scores were significantly correlated with scores on the do–imagine task ($r = .62$, p < 0.01).[2]

Suggestibility Task. During the first questioning session for each event, children's responses to whether or not events occurred were relatively accurate. Most children accurately agreed that true events had occurred. Fewer than one quarter of children's responses to questions about false events were inaccurate assents. Across the 5-week period of questioning, children's rates of acquiescence to false events grew substantially, in line with results from similar multiple-interview paradigms and expectations given the suggestive interviewing techniques (e.g., Bruck et al., 1997; Ceci, Loftus, et al., 1994). By the fifth

---

[2]All correlations reported in the results of Experiments 1 and 2 are simple correlations. When age was partialled out, none of the correlations changed significantly.

interview, children assented to more than three-quarters of the questions the experimenter asked about the occurrence of false events. The correlations between the source-monitoring tasks and the suggestibility task indicated relationships between these measures in the predicted direction, although not all were significant. As expected, the total number of assents to true events across the five sessions was not significantly correlated with any index of source monitoring. However, the number of assents to false events showed a highly significant negative correlation with the immediate source task in the drawer procedure ($r = -.59$, $p < .001$). Performance on the delayed source task in the drawer procedure and on the do–imagine source task were correlated with suggestibility scores in the same direction, but were not significant predictors (all $ps > .20$). Interestingly, assents to false events during the first interview (our baseline measure of acquiescence) also showed a high negative correlation with immediate source-monitoring scores on the drawer task ($r = -.56$, $p < .01$). This baseline suggestibility measure was not significantly related to any other source-monitoring variable (all $ps > 20$). Finally, in order to assess whether the foregoing correlations were simply a reflection of better performance by some children on any general memory task, we considered the correlations that included a nonsource memory measure—children's ability to recall from the do–imagine task. This measure showed no relationship to any of the source-monitoring or suggestibility measures.

Thus, Experiment 1 provided support for the hypothesis that performance on some tasks involving source monitoring was predictive of performance on a suggestibility task in a small sample of preschool children. To explore this notion further with a larger sample and additional suggestibility measures, we conducted Experiment 2.

EXPERIMENT 2: A FURTHER EXPLORATION OF INDIVIDUAL DIFFERENCES

Outline of Study

Forty-five children, ages 3 to 5 years ($M = 48$ months) participated. Participants were given two source-monitoring measures and two suggestibility measures.

Source-Monitoring Tasks. The two source-monitoring measures were identical to those in Experiment 1. However, we added instructions at the beginning of the drawer task to ensure that children understood the tasks and would perform as well as possible. At the outset of the drawer task, the experimenter showed each participant the drawers. The experimenter told the child that he or she would learn what was inside each drawer by either seeing the object with her or his own eyes, hearing about the identity of the object from the experimenter, or inferring the identity of the object from a clue. Before the do–imagine task, the experimenter explained to each child the difference between doing and imagining an action and demonstrated an example of each, as in Experiment 1.

Suggestibility Tasks. The first suggestibility task was a multiple-interview design much like the task in Experiment 1. Suggestibility was measured longitudinally over a 7-week period. Children were questioned about six different events once per week in a single session. Three of the events were "true events" that all of the children had experienced and three were "false events" that none of the children had experienced (e.g., one of the false events involved the children's teacher finding $100 under the slide on the playground).

During the first week of questioning, the experimenter told each child that she was trying to find out about some things that children saw happen at school. The experimenter told the child that the children's teacher had informed her that children saw some of the events she was going to ask about and that they did not see others. Each child was carefully instructed to say "yes" if asked about an event that they had seen and "no" if asked about an event they did not see. The experimenter further instructed the child that some of the questions should be answered "yes" and some should be answered "no" to minimize the effects of social pressure to acquiesce to the events. These instructions were repeated at the beginning of each questioning session throughout the procedure.

For the next 5 weeks, the experimenter asked each child again about whether she had seen each of the events. If a child assented, the experimenter provided the child with a perceptual detail about the event embedded in a question. For example, each child was asked "Did you see your teacher find $100 under the slide?" If the child assented to this question, the experimenter would then provide a detail about the event, such as "She was wearing a red dress, wasn't she?"; if a child denied seeing the event, the experimenter asked the child to "think real hard and pretend that you saw the event." Subsequently, the experimenter provided the same perceptual detail that was provided to children who assented to the event. Each week of questioning, a different perceptual detail was scripted in advance, and each week the detail provided was the same for all children. During the final interview, a new experimenter questioned each child about whether or not the events had occurred. If the child assented, the experimenter said "I wasn't there that day. Tell me something about that." In addition, assenting children were asked whether they had seen the events occur with their own eyes. If a child denied the occurrence of an event, the experimenter asked "Can you tell me something about that?" Thus, in the overall procedure, each participant had seven opportunities to either deny or acquiesce to the occurrence of each of the six events. Interviews were recorded on audiotape and free narratives were transcribed.

A second suggestibility task was modeled after a traditional misinformation paradigm (Ceci et al., 1987; Loftus et al., 1992). Children were shown an illustrated story in a slide show format as a group. Two days later, an experimenter met with each child individually and asked questions about the story that included misleading information about events that occurred in the story (e.g., asking "Wasn't that fun when Max ate pizza with his friends?" when Max ate spaghetti in the story). A week after the original story presentation, children were given a forced choice recognition test asking them to choose between pictures illustrating events that did and did not happen in the story. The pictures of the actual events in the story were created from the original slides, and the pictures of the suggested events were alterations of the originals created using computer technology. During the test session children were also given simple recognition tests asking them to chose between pictures of characters that had appeared in the story and characters that had not, matched on salient physical characteristics.

Results and Discussion

Source-Monitoring Tasks. Results of the source-monitoring measures indicated that children's performance was at levels similar to those reported in Experiment 1. On the drawer task, children made a large number of errors on both the immediate and delayed source memory questions, and they again performed at levels well below Foley and Johnson's (1985) older participants on the do–imagine source task.

The source-monitoring measures in this experiment showed a pattern of highly significant intercorrelations in the predicted direction. As in Experiment 1, immediate and delayed source memory questions in the drawer task were positively correlated with each other ($r = 0.85, p < .001$). Each of these measures was also positively correlated with performance on the do–imagine task (immediate: $r = 0.76, p < .001$, delayed: $r = 0.75, p < .001$). Hence, in this larger sample of young children who were well instructed prior to each task, these diverse measures of source-monitoring skill appeared closely connected.

Suggestibility Tasks. Results of the multiple interview "true–false event task" in this study paralleled those of the suggestibility task in Experiment 1, in that acquiescence to false events climbed across interviews. During the baseline interview children virtually always assented to true events, and also assented to approximately one-third of false events. By the final interview, children assented to more than three-quarters of false events. The two suggestibility tasks children engaged in during this study also showed a substantial relationship to each other. Children's total assents to false events during the true–false event task were negatively related to their correct answers in the final interview of the misinformation paradigm ($r = -.34, p < .05$). In other words, children who were more likely to assent to false events on the first suggestibility task were also less likely to provide correct answers in the face of misinformation on the second suggestibility task. This finding suggests that as predicted, these two types of tasks indeed reflect a global vulnerability to suggestion that accounts for their relationship.

Using the same measures, the pattern of correlations between the source-monitoring tasks and the suggestibility tasks indicated a robust relationship between the two kinds of tasks in the predicted direction. In fact, each source-monitoring measure was significantly related to each of the two measures of suggestibility. (Note that the direction of the correlations changed depending on the measures; in every case, better source monitoring predicted greater resistance to suggestion.) Immediate source recall in the drawer task was correlated with assents to false events on the true–false event task ($r = -.62, p < .001$) and with resistance to misleading information on the misinformation task ($r = 0.48, p < .001$). Delayed source recall in the drawer task was correlated with assents to false events on the true–false event task ($r = -.54, p < .001$) and with resistance to misleading information on the misinformation task ($r = 0.55, p < .001$). Finally, performance on the do–imagine task, measured by the number of actions correctly identified as performed or imagined, was correlated with assents to false events on the true–false event task ($r = -.63, p < .001$) and the ability to resist misleading information on the misinformation task ($r = 0.33, p < .05$).

Finally, we wished to observe measures of general memory not designed to rely on source information. The measure of simple recognition taken during the misinformation task (and unrelated to source memory) showed no relationship with any measure of source monitoring or suggestibility (ps > .20). The ability to recall and list actions performed and imagined was also unrelated to source performance on the do–imagine task, but it was significantly correlated with both immediate ($r = 0.38, p < .01$) and delayed ($r = 0.32, p < .01$) source memory on the drawer task. This recall task showed no relationship with either measure of suggestibility (p's > .20).

In summary, most, but not all, of the correlations between simple measures of general memory and source memory failed to approach significance, and this is consistent with other claims and empirical demonstrations of a dissociation between source monitoring and old–new recognition memory (e.g., Foley & Johnson, 1985; Johnson et al., 1993; Roberts & Blades, 1995). Similarly, none of the correlations between general memory and suggestibility measures approached significance. This allows a measure of confidence that the pattern of highly significant correlations between source memory and suggestibility tasks is unlikely to be due to a general memory factor. Instead, it is likely that these tasks correlate with each other because individual differences in suggestibility are at least partly a function of children's ability to remember the context in which they learned about events and information stored in memory and to make reliable attributions about source on the basis of those cues.

EXPERIMENT 3: REINFORCING THE CONNECTION BETWEEN INFORMATION AND ITS SOURCE

The preceding studies provided strong correlational evidence that individual differences in source-monitoring abilities play a significant role in children's suggestibility. A logical further question is whether reinforcing the relationship between a memory and its source shortly after an event can improve children's subsequent source memory and resistance to suggestions regarding that event. To the extent that the salience of the source of a memory can be empirically strengthened near the time of presentation, children's eventual memories may reflect this in both better identification of the source and less vulnerability to distortion from intervening misinformation. We examined this prediction in a recent study of preschoolers (Dixon, 1996).

Outline of Study

Thirty-six 3- to 4-year-olds ($M = 44$ months) and thirty-six 5- to 6-year-olds ($M = 65$ months) participated. (For ease of discussion, the groups are referred to as the 3- and 5-year-old groups.) The initial presentation of information took place when children met individually with a researcher, and was the same for all children. During a 25-minute session, children watched a video about a character named "Frog," heard a story about "Frog," and then played with a toy "Frog" and other toys in a scripted interaction with the interviewer. Order of presentations varied across participants according to a Latin Square design. A giant stuffed elephant named "Sophie" was placed next to children at the outset, and they were told that Sophie was going to watch and listen to Frog's adventures too. Each source (video, story, toys) presented children with information about a variety of activities Frog engaged in as part of a narrative (e.g., Frog poured ice water over his head, asked his friend to tell him a story, and tripped over a bucket). After the presentation of information through these three sources, the treatment that children received varied according to whether they had been randomly assigned to one of three conditions: source reinforced, memory reinforced, or control.

For children in the source-reinforced condition, after all of the presentations were complete, the researcher talked to the child about each central item of information (i.e., Frog's activities, colors of objects, names of characters) that had been presented. The researcher began the conversation by stating the source of the information she was about to review (e.g., "In the video we saw ... "), as well as pointing her finger at the source of the information (i.e., pointing at the book, toys, or video machine). The researcher then finished the sentence with the information of interest (e.g., "In the video we saw Toad and his friend drinking tea") and asked the child "Now where did we see this?" The child answered with the information the researcher had just provided (e.g., "in the video") and the researcher repeated this information following the child's answer (e.g., "That's right, in the video"). In the *memory-reinforced* condition, the experimenter repeated the same points, but the source statements were replaced by statements that did not refer to the source (e.g., "Today we learned that ... Do you remember that happening?"). In the *control* condition there was no reinforcement of the memory or the source; the researcher simply chatted with the children for several minutes about unrelated topics.

The logic of this design was to focus the attention of children in the source-reinforcement condition on the connection between where each item of information was obtained and the information itself. By reminding children of the source of each memory in this way, we simultaneously reinforced the content of each memory item, in which case improvement in source memory or resistance to suggestibility could be attributable to general strengthening of the memory trace for the original items of information. Thus, for the purpose of comparison we added the memory-reinforced condition, in which children received reinforcement of the content of the presentations only, and not of the sources.

A 5-minute distracter task followed the researcher's discussion with the children, and then the researcher told children that Sophie the stuffed elephant had something to tell them. The researcher occupied herself out of earshot in an adjoining room while Sophie "spoke." Sophie, via a tape recorder hidden on the stuffed toy, presented a version of the events that included misleading information. Sophie talked about the events in a chatty narrative that was sprinkled with questions to the children about matters unrelated to the target information in order to keep their attention (e.g., "Frog had to climb onto his big blue bed, but he couldn't! It was nice of Tim to help him, don't you think so, too? Oh, dear, my big red bow is crooked; do you think you could straighten it for me?"). The critical misinformation relevant to each of the three presentations included a color change, a name change, and a change in an action Frog performed. Thus, Sophie provided nine misleading statements in total. Following Sophie's narrative, children were dismissed. Thirty minutes later, they returned to the experimental room and the researcher asked nine dual-choice questions that included the original and suggested items, each followed by a forced-choice source question, for example, "Did Frog fall on a bucket or slip on a stone? How do you know that—did you see it on the video, did you hear it in the storybook, did you play with it with the toys, or are you just guessing?" Pilot work indicated that children in this age range understood the question.

Results and Discussion

Developmental Differences. The results of this study provide several insights into source monitoring and suggestibility across the preschool years, although they were not wholly in line with predictions. Consistent with past findings (e.g., Gopnik & Graf, 1988; Taylor et al., 1994), during the final questioning period 5-year-olds recalled a significantly greater number of original items and their associated sources than 3-year-olds, $F(2, 66) = 4.58, p < .02$. Indeed, 3-year-olds performed poorly when answers to both memory and source questions were combined, averaging 1.75 out of a possible 9 completely correct answers (i.e., identifying both the original item and the correct source). Three-year-olds' item memory was at chance level ($M = 4.44$ correct, 49% correct in a 2 choice paradigm) and their memory for sources was just above chance ($M = 3.01$ sources correct, 33.3% in a 4 choice paradigm). These results indicate that as a group, 3-year-olds were highly vulnerable to suggestion, equally often reporting the misleading information that had been suggested to them as the original item information. In addition, 3-year-olds were poor at identifying the sources of the items in question.

Analyses of children's "total correct" (item and source) answers revealed a significant main effect for condition, $F(2, 66) = 3.18, p < .05$, qualified by a marginally significant age by condition interaction, $F(2,66) = 2.73, p < .07$. Turning first to the 3-year-olds, these young participants showed no improvement when provided with reinforcement for either memory or source; analyses revealed that their "total correct" scores were equivalent across the source-reinforced, memory-reinforced, and control conditions ($Ms = 2.08, 1.42, 1.75$, respectively). Moreover, this pattern of no differences across conditions was mirrored when the data were separately analyzed in terms of memory items correct ($Ms = 4.71, 4.05, 4.52$, respectively) and sources correct ($Ms = 3.30, 2.76, 3.11$, respectively). In essence, the manipulations made little difference to any aspect of memory for which the 3-year-olds were tested. These results echo findings from other researchers who have attempted to improve 3-year-olds' performance on source-monitoring tests (Gopnik & Graf, 1988), and on appearance–reality and false belief tasks (Flavell, Green, & Flavell, 1986; Perner, Leekam, & Wimmer, 1987). The results underscore the limited source-monitoring abilities 3-year-olds possess for memory tasks that reflect a relatively high level of complexity, even when they are provided with reinforcing source information after acquisition. The findings also affirm that despite repetition of the original items shortly following acquisition, these very young children's memories were vulnerable to intrusion from misleading information.

A further point is that for most 3-year-olds, the sources of their correct answers seemed to be uncoupled from the answers themselves. When 3-year-olds answered the item questions correctly, they answered 39% of the associated source questions correctly. Although this is above the 25% chance mark for selection among four choices (video, story, toys, or guessing), importantly, it means that usually when 3-year-olds were correct, source knowledge did not support their insights. Furthermore, when 3-year-olds were incorrect in their item selection, 27% of their source answers were correct. Thus, whether they were correct or not in their content knowledge, these young children were far more likely to identify an incorrect than a correct source.

Observation of participants during the task strikingly illustrated that most 3-year-olds had yet to grasp the full causal connection between knowing an answer, and how they learned it. For example, when asked "What color was the gas pump, purple or yellow?" some

3-year-olds looked around the room to see if they could locate the gas pump in order to check the color. This behavior suggested that the children correctly realized the pump was a toy that they had just played with. However, when the researcher asked them the associated source question, the same 3-year-olds were unable to recognize that they knew the answer *because* they had played with the toy. Although they remembered playing with toys, these children's answers did not reflect an understanding that playing was the source of their knowledge. This anecdotal point supports the conclusions theorists have drawn from other paradigms, namely that children's understanding of the origins of their own beliefs is still rudimentary during the early preschool years (Flavell, Green, & Flavell, 1995; Perner & Ruffman, 1995). It also supports insights from Robinson (chap. 3, this volume), who found that young children could use conflicting sources of knowledge appropriately (e.g., children trusted what they saw before trusting what a naïve adult said) but absolutely could not reflect on how they knew different pieces of information (i.e., did they see or were they told the information?).

Five-year-olds' performance was above chance level for both memory and source answers, averaging 4.33 totally correct (item and source) answers out of 9 possible. As noted, 5-year-olds' performance was significantly better than 3-year-olds' across all three conditions for both item ($M = 6.40$ correct, 71% in a 2-choice paradigm) and source information ($M = 5.41$ correct, 60% correct in a 4-choice paradigm). In contrast with the pattern of findings for 3-year-olds, 5-year-olds' "totally correct" scores showed significant gains over the control condition ($M = 3.00$) in both the source-reinforced ($M = 5.17$) and memory-reinforced ($M = 4.83$) conditions, Tukey's ps $< .05$. Although the pattern of means was in the predicted direction (participants in the source-reinforced condition scored slightly higher than those in the memory-reinforced condition in terms of totally correct answers) there was no significant difference between source-reinforced and memory-reinforced groups. When the number of correct memory items was analyzed separately, the pattern of results for 5-year-olds mirrored their pattern for "totally correct" answers. Source-reinforced ($M = 7.01$) and memory-reinforced ($M = 7.03$) groups did not differ from each other, but both were significantly different from controls ($M = 4.91$), Tukey's $p < .05$. The source memory data for the entire sample of 3- and 5-year-olds combined revealed similar trends, although only the age effect reached significance and the Age x Condition interaction did not. Among 5-year-olds, as among three-year-olds, the mean differences among the conditions in post-hoc analyses of the source memory data did not reach significance (Ms = 6.22, 5.90, 4.52, for 5-year-old source reinforced, memory reinforced, and controls, respectively). Nonetheless, source and item data were more closely connected than in the case of 3-year-olds. When 5-year-olds answered the item questions correctly, they also answered 68% of the associated source questions correctly. However, when they answered the item questions incorrectly, they answered only 39% of source questions correctly. In both cases, then, performance on source identification was above the 25% chance mark. Critically, however, when 5-year-old children knew the correct item answer they were far more likely than not to be able to identify the source. When they did not choose the correct item answer, whether because of intrusions from misinformation or because they were mistaken for other reasons, more often than not they were unable to recognize the correct source.

The age trends in these data are consistent with the hypothesis that source-monitoring abilities develop on a continuum from simple, rudimentary skills to more complex ones, with the latter being acquired at a later age (Flavell et al., 1989; O'Neill & Gopnik, 1991; see chap. 2, this volume). Three-year-olds have been shown to perform well on simple, straightforward tasks involving the relationship between one single event and source, such as in the Pillow (1989) and Pratt and Bryant (1990) tasks (e.g. recognizing that looking in a box leads to knowing its contents). However, the majority of children did not master more complex tasks until 4 to 5 years of age, such as differentiating among three possible sources, as in the Gopnik and Graf (1988) and O'Neill and Gopnik (1991) tasks. In the present study, the incorporation of misleading questions and a 30-minute time delay between the initial presentation and memory testing added to the difficulty of the source-monitoring task. Thus the task may have overtaxed 3-year-olds' nascent capacity to identify sources, which, like many emerging capacities, appears fragile and limited in its expression at this early stage (Flavell et al., 1989; Roberts & Blades, 1995; chap. 3, this volume).

Nonetheless, there was considerable range in 3-year-old children's performance. A minority of 3-year-olds fared well on the source task, achieving correct scores as high as 7 out of 9. Consistent with findings from Experiments 1 and 2 and others in the literature, this suggests that the ability to differentiate between several source choices can be present by age 3 (Gopnik & Graf, 1988). In other studies, a minority of 3-year-olds was able to master conceptually similar tasks, such as appearance–reality, false belief, and representational change problems (Flavell et al., 1986; Gopnik & Astington, 1988; Perner et al., 1987).

This pattern of findings confirms that by age 5 children have made significant progress in handling complex source-monitoring tasks, with or without the source being brought to their conscious attention. Contradicting hopes at the outset of the experiment, source-reinforcement as operationalized here did not have the effect of improving children's source memory beyond increasing their general ability to retrieve item information. The memory reinforcement condition was not designed to remind children of the source, but only of the content of the presentations. However, for 5-year-olds, unlike for 3-year-olds, the content and source may have been bound closely enough in memory that a reminder of content automatically served as a reminder of source. This would account for the nonsignificant but suggestive trend from the 5-year-olds that source data followed the same pattern as memory data, with superior performance in both experimental conditions in comparison with controls.

Although the experimental manipulations had little effect of any kind on 3-year-olds' memories, they helped 5-year-olds resist the effects of misleading information. Among 5-year-olds, strengthening the trace for the original items improved resistance to suggestion across the board, whether or not the source was emphasized. Because there was no significant difference between the source-reinforced and memory-reinforced groups in either memory or source scores, it appears that the source manipulation was ineffective in helping children to resist suggestion over and above strengthening their memory for the original items.

Thierry, Spence, and Memon (chap. 7, this volume) reported a study with conceptual similarities to Experiment 3 that gives further perspective to these results. The researchers observed whether asking 3- to 6-year-old children source questions immediately following their viewing of a series of events in either a live or video format improved resistance to misleading information after a one week delay. The experimental condition most relevant to the present discussion is one in which children received misleading information about details of observed events. The findings contrast with the present results, in that 3-year-olds' suggestibility, but not 5-year-olds' suggestibility, was reduced by "source reinforcement" (in Thierry et al.'s study, questions about the source of event information shortly after the events). However, there are several procedural differences that limit comparison of the results. Thierry et al. tested resistance to misinformation after a week's delay, in contrast to the present study's half-hour delay between source reinforcement and questioning. Also, the potential sources in Thierry et al.'s study were fewer, perhaps making the tasks easier for 3-year-olds. Notably, in Thierry et al.'s study, source reinforcement did not boost the 3-year-olds' performance by inspiring them to resist suggestibility with more correct item answers, but instead boosted performance by decreasing the number of incorrect answers and increasing the number of times children chose "don't know." In the present study, children were asked directly to choose between two item choices, as opposed to Thierry et al.'s yes–no recognition paradigm in which children were reminded of a "don't know" option and warned that some information might not be correct. Thus, in the present study children did not provide "don't know" answers, obscuring the kind of subtle effect that Thierry et al. reported among 3-year-olds.

Thierry et al. (chap. 7, this volume) found no differences between control and experimental (i.e., source reinforced) 5-year-olds in the ability to resist misleading information. The authors speculated that the equality between these groups was due to the fact that control 5-year-olds spontaneously rehearsed source information, even when it was not explicitly probed. This rehearsal may have helped them to keep intact and rely on accurate verbatim traces at test. In Thierry et al.'s study, the control group was conceptually equivalent to the "memory reinforced" group in Experiment 3, as children in the control group were asked factual recognition questions instead of the source questions as part of the manipulation. Thus, Thierry et al.'s control and experimental children had equally strong memories of the original events.

Thierry et al.'s (chap. 7, this volume) explanation for the lack of differences between their 5-year-old groups may also apply to the similarity in Experiment 3 between "memory reinforced" and "source reinforced" groups who also had equally strong memories of the original events. In Experiment 3, 5-year-olds in both experimental groups may have spontaneously rehearsed source information in light of their strong original memories. Five-year-olds in the Experiment 3 control condition were at a distinct disadvantage (unlike any group in Thierry et al.'s study) because they received no reinforcement of the original information in any form, and would thus be expected to have weaker traces for the original information. The fact that they performed poorly on the suggestibility task in comparison with both of the other groups may be a function of the weaker original trace. Trace theorists assume that the incorporation of misleading information occurs in part as a function of trace strength, with weak traces being especially vulnerable to destruction or competition (Ceci & Bruck, 1993). Supporting this, research has also shown that children with weaker original memories of an event are less able to resist suggestions about that event (King & Yuille, 1987; Warren, Hulse-Trotter, & Tubbs, 1991). Unfortunately, the specific role that source attributions played in improving resistance to suggestion in this study, over and above the general strengthening of the memory trace, cannot be determined.

Differences in the Saliency of Sources.   There were no significant variations in children's item memory performance according to the source from which they had learned the items. However, answers to the source memory questions indicated that certain sources were more difficult for young children to identify than others. Children of both ages were most often correct in their source identification when the source was the video (61% correct), followed by participation with the toys (53% correct), and storybook (28% correct) experiences, respectively. This finding is consistent with suggestions that memory retention is influenced by the degree of sensory information contained in the to-be-remembered event (Foley & Johnson, 1985). Furthermore, it is consistent with suggestions that the quality of a memory, particularly the amount of perceptual detail it contains, contributes to the ease with which its source can be identified later (Johnson et al., 1993). The video and participation experiences may have offered a richer array of perceptual details for children to observe than did the storybook. Furthermore, in the participation condition, children's personal involvement may have promoted attention and active processing in a manner that enhanced subsequent source identification (Baker-Ward, Hess, & Flannagan, 1990; Parker, 1995; Roberts & Blades, 1998; Tobey & Goodman, 1992).

In summary, Experiment 3 demonstrated that source-monitoring abilities, although present in rudimentary form in some 3-year-olds, had undergone significant development by age 5. The data pointed to a different relationship between item and source information among younger and older preschoolers. Notably, strengthening older children's memory for either item information alone or item information accompanied by source information assisted their source memory. This is consistent with the possibility that older children knew better than younger children how to use cues derived from item memory to help them make correct source attributions. Children in both age groups had the easiest time remembering source information for events presented in video and participatory contexts.

CONCLUSIONS

The results of the three experiments discussed in this chapter highlight a number of conceptual points about children's source monitoring and suggestibility. First, source-monitoring skills showed clear improvement across the brief developmental period from 3- to 6-years, as other studies in the literature have also indicated (e.g., Foley, Johnson & Raye, 1983; Roberts & Blades, 1995; Welch-Ross, 1995). In addition to age comparisons within our samples, performance of 4-year-olds on the do–imagine tasks of Experiments 1 and 2 can be compared with performance of the youngest children in Foley and Johnson's (1985) sample. Observation of the difference between these samples indicates that improvement occurs between the earlier preschool years and 6 years of age in the ability to discriminate performed from imagined actions.

Children in the present samples performed poorly on Gopnik and Graf's (1988) classic drawer task compared with the original participants, despite our attempts to replicate the method in all significant aspects (e.g., the drawers used in the present experiments were created according to Gopnik & Graf's specifications, and participants in Experiment 1 were trained according to their instructions). Participants from Experiments 1 and 2 came from a number of preschools, and may have reflected a broader SES base than Gopnik and Graf's higher SES participants. Attempts to quantify SES effects on the major variables in our studies did not qualify the pattern of results we described. However, we speculate (as did Robinson, this volume) that SES may represent a dimension that explains some of the difference in performance between our samples and the original.

Data from Experiments 1 and 2 also underscore a point about children's suggestibility that has not been demonstrated previously in the empirical literature. Within a sample of preschool-aged children, vulnerability to misleading information in a laboratory-style misinformation paradigm predicted performance on a suggestibility task that involved multiple exposures to leading questions about naturally occurring events. This is potentially quite important forensically, because it suggests a relationship between the type of suggestibility effects that are likely to be present in the real world and the effects that are most often tested in the laboratory. We would like to offer the caveat that from an applied perspective, the data do not support a simple, testable assessment of children's suggestibility. It would be unwise to try to predict an individual child's performance on a given real-world suggestibility task from source-monitoring measures, for example. Many factors are involved in every real-world situation in which children's suggestibility is important, and source-monitoring skill is only one of these (Ceci & Bruck, 1993).

The results of these experiments confirm that some substantial portion of the variance in children's suggestibility is likely to be cognitive, as past work has hinted. Within the field of scholarship on children's suggestibility, researchers are continuing to debate the question of to what extent suggestibility is social, and to what extent suggestion affects memory itself (Loftus et al., 1992; McCloskey & Zaragoza, 1985; Tversky & Tuchin, 1989). Although we cannot draw a conclusion about the permanence of memory impairment from the foregoing data, these findings support the concept that some participants experience a significant effect of misinformation on stored information.

In Experiments 1 and 2, we did not include the control group that would usually be included in a misinformation paradigm for comparison purposes (see Loftus et al., 1992, for examples). That is, we did not test a group of participants (or include a within-subjects manipulation) in which children were exposed to the original story, did not receive misinformation, and were then given the same test procedure as participants in the experimental group. Similarly, in Experiment 3 we did not include a group of children who received no misinformation about narrative details. We did not include such conditions in the three foregoing studies because a wealth of studies has indicated that misinformation influences preschoolers' reports of past events under conditions similar to those we provided. We observed variation in the degree to which this effect varied across individuals (in Experiments 1 and 2) and across reinforcement conditions (in Experiment 3). In Experiments 1 and 2, we predicted individual differences in these effects that were related in theory to vulnerability to suggestion. Thus we did not require further direct evidence that variations in children's reports were due to their susceptibility to the suggestions we provided, as opposed to erroneous remembering for other reasons. Given the pattern of results, we have confidence that our misinformation manipulations were effective in distorting children's reports.

Most importantly, the findings of Experiments 1 and 2 demonstrated a particular connection between classic source-monitoring tasks and measures of children's suggestibility. Theorists have thought about suggestibility as incorporating source-monitoring processes, such that individuals given leading questions and misinformation generate thoughts or images of events that they later confuse with actual experiences (e.g., Ceci, Loftus et al., 1994; Leichtman & Ceci, 1995; Schacter et al., 1995). For example, Zaragoza and colleagues conducted a series of studies demonstrating that misled participants of all ages sometimes come to believe they remember actually seeing items that were only suggested to them, a clear source misattribution effect (Ackil & Zaragoza, 1995; Zaragoza & Lane, 1994). However, such demonstrations of the role that source monitoring plays during particular suggestibility tasks leave open the question posed in the present studies: Does general source-monitoring ability predict the degree of suggestibility, over and above age, when these two factors are indexed on entirely different tasks? The robust correlations between each of the source-monitoring tasks and each of the suggestibility tasks in Experiment 2, the similar but less pervasive pattern in Experiment 1, as well as evidence in other studies (chap. 9, this volume) provide evidence that this is the case.

Given the significant relationship between children's source-monitoring skills and their vulnerability to suggestion on several tasks that were presented close together in time, an obvious question is what accounts for this effect. As we described in the introduction, we hypothesized at the outset that children's frontal lobe development might be a crucial mediator of both source monitoring and suggestibility task performance. As Schacter et al. (1995) described, adult patients with prefrontal damage show poor source-monitoring skills and also provide reports of events that share some of the qualities of children's misinformed narratives. Unfortunately, specifying the developmental status of any particular child's frontal lobe functioning is, at present, difficult. There are a number of behavioral measures of prefrontal function, and as Drummey and Newcombe (1999) demonstrated, some of these are moderately predictive of source-monitoring skills. However, there is no effective neuropsychological test of prefrontal function that can definitively characterize development of this brain region. Furthermore, knowledge of the developmental trajectory of the prefrontal area is still incomplete. Huttenlocher (1990) has indicated that development of this area continues until adolescence, and children the age of those in our samples would be expected to display prefrontal immaturity. Again, however, how to characterize the developmental status of individual children is still a question. Furthermore, eventually it may be important to characterize the interaction of the developmental status of prefrontal cortex and other brain regions involved in suggestibility performance.

This description of frontal lobe involvement in source monitoring and suggestibility implies that part of the relationship between these two kinds of measures is maturational. In this case, individual differences in performance can be thought of as a function of statelike characterstics that may change as each child grows older. However, it is critical to acknowledge that traitlike individual difference factors are also likely to constrain performance on each type of task. Frontal function itself may vary across individuals during childhood and once maturity is reached in pertinent ways. Furthermore, as researchers have noted, temperament, dissociation tendencies, imagery absorption, mental-state reasoning, and other cognitive and personality factors not evaluated in the present experiments are likely to play a role in suggestibility performance (Ceci & Bruck, 1993; Eisen, Goodman, Davis, & Qin, 1998; chaps. 8 and 9, this volume), and perhaps in some more sanitized source tasks as well.

Although the original intention in Experiment 3 was to show that reinforcing the source could improve suggestibility in young children, our findings instead underscore the conclusions we drew from Experiments 1 and 2, consistent with other literature. Namely, children's source-monitoring skills may be heavily constrained by maturational factors, such that even verbally reinforcing the source had little effect for very young children. The findings of Experiment 3 illustrate the limits of individual children's source monitoring within the context of a suggestibility task. Despite efforts to verbally point out to children the origins of their acquired event knowledge shortly after encoding, neither 3- nor 5-year-olds' source memory significantly improved from this manipulation alone. The findings indicate that 5- to 6-year-olds' performance on both suggestibility and source memory tasks benefitted from reinforcement of just the item or both the item and the source. However, 3-year-olds' source memory performance was impervious to both manipulations, and thus it is not surprising that their ability to resist suggestion was also unaffected. Thierry et al.'s findings (chap. 7, this volume) supported this, at least insofar as reminding children of the source did not significantly affect the ability to identify correct original information after misleading questions. Consistent with other data (e.g., Taylor et al., 1994), 5-year-olds may be at a developmental level at which context is more tightly bound with acquired information than is the case among 3-year-olds. Nonetheless, children of both ages were affected by the nature of the source, providing more correct source answers when the source was a video or interaction with a toy than when it was a storybook.

In closing, the most spectacular effects of preschoolers' impoverished source-monitoring skills may arise in the forensic context of children's eyewitness testimony. When children are exposed to misleading information, questioning that inspires visualization of nonevents, or conflicting event reports across multiple sessions, the fragile links between facts and the sources of their acquisition may become blurred in memory. Thus, children may come to report, and in some cases to believe, that events occurred that never did. The consequences of such beliefs within the legal arena can be tragic.

However, there may be positive benefits to the same relationship between source monitoring and suggestibility, as other contributors to this volume have noted. For example, Ratner and colleagues (chap. 4, this volume) demonstrated that source-monitoring errors indexed greater learning in a collaborative context. Similarly, the relationship between source monitoring and suggestibility has been exploited for years by caregivers in many civilizations. The weak link between source and knowledge in children's memory makes it easier for parents to convince children of information that enforces proper behavior. For example, on Woleai Atoll in Micronesia, children live near thick woods in which they could become injured or lost. Parents teach their young children that ghost-like creatures called yalus live in the woods and will come after children if they enter by themselves. Many young children find indications of the yalus' existence in the world around them and some believe that they have seen the creatures with their own eyes, which keeps them a respectful distance from the woods (Douglass, 1998). Likewise, some preschool children in Western cultures come to believe that they have actually seen Santa Claus or the Tooth Fairy visit their homes. Thus, young children's suggestibility, which emerges as a function in part of immature source-monitoring abilities, may serve post hoc to reinforce meaningful cultural myths and keep children from harm.

REFERENCES

Ackil, J. K., & Zaragoza, M. S. (1995). Developmental differences in eyewitness suggestibility and memory for source. *Journal of Experimental Child Psychology, 60*, 57–83.

Baker-Ward, L., Hess, T. M., & Flannagan, D. A. (1990). The effects of involvement on children's memory for events. *Cognitive Development, 5*, 55–69.

Bartlett, F. C. (1932/1954). *Remembering: A study in experimental and social psychology.* Cambridge: Cambridge University Press.

Bruck, M., Hembrooke, H., & Ceci, S. J. (1997). Children's reports of pleasant and unpleasant events. In J. D. Read and S. D. Lindsay (Eds.). *Recollections of trauma: Scientific evidence and clinical practice.* (NATO ASI Series: Series A: Life Sciences, Vol. 291, pp. 191–219). New York: Plenum.

Ceci, S. J., & Bruck, M. (1993). The suggestibility of the child witness: A historical review and synthesis. *Psychological Bulletin, 113*, 403–439.

Ceci, S. J., & Bruck, M. (1995). *Jeopardy in the courtroom: A scientific analysis of children's testimony.* Washington, DC.: American Psychological Association.

Ceci, S. J., Huffman, M.L. Smith E., & Loftus, E. F. (1994). Repeatedly thinking about nonevents. *Consciousness and Cognition, 3*, 388–407.

Ceci, S. J., Loftus, E. F., Leichtman, M. D., & Bruck, M. (1994). The role of source misattributions in the creation of false beliefs among preschoolers. *International Journal of Clinical and Experimental Hypnosis, 42*, 304–320.

Ceci, S. J., Ross, D. F., & Toglia, M. P. (1987). Suggestibility of children's memory: Psycholegal implications. *Journal of Experimental Psychology: General, 116*, 38–49.

Dixon, A. (1996). *The effect of source reinforcement on preschoolers' ability to resist suggestible information.* Unpublished Master's thesis, Harvard University Extension School.

Douglass, A. R. (1998). *Childrearing and adoption on Woleai Atoll: Attachment and young children's responses to separation.* Unpublished doctoral dissertation, Harvard University.

Drummey, A. B., & Newcombe, N. (1999). *Prefrontal cortex development and changes in episodic memory.* Manuscript submitted for publication.

Eisen, M. L., Goodman, G. S., Davis, S. L., & Qin, J. (1998). Individual differences in maltreated children's memory and suggestibility. In L. M. Williams & V. Banyard (Eds.), *Trauma and memory* (pp. 31–46). Thousand Oaks, CA: Sage.

Flavell, J. H., Green, F. L., & Flavell, E. R. (1985). The road not taken: Understanding the implications of initial uncertainty in evaluating spatial directions. *Developmental Psychology, 21*, 207–216.

Flavell, J. H, Green, F. L, & Flavell, E. R. (1986). Development of knowledge about the appearance–reality distinction. *Monographs of the Society for Research in Child Development, 51*, 1–68.

Flavell, J. H., Green, F. L., & Flavell, E. R. (1989). Young children's ability to differentiate appearance-reality and level 2 perspectives in the tactile modality. *Child Development, 60*, 201–213.

Foley, M. A., & Johnson, M. K. (1985). Confusions between memories for performed and imagined actions: A developmental comparison. *Child Development, 56*, 1145–1155.

Foley, M. A., Johnson, M. K., & Raye, C. L. (1983). Age-related changes in confusion between memories for thoughts and memories for speech. *Child Development, 54*, 51–60.

Gopnik, A., & Astington, J. W. (1988). Children's understanding of representational change and its relation to the understanding of false belief and the appearance-reality distinction. *Child Development, 59*, 26–37.

Gopnik, A., & Graf, P. (1988). Knowing how you know: Young children's ability to identify and remember the sources of their beliefs. *Child Development, 59*, 1366–1371.

Huttenlocher, P. R. (1990). Morphometric study of human cerebral cortex development. *Neuropsychologia, 28*, 517–527.

Johnson, M. K., Hashtroudi, S., & Lindsay, D. S. (1993). Source monitoring. *Psychological Bulletin, 114*, 3–28.

King, M., & Yuille, J. (1987). Suggestibility and the child witness. In S. J. Ceci, M. Toglia, & D. Ross (Eds.), *Children's eyewitness memory* (pp. 24–35). New-York: Springer-Verlag.

Leichtman, M. D., & Ceci, S. J. (1995). The effects of stereotypes and suggestions on preschoolers' reports. *Developmental Psychology, 31*, 568–578.

Leichtman, M. D., & Morse, M. B. (1997, April). *Individual differences in preschoolers' suggestibility: Identifying the source.* Paper presented at the biennial meeting of the Society for Research in Child Development, Washington, DC.

Lepore, S. J., & Sesco, B. (1994). Distorting children's reports and interpretation of events through suggestion. *Applied Psychology, 79*, 108–120.

Lindsay, D. S., & Johnson, M. (1987). Reality monitoring and suggestibility: Children's ability to discriminate among memories from different sources.

In S. J. Ceci, M. P. Toglia, & D. F. Ross (Eds.), *Children's eyewitness memory.* (pp. 92–121) New York: Springer-Verlag.

Loftus, E. F. (1991). Made in memory: Distortions of recollection after misleading information. In G. Bower (Ed.), *Psychology of learning and motivation: Vol. 27* (pp. 187–215). New York: Academic Press.

Loftus, E. F., Hoffman, H. G., & Wagenaar, W. A. (1992). The misinformation effect: Transformations in memory induced by postevent information. In M. L. Howe, C. J. Brainerd, & V. F. Reyna (Eds.), *Development of long-term retention* (pp. 159–183). New York: Springer-Verlag.

Loftus, E. F., & Palmer, J. C. (1974). Reconstruction of automobile destruction: An example of the interaction between language and memory. *Journal of Verbal Learning and Verbal Behavior, 13,* 585–589.

McCloskey, M., & Zaragoza, M. (1985). Misleading postevent information and memory for events: Arguments and evidence against memory impairment hypothesis. *Journal of Experimental Psychology: General, 114,* 1–16.

Neisser, U., & Harsch, N. (1992). Phantom flashbulbs: False recollections of hearing the news about Challenger. In E. Winograd & U. Neisser (Eds.), *Affect and accuracy in recall: Studies of flashbulb memories* (pp. 9–31). New York: Cambridge University Press.

O'Neill, D. K., & Gopnik, A. (1991). Young children's ability to identify the sources of their beliefs. *Developmental Psychology, 27,* 390–397.

Parker, J. F. (1995). Age differences in source monitoring of performed and imagined actions on immediate and delayed tests. *Journal of Experimental Child Psychology, 60,* 84–101.

Payne, D. G., Toglia, M. P., & Anastasi, J. S. (1994). Recognition performance level and the magnitude of the misinformation effect in eyewitness memory. *Psychonomic Bulletin & Review, 1,* 376–382.

Perner, J., Leekam, S., & Wimmer, H. (1987). Three-year-olds' difficulty with false belief: The case for a conceptual deficit. *British Journal of Developmental Psychology, 5,* 125–137.

Perner, J., & Ruffman, T. (1995). Episodic memory and autonoetic consciousness: Developmental evidence and a theory of childhood amnesia. *Journal of Experimental Child Psychology, 59,* 516–548.

Pillow, B. H. (1989). Early understanding of perception as a source on knowledge. *Journal of Experimental Child Psychology, 47,* 116–129.

Poole, D. A., & Lindsay, D. S. (1995). Interviewing preschoolers: Effects of nonsuggestive techniques, parental coaching, and leading questions on reports of nonexperienced events. *Journal of Experimental Child Psychology, 60,* 129–154.

Pratt, C., & Bryant, P. (1990). Young children understand that looking leads to knowing (so long as they are looking into a single barrel). *Child Development, 61,* 973–982.

Reyna, V. F., & Lloyd, F. (1997). Theories of false memory in children and adults. *Learning and Individual Differences, 9,* 95–124.

Roberts, K. P., & Blades, M. (1995). Children's discriminations of memories for actual and pretend actions in a hiding task. *British Journal of Developmental Psychology, 13,* 321–333.

Roberts, K. P., & Blades, M. (1996). Children's eyewitness testimony for real-life and fantasy events. In N. K. Clark & G. M. Stephenson (Eds.), *Investigative and forensic decision making* (Vol. 26, pp. 52–57). Leicester, UK: British Psychological Society.

Roberts, K. P., & Blades, M. (1998). The effects of interacting with events on children's eyewitness memory and source monitoring. *Applied Cognitive Psychology, 12,* 489–503.

Schacter, D. L. (1995). Memory distortion: History and current status. In D. L. Schacter (Ed.), *Memory Distortion* (pp. 1–43). Cambridge, MA: Harvard University Press.

Schacter, D. L., Kagan, J., & Leichtman, M. D. (1995). True and false memories in children and adults: A cognitive neuroscience perspective. *Psychology, Public Policy and Law, 1,* 411–428.

Schacter, D. S., Harbluk, J. L., & McLachlan, D. R. (1984). Retrieval without recollection: An experimental analysis of source amnesia. *Journal of Verbal Learning and Verbal Behavior, 23,* 593–611.

Taylor, M., Esbensen, B. M., & Bennet, R. T. (1994). Children's understanding of knowledge acquisition: The tendency for children to report they have always known what they have just learned. *Child Development, 65,* 1581–1604.

Tobey, A. E., & Goodman, G. S. (1992). Children's eyewitness memory: effects of participation and forensic context. *Child Abuse and Neglect, 16,* 779–797.

Tversky, B., & Tuchin, M. (1989). A reconciliation of the evidence on eyewitness testimony: Comments on McCloskey and Zaragoza. *Journal of Experimental Psychology: General, 118,* 86–91.

Warren, A. R., Hulse-Trotter, K., & Tubbs, E. (1991). Inducing resistance to suggestibility in children. *Law and Human Behavior, 15,* 273–285.

Welch-Ross, M. K. (1995). Developmental changes in preschoolers' ability to distinguish memories of performed, pretended and imagined actions. *Cognitive Development, 10,* 421–441.

Welch-Ross, M. K., Diecidue, K., & Miller, S. A. (1997). Young children's understanding of conflicting mental representation predicts suggestibility. *Developmental Psychology, 33,* 43–53.

White, T. L, Leichtman, M. D, Ceci, S. J. (1997). The good, the bad, and the ugly: Accuracy, inaccuracy, and elaboration in preschoolers' reports about a past event. *Applied Cognitive Psychology, 11,* S37–S54.

Wright, D. (1993). Recall of the Hillsborough Disaster over time: Systematic biases of flashbulb memories. *Applied Cognitive Psychology, 7,* 129–138.

Zaragoza, M. S., & Lane, S. M. (1994). Source misattributions and the suggestibility of eyewitness memory. *Journal of Experimental Psychology: Learning, Memory and Cognition, 20,* 934–946.

11

The Study of Developmental Differences in Face Identification Accuracy as Instances of Source-Monitoring Judgments

Mary Ann Foley
Hugh J. Foley
Kim Cormier
Skidmore College

OVERVIEW

The devastating effects of inaccurate face identification are many and varied, but were brought to public attention recently by a tragic incident of misidentification occurring in New York City. On February 4, 1999, law enforcement officials on the city's streets gunned down an innocent individual bearing some facial similarity to a dangerous criminal. Although face identification ability and its failure have been studied extensively, we are far from understanding and predicting these kinds of misidentifications. This chapter focuses on processes thought to mediate face identification with the goal of exploring, within the source-monitoring framework, what these processes might involve. In the eyewitness literature, the expression "face identification ability" may refer to memory for who was seen as well as memory for the way in which a person was seen. However, in this chapter, we use the term *face identification* to refer to source judgments (i.e., is the face exactly the same or different from how it was seen before) rather than old–new recognition judgments.

The study of memory for source, or *source monitoring* (Johnson, Hashtroudi, & Lindsay, 1993) includes a wide range of judgments. These judgments may involve consideration of memories arising from very different sources (e.g., perception and imagination), two perceptual sources that are easily distinguishable (e.g., distinguishing between speakers whose voices sound quite different, two texts drawn from quite different resources), or two cognitive sources that are also relatively distinguishable (e.g., cognitive operations like reading and imagining). They may also involve judgments within the same class of source, which are not as readily distinguishable (e.g., discriminations between two speakers whose voices sound quite similar, spontaneous vs. deliberately generated imagery). Face identification assessed by same–different judgments about the way in which faces were experienced may be thought of as an instance of source-monitoring judgments involving discrimination between the way in which the same source (face) was experienced on two occasions (same or different). We suggest that source-monitoring judgments offer an intriguing way to test hypotheses about the nature of processes mediating face identification ability. Beginning with an overview of the way in which our previous source-monitoring studies about object identification processes led us to the approach outlined in this chapter, we then report two new developmental studies intended as illustrations of the heuristic potential of this approach.

SOURCE-MONITORING JUDGMENTS AS EVIDENCE FOR IMPLICIT IMAGINAL PROCESSING

According to the source-monitoring framework (Johnson & Raye, 1981; Johnson et al., 1993), cognitive operations (e.g., reading, inferencing, imagining) are sometimes represented in memory, and may affect both memory for content (e.g., what a story was about) as well as memory for its source (e.g., who narrated the story or some aspect of the story). While reading or listening to words, sentences, or texts, individuals may draw inferences not explicitly stated or they may experience implicit images evoked by the text. Subsequently, when asked to report what they actually read or heard, they may mistakenly claim they "heard" remarks that were only inferred, or that they "saw" pictures that were actually implicit images. These confusions result in a reduction in the accuracy of source-monitoring judgments, a reduction attributed to the automatic nature of the cognitive operations giving rise to the images (e.g., Foley, Durso, Wilder, & Friedman, 1991; Johnson et al., 1993). When these processes are more deliberate in nature (e.g., deliberately generating images), source monitoring is considerably better (Foley & Foley, 1999; Foley et al., 1991; Johnson, Raye, Foley, & Foley, 1981).

Children's source judgments are similarly affected by the automatic nature of cognitive operations (Foley, 1998; Foley et al., 1991). For example, after 6-year-olds see pictures and words referring to familiar objects, if they simply respond to those objects by describing actions they might perform with the objects, they are subsequently confused about the way in which the objects were presented. In particular, they mistakenly claim that words were presented as pictures more often than the reverse. These picture–word confusions are interpreted as evidence for implicit imaginal processing. If images of the objects are evoked while reading the words, these images may later be mistakenly remembered as pictures. Source-monitoring errors about pictures and words are considerably reduced if children are explicitly asked to create images during the initial viewing. Notably, children's source-monitoring errors in this context are not greater than those of adults (Foley et al., 1991). Thus, both children and adults experience implicit imaginal processing, and this kind of activation leads to subsequent reduction in source-monitoring performance. This research on the effects of implicit processing (e.g., imaginal, inferential) led us to expect that source judgments might be a promising way to test hypotheses about the basis of object identification under conditions of incomplete visual information.

Does Incomplete Pictorial Information Also Elicit Implicit Imaginal Processing

Individuals' recognition of familiar objects is remarkably good, even under conditions of incomplete information (Matlin & Foley, 1997). When presented with pictures of familiar objects made incomplete because the renderings are fragmented (e.g., Snodgrass & Feenan, 1990) or partially deleted (e.g., Biederman, 1987), adults are nonetheless able to identify the objects portrayed. In these contexts, individuals are described as "filling in" the missing portions of pictorial renderings, and this filling-in process presumably leads to object identification. Although the basis for these closure effects is still a matter of considerable debate (e.g., Churchland & Ramachandran, 1997; Dennett, 1992; Foley, Foley, Durso, & Smith, 1997; Foley, Korenman, & Foley, 1999; Kimchi, 1992), one explanation invokes the activation of implicit imaginal processing as a mechanism of closure.

We reasoned that if incomplete pictures of objects evoke implicit imaginal processes (e.g., "filling in" missing portions of pictures), then individuals should be confused about whether they had experienced that object as complete or incomplete. In particular, if presented with incomplete visual information, they may later report the information was actually seen as complete in form. In our earlier studies, deleting portions of pictures of familiar objects created incomplete visual information (Foley et al., 1997). After viewing complete and incomplete pictures under a variety of encoding conditions, adults were surprised with a source-monitoring task in which they were asked to remember the way in which they experienced those pictures initially. Adults were considerably confused about the way in which they had seen the pictures, and their confusion was expressed as a bias to report that incomplete pictures were experienced as complete rather than the reverse. This bias (producing lower source-monitoring scores for incomplete pictures compared with completed pictures) was observed whether pictures were rendered incomplete by deletion or occlusion (Foley et al., 1997; Foley et al., 1999). We interpreted this bias as evidence for the activation of imaginal completion processes, lending support for the notion that closure processes may involve filling-in processes.

WHAT IF THE INCOMPLETE PICTURES ARE FACES?

The face identification literature provides some suggestion that similar filling-in processes may be evoked in response to incomplete faces. Comparisons of the effects of deleting internal (eyes, mouth, nose) and external (hairline, chin) features of faces have been reported for both face recognition and priming studies (Brunas, Young, & Ellis, 1990; Campbell, Walker, & Baron-Cohen, 1995; Cohen, Shepherd, Ellis, & Craw, 1994; Ellis, 1990; Ellis, Burton, Young, & Flude, 1997; Ellis, Ellis, & Hosie, 1993; Shapiro & Penrod, 1986; Wells & Turtle, 1989). In priming studies, for example, partial photographs of unfamiliar faces serve as effective primes whether portions deleted include internal or external parts of faces (Brunas et al., 1990). These priming effects suggest that incomplete pictures of faces may activate more complete representations or configurations for the faces.

To test this idea more directly, in our preliminary face identification studies, we showed adults pictures of faces, some of which were cropped along the midline. Given the results from our object identification studies, we predicted that if individuals were seeing the incomplete faces as complete in their mind's eye, they would be confused about the way in which they initially saw the faces. In particular, we predicted that they would claim incomplete faces were actually seen as complete in form, and indeed this was the case (Foley et al., 1997).

More recently, one of our students (Pallotta, 1997) rendered both familiar and unfamiliar faces incomplete by using an occluding object (a book partially covering the faces). Whether cropping or occluding portions of faces, once again, the bias to claim incomplete versions were seen as complete in form was evident, particularly for familiar faces. We interpret this bias about incomplete faces in the same way that we interpreted a similar bias to claim pictures of incomplete objects were seen as complete. That is, the incomplete pictorial information seems to elicit filling-in processes leading to the impression that a complete picture was seen when it was not. Thus, adults seem to process incomplete faces holistically, experiencing more complete configurations in their mind's eye. Configurational processes are often invoked to account for face identification ability, and what intrigues us about these explanatory mechanisms is their similarity to those invoked to account for object identification under conditions of incomplete visual information.

CONFIGURATIONAL PROCESSING: A KIND OF FILLING-IN PROCESS?

More specifically, two versions of configurational processing currently hold the attention of investigators (e.g., Carey, 1992; Carey & Diamond, 1977, 1994; Carey, Diamond, & Woods, 1980; Chung & Thompson, 1995; Diamond & Carey, 1977; Hole, 1994; Rhodes & Tremewan, 1994; Tanaka & Farah, 1993). One version, referred to as *first-order* configurational processing, is described as the abstraction of holistic or gestaltlike representations for faces (Carey, 1992; Tanaka & Farah, 1993). From this point of view, when faces are partially covered by paraphernalia, adults abstract holistic or gestaltlike representations. *Second-order* configurational processing, a more precise version, suggests that adults notice relationships among features that are relatively invariant (e.g., "large wide-set eyes for such a long narrow face," Diamond & Carey, 1986, p. 108), perhaps recognizing people by their facial idiosyncrasies. The independent contributions of these two kinds of processes to face identification remains to be specified (e.g., Carey & Diamond, 1994; Chung & Thomson, 1995). For present purposes, however, the important point to notice is that both versions suggest that adults may well be looking beyond the missing information, seeing more complete facial configurations in their mind's eye (Baenninger, 1994; Carey & Diamond, 1994; Chung & Thomson, 1995).

DOES LOOKING BEYOND ALSO INVOLVE FILLING-IN?

Configurational processes are also invoked to account for the effects on face identification (both old–new and source judgments) of paraphernalia. Paraphernalia include features "added on" to faces, such as hats and dark glasses, as well as features "attached" to the faces such as beards and moustaches. Although sometimes also referred to as disguises, we prefer the term "paraphernalia" because, as we will discuss later, the extent to which these add ons and attachments are interpreted as disguise may well depend on contextual factors. Paraphernalia covering portions of faces (e.g., beards and sunglasses), as well as changes in viewing perspective, often detract from face identification performance (e.g., Baenninger, 1994; Bruce & Humphreys, 1994; Davies & Flin, 1984; Ellis, 1992; Patterson & Baddeley, 1977). These disruptive effects are often exaggerated for young children (e.g., Carey & Diamond, 1977; Diamond & Carey, 1977; Ellis, 1990, 1992). Developmental differences in memory for faces are reported across a wide range of circumstances (Carey & Diamond, 1994; Lie & Newcombe, 1999), but there are also instances in which young children do as well as older individuals in remembering faces (e.g., Goodman & Reed, 1986). Young children are thought to process faces in a piecemeal fashion, focusing on featural information rather than configurational information, and this difference in focus is thought to mediate age deficits in face identification (Carey & Diamond, 1977; Diamond & Carey, 1977). Indeed, young children are so captivated by facial coverings (e.g., large floppy hats), that they think they saw a distractor face previously if it is shown wearing a partial covering that they did see before but worn by someone else. For example, in a frequently cited study along these lines, 6-year-olds' accuracy is quite poor (about 25%) whereas older children's performance is much better (about 75% accurate for 10-year-olds), presumably because young children select faces on the basis of paraphernalia (Carey & Diamond, 1977).

Numerous developmental studies have reported age trends in the recognition of unfamiliar faces (see Chung & Thomson, 1995, for a review). Although originally interpreted as evidence that young children were incapable of configurational processing (e.g., Carey & Diamond, 1977), recent evidence suggests that the age trends reflect young children's susceptibility to the presence of salient coverings rather than an inability to process faces configurationally (e.g., Baenninger, 1994; Campbell et al., 1995; Carey & Diamond, 1994; Flin, 1985; Flin & Dziurawiec, 1989). When the striking quality of a piece of paraphernalia that partially covers a face is reduced, for example, by keeping the kind of covering constant across faces, young children's face identification can be comparable to that of adults (Baenninger, 1994; Flin, 1985;). These findings suggest that young children can be induced to look beyond the covering, processing faces more holistically (Baenninger, 1994). Although, again, what it means to process holistic or featural information is not fully specified in the literature (Tanaka & Sengco, 1997). Discussions of developmental differences in face identification ability nevertheless lead to interesting questions about what "looking beyond" paraphernalia might mean as well as questions about the memory status of the paraphernalia.

If looking beyond paraphernalia means viewers are filling in missing portions of faces occluded by add ons, for example, then viewers should be confused when later asked to report how they saw faces, in full or partially covered versions. This confusion might also be expected to resemble confusions about whether a face was presented in full view or partially cropped. We examine memory for each type of incomplete visual information about faces in Studies 1 and 2. From a source-monitoring perspective, the activation processes mediating filling in are relatively automatic and less attention-deploying, leading to the expectation that, in both studies, viewers will be confused about the way in which they saw faces initially. But will the pattern of confusions in the two studies be the same? If the filling-in processes lead viewers to overlook the incomplete information, the filling-in processes may lead to the impression of a more complete facial configuration, whether the information is missing because some of the face is cropped or partially covered. In this case, we would expect similar confusion patterns in Studies 1 and 2. Because face identification ability often varies for children and adults, these patterns might also be expected to be age dependent. These possibilities provide the focus for our developmental studies of face identification ability.

OVERVIEW OF OUR DEVELOPMENTAL SOURCE-MONITORING STUDIES OF FACE IDENTIFICATION

At encoding, children and adults were shown unfamiliar computer-generated faces that were identical in the two studies. Half of the faces were seen wearing paraphernalia and half were not. Within each paraphernalia condition (present or absent), half of the faces were complete in form and half were incomplete, missing their left or right side, cropped along the midline (see Fig. 11.1 for examples). The difference between the two studies focused on the nature of change introduced at test, and, therefore, the focus of the source-monitoring judgment. In Study 1, adults and children were asked to make same–different judgments focusing on paraphernalia (see Fig. 11.2 for examples). Half the composites looked the same at encoding and

No Paraphernalia   Paraphernalia

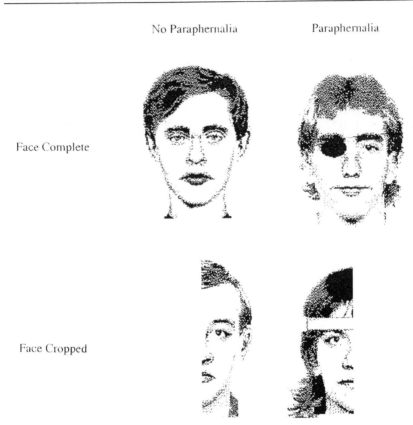

Face Complete

Face Cropped

FIG. 11.1. Examples of composite faces presented during encoding (Studies 1 and 2).

test, with the paraphernalia unchanged, but the other half looked different (e.g., glasses present during encoding were removed in the test version). This created four different categories of faces, those looking the same at encoding and test (with or without paraphernalia) and those looking different (paraphernalia added or deleted). Materials were counterbalanced so that each face occurred equally often in each of these four categories. In Study 1, then, the complete–incomplete face manipulation was held constant at encoding and test. In Study 2, other adults and children were asked to make same–different judgments focusing on face completeness (e.g., half of the complete faces presented during encoding were shown with one side of the face removed at test; see Fig. 11.3 for examples). In this case, the paraphernalia (present or absent) manipulation was held constant from encoding to test.

Encoding Version   Test Version

Same

Different

Same

Different

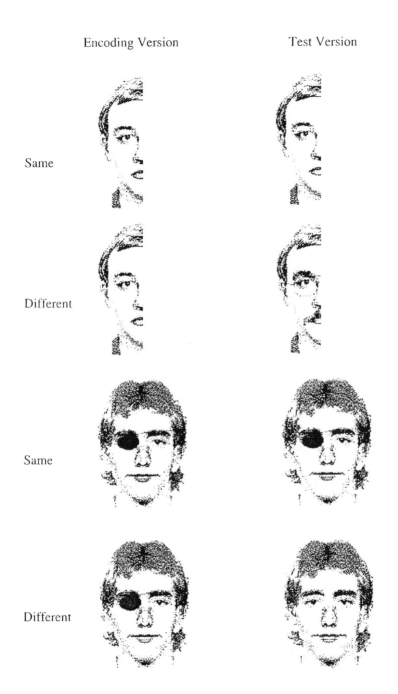

FIG. 11.2. Examples of test faces presented in Study 1, with changes focused on paraphernalia (added or deleted from the encoding versions) and completeness manipulation constant.

Encoding Version　　　　Test Version

Same

Different

Same

Different

FIG. 11.3. Examples of test faces presented in Study 2, with changes focused on completeness (cropped from or added to the encoding versions) and paraphernalia held constant.

What Might This Person Like to Do? The Encoding Phase of Each Study

In each study, adults and children were first asked to look at the booklet of unfamiliar face composites, describing what each individual in the composite might like to do for work or as a hobby. This cover task was selected for two reasons: (a) We know that recognition of unfamiliar faces is not particularly good (Faw, 1992) and we wanted to avoid floor effects, and (b) Hanley, Pearson, and Howard (1990) reported that asking adults to describe likely occupations led to better recognition memory for faces than other kinds of cover tasks. Moreover, we thought that this kind of cover task might increase the likelihood that adults and children would integrate the paraphernalia with the composite when offering their suggestions (e.g., reporting that a male wearing a beret "likes to paint pictures"), and responses were consistent with this expectation. The encoding task was self-paced, with the experimenter recording participants' remarks. This first phase took approximately 10 minutes to complete and was followed by a 3-minute distraction period during which the experimenter engaged in conversation with participants. Adults and children were then surprised by a source-monitoring same–different judgment.

Creating Composite Faces for Studies 1 and 2

Forty-eight composite male faces were created using Mac-a-Mug Pro software. The computer-generated faces were created in various ways, combining six kinds of facial features (i.e., eyes, nose, chin, mouth, hair, and ears) along with features serving as paraphernalia (mustaches, beards, glasses, and hats). Except for repeating a few noses and ears available in the software package, the facial features selected were unique to each composite face. For each composite face, two versions were constructed, one without paraphernalia and one with one or two pieces of paraphernalia partially covering the face (e.g., moustache, beard, sunglasses, hat). Furthermore, for each composite (with or without paraphernalia), one version was complete in form and the other was cropped in half so that one side of the face was deleted. These manipulations created four versions for each composite face: Face complete with no paraphernalia, Face complete with paraphernalia, Half face with no paraphernalia, Half face with paraphernalia (see Fig. 11.1 for examples). For the cropped versions of faces, the left and right sides were deleted with equal frequency. Materials were counterbalanced, with each version occurring equally often across participants. Twenty-four of the 48 faces, along with four practice faces, were included in the first part of the session. All 24 faces were presented from the frontal perspective. Of the 12 uncovered faces (no paraphernalia), 6 were complete and 6 were incomplete. Of the 12 partially covered faces (with paraphernalia), 6 were complete and 6 were incomplete. In both studies, for both encoding and test phases, the face composites were presented in booklet form, each in the center of an 8 ½ in. × 11 in. piece of white paper. Following a brief distractor period, during which time the experimenter and participant conversed about school-related activities, adults and children were surprised with one of two source-monitoring tests.

The Source-Monitoring Tests: Focus on Paraphernalia or Completeness

Participants were asked to look at each face in a second booklet and indicate whether or not it was a composite face that they had seen in the first part of the session. If they thought they had seen the face during the first part of the session, they were also asked to indicate whether it looked exactly the same as or different from the original version. For the source tests, 24 faces served as distractors, and were presented in random order with the 24 targets. Of the 24 original faces, 12 were presented in exactly the same way in which they were originally viewed. Twelve other original faces were presented differently. In Study 1, of the faces that were originally presented without paraphernalia, half were presented in the same way, and half were shown with paraphernalia added (see examples in Fig. 11.2). Similarly, of the faces originally presented with paraphernalia, half were presented in the same way and half were shown without the paraphernalia. Additions and deletions were counterbalanced so that all faces occurred in all combinations (e.g., change involved addition or deletion) across participants. In Study 2, the same 48 composite faces created for Study 1 were presented here as well. In this case, what varied was whether faces were seen complete or incomplete during encoding or test (see Fig. 11.3 for examples). None of the pieces of paraphernalia on the distractor faces was seen previously as paraphernalia on the target composite faces.

STUDY 1: SAME DIFFERENT JUDGMENTS ABOUT PARAPHERNALIA

What pattern of performance might we expect on the identification test in Study 1 if viewers are processing faces configurationally, essentially looking beyond the paraphernalia? If, in their mind's eye, adults are seeing complete configurational representations of faces whether or not partially covered by paraphernalia, they should be quite confused about the way in which they saw the faces initially. Moreover, the nature of the change from encoding to test should have little effect on performance because the encoded representations would not include paraphernalia information. On the other hand, if looking beyond paraphernalia elicits a configurational representation, but this representation retains information about the paraphernalia, then the relationship between the encoding and test versions should indeed affect performance. Thus, if we found that source-monitoring judgments were better when the version seen at encoding and test was identical, it would be difficult to argue that looking beyond involves a failure to encode information about paraphernalia. Furthermore, if young children are overly attentive to paraphernalia cues compared with adults, we might actually expect them to do better than adults when the basis of the source-identification decision could be made on the basis of the paraphernalia. In this case, then, children's performance might be particularly good when the paraphernalia are the same at encoding and test, but, in turn, their performance might be hurt more than adults' by the introduction of changes in paraphernalia from encoding to test.

Twelve first graders and 12 fourth graders from Division Street Elementary School in Saratoga Springs participated in this study. Their mean ages were 6 years, 5 months and 9 years, 6 months. Parental consent was obtained for each child. The 12 adult participants were undergraduates enrolled in introductory psychology classes at Skidmore College. These undergraduates each received extra credit for their participation.

Predictions and Outcomes Compared

Analyses of variance were calculated on three main dependent variables: Source-Monitoring Judgments, Proportion Hits, and False Positives. When appropriate, the Tukey-Kramer post hoc test was used.

Source-Monitoring Judgments: Identification Scores. Responses to the target faces were assessed by computing an identification score, that is, the number of targets whose presentation–test combination was correctly classified (i.e., as "same" or "different") divided by the number recognized as old. Essentially, this measure focuses on faces correctly recognized as old, assessing sensitivity to the ways in which faces were presented. An analysis of variance including Age, Paraphernalia (Present vs. Absent at Encoding), Completeness of Face (Complete vs. Incomplete), and Test Version (Same or Different from

Paraphernalia Encoding Version) as factors produced three significant effects. Notably, age was not one of these factors, nor did it interact with any factors that were significant. The mean identification
scores were 0.71, 0.66, and 0.63 for 6-year-olds, 9-year-olds, and
adults, respectively.

There was a main effect for Paraphernalia, $F(1,31) = 8.78$, $MSE =$
0.08, $p = 0.006$; for Test Version, $F(1,31) = 24.69$, MSE $= 0.02$, $p =$
0.001; and a two-way interaction between these factors, $F(1,31) =$
13.46, $MSE = 0.05$, $p = 0.001$. As shown in Table 11.1, and confirmed by post hoc tests, if target faces were recognized as old, adults
and children were relatively good at reporting "the face looks the
same" (about 80%) if the versions were the same at encoding and test,
regardless of the presence or absence of paraphernalia. However,
when change was introduced, identification performance decreased,
and this decrease was greater when judging faces from which paraphernalia had been removed. Notably, this effect was not age-depend-
ent. Finally, identification performance did not vary for complete and
incomplete composites ($Ms = 0.66$ and 0.58, respectively), nor did
this encoding manipulation interact with other factors.

Proportion Hits: Recognizing Target Faces. The identification test
was also scored to create a measure of recognition of target faces, that

TABLE 11.1

Memory for Faces: Focus on Paraphernalia (Study 1)

	Test Version Relative To Encoding	
	Same	Changed
SM Identification Scores		
Encoding Version		
Face Without Paraphernalia	0.82	0.66
Face With Paraphernalia	0.81	0.38
Proportion Hits		
Encoding Version		
Face Without Paraphernalia	0.73	0.57
Face With Paraphernalia	0.78	0.45

Note. SM = source monitoring.

is, the proportion of faces correctly recognized as target faces, ignoring whether or not they were correctly classified as looking the same or different. In an analysis including Age (6-year-olds, 9-year-olds, and adults), Paraphernalia (Present vs. Absent at Encoding), Completeness of Face (Complete vs. Half Faces), and Test Version (Same or Different from Paraphernalia Encoding Version), a main effect for age was observed, $F(2, 33) = 8.22, MSE = 0.18, p = 0.001$. Although no age group performed particularly well, on average, recognition was better the older the participant; the average proportions were 0.51, 0.63, and 0.76 for 6-year-olds, 9-year-olds, and adults, respectively. Most important for our purposes, however, this age trend did not interact with other factors. In summary, although children were not as good as adults at recognizing composite faces they had seen before, once correctly recognized, they were as good as adults in remembering how they had seen those composite faces.

There was a main effect for Test Version, $F(1,33) = 41.71, MSE = 0.11, p = 0.001$, and a significant two-way interaction between Test Version and Paraphernalia Encoding Version, $F(1,33) = 3.01, MSE = 0.12, p = 0.05$. As shown in Table 11.1, and confirmed by post hoc tests, recognition of target faces was comparable when the versions presented during encoding and test were the same (about 75% accurate). However, when change was introduced between encoding and test versions, recognition of targets was much worse, particularly when the change involved the removal of paraphernalia (i.e., paraphernalia at encoding but removed at test). Finally, recognition did not vary for complete and incomplete composites; the means were 0.65 and 0.61, respectively.

False Positives: False Claims About Distractors. Responses to new faces misidentified as old were analyzed to see if there was any bias to report "looks the same" or "looks different." An analysis of variance including Age, Paraphernalia on Distractor (Present or Not), Completeness (Complete vs. Half), and Type of Response Error ("Same" vs. "Different" response on number of false positives) showed only one significant effect. The interaction between age and paraphernalia was significant, $F(1,33) = 5.19, MSE = 0.04, p = 0.01$. The number of false positives committed was relatively low, but children were more likely to claim a new face had been seen before if it was partially covered by paraphernalia than if it was not, and the reverse was the case for adults. The mean false positive scores for faces with and without paraphernalia were: 0.24 and 0.18; 0.38 and 0.21; and 0.24 and 0.33, for 6-year-olds, 9-year-olds, and adults, respectively. (Note, these values are based on the mean number of false positives averaged across participants. Thus, on average, people made fewer than one false positive.) The false positives indicate that the confusion leading to reduction in the source-monitoring accuracy reported earlier did not reflect a response bias (e.g., to report "same" when in doubt), consistent with our previous work (Foley et al., 1997; Foley & Foley, 1998; Johnson et al., 1981).

Summary of Study 1

The results of Study 1 suggest that both adults and children may indeed be "looking beyond" paraphernalia when processing faces, because they both exhibit some confusion on the same–different identification test. For both recognition memory for composites and for source memory, or memory for the way in which the composites were presented, we showed a clear decrement in performance when the versions seen at encoding and test differed. This decrement was most striking for changes involving the deletion of paraphernalia. Notably, however, these effects were not age dependent. Although we did find age differences in recognition memory for faces, there were no age differences in judgments about versions seen if the faces were recognized as seen previously.

However, our results also suggest that information about the paraphernalia did not go unnoticed because changes in the paraphernalia affected source judgments. If "looking beyond" paraphernalia elicits a configurational representation, but this representation includes information about what is "looked beyond," then the versions seen at encoding and test should affect performance, and, indeed they did. Source-monitoring judgments were better for versions that were identical at encoding and test. Before further discussing the significance of these findings, we turn to Study 2 to see if similar confusion patterns are observed when judgments focus on the completeness of the faces.

STUDY 2: SAME DIFFERENT JUDGMENTS
ABOUT COMPLETENESS OF FACES

If adults and children are filling in the missing portions of faces, seeing half faces as complete in their mind's eye, they should be confused when making same–different judgments. In particular, they should report "same" when faces that were presented as incomplete during encoding are later presented as complete in form. Moreover, if the process involves looking beyond paraphernalia, the presence of these paraphernalia cues should not facilitate performance, at least for adults.

Sixteen first graders and 16 fourth graders from Division Street Elementary School in Saratoga Springs participated in this study. Their mean ages were 6 years, 8 months and 9 years, 7 months. Parental consent was obtained for each child. The 16 adult participants were undergraduates enrolled in introductory psychology classes at Skidmore College. These undergraduates each received extra credit for their participation. None of these individuals participated in the other study reported in this chapter.

Predictions and Outcomes Compared

Analyses of variance were calculated on the three main dependent variables: Source-Monitoring Judgments, Proportion Hits, and False Positives. When appropriate, the Tukey-Kramer post hoc test was used.

Source-Monitoring Judgments: Identification Scores. Responses to the target faces were again assessed by computing an identification score of the number of targets whose presentation–test combination was correctly classified (i.e., as "same" or "different") divided by the number recognized as old. In an analysis including Age (6-year-olds, 9-year-olds, and adults), Completeness at Encoding (Complete vs. Half Face), Paraphernalia (Present vs. Absent), and Test Version (Same or Different from Completeness Version at Encoding), again, there was no effect for age, nor interactions with this factor. The mean identification scores were 0.69, 0.69, and 0.70, for 6-year-olds, 9-year-olds, and adults, respectively.

There was a main effect for Completeness at Encoding, $F(1,39) = 5.88$, $MSE = 0.08$, $p = 0.006$; Test Version, $F(1,39) = 9.64$, $MSE = 0.18$, $p = 0.003$; and a two-way interaction between these factors, $F(1,39) = 5.52$, $MSE = 0.05$, $p = 0.003$. Subsequent tests showed that complete faces were identified better than those with one side deleted when encoding and test versions were the same. This advantage indicates that the tendency to inaccurately report the face looked different was exaggerated when incomplete faces were seen; again, at test, such an error would be expected if incomplete faces induced more complete representations during encoding, representations that would differ from the versions experienced at test. Notably, this advantage for completed faces disappeared when faces changed between encoding and test (see Table 11.2). Finally, faces that were shown wearing paraphernalia at encoding were identified better than those that were not, $F(1,39) = 16.49$, $p = 0.001$, but this encoding manipulation did not interact with the preceding results. The means were 0.75 and 0.65 for faces presented with or without paraphernalia, respectively.

TABLE 11.2

Memory for Faces: Focus on Completeness of Faces (Study 2)

	Presentation Mode at Test	
	Same	Changed
SM Identification Scores		
Encoding Version		
Face Complete	0.88	0.61
Face Cropped at Midline	0.71	0.58
Proportion Hits		
Encoding Version		
Face Complete	0.76	0.69
Face Cropped at Midline	0.71	0.55

Note. SM = source monitoring

Proportion Hits: Recognizing Target Faces. The identification test was also scored to create a measure of recognition of target composites, that is, the proportion of composite faces correctly recognized as target composite faces, ignoring whether or not they were correctly classified as looking the same or different. In an analysis including Age (6-year-olds, 9-year-olds, and adults), Encoding Version (Complete vs. Cropped), Paraphernalia (Present vs. Absent), and Test Version (Same or Different from Encoding Version), there were four significant main effects but no interactions. Again, recognition of targets varied with age, $F(2, 45) = 21.75, MSE = 0.21, p = 0.001$. Recognition of target faces was better the older the participant; the average proportions were 0.49, 0.69, and 0.81, for 6-year-olds, 9-year-olds, and adults, respectively.

There was also a main effect for Completeness Version at Encoding, $F(1,45) = 9.56, MSE = 0.08, p = 0.003$; a main effect for Paraphernalia (present or absent), $F(1,45) = 4.43, MSE = 0.06, p = 0.04$; and a main effect for Test Version, $F(1,45) = 20.35, MSE = 0.06, p = 0.001$. Unlike Study 1, recognition was better for faces that were seen in their complete form than for those that were incomplete ($Ms = 0.72$ and 0.63). Recognition was also better for faces presented in the same way at encoding and test ($Ms = 0.73$ and 0.62 for same and different, respectively). Finally, recognition was better for faces partially covered by paraphernalia than for those shown without paraphernalia ($Ms =$ 0.70 and 0.65, respectively).

False Positives: False Claims About Distractors.   Responses to new faces misidentified as old were analyzed to see if there was any bias to report "looks the same" or "looks different" when distractors were presented complete or cropped in form. An analysis of variance including Age, Paraphernalia (Present or Not), Completeness (Complete or Half Faces), and Type of Response Error ("Same" vs. "Different" response) showed only two significant effects. The number of false positives committed was relatively low, but they were lower for faces presented complete in form ($M = 0.07$) than for those with half the face missing ($M = 0.22$), $F(1,45) = 21.50$, $MSE = 0.01$, $p = 0.001$. Furthermore, there was an interaction between age and type of response error, that is, falsely reporting "same" or "different." Six-year-olds tended to report "looks the same" more than "looks different" whereas the two older age groups did not. The means for incorrect reports of "same" and "different" were 0.11 and 0.07; 0.08 and 0.09; and 0.08 and 0.15 for 6-year-olds, 9-year-olds and adults, respectively.

Summary of Study 2

Although comparable across the three age groups, face identification accuracy about the way in which faces were presented was affected by the completeness manipulation in this second study. When there was no change in version from encoding to test, performance was better for complete faces than incomplete ones, suggesting incomplete faces were experienced as "complete" during encoding. Similar patterns were observed for memory for the faces themselves as the recognition findings suggest. Notably, the presence of paraphernalia at encoding, held constant at test, facilitated performance, but this effect did not interact with the completeness manipulation.

INTERPRETATION OF THE RESULTS

Configurational Processing: A Filling In Process?

Our results are intriguing in their suggestion that at least some configurational processing may depend on filling-in processes. The fact that we observe confusion about the way in which faces were seen is consistent with this claim. In Study 2, adults and children were confused about the way in which they initially saw complete and incomplete faces, and this confusion was expressed in relatively low same–different source-monitoring judgments—particularly when changes between the encoding and test versions were introduced. When viewing faces, if individuals are experiencing completed facial configurations in their mind's eye, this confusion pattern would be expected. The confusion we observed in Study 2 between complete and incomplete faces, and the advantage observed for complete faces viewed as such during encoding and test, is consistent with our previous work (e.g., Foley et al., 1997) and suggests that incomplete faces activate filling-in processes.

Another aspect of our work reported previously is consistent with the claim that at least some configurational processing may depend on filling-in processes. As we mentioned, when faces are presented complete or incomplete in form (with no paraphernalia involved), adults are later confused when asked how they saw the faces. Specifically, they claim incomplete faces were "seen" as complete, producing lower source-monitoring scores for incomplete faces. However, this bias is unaffected by encoding tasks. Whether adults attend to configural aspects of faces (e.g., producing ratings for how much faces resemble people they actually know) or featural aspects (e.g., rating the distinctiveness of features), this bias occurs at a comparable level across the encoding tasks (Foley et al., 1997, Experiment 4). This finding is consistent with the suggestion that filling-in processes are important for the processing of configurational information, whether that configural information is gestaltlike (first order) or relational (second order) in nature.

The results of the present studies indicate that, in the study of face identification ability, we must attend to the way in which incomplete information is created. If filling-in processes involve "looking beyond" missing visual information, then source-monitoring judgments should be similarly affected by what is overlooked, namely, missing portions of faces covered by paraphernalia (Study 1) or missing portions deleted by cropping (Study 2), but they were not. When incomplete visual information involved the explicit removal of portions of the faces themselves (Study 2), the pattern of performance differed from that observed when it involved partially covering portions of faces (Study 1). The effects of restoring completed faces at test differed for the two studies. Removing add ons or attachments from faces, making more of the faces visible, reduced the accuracy of source-monitoring judgments (from 81% to 38%, see Table 11.1, Study 1). Essentially, when paraphernalia were removed, viewers were more likely to report that the faces "looked the same as before," thinking they had seen them fully in view, when this was not the case. Restoring half the face by showing a completed version at test also caused a decrement in performance (from 71% to 58%, see Table 11.2), however it was nowhere near as pronounced as that observed in Study 1. Thus, these "filling-in" and "looking beyond" processes may be involved in face identification, but they may well represent different kinds of processing. Whether impressions of overall configurations take precedence over the analysis of parts of faces, or perhaps, operate as prerequisites, is a matter of long-standing debate in the object identification literature (Kimchi, 1992). Our studies of incomplete visual information within a source-monitoring framework emphasize the importance of specifying what is meant by the parts themselves.

Paraphernalia and Their Memory Status

The first study in this chapter as well as our previous work (Foley & Foley, 1998) and that of others (e.g., Diamond & Carey, 1977; Reynolds & Pezdek, 1992) clearly demonstrate the profound effects on face identification of various kinds of paraphernalia. Furthermore, as others have shown, some types of paraphernalia are more disruptive to face identification than others (e.g., eyeglasses or beards; Matthews, 1978; McKelvie, 1993; Patterson & Baddeley, 1977; Reynolds & Pezdek, 1992; Terry, 1994). Although there are numerous studies of the effects of specific facial features on identification ability, the systematic comparison of the effects of different kinds of paraphernalia (add ons vs. attachments to faces) as well as their placement (e.g., portions of faces concealed) are noticeably absent. Similarly, although the effects of change in version (e.g., deletions vs. additions) are sometimes examined (e.g., Baenninger, 1994; Carey & Diamond, 1977; Patterson & Baddeley, 1977), more systematic comparisons involving the nature of the changes are yet to be reported.

Our work suggests the intriguing possibility that these effects of paraphernalia (e.g., kind of change and specificity of change) may also depend on the interpretation of those paraphernalia. In Study 1, after thinking about the kind of work or hobbies the person represented by the face composite might like to do, adults' and children's judgments were not affected by the presence of paraphernalia if the versions of the composite seen at encoding and test were the same. In a previous study in which adults first rated their impressions of the likelihood the face was that of a criminal, their source-monitoring judgments were very much affected by the presence of paraphernalia, and by its removal (Foley & Foley, 1998). Because the materials were very simi-

TABLE 11.3

Source-Monitoring Judgments Focused on Paraphernalia:
From Foley and Foley (1998)

	Test Version Relative To Encoding	
	Same	Changed
SM Identification Scores		
Encoding Version		
Face Without Paraphernalia	.68	.76
Face With Paraphernalia	.49	.53

Note. SM = source monitoring

lar to those used here, we summarize the findings from our previous
study in Table 11.3. As is clear from the table, source-monitoring
judgments were quite poor when paraphernalia were partially covering the faces, and the introduction of a change involving the removal of
paraphernalia had a greater effect than that involving additions (Foley
& Foley, 1998). Perhaps paraphernalia are incorporated into a facial
configuration just as other facial features are incorporated into the
configuration, and this tendency might be increased by particular
kinds of encoding tasks. In short, our findings for the effects of paraphernalia suggest that asking people if a face was shown with glasses
on (or not) is a task that would not necessarily be made easier because
the people implicitly filled in half the face. And, in Study 1, they were
not. Moreover, the effects we did observe were independent of the
completeness manipulation at encoding (Study 1).

Children s Source Monitoring

Our studies also invite explorations of these effects of paraphernalia
within a developmental context. Expectations of developmental differences in source-monitoring judgments about face identification
follow from two lines of research. One major theme of this chapter
highlights age trends and the way in which explanations for these differences might lead one to expect developmental differences in
same–different judgments about faces (e.g., Carey & Diamond,
1977). But age trends in our studies were only evident in memory for
faces that were seen (recognition memory), not for the particular way
in which faces were seen (source-monitoring identification). Their

absence in source judgments is particularly interesting in light of other recent work. As we mentioned earlier in the chapter, when the striking quality of paraphernalia is reduced by keeping the kind of covering constant across faces, young children's identification performance is comparable to adults (Baenninger, 1994). In our Study 1, however, the paraphernalia used was not held constant, yet we still found comparable performance across age groups similar to those compared in previous work.

Nevertheless, other aspects of the source-monitoring literature could lead to expectations of age differences in face identification. As we mentioned earlier, when memories arising from two perceptual sources are quite similar, decisions about source (e.g., which speaker said what) are more difficult, leading to errors in source judgments (e.g., Foley & Johnson, 1985; Lindsay, Johnson, & Kwon, 1991; chap. 6, this volume). Furthermore, young children seem to be particularly disadvantaged by these kinds of similarity effects (Foley & Ratner, 1998a; Lindsay et al., 1991). We conceptualize face identification ability as an instance of source monitoring when individuals are asked to report not just who they saw but the way in which the person appeared. In this latter instance, the perceptual source is the same (the person's face) and the judgment focuses on the nature of the renderings (same or different), presumably a more difficult judgment than distinguishing between sources. Thus, young children might be expected to have particular difficulty with these kinds of judgments.

However, the study of source-monitoring differences also suggests that the extent to which developmental differences are observed is not simply a function of the type of judgment (e.g., two perceptual sources, two self-generated sources like performing and imagining actions). Rather, the specific kinds of memories involved in the judgments bear consideration, emphasizing the sensitivity of source judgments to contextual factors. Although young children are more confused than older individuals about what they did and what they imagined doing (Foley & Johnson, 1985; Foley, Johnson, & Raye, 1983), this is not uniformly the case (Foley, Aman, & Gutch, 1987; Foley & Ratner, 1998a, 1998b; Foley, Santini, & Sopasakis, 1989). Rather, the goal guiding the activities has important implications for do–imagine confusions (Foley & Ratner, in press; Foley & Ratner 1998b; Ratner, Foley, & Gimpert, this volume, Study 1) as does action consequence (Foley et al., 1987). Self–other judgments are clearly sensitive to the nature of goals mediating the self–other actions (Foley & Ratner, 1998b; Foley & Ratner, in press; chap. 4, this volume, Studies 2 and 3).

Our "failure" to observe developmental differences in face identification (Study 1) is not an anomaly. As others have pointed out, children are not always uniformly worse than adults when asked to identify culprits (cf. Goodman & Reed, 1986; Marin, Holmes, Guth, & Kovac, 1979). Moreover, the absence of developmental differences in source-judgments in the present studies does not preclude the possibility of observing age trends in source-monitoring judgments about faces. In our studies, the paraphernalia could serve as discriminative cues because there was no overlap between those used on targets and on distractors. Although eyeglasses occurred in both sets, for example, the versions were unique to each. Thus, adults and children could make their judgments on the basis of memory for versions of paraphernalia. However, remembering that a face was shown with sunglasses would not help memory if the change introduced was in the type of glasses rather than their presence (or absence). Age trends may well be more apparent under more demanding judgment conditions of this sort (e.g., changes in the kinds of glasses).

When Paraphernalia Serves to Disguise: A Matter of Interpretation?

The effects of paraphernalia are often interpreted as effects of disguise on face identification, but this interpretation may be more in the eye of the experimenter than that of the person whose memory is under investigation. Our studies of face identification, therefore, have interesting implications for the interpretation of the effects of facial coverings (as occluders, parts of faces, or disguises). Because perpetrators frequently use different kinds of paraphernalia as disguise, and because identi-kit packages also seek identification by the selection of different kinds of paraphernalia, it seems important to examine further the specificity of memory for paraphernalia along these lines. Furthermore, the interpretation of paraphernalia as disguises may depend on the encoding context. At the very least, paraphernalia may sometimes be interpreted as parts of the face configuration itself rather than as "add ons."

The value of investigative source monitoring in the context of *verbal* eyewitness reports has been amply demonstrated already in this volume (see chaps. 6, 7, 8, 9, and 10, this volume). From the research reviewed in this chapter, however, it is clear that the source-monitoring framework (Johnson et al., 1993) is also a useful and productive guide to the investigation of nonverbal processes involved in eyewitness memory, namely, face identification. Moreover, we have reviewed both theoretical and practical implications of this research program.

REFERENCES

Baenninger, M. A. (1994). The development of face recognition: Featural or configurational processing. *Journal of Experimental Child Psychology, 57*, 377–396.

Biederman, I. (1987). Recognition-by-components: A theory of human image understanding. *Psychological Review, 94*, 115–147.

Bruce, V., & Humphreys, G. W. (Eds.). (1994). *Object and face recognition.* Hillsdale, NJ: Lawrence Erlbaum Associates.

Brunas, J., Young, A. W., & Ellis, A. W. (1990). Repetition priming from incomplete faces: Evidence for part to whole completion. *British Journal of Psychology, 81*, 43–56.

Campbell, R., Walker, J., & Baron-Cohen, S. (1995). The development of differential use of inner and outer face features in familiar face identification. *Journal of Experimental Child Psychology, 59*, 196–210.

Carey, S. (1992). Becoming a face expert. In V. Bruce, & A. Cowey, A. (Eds.), *Processing the facial image.* (pp. 95–103). Oxford, UK: Clarendon Press/Oxford University Press.

Carey, S., & Diamond, R. (1977). From piecemeal to configurational representation of faces. *Science, 195*, 312–314.

Carey, S., & Diamond, R. (1994). Are faces perceived as configurations more by adults than by children? *Visual Cognition, 1*, 253–274.

Carey, S., Diamond, R., & Woods, B. (1980). The development of face recognition: A maturational component? *Developmental Psychology, 16*, 257–269.

Chung, M. S., & Thomson, D. M. (1995). Development of face recognition. *British Journal of Psychology, 86*, 55–87.

Churchland, P. S., & Ramanchandran, V. S. (1997). Filling in: Why Dennett is wrong. In K. Atkins (Ed.), *Perception* (pp. 132–157). New York: Oxford University Press.

Cohen, N.P., Shepherd, J. W., Ellis, H. D., & Craw, I. (1994). Masking of faces by facial and non-facial stimuli. *Visual Cognition, 1*, 227–251.

Davies, G., & Flin, R. (1984). The man behind the mask—disguise and face recognition. *Human Learning, 3*, 83–95.

Dennett, D. (1992). Filling in versus finding out: A ubiquitous confusion in cognitive science. In P. van den Broek, H .L. Pick, Jr., & D. Knill (Eds.), *Cognition: Conceptual and methodological issues.* Washington, DC: American Psychological Association.

Diamond, R., & Carey, S. (1977). Developmental changes in the representation of faces. *Journal of Experimental Child Psychology, 23*, 1–22.

Diamond, S., & Carey, S. (1986). Why faces are and are not special: An effect of expertise. *Journal of Experimental Psychology: General, 115*, 107–117.

Ellis, H. D. (1990). Developmental trends in face recognition. *The Psychologist: Bulletin of British Psychological Society, 3*, 114–119.

Ellis, H. D. (1992). The development of face processing skills. *Philosophical Transactions of the Royal Society, Series B, 335*, 105–111.

Ellis, A., Burton, A. M., Young, A., & Flude, B. M. (1997). Repetition priming between parts and wholes: Tests of a computational model of familiar face recognition. *British Journal of Psychology, 88*, 579–608.

Ellis, H. D., Ellis, D. M., & Hosie, J. A. (1993). Priming effects in children's face recognition. *British Journal of Psychology, 84*, 101–110.

Faw, H. W. (1992). Recognition of unfamiliar faces: Procedural and methodological considerations. *British Journal of Psychology, 83*, 25–37.

Flin, R.H. (1985). Development of face recognition: An encoding switch? *British Journal of Psychology, 76*, 123–134.

Flin, R. H., & Dziurawiec, S. (1989). Developmental factors in face recognition. In A. Young & H. Ellis (Eds.), *Handbook of research on face processing* (pp. 335–378). Amsterdam: Elsevier.

Foley, M. A. (1998). What the study of source monitoring suggests about the role of imagery in children's thinking and remembering. Invited chapter in J. Bideaud & Y. Courbois (Eds.), *Image mentale et development* (pp. 37–54). Presses Universitaires de France.

Foley, M. A., Aman, C., Gutch, D. (1987) Discriminating between action memories: Children's use of kinesthetic cues and visible consequences. *Journal of Experimental Child Psychology, 44*, 335–347.

Foley, M. A., Durso, F. T., Wilder, A., & Friedman, R. (1991). Developmental comparisons of explicit versus implicit imagery and reality monitoring. *Journal of Experimental Child Psychology, 51*, 1–13.

Foley, M. A., & Foley, H. J. (1998). A study of face identification: Are people looking "beyond" disguises? In M. J. Intons-Peterson & D. Best (Eds.), *Challenges and controversies: Memory distortions and their prevention* (pp. 29–47). Mahwah, NJ: Lawrence Erlbaum Associates.

Foley, M. A., & Foley, H. J. (1999) *Observing a memory advantage for difficult problem solving: An indication that effort indeed matters.* Manuscript under review.

Foley, M. A., Foley, H. J., Durso, F. T., & Smith, K. (1997). Investigations of closure processes: What's closing? *Memory & Cognition, 25*, 140–155.

Foley, M. A., & Johnson, M. K. (1985) Confusions between memories for performed and imagined actions: A developmental comparison. *Child Development, 56*, 1145–1155.

Foley, M. A., Johnson, M. K., & Raye, C. L. (1983) Age-related changes in confusion between memories for thoughts and memories for speech. *Child Development, 54*, 51–60.

Foley, M. A., Korenman, L., & Foley, H. J. (1999). *Further investigations of closure processes: Remembering cartoon characters in a Where's Waldo search task.* Manuscript under review.

Foley, M. A., & Ratner, H. H. (1998a). Distinguishing between memories for thoughts and deeds: The role of prospective processing in children's source monitoring. *British Journal of Developmental Psychology, 16*, 465–484.

Foley, M. A., & Ratner, H. H. (1998b). Children's recoding in memory for collaboration: A way of learning from others. *Cognitive Development, 13*, 91–108.

Foley, M. A., & Ratner, H. H. (in press) The role of action-based structures in activity memory. Invited chapter to appear in H. D. Zimmer & R. Cohen (Eds.), *Memory for movement: Actions speak louder than words.* New York: Oxford University Press, Counterpoint Series.

Foley, M. A., Santini, C., & Sopasakis, M. (1989) Discriminating between memories: Evidence for children's spontaneous elaborations. *Journal of Experimental Child Psychology, 48*, 146–149.

Goodman, G. S., & Reed, R.S. (1986) Age differences in eyewitness testimony. *Law and Human Behavior, 10*, 317–332.

Hanley, J. R., Pearson, N.A., & Howard, L.A. (1991). The effects of different types of encoding tasks on memory for famous faces and names. *Quarterly Journal of Experimental Psychology, 42*, 741–762.

Hole, G. J. (1994). Configurational factors in the perception of unfamiliar faces. *Perception, 23*, 65–74.

Johnson, M. K., Hashtroudi, S., & Lindsay, D. S. (1993). Source monitoring. *Psychological Bulletin, 114*, 3–28.

Johnson, M. K., Raye, C. L., Foley, H. J., & Foley, M. A. (1981). Cognitive operations and decision biases in reality monitoring. *American Journal of Psychology, 94*, 37–64.

Kimchi, R. (1992). Primacy of wholistic processing and global/local paradigm: A critical review. *Psychological Bulletin, 112*, 24–38.

Lie, E., & Newcombe, N.S. (1999). Elementary school children's explicit and implicit memory for faces of preschool classmates. *Developmental Psychology, 35*, 102–112.

Lindsay, S. D., Johnson, M. K., & Kwon, P. (1991). Developmental changes in children's source monitoring. *Journal of Experimental Psychology, 52*, 297–318.

Marin, V. M., Holmes, D. L., Guth, M., & Kovac, P. (1979). The potential of children as eyewitnesses. *Law and Behavior, 3*, 295–305.

Matlin, M. & Foley, H. J. (1997). *Sensation and Perception*. New York: Allyn & Bacon.

Matthews, M. L. (1978). Discrimination of Identi-kit constructions of faces: Evidence for a dual-processing strategy. *Perception and Psychophysics, 23*, 153–161.

McKelvie, S. J. (1993). Effects of spectacles on recognition memory for faces: Evidence from a distractor-free test. *Bulletin of Psychonomic Society, 31*, 475–477.

Pallotta, S. (1997). *Recognizing complete and incomplete faces: Does familiarity have an effect?* Senior honors thesis, Skidmore College, Saratoga Springs, NY.

Patterson, K. E., & Baddeley, A. D. (1977). When face recognition fails. *Journal of Experimental Psychology: Human Learning and Memory, 3*, 406–417.

Reynolds, J. K., & Pezdek, K. (1992). Face recognition memory: The effects of exposure duration and encoding instruction. *Applied Cognitive Psychology, 6*, 279–292.

Rhodes, G., & Tremewan, T. (1994). Understanding face recognition: caricature effects, inversion, and the homogeneity problem. In V. Bruce & G. W. Humphreys (Eds.), *Object and face recognition: Special issue in visual cognition* (pp. 275–313). Hillsdale, NJ: Lawrence Erlbaum Associates.

Shapiro, P. N., & Penrod, S. (1986). Meta-analysis of facial identification studies. *Psychological Bulletin, 100*, 139–156.

Snodgrass, J. G., & Feenan, K. (1990). Priming effects in picture fragment completion: Support for the perceptual closure hypothesis. *Journal of Experimental Psychology: General, 119*, 276–296.

Tanaka, J. W., & Farah, M. J. (1993). Parts and wholes in face recognition. *Quarterly Journal of Experimental Psychology, 46A*, 225–245..

Tanaka, J. W., & Sengco, J. A. (1997). Features and their configuration in face recognition. *Memory & Cognition, 25,* 583–592.

Terry, R. L. (1994). Effects of facial transformations on accuracy of recognition. *Journal of Social Psychology, 134,* 483–492.

Wells, G. L., & Turtle, J. W. (1989). What is the best way to encode faces? From A.W. Young & H. D. Ellis, (Eds.), *Handbook of research on face processing* (pp. 163–168). North Holland: Elsevier.

12

Conclusions: Children's Source Monitoring

Kim P. Roberts
*National Institute of Child Health
and Human Development*

The contributors to this book have reported exciting, ingenious, and useful research programs on children's source monitoring in many different contexts. This chapter draws together some of the common themes in the book, and makes suggestions for further research in this area of children's cognition. Rather than repeat in detail the points made earlier in the volume, this chapter makes holistic comments on the field in response to the work reported in the preceding chapters, and readers are urged to the refer to the actual chapters for details of the studies and discussions. In the first half of the chapter, I highlight the development in our understanding of children's source monitoring over recent years. Particularly, I focus on the wealth of source discriminations that are currently under investigation, the usefulness of the conclusions drawn, the adaptive value of source-monitoring errors, and the need to study source monitoring in context. In the second half of the chapter, I turn to those questions that are not fully answered by current research, including techniques to train children to monitor source, distinguishing between multiple (i.e., more than two) sources, and the relationship between source monitoring and the social and emotional aspects of children's development.

Source-Monitoring Judgments

In the pioneering days of research on developmental differences in source-monitoring skills, researchers investigated how children make relatively simple source distinctions, for example, distinguishing between spoken words and imagined words (Foley, Johnson, & Raye, 1983). Since then, researchers have expanded their laboratory techniques so that there is now a variety of ways to (explicitly or implicitly) measure children's source monitoring. Investigations of "simple source distinctions" remain productive ways to estimate cognitive functioning in children, but from the wealth of research since these early investigations we know that there is a whole host of source distinctions that children have to make in their everyday lives. As well as distinctions for details at a low level (e.g., "Did my Dad say I could stay off school or did Mom say that?"), distinctions have to be made at a higher level such as when attributing source to entire events (e.g., "Did the Maple Leafs hockey team really win the Stanley Cup or was that just a dream?"—hint: Since 1967, it was just a dream). In the preceding chapters in this book, a variety of the source distinctions necessary for children to make were documented, although this was by no means an exhaustive list. As discussed in chapter 1 this volume, the source distinction required at any one time depends not only on the characteristics of the different sources to be distinguished, but also on the particular cognitive or social demands of each situation (see Marsh & Hicks, 1998). Each author has contextualized their research in a domain that is important for children's lives. What stands out from the chapters is a sense of the many different ways that children are exposed to information in the world and the need for them to make accurate source distinctions to make sense of this constant flow of information. We see that children learn, among other things, from what adults tell them (chaps. 3, 5, 7, 8, and 9, this volume), from what adults do (chaps. 4 and 5, this volume), from what they see and hear on television (chaps. 6, 7, and 10, this volume), from pictures and stories that they see (chaps. 4, 5, 9, 10, and 11, this volume), in addition to their direct experience. The way that children learn from these different sources, then, has implications for the development of declarative knowledge (e.g., facts learned from television, chaps. 6 and 7, this volume), procedural knowledge (e.g., organizational skills, chap. 4, this volume), autobiographical memory (e.g., being touched in playschool, chap. 8, this volume) and event memory (e.g., chap. 10, this volume). There are many factors that are important in children's learning and memory for all of the listed examples and the authors have presented convincing arguments to show that source-monitoring expertise is one of them.

Applications of Source-Monitoring Research

There are two areas of application that stand out from the work reported in this volume: Eyewitness memory and education.

Eyewitness Memory. With regard to eyewitnesses, inaccurate source attributions can have negative effects (see chap. 8, this volume, for a review). For example, some contributors reported that children's reports of events in which they have been actively involved can be contaminated with information gleaned from television, if they are similar (chap. 6, this volume) or gist consistent (chap. 7, this volume). As another example, consider a situation in which adults (e.g., investigative interviewers, parents) misconstrue or even invent details during an interview conducted to elicit the child's account about an experienced event, a situation that was artificially created in the laboratory by several contributors to this volume. All of the researchers who misled children about particular details found that some children assented (inaccurately) that the misleading details actually occurred in the event (chaps. 7, 8, 9, and 10, this volume). Although there are several reasons why this suggestibility effect may have occurred (and interested readers are urged to refer to the actual chapters as well as contemporary reviews, (e.g., Ceci & Bruck, 1998; Poole & Lamb, 1998), many researchers have asserted that source misattribution is wholly or partly responsible because children inaccurately attribute memory for details to the actual event rather than to the postevent misinformation sessions to which they have been exposed (e.g., Ceci, Loftus, Leichtman, & Bruck, 1996; Lindsay & Johnson, 1987; Roberts & Blades, 1996). The contributors to this volume have demonstrated some of the circumstances under which source misattributions may be responsible for inaccurate reports of an experienced event. For example, Welch-Ross (chap. 9, this volume) provides evidence that source misattribution is a likely explanation for suggestibility effects if children lack an explicit awareness that knowledge originates with particular experiences. Correlations of individual differences in source monitoring and resistance to misleading suggestions were also provided by Leichtman and colleagues (Leichtman et al., this volume). Finally, chapters 7 and 10, this volume, both provide evidence indicating that it may be possible to inoculate children against acquiescing to suggestions by reinforcing the connection between information and source prior to a memory interview.

As well as the relationship between source misattributions and inaccuracies in verbal reports of events, (chap. 11, this volume) discussed how source-monitoring judgments can inform us about face identification processes. Although research on children's face recognition is a relatively large and growing area, it is not as theoretically rich as some other areas of eyewitness research. In their chapter, Foley and colleagues provided inspiration for using source-monitoring theory (Johnson, Hashtroudi, & Lindsay, 1993; Johnson & Raye,

1981) to guide a research program in this area, particularly with regard to understanding the processes that occur when faces are perceived. In particular, they showed that although there was a
developmental increase in accurate recognition of faces, children
were no worse than adults when asked to identify whether the face at
test was the same or different as initially presented after the original
image was changed by adding or removing "paraphernalia" (e.g.,
scarves, sunglasses, facial hair), or even explicitly deleting portions of
the face. Children may be called on to identify suspects in many instances such as in the case of kidnaping, hit-and-run accidents, as
well as when they are incidental witnesses to events, such as during
robberies. In many of these incidents, faces may be disguised. Foley et
al.'s results suggest that paraphernalia may not be perceived as an
"add on" but rather as an integral part of the face and so it is imperative to fully understand mechanisms of closure processes.

Education.   With regards to education, children need to learn to
assign appropriate weight to different sources of information (e.g., information from parents, teachers, textbooks, television, peers) otherwise their knowledge and memories would be hopelessly
contaminated by inaccuracies and "noise." Even if children assign appropriate weight to sources (and research by Robinson, this volume,
suggests that even young children can do this in some circumstances),
their knowledge and expertise will reflect hybrids of information from
different sources when children forget or confuse those sources from
which they learned the information. Even if children can assess the
credibility of different sources at the time of encoding, over time, they
may not retain this information and consequently assign credible status to noncredible information (c.f., the sleeper effect, Leippe, Greenwald, & Baumgardner, 1982). Source distinctions, then, are part of
children's everyday existence both in formal and informal educational
settings, and the accuracy of children's source distinctions will have
significant effects on the content of their knowledge base and beliefs
about the world. Investigations of source-monitoring skills in special
populations may also prove to be beneficial in an educational setting,
and Lorsbach (chap. 5, this volume) reviews the small number of
studies in this area. Drawing on the results of research on source
monitoring and memory in children with learning difficulties,
Lorsbach presents a hypothesis that these children may be disadvantaged in situations that require reflective processing. Improving our
understanding of the cognitive profile of children with learning difficulties will enable practitioners, educators, and parents to provide
services more closely tied to children's special needs. In addition,

studying impairments in source monitoring provides a window on the cognitive mechanisms that mediate this skill in children with and without special educational needs.

The Adaptive Value of Source-Monitoring Judgments

Although there are clearly negative effects when children (and adults) make inaccurate source attributions, it is now becoming clear through research programs (e.g., chap. 4, this volume) that there is sometimes adaptive value in source errors. As described in chapter 4, "these errors may then index cognitive operations that are highly adaptive, promoting more complex modes of functioning, rather than markers of processes that only result in poorer performance in some domain" (Ratner et al., this volume, p. 89).

As previously mentioned, children learn from many different sources in the world and sometimes the source of the information may be forgotten or confused. Source errors may serve a function in a social context to reinforce cultural myths or threats of harm (chap. 10, this volume), or to increase children's knowledge base (chap. 10, this volume). For example, a child may learn that frogs like water but be amnesic regarding whether their mom or preschool teacher taught them the fact. The lack of attention paid to encoding the source of the information (hence, providing little information to use in a later source attribution) may be a mechanism that enhances the ease with which information is assimilated. At this early stage, when children have so much to learn, valuable processing resources may need to be spent on absorbing information around them rather than on source judgments. The lack of accurate source attribution in this instance is not a problem, as both sources are credible. Similarly, when children watch educational programs on television such as *National Geographic*, there are generally no detrimental consequences to their knowledge base if they confuse information seen in such a television program with information they read about in a *National Geographic* magazine. Negative effects may result, however, when children are exposed to television programs that distort features of the world and children confuse this with information from more credible sources (chap. 6, this volume).

The research discussed in chapter 4, this volume, provides the clearest example to date of the adaptive value of one kind of source error—reality-monitoring confusions—and its beneficial effects on young children's learning in collaborative contexts. In their research, they find that children who tend to inaccurately claim that they performed actions that an adult actually performed are more likely to learn from the interactive exchange than are children who are more accurate at making self–other distinctions. A series of studies designed to index these individual differences in misattributions has revealed that the "good learners" actually recode the adults' actions as their own, thus enabling them to use the consequent knowledge in future tasks. In other research, (e.g., Ackkerman, 1992, 1994), increases in children's inferential reasoning have come at the expense of their ability to accurately identify the source of the information used in the reasoning.

If there were evolutionary value in source misattributions for the reasons outlined previously (i.e., ease of assimilation of knowledge, appropriation), we would expect to see most source misattributions occurring when the need to learn facts or procedures is greatest. In humans, this could arguably be during the preschool years. Research appears to support this idea: Those who have investigated source monitoring in young children below age 6 report higher rates of inaccuracy for these younger children in response to traditional source-monitoring questions compared with the inaccuracy rates of older children and adults (e.g., Roberts & Blades, 1995; Welch-Ross, 1995). Similarly, many of the contributors to this volume have argued that some of the most important developments in source monitoring take place during the 3- to 6-year-old age range (e.g., chaps. 3, 6, 9, and 10, this volume).

Robinson (chap 3, this volume) documents a series of studies neatly illustrating how young children (i.e., below 5 years) cannot reflect on their knowledge. They can, however, use different sources of information appropriately, which suggests that source monitoring (i.e., making accurate attributions for memories of learned information) may not be essential for the goal of expanding one's knowledge base in early childhood, provided that children can judge which sources are useful. Specifically, Robinson found that children knew not to trust an adult's utterance about the identity of an object when the adult had not actually seen the object. In other studies, making the sources of different information explicit to young children did not decrease their source confusions any more than by reminding children of the content of the events, either through a reinforcing procedure (chap. 10, this volume) or through recognition questions (chap. 9, this volume). There seems to be a striking consensus, that young children seem able to use knowledge appropriately, but have no access to how they used those sources or the metacognitive awareness of which cues are useful.

Evolutionary theories of human behavior cannot be disproved, however. If source amnesia or source misattributions contribute to learning, perhaps it would be possible to track the rates of source misattribution errors in adults as they learn new tasks. In this instance, more source errors would be expected at the beginning of training when the need for learning is greatest, and the rate of these errors should fall as the learning reaches optimal levels. What is clear is that value judgments about source errors need to be made with respect to the context. In forensic situations when a child is required to retrieve accurate, verbatim information from event memory and reject misleading information, errors are clearly troublesome; when children are acquiring declarative or procedural knowledge, source errors can be beneficial. At present, there is little direct evidence of the adaptive value of source errors with respect to children's acquisition of social and cultural norms. In research with adults, however, reality monitoring has been implicated in the development and persistence of some social phenomena, such as stereotypes (Slusher & Anderson, 1987), and the contribution of source monitoring to the perpetuation of social norms awaits further research.

Assessment Techniques

The preceding chapters provided examples of the wealth of implicit and explicit techniques that have been developed to measure children's source monitoring. Many of the contributors to this volume document how they explicitly measured children's source attributions using traditional source-monitoring questions in which children are presented with a forced choice between the relevant sources (e.g., chaps. 5, 7, 9, and 10, this volume). For example, Leichtman and colleagues (chap. 10) presented children with a list of sources (video, story, toys) and asked the children to choose the source in which a particular detail was presented. Other researchers have used more implicit tests of source monitoring (e.g., chaps. 6 and 7, this volume) in which children are given a task to perform that requires them to make source attributions in order to accurately carry out the task. For example, Roberts and Blades (chap. 6) asked children to report everything they remembered about an event, a task that necessitated inhibiting details remembered from a similar, related event. Thierry and her colleagues (chap. 7) presented children with misleading questions that confused details from two events; this necessitated accurate source attribution for the details before an accurate response to the misleading question could be given.

   As with many areas of children's development, different measurement tools reveal different aspects of the phenomena of interest. For example, researchers of children's eyewitness or autobiographical reports know that children's memory when measured using open-ended questions appears incomplete, but nevertheless usually accurate (e.g., Fivush &

Schwarz-Mueller, 1998; Fivush & Shukat, 1995) unless they have been subjected to suggestive procedures between the event and describing their memory (e.g., Ceci, Loftus, et al., 1994). When children are questioned with coercive questions containing inaccurate information, however, they may acquiesce to the misleading information (see Ceci & Bruck, 1993, 1995) leading to an assessment that children do not remember events well at all. Roberts and Blades (chap. 6, this volume) report similar patterns for source errors, namely that there was more evidence of source confusions when children answered focused and suggestive questions than when they were allowed to spontaneously report what they remembered. The measures used to assess children's source monitoring need to be carefully chosen depending on the particular research questions, and examples of a variety of techniques are contained in this volume.

One of the challenges facing researchers is assessing source monitoring in preschool children. Some researchers have successfully used traditional source-monitoring questions (e.g., asking "Did you do that or did Jessie do that?" when distinguishing between self- and other-performed actions; (chaps. 3 and 4, this volume). Others have needed to supplement the verbal questions with props (chap. 7, this volume). Still, others have avoided the need to switch between memories of two events (as in dual-choice source-monitoring questions) and assessed memory for one source at a time using cued recall questions from which it is possible to decipher from the child's response from which source she or he is retrieving information (chap. 6, this volume).

One of the difficulties with traditional source questions is that they inevitably give the child a forced choice between the relevant sources (usually two), a procedure that can inflate the number of correct source attributions that were produced by guessing. Although this would be true for any age group, younger children may feel more pressured to guess so that they can provide an authoritative adult with an answer to their question. Because of perceived experimental pressure, a forced-choice procedure may also mask another kind of source-monitoring failure, that of amnesia for source, because the child feels compelled to answer even if they cannot make a source attribution. Another difficulty with listing multiple sources in a question is that children tend to choose the last option in a sequence more than the other options (Walker, 1997), and so results may also be skewed this way.

Although it seems a promising alternative, using open-ended prompts to elicit source reasoning by young children may not, however, be feasible given the results reported by Robinson (chap. 3, this volume). She found that 3- to 4-year-olds had difficulty answering open-ended source probes such as "How did you know it was a X?" although they could provide an answer to a forced-choice question such as "Did you see it, or did I tell you it was a X?" This meant that source errors were reported only in response to the "traditional" source-monitoring questions. The methodological considerations of using traditional, forced-choice source questions are not insurmountable, however. For example, the order of two options can be counterbalanced so that each choice appears at the end of a question equally often. Also, preliminary practice in answering the source questions can be used as a "check" that children are actually considering the sources rather than "yeah-saying." A careful and thorough analysis of alternative explanations can also improve the validity of conclusions regarding young children's source monitoring, as shown in chapter 3, this volume. Another useful technique to assess whether response biases are operating above and beyond experimental treatments (and also informative in its own right) is to analyze the patterns of source misattributions. Ratner et al. (chap. 4, this volume) found source misattributions for other-performed actions but not self-performed actions, and Lorsbach (chap. 5, this volume) reported that children asserted that a falsely recognized distracter was presented as a word more than they claimed it was presented as a picture. As response options were counterbalanced, these patterns of errors were clearly not due to response biases.

Another consideration of forced-choice questions containing multiple options is that they can be verbally demanding for young children. As argued in chapter 3, this volume, most assessments of children's source monitoring require children to make verbally explicit the source of information, and this may mask any working knowledge that they have. Indeed, Roberts and Blades (1995) found that, when tested with a behavioral measure, 3-year-olds could (at short delays) discriminate between actions that they had performed and those that they had pretended to perform during a hiding game; in contrast, their source monitoring appeared significantly poorer than older children's and adults' when tested with a traditional verbal source discrimination test. Similarly, Lorsbach (chap. 5, this volume) notes that children with learning difficulties have a verbal memory deficit compared with children without such disabilities, and he hypothesized that their deficits in source monitoring may also be limited to verbal processing, a hypothesis that awaits exploration. There are clearly opportunities and the need for developmental psychologists to create a variety of testing procedures to provide a richer picture of children's source monitoring.

The development of ways to adequately assess children's source monitoring can also be channeled in practical ways. The need for victims and witnesses to distinguish between events that they have actually perceived (e.g., seen with their own eyes) and those that have not occurred (e.g. events they have imagined, events that were suggested), as well as distinctions between one event and another have been amply discussed by many of the contributors (chaps. 3, 6, 7, 8, 9, and 10, this volume). As reviewed in the previous chapters, one of the crucial tasks of an investigative interviewer is to elicit an account about the alleged incidents that is as minimally contaminated as possible with details gleaned from other sources. One response to this dilemma is to ask children whether an event really happened to help them discriminate between the actual event(s) and contaminating sources. This approach may not always be helpful, however, because children's pragmatic understanding of the term "really" may be quite different than an adult's, as in the case where a child's mom "really" told her to invent a story (Poole & Lindsay, 1999a). At the very least, investigators are urged to bear in mind these conflicts when working with young children and to endeavor to explore new methodologies.

Source Monitoring in Context

Another development observed from the work reported in this volume is that investigating children's source monitoring with respect to its context has deepened our understanding of children's cognition. For example, early developmental studies of source monitoring showed that, by age 6, children were as competent as adults at accurately distinguishing between memories of isolated actions that they had carried out and those performed by an adult confederate (Foley & Johnson, 1985). More recent investigations of this same kind of reality monitoring have revealed individual differences that have a significant impact on what children learn from collaborative activities (chap. 4, this volume). Ratner, Foley, and colleagues' (chap. 4) work also revealed the importance of considering source monitoring with respect to the goal-related nature of the task, and this was also reflected in chapter 11, this volume, on face processing. Studies carried out in the context of event memory have also contributed to our understanding of the mechanisms involved in source monitoring (e.g., chap. 9, this volume). Examining spontaneous source monitoring carried out in the pursuit of another goal is likely to yield results that are indicative of the everyday source monitoring performed by children and adults.

In summary, the findings discussed throughout this volume have revealed that source monitoring impacts children's declarative and episodic memory in many ways. Important developments in source monitoring take place in the preschool years, and this is concurrent with other developments, such as representational understanding. Source monitoring is sensitive to situational and individual factors, and it is hoped that in future research these interactions can be more fully understood. One of the mechanisms that appears to contribute to inaccuracies in source monitoring is the lack of reflective processing evidenced by young children and those with learning difficulties. This is discussed further in the following sections on contemporary research questions about children's source monitoring.

Training Source-Monitoring Skills

A useful technique for understanding the mechanisms involved in a skill is to train people in that skill according to hypotheses about those mechanisms. For example, consider a study designed to test the hypothesis that strengthening leg muscles enables babies to walk: A program of daily leg exercises was carried out with a group of babies and their walking was compared with that of another group of babies who were not given any special treatment during the training period. If a training effect was observed (such that the exercise group learned to walk faster than the no-exercise group), then we could conclude that, all things being equal, strong leg muscles lead to walking skills. Training studies, therefore, can inform us about the mechanisms of children's cognition by allowing us to increase or decrease the parameters of competence to see what helps and what hinders source-monitoring accuracy.

Based on the hypothesis that orienting children to source would improve their source monitoring (e.g., Lindsay & Johnson, 1987, 1989; Zaragoza & Koshmider, 1989), Thierry and colleagues (chap. 7, this volume) and Leichtman and colleagues (chap. 10, this volume), in independent investigations, exposed children to information from multiple sources and reinforced the link between the information and the source from which it came. Thierry et al. (this volume) compared information from television and real-life demonstrations; Leichtman et al. compared information from television, a storybook, and direct participation with toys. Each investigation was contextualized within a misinformation paradigm to enable conclusions about children's suggestibility. Both groups reported a decrease in errors after the source-reinforcement, but the results were not as strong as expected: Thierry et al. reported a decrease in suggestibility, but this was mainly restricted to the 3- to 4-year-olds; Leichtman et al. reported a decrease in suggestibility, but no more than a comparison group for whom memory of the events was reinforced without mention of source. Similarly, Welch-Ross (chap. 9, this volume) found that children who answered recognition questions well also answered source-monitoring questions well—there was no advantage to cuing children to source on their responses to recognition questions.

In another investigation, Poole and Lindsay (1999a) found that older (6 to 8 years), but not younger (3 to 5 years) children benefitted from an orientation to the sources from which information was learned. Specifically, children were exposed to real-life science demonstrations, and then their parents read a story about the demonstrations to them three months later in which some events were described that never actually occurred. The children were later asked to give narrative descriptions and answered leading questions about the real-life demonstrations. Some of the children reported the fictitious events heard in the story as if they had actually happened. When it was made clear to the children that there was a story as well as the actual demonstrations, some of the older children retracted the story details, but the younger children did so much less frequently.

Given that several of the authors indicated that children who make source misattributions have difficulty with reflective processing (e.g., chaps. 3, 5, and 10, this volume), it may be that very young children (e.g., 3-year-olds) simply cannot benefit from efforts to make the source explicit. Perhaps young children do not appreciate the value of using source information. Indeed, if children do not appreciate that specific experiences lead to knowing specific kinds of information they may see little need to engage in attributional reasoning about source (see chaps. 3 and 9, this volume). If children lack the kinds of representational understanding outlined in chapter 9, then they also may not be able to use the same heuristics that adults use when attributing source. Take the example described by Johnson et al. (1993) in how some people may be able to avoid making a source error of claiming that they have a memory of an event if they can also reason that they were not there. Young children who do not understand the experience–knowing connection (e.g., Wimmer, Hogrefe, & Perner, 1988), may not be able to reason this way. In addition, the frontal lobe is involved in source-monitoring decisions (see Johnson et al., 1993) and Schacter and colleagues (e.g., Schacter, Kagan, & Leichtman, 1995) have suggested that children's source-monitoring problems stem from immature development of the prefrontal regions. Some children may simply not possess the "hardware" for source monitoring and, thus, training may be ineffective.

Given that one of the likely causal mechanisms for suggestibility is inaccurate source monitoring because a child may misattribute a detail from, say, a suggestive interview to their memory of an actual event, the development of source-monitoring training techniques also has great practical and legal implications. This may be especially important in "tell me everything" interviewing protocols such as the cognitive interview (Fisher & Greiselman, 1992)or the NICHD protocol (see Poole & Lamb, 1998) in which children are repeatedly encouraged with open-ended prompts to report every detail that they can recall. Source-monitoring judgments are more accurate when stringent decision-making criteria are applied (Johnson et al., 1993), and "report everything" requests may encourage children to report any detail that springs to mind without a thorough appraisal of its source. Of course, increases in information spontaneously produced by children is a desirable outcome in a forensic interview because children are known to be most accurate in their responses to open-ended prompts (e.g., and the more information child witnesses report, the more information police officers have to use in their investigation. Given the results found in chapters 7, 8, 9, and 10, this volume, as well as other researchers who have argued about causal links between source-monitoring accuracy and suggestibility (e.g., Ackil & Zaragoza, 1995; Ceci, Huffman, et al., 1994; Ceci, Loftus, et al., 1994; Lindsay & Johnson, 1987), careful attention needs to be paid to the precise nature of free recall requests in terms of the cognitive mechanisms that precede and accompany responses to these kinds of probes.

Leichtman et al.'s (chap. 10, this volume), Poole and Lindsay's (1999a), and Thierry et al.'s (chap. 7, this volume) results are encouraging and suggest that the stringency of the criteria used when answering event memory interviews can be manipulated. The kinds of procedure used in their studies may be difficult to reproduce in the field of investigative interviewing, however. In all three studies, the sources to which the children had been exposed were known and so it was possible to orient children specifically to the different sources. Although alternative sources are sometimes known in some investigations of sexual abuse (e.g., contamination from peers in the case of suspected group abuse, exposure to educational programs about inappropriate touch, or exposure to pornographic videos), for the most part, the different and potentially contaminating sources that children may have been exposed to are unknown. The challenge remains, then, to develop techniques that can train children to "gate out" (Poole & Lindsay, 1999a) competing sources themselves. In a recent study, attempts to train children to monitor their memories spontaneously was unsuccessful as measured by children's responses to yes/no questions (Poole & Lindsay, 1999b).

Source-monitoring training, then, is an obvious path to pursue for both theoretical and practical reasons. However, research in this area is still in its early stages and recommendations for investigative interviewing in the field should be approached with caution. One potential disadvantage of training children to improve their source-monitoring accuracy is that the increased stringency of the source decision-making process may reduce the amount of information that they report if they choose to report information only if they are absolutely sure of its source. Imagine, for example, that a child has claimed that she was sexually abused by her grandfather at their vacation home. She is asked if there were any other people nearby at the time when the alleged incident was said to have occurred. She can remember her sister playing outside, but is not sure whether this was the time that her grandfather abused her or another time when he did not abuse her. Whether she reports this remembered detail may depend on instructions laid out earlier in the interview (report everything, report only what you are sure happened that time). If she has been primed to use strict source decision criteria, then she may decide not to report the detail. This would mean, however, that she may be dissuaded from reporting many other details, leading to a skeletal report from which it is difficult to corroborate any details and the investigation comes to a halt. A possible hybrid of the techniques previously discussed is to first elicit a free recall account of the incidents, and then to revisit the details in the child's testimony after he or she has been instructed in stringent source monitoring. These are merely speculations, however, and much more research is clearly needed before the true effects of source training on children's reports can be evaluated.

Although, improving children's source-monitoring accuracy seems to be a beneficial goal in the legal context, it is necessary to bear in mind the points raised by the contributors to this volume about the value of source errors in some circumstances. Going back to the hypothetical learning-to-walk training exercise, it may not be in some babies' best interests to encourage walking through a training program. For example, if a child's bones are not formed enough that they will keep their shape when weight is placed on them, then walking could have undesirable consequences. Similarly, we have seen that source errors can serve adaptive functions: Ratner et al. (chap. 4, this volume) argues convincingly that children can learn through recoding another person's actions as their own. To manipulate source confusions, then, may have negative implications for other cognitive developments. Given that Poole and Lindsay (1999b) found that source-monitoring training effects did not generalize when the children were required to spontaneously monitor their memories, however, global deficits may be unlikely. Furthermore, it should also be noted that children develop different cognitive skills at different times (e.g., Siegler, 1988), and source-monitoring development also does not show an all-or-none quality (see chap. 2, this volume). A consideration of the ethical soundness of training procedures should be utmost in researchers' minds, however.

Source Monitoring Memories of Multiple Events

Another consideration and challenge for our understanding of source monitoring is to further investigate how children process multiple sources such as an event that they have experienced three, four, five or more times. In most investigations of children's source monitoring, children's ability to distinguish between memories of two different sources has been studied. In everyday life, however, there are times when children are required to distinguish between memories from more than two sources, for example, when a child alleges multiple incidents of sexual abuse. Research on the development of scripts can inform us on children's memories for multiple sources (see Farrar & Goodman, 1992; Hudson, Fivush, & Kuebli, 1992; Nelson, 1986; for reviews). From these investigations, we know that after multiple exposures to similar events, children develop generalized event representations that enable them to organize and retrieve information common to the occurrences. Forming scripts, however, can also lead to memory errors that are likely to take the form of source confusions because details from similar occurrences are reported as if they occurred in a target occurrence (e.g., Powell & Thomson, 1996). According to script theories, this is because common features of occurrences are abstracted with repeated experience, and specific instantiations are retained as "slot fillers" for the specific details (Hudson et al., 1992), and so children remember the common features well but have difficulty identifying the particular instantiation to fit the "slot." As Powell and Thomson (1996) noted, source-monitoring theory explains how children can remember the content of memories but confuse in which instance those details were experienced (e.g., claiming that a detail was present in the first event when it was actually experienced in the second event). Script theory, however, better explains how specific occurrences are merged into one general event representation.

Specifying the relationship between multiple (i.e., more than two) experiences and suggestibility is still in its infancy. In a recent investigation, it was demonstrated that errors made by children who experienced an event between four and six times versus those made by children who experienced an event just once showed distinct patterns (Powell et al., 1999). After repeated experience, children resisted suggestions about details that did not happen in any of the events more than others who had watched an event just once; however, they did confuse the different events. Importantly, the accuracy of children's memories of different events depended on whether the details varied across the occurrences. Memory for invariant details is good (Connolly & Lindsay, 1997; Powell et al., 1999), whereas source confusions are evident for those details that vary each time. It is hoped that the next generation of source-monitoring research could clarify the ways in which adults and children distinguish between details that they have encountered on multiple occasions. The need for research is further exemplified given the potential problems of forced-choice source-monitoring questions mentioned in this chapter, as well as the need for source-monitoring training techniques in the field. Many allegations of sexual and physical abuse involve multiple incidents for which children are likely to have scripted memories. In particular, understanding whether and how source monitoring affects the development of scripts will be particularly informative for our understanding of children's multiple event memories, for example, source confusions may contribute to the integration and gist abstraction of scripts.

Children s Social and Emotional Lives

There are currently few studies of children's source monitoring in a social context. As suggested in the chapter 1, this volume, source confusions can indirectly harm personal relationships if one is constantly confusing who told them which pieces of information, for example. As suggested in chapter 10, this volume, however, source confusions can also function to reinforce social and cultural norms. In contrast to investigations with children, source-monitoring skills have been implicated in many different social phenomena with adults, such as arguments (Ross & Holmberg, 1990), client–therapist relationships (Lindsay & Read, 1994), and memories for conversations (Brown, Jones, & Davis, 1995). Also, judgments of the source (perceived vs. imagined) of other peoples' memories is affected by social factors, such as the interpersonal context in which the judgment took place. Although increased perceptual and emotional detail in an account usually signals a memory of an event that actually occurred, Johnson and colleagues did not find this to be the case when suspicions about the veracity of the account were induced in those making the judgment (Johnson, Bush, & Mitchell, 1998). Understanding how source monitoring mediates aspects of children's social–cognitive understanding is important, for example, in understanding how young children develop theories about other peoples' minds. How do children use the cues in their own source-monitoring judgments to reason about what other people are thinking?

The role of source monitoring in children's emotional lives is also worthy of study. Given the relationship between source monitoring, suggestibility, and children's eyewitness reports (e.g., chaps. 7, 9, and 10, this volume), an important question is how emotional state affects source discriminations of traumatic memories? In several studies with adults, researchers have found that focusing on emotional content may impair later source monitoring, even if it improves memory for the content (Hashtroudi, Johnson, Vnek, & Ferguson, 1994; Johnson, Nolde, & De Leonardis, 1996). These findings raise important issues about children's source monitoring for emotionally-engaging memories, as well as wider issues about the generalizability of laboratory findings to crucial situations, such as investigations of sexual abuse. For example, if a child involved in an investigation of sexual abuse is also in therapy related to the abuse, then rehearsal of their memories is likely to change the qualitative profiles in important ways. This, in turn, is likely to have a significant impact on their source monitoring of events that they actually experienced versus information gleaned from other sources. Further research on the functional significance of source monitoring is likely to produce findings of great interest for our understanding of children's social and emotional development.

SUMMARY

Since the first studies published in the early 1980s, a significant amount of research has been generated on the nature and development of source-monitoring processes in children. The focus of research has shifted from studying source monitoring as an isolated skill, to understanding how the processes involved in the source decision process (from encoding to attribution) affect representations in important ways. The results of the research effort reveal that source-monitoring skills emerge during the preschool years, although very young children may have a working understanding about the different sources of information before they can reflect or verbally report on their source attributional reasoning. The development of source monitoring continues throughout the life span and children may master some types of source distinctions before others. Source-monitoring skills impact many areas of children's lives. At present, their impact is best understood in relation to other aspects of children's cognition, such as event memory. In some circumstances, source confusions have detrimental effects (e.g., in their eyewitness reports), and, in others, beneficial effects (e.g., in collaborative learning contexts). The role of source-monitoring skills in reinforcing social behavior is, at present, not well understood. The contributors to this volume have shared state-of-the-art research programs that explore a wide range of source-monitoring phenomena. Their conclusions have implications for the educational and legal arenas. The work reported also raises many challenges for future research. Tracking the precise mechanisms involved in children's source confusions is one of them. Are children aware of the need to monitor the sources of their memories? Do children encode information in such a way that it can be effectively used in source reasoning? Can children be trained in the metacognitive awareness of when they need to distinguish between different memories? Can children alter the weight of the criteria used in source judgments? It is hoped that these and other questions will be answered in the next wave of source-monitoring research, and that this knowledge can be put to practical use in children's lives.

REFERENCES

Ackerman, B. P. (1992). The sources of children's source errors in judging causal inferences. *Journal of Experimental Child Psychology, 54*, 90–119.

Ackerman, B. P. (1994). Children's source errors in referential communication. *Journal of Experimental Child Psychology, 58*, 432–464.

Ackil, J. K., & Zaragoza, M. S. (1995). Developmental differences in eyewitness suggestibility and memory for source. *Journal of Experimental Child Psychology, 60* 57–83.

Brown, A. S., Jones, E. M., & Davis, T. L. (1995). Age differences in conversational source monitoring. *Psychology and Aging, 10*, 111–122.

Ceci, S. J., & Bruck, M. (1993). The suggestibility of the child witness: A historical review and synthesis. *Psychological Bulletin, 113*, 403–439.

Ceci, S. J., & Bruck, M. (1995). *Jeopardy in the courtroom.* Washington, DC: American Psychological Association.

Ceci, S. J., & Bruck, M. (1998). Children's testimony: Applied and basic issues. In W. Damon, I. E. Sigel, & K. A. Renninger (Eds.), *Handbook of child psychology: Vol. 4 (5th ed., pp 713–773).* New York: Wiley.

Ceci, S. J., Huffman, M. L. C., Smith, E., & Loftus, E. F. (1994). Repeatedly thinking about a non-event: Source misattributions among preschoolers. *Consciousness and Cognition, 3*, 388–407.

Ceci, S. J. Loftus, E. F., Leichtman, M. D., & Bruck, M. (1994). The possible role of source misattributions in the creation of false beliefs among preschoolers. *International Journal of Clinical and Experimental Hypnosis, 42*, 304–320.

Connolly, D. A., & Lindsay, D. S. (1997, April). *The influence of postevent misinformation on children's reports of an unique event versus an instance of a repeated event.* Presented at the biennial meeting of the Society for Research in Child Development, Washington, DC.

Dent, H. R., & Stephenson, G. M. (1979). An experimental study of the effectiveness of different techniques of questioning child witnesses. *British Journal of Social and Clinical Psychology, 18*, 41–51.

Farrar, M. J., & Goodman, G. S. (1992). Developmental changes in event memory. *Child Development, 63*, 173–187.

Fisher, R. P., & Geiselman, R. E. (1992). *Memory-enhancing techniques for investigative interviewing: The cognitive interview.* Springfield, IL: Charles C. Thomas.

Fivush, R., & Schwarzmueller, A. (1998). Children remember childhood: Implications for childhood amnesia. *Applied Cognitive Psychology, 12*, 455–473.

Fivush, R., & Shukat, J. R. (1995). Content, consistency, and coherence of early autobiographical recall. In M. S. Zaragoza, J. R. Graham, G. C. N. Hall, R. Hirschman, & Y. N. Ben-Porath (Eds.), *Memory and testimony in the child witness,*(pp. 5–23). Thousand Oaks: Sage.

Foley, M. A., & Johnson, M. K. (1985). Confusions between memories for performed and imagined actions: A developmental comparison. *Child Development, 56*, 1145–1155.

Foley, M. A., Johnson, M. K., & Raye, C. L. (1983). Age-related changes in confusion between memories for thoughts and memories for speech. *Child Development, 54*, 51–60.

Hashtroudi, S., Johnson, M. K., Vnek, R., & Ferguson, S. A. (1994). Aging and the effects of affective and factual focus on source monitoring and recall. *Psychology and Aging, 9*, 160–170.

Hudson, J. A., Fivush, R., & Kuebli, J. (1992). Scripts and episodes: The development of event memory. *Applied Cognitive Psychology, 6*, 483–505.

Johnson, M. K., Bush, J. G., & Mitchell, K. J. (1998). Interpersonal reality monitoring: Judging the sources of other people's memories. *Social cognition, 16*, 199–224.

Johnson, M. K., Hashtroudi, S., & Lindsay, D. S. (1993). Source monitoring. *Psychological Bulletin, 114*, 3–28.

Johnson, M. K., Nolde, S. F., & De Leonardis, D. M. (1996). Emotional focus and source monitoring. *Journal of Memory and Language, 35*, 135–156.

Johnson, M. K., & Raye, C. L. (1981). Reality monitoring. *Psychological Review, 88*, 67–85.

Leippe, M. R., Greenwald, A. G., & Baumgardner, M. H. (1982). Delayed persuasion as a consequence of associative interference: A context effect. *Personality and Social Psychology Bulletin, 8*, 644–650.

Lindsay, D. S., & Johnson, M. K. (1987). Reality monitoring and suggestibility: Children's ability to discriminate among memories from different sources. In S. J. Ceci, M. P. Toglia, & D. F. Ross (Eds.), *Children's eyewitness memory* (pp. 92–121. New York: Springer-Verlag.

Lindsay, D. S., & Johnson, M. K. (1989). The eyewitness suggestibility effect and memory for source. *Memory and Cognition, 17*, 349–358.

Lindsay, D. S., & Read, J. D. (1994). Psychotherapy and memories of childhood sexual abuse: A cognitive perspective. *Applied Cognitive Psychology, 8*, 281–338.

Marsh, R. L., & Hicks, J. L. (1998). Test formats change source-monitoring decision processes. *Journal of Experimental Psychology, Learning, Memory and Cognition, 24*, 1137–1151.

Nelson, K. (1986). *Event knowledge: Structure and function in development.* Hillsdale, NJ: Lawrence Erlbaum Associates.

Poole, D. A., & Lamb, M. E. (1998). *Investigative interviews of children: A guide for helping professionals.* Washington, DC: American Psychological Association.

Poole, D. A., & Lindsay, D. S. (1999a). *Children's eyewitness reports after exposure to misinformation from parents.* Manuscript under review.

Poole, D. A., & Lindsay, D. S. (1999b, April). Counteracting the effects of contamination of children's eyewitness reports. In A. R. Warren & D. A. Poole (Chairs), *Eliciting accurate testimony from children: What works, what doesn't, and why?* Symposium conducted at the biennial meeting of the Society for Research in Child Development, Albuquerque, NM.

Powell, M. B., Roberts, K. P., Ceci, S. J., & Hembrooke, H. H. (1999). The effects of repeated experience on children's suggestibility. *Developmental Psychology, 35,* 1462–1477.

Powell, M. B., & Thomson, D. M. (1996). Children's memory of an occurrence of a repeated event: Effects of age, repetition, and retention interval across three question types. *Child Development, 67,* 1988–2004.

Roberts, K. P., & Blades, M. (1995). Children's discriminations of memories for actual and pretend actions in a hiding task. *British Journal of Developmental Psychology, 13,* 321–333.

Roberts, K. P., & Blades, M. (1996). Children's memories of events on TV and witnessed in real life. In H. Gray, N. Foreman, & N. Hayes (Eds.), *Psychology in a changing Europe* (pp. 283–286). Moscow: Innostraniya Psichologiya [Foreign Psychology].

Ross, M., & Holmberg, D. (1990). Recounting the past: Gender differences in the recall of events in the history of a close relationship. In J. M. Olson, & M. Zanna (Eds.), *Self-inference processes: The Ontario symposium: Vol. 6., Personality and Social Psychology* (pp. 135–152). Hillsdale, NJ: Lawrence Erlbaum Associates.

Schacter, D. L., Kagan, J., & Leichtman, M. D. (1995). True and false memories in children and adults: A cognitive neuroscience perspective. *Psychology, Public Policy and Law, 1,* 411–428.

Siegler, R. S. (1988). Mechanisms of cognitive development. *Annual Review of Psychology, 40,* 353–379.

Slusher, M. P., & Anderson, C. A. (1987). When reality monitoring fails: The role of imagination in stereotype maintenance. *Journal of Personality and Social Psychology, 52,* 653–662.

Walker, N. (1997, April). Should we question how we question children during child abuse investigations? In M. Bruck & H. Hembrooke (Chairs), *Beyond suggestibility: Interviews, interviewers, and the information they elicit from children.* Symposium conducted at the biennial meeting of the Society for Research in Child Development, Washington, DC.

Welch-Ross, M. K. (1995). Developmental changes in preschoolers' ability to distinguish between memories of performed, pretended, and imagined actions. *Cognitive Development, 10,* 421–441.

Wimmer, H., Hogrefe, A., & Perner, J. (1988). Children's understanding of informational access as a source of knowledge. *Child Development, 59,* 386–396.

Zaragoza, M. S., Koshmider III, J. W. (1989). Misled subjects may know more than their performance implies. *Journal of Experimental Psychology: Learning, Memory, and Cognition, 15,* 246–255.

About the Contributors

Kristen Weede Alexander, BA
Kristen Alexander is a doctoral student in the Division of Human Development and Family Studies at the University of California, Davis. She received her bachelor's degree in human development from University of California, Riverside in 1995. Much of her research concerns children's cognitive and memory development.

Mark Blades, PhD
After receiving his PhD from the University of Sheffield in the UK, Mark Blades joined the Faculty there and is currently an Associate Professor of Developmental Psychology. He teaches undergraduate and graduate classes on children's cognitive development. He has published widely on spatial cognition, and has supervised several dissertations on the various skills of child witnesses, including source monitoring, color memory, and children's understanding of the legal system.

Kim Cormier, MA
Kim Cormier completed her BA degree in 1997 at Skidmore College. The studies reported in this chapter were part of her senior thesis research. Kim just completed her master's degree in school psychology from the University of Massachusetts at Amherst.

Angela Dixon, MA
Angela Dixon is a PhD candidate in the Department of Psychology at the University of Sydney, Australia. She received a BA from the University of Melbourne, and an MA from Harvard University Extension School.

Hugh J. Foley, PhD
Hugh J. Foley is an Associate Professor in the Department of Psychology at Skidmore College in Saratoga Springs, NY. He received his PhD from the State University of New York at Stony Brook. His research interests include the study of the mechanisms of perceptual closure, contextual effects on psychophysical judgments, and decision making.

Mary Ann Foley, PhD
Mary Ann Foley is Professor in the Department of Psychology at Skidmore College in Saratoga Springs, NY. She received her PhD from the State University of New York at Stony Brook. She has been investigating children's source-monitoring abilities for more than 15 years. In recent years, her research demonstrates the heuristic value of the source-monitoring framework for addressing a wide range of theoretical questions.

Nicole R. Gimpert, BA
Nicole R. Gimpert recently completed her BA degree with honors at Wayne State University.

Gail S. Goodman, PhD
Gail Goodman is Professor of Psychology at the University of California, Davis. Her research on children's eyewitness memory has been supported by numerous federal grants and cited in U.S. Supreme Court decisions. She has served as President of Division 41 (Psychology and Law), Division 37 (Child, Youth, and Family Services), and the Section on Child Maltreatment of Division 37 of the American Psychological Association.

Michelle D. Leichtman, PhD
Michelle D. Leichtman is an Associate Professor in the Department of Psychology, Harvard University. She received a BA from Wellesley College, and a PhD from Cornell University.

Thomas C. Lorsbach, PhD
Tom Lorsbach obtained his PhD from the University of Missouri–Columbia. He is currently a Professor in the Department of Special Education and Communication Disorders at the University of Nebraska at Omaha. His research interests generally include developmental and individual differences in attention and memory. Most recently, his research efforts have been devoted to the study of source monitoring and attentional inhibition.

Amina Memon, PhD

Amina Memon graduated in Psychology from University of East London in 1982 and obtained her PhD in Experimental Psychology in 1985. She has published widely in the field of eyewitness memory and investigative interviewing, and recently completed her first text on Psychology and Law (McGraw Hill). Dr. Memon is currently an Associate Professor of Psychology at the University of Aberdeen in Scotland.

Marjorie B. Morse, JD

Marjorie B. Morse is a PhD candidate in the Department of Psychology, Harvard University. She received a BA from Stanford University and a JD from Columbia University.

Jodi A. Quas, PhD

Jodi Quas is a postdoctoral fellow at the University of California, Berkeley in the Institute of Human Development. Her research concerns children's memory for emotional events, the influence of social support and attachment on children's memory and suggestibility, and consequences of maltreatment and legal involvement on child victims. Her research has been supported by federal grants, and she has co-authored several articles and chapters on her work.

Hilary Horn Ratner, PhD

Hilary Horn Ratner is Professor of Psychology and Associate Dean of the Graduate School at Wayne State University. She joined the faculty in 1981 after completing her PhD in 1979 at the University of Massachusetts, Amherst, and an Individual National Research Service Award Postdoctoral Fellowship at the University of Chicago in 1981. Her primary research interests have focused on memory development and she has received funding from the National Institute on Aging, the National Science Foundation, the Maternal and Child Health Bureau, the Wellcome Trust, and the McGregor Foundation. She serves as a member of the editorial boards of the Journal of Experimental Child Psychology and the Merrill-Palmer Quarterly. She is a fellow of the American Psychological Association.

Kim P. Roberts, PhD

Kim Roberts is currently a Visiting Fellow at the National Institute of Child Health and Human Development in Bethesda, Maryland. She received her PhD in Developmental Psychology from the University of Sheffield, United Kingdom. She has conducted research on children's source monitoring and eyewitness memory in both the lab and investigative interviews in the field. She holds grants from the Economic and Social Research Council (UK) and the Australian Research Council.

Elizabeth J. Robinson, PhD

Elizabeth Robinson is Professor of Developmental Psychology at the University of Birmingham in the United Kingdom. She received her PhD from the University of London. She has published extensively on various aspects of children's cognitive development, in particular on children's understanding of communication. Recently, her research interests have extended to include other aspects of children's theory of mind such as understanding the sources of knowledge, pictures, false belief, and counterfactual reasoning.

Jennifer M. Schaaf, MA

Jennifer Schaaf is an advanced doctoral student in Cognitive Psychology at the University of California, Davis. Her research interests include children's eyewitness memory and suggestibility as well as associated individual differences, and interviewing techniques for children.

Rainer Speigel, MA

Rainer Speigel is a PhD candidate at Emmanuel College, Cambridge University, United Kingdom. He received BA and MA degrees from the University of Trier, Germany.

Melanie J. Spence, PhD

Melanie Spence is an Associate Professor of Psychology in the School of Human Development at the University of Texas at Dallas. She received MA and PhD degrees in Experimental Psychology from the University of North Carolina at Greensboro. Her research interests include memory development in infants and young children, and the relationship between infants' processing of speech and voice information and later language acquisition.

Karen L. Thierry, BA

Karen Thierry is a PhD candidate in the School of Human Development at the University of Texas at Dallas. She received her BA in Psychology from the University of Notre Dame. Currently her primary research interest is young children's memory development, particularly as it relates to eyewitness testimony.

Melissa Welch-Ross, PhD

Melissa Welch-Ross, PhD is Assistant Research Professor of Psychology at Georgia State University. She has published articles on the development of source monitoring skills, theory of mind, autobiographical memory, and the suggestibility of children. A focus of her research is on the relation of metacognition and social cognition to the development of personal event memory. She holds a FIRST Award from NIMH for the study of preschoolers' autobiographical memory.

Author Index

Subject Index